Historical Sociology of Intern: ¹ ᴰ ⸗¹⸗⸗ⁱ⸗ⁿ⸗

CW00501549

International relations theorists are in·
sociology as a means both of broadenii
and of critiquing mainstream thinking.
a rudimentary understanding of what
it can offer the subject. This book act:
ciology, considering a range of issues, incluaing a⸺⸺⸺ ⸺
variants of historical sociology; how they can be applied to international
relations; why international relations theorists should engage with these
approaches; and how historical sociological insight can enhance and reconfigure the study of international relations. In addition to describing
the seven major approaches – neo-Weberianism, constructivism, critical historical materialism, critical theory, postmodernism, structural
realism and world systems theory – the volume's introductory and concluding chapters set out in detail an approach and research agenda that
revolve around what the editors call 'world sociology'.

STEPHEN HOBDEN is Lecturer in the Department of International
Politics, University of Wales, Aberystwyth. He is the author of *International Relations and Historical Sociology*.

JOHN M. HOBSON is Senior Lecturer in International Relations at the
University of Sydney. His publications include *The State and International Relations* (2000), *The Wealth of States: A Comparative Sociology
of International Economic and Political Change* (1997) and *States and
Economic Development* (1995; co-authored with Linda Weiss).

Historical Sociology of International Relations

Edited by

Stephen Hobden and John M. Hobson

CAMBRIDGE
UNIVERSITY PRESS

PUBLISHED BY THE PRESS SYNDICATE OF THE UNIVERSITY OF CAMBRIDGE
The Pitt Building, Trumpington Street, Cambridge, United Kingdom

CAMBRIDGE UNIVERSITY PRESS
The Edinburgh Building, Cambridge CB2 2RU, UK
40 West 20th Street, New York, NY 10011-4211, USA
477 Williamstown Road, Port Melbourne, VIC 3207, Australia
Ruiz de Alarcón 13, 28014 Madrid, Spain
Dock House, The Waterfront, Cape Town 8001, South Africa

http://www.cambridge.org

First published 2002

Printed in the United Kingdom at the University Press, Cambridge

Typeface Plantin 10/12 pt.   *System* LaTeX 2$_\varepsilon$ [TB]

A catalogue record for this book is available from the British Library

Library of Congress Cataloguing in Publication Data
Historical sociology of international relations / edited by Stephen Hobden &
John M. Hobson.
     p.   cm.
Includes bibliographical references and index.
ISBN 0 521 80870 7 (hb) – ISBN 0 521 00476 4 (pb)
1. International relations – Sociological aspects – History.   2. Historical
sociology.   I. Hobden, Stephen, 1956–   II. Hobson, John M.
JZ1251.H57   2001
327 – dc21   2001035361

ISBN 0 521 80870 7 hardback
ISBN 0 521 00476 4 paperback

Contents

Contributors

MICHAEL BARNETT is an Associate Professor of Political Science at the University of Wisconsin.

BARRY BUZAN is Professor of International Relations at the University of Westminster, London.

A. CLAIRE CUTLER is an Associate Professor at the University of Victoria.

BARRY K. GILLS is a Senior Lecturer in International Relations at the University of Newcastle.

FRED HALLIDAY is Professor of International Relations at the London School of Economics.

STEPHEN HOBDEN is a Lecturer in International Politics at the University of Wales, Aberystwyth.

JOHN M. HOBSON is a Senior Lecturer in International Relations at the University of Sydney.

ANDREW LINKLATER is Woodrow Wilson Professor of International Politics at the University of Wales, Aberystwyth.

RICHARD LITTLE is Professor of International Relations at the University of Bristol.

CHRISTIAN REUS-SMIT is a Senior Fellow, Department of International Relations, Research School of Pacific and Asian Studies, the Australian National University.

MARTIN SHAW is Professor of International Relations at the University of Sussex.

STEVE SMITH is Professor of International Politics at the University of Wales, Aberystwyth.

Preface and acknowledgements

The idea for this book came in 1997, when Steve Hobden and John Hobson were carrying on an e-mail discussion about historical sociology and international relations. We were struck by just how many books were currently emerging, and indeed were about to be published, in this new and exciting area. It seemed that historical sociology was undergoing something of a 'renaissance', with not only new work being undertaken, but also a whole range of genuinely innovative approaches suddenly emerging. Indeed, it was apparent that at least seven major historical sociological approaches of international relations had appeared by the end of the 1990s. And yet, what particularly struck us was that while many international relations scholars were beginning to talk and think about drawing on historical sociology, not only was there little appreciation in the wider international relations community of just *how far* this renaissance had come, but equally, there was, in general, little understanding of what historical sociology has to offer international relations. It seemed to us that this was not a function of a lack of interest, given that references to historical sociology are frequently made in the general literature. Rather, it was due in part to the fact that an adequate summary did not then exist of the various approaches on offer; a summary which also needed to explain how they could be applied to international relations, and with what effects. In the light of this, it seemed to us a particularly opportune time to take stock of this 'renaissance'. We, therefore, planned to produce an edited volume which would showcase to a wider audience not only what these new approaches comprise, but equally, what they have to offer, how they can be applied to the study of international relations, and why we believe that international relations theorists can benefit from such an engagement. Additionally we hoped to demonstrate how such insights could not only enhance, but also reconfigure, the discipline. The immediate question then was: how best to achieve this?

We decided that it would be best to hold a conference, in which we would ask some of the leading scholars who are working at the interface of these two disciplines to contribute to this project in a single forum.

All but one of the chapters in this volume were first presented at that conference, which was held in Aberystwyth in the summer of 1999. We were particularly fortunate that the majority of the people whom we had singled out as potential contributors agreed to come along and contribute a paper.

We were to find that we would be involved in no less than four intensive stages of intellectual and organisational planning. First, having constructed an intellectual outline of the whole project, we wrote to each of our contributors and specified a particular area that we wanted them to write on, in order to ensure consistency. We also specified the purpose of the conference, and asked them to think about this when writing their papers. Second, we specified a strict deadline for the 'first-draft' papers to arrive, so that we could then circulate them to all the other paper-givers in advance of the conference. We then carefully read each of the papers and made fairly detailed comments that we wanted them to consider when rewriting them after the conference (all of which were discussed individually with each of the paper-givers at the conference). Third, of course, was the conference itself, which was, we believe, very successful, not just in terms of the quality of discussion, but also for its intellectually constructive atmosphere. We were also particularly pleased that all of the paper-givers had kept to our requested specifications. We then specified a strict deadline for the final versions to be submitted. Finally we entered a fourth stage in which we spent almost six months both formatting and editing the papers to make them into one fluent book, as well as writing our introductions and conclusion – with the latter drawing all of the approaches laid out in this volume into one single school, that we label 'world sociology'.

In agreeing to host and fund the bulk of the conference we owe a considerable debt both to the Department of International Politics at Aberystwyth and to Professor Steve Smith (who was then head of department, and is now the university's Pro-Vice Chancellor). We would like in particular, therefore, to thank Steve Smith for all the support, which, with his usual unceasing enthusiasm, he has given to the project. For all their assistance and advice during the planning phases of the conference, we would also like to express our gratitude to Caroline Haste, the department's administrator, Elaine Lowe, the departmental secretary, and Professor Colin McInnes, the Director of Research.

This is also our opportunity to thank all the contributors to the volume, both for agreeing to take part in the conference and for providing their papers and subsequent chapters in such a timely fashion. We would also like to say a special 'thank you' to Claire Cutler who agreed subsequently to the conference to contribute a chapter on neo-Gramscian historical sociology. We thank the various members of staff and graduate students both from Aberystwyth and from elsewhere who attended the conference; their input added enormously to the intellectual success of the meeting, as well as to its conviviality.

We also would like to thank the team at Cambridge University Press for their involvement in getting the manuscript into print. The extensive comments and constructive suggestions from the two CUP reviewers contributed enormously to strengthening the volume, and we have sought to accommodate their suggestions wherever possible. Finally, we would like to acknowledge our debt to John Haslam, our commissioning editor at Cambridge University Press, for all his support, advice and characteristic efficiency throughout.

Aberystwyth and Sydney   STEPHEN HOBDEN AND
                                                              JOHN M. HOBSON

Part I

Introduction: Bringing historical sociology back into international relations

1 What's at stake in 'bringing historical sociology *back* into international relations'? Transcending 'chronofetishism' and 'tempocentrism' in international relations

John M. Hobson

Introduction: the growing convergence of historical sociology and international relations

Since the late 1970s historical sociology has been implicitly moving towards international relations, while, since the early 1980s, international relations has begun to explicitly move towards historical sociology. Although Theda Skocpol (1979) most famously insisted that the 'international' should be brought into historical sociology, it is clear that such a move was already in the air (e.g., Frank, 1967; Wallerstein, 1974; Tilly, 1975a; Bendix, 1978; Poggi, 1978), and had in fact been waiting in the wings ever since the early 1900s – e.g., Weber (1978, originally published in 1922), Elias (1994[1939]) and Hintze (1975), the last comprising a series of essays which were originally published between 1896 and 1937. Moreover, this move has since gathered some momentum within historical sociology (Giddens, 1985; Mann, 1986, 1993; Tilly, 1990; Goldstone, 1991). And on the other side of the 'border', a few international relations theorists began to look to historical sociology in the very early 1980s, as a means of enhancing and reconfiguring their discipline (e.g., Ruggie, 1983; Cox, 1986; cf. Ashley, 1986); this is a development that has gathered momentum through the 1980s and 1990s (e.g., Halliday, 1987, 1994, 1999; Jarvis, 1989; Linklater, 1990, 1998; Scholte, 1993; Buzan, Jones and Little, 1993; Thomson, 1994; Spruyt, 1994; Rosenberg, 1994; Ferguson and Mansbach, 1996; Frank and Gills, 1996; Hobson, 1997, 1998a; Hobden, 1998, 1999a, 1999b; Reus-Smit, 1999; M. Hall, 1999; R. Hall, 1999). It is both *significant* that historical sociologists working outside international relations have been slow to pick

I wish to express special thanks to Steve Hobden for his generous help, which has proved invaluable in the writing of this chapter. I gratefully acknowledge the comments made by the contributors to this volume during the conference. Naturally, I remain responsible for the final product and any of its errors or omissions.

up on the complementary developments within international relations, and *unfortunate*, given that such oversight arguably comes at a significant cost (see Hobson, Smith, Halliday and Hobson & Hobden, this volume). Historical sociologists would do well, therefore, to follow the progress of their 'cousins' within international relations. Nevertheless, it seems fair to state that the 'boundaries between those writers in international relations who are interested in taking a historical sociological approach and the macro-sociologists in Historical Sociology are . . . breaking down' (Hobden, 1998: 196).

However, despite this growing momentum of interest in historical sociology within international relations, and despite the fact that historical sociology is often mentioned, or referred to, by international relations scholars, no 'take-off' is as yet in evidence. Moreover, there is as yet only a very rudimentary understanding of what historical sociology is, and what it has to offer international relations – in much the same way that historical sociologists have only a very rudimentary understanding of international relations and what it has to offer them. It is as if historical sociology is *seen* by international relations scholars, but not *heard*. And while international relations is currently undergoing a 'sociological turn', often equated with the rise of constructivism, we argue here that the 'sociological turn' can only be *fully* realised by bringing 'history' back in. Indeed the primary purpose of this volume is its calling for an '*historical* sociological turn' in international relations. The volume, therefore, acts as a kind of *historical sociology manifesto*, which can relay to the wider international relations audience what some of the major variants of historical sociology look like; show how they can be applied to international relations; explain why international relations theorists *should* engage with historical sociology; and demonstrate how historical sociological insight can enhance and reconfigure the study of international relations. In the process, we hope that historical sociology might shift from its current peripheral position closer to the centre of the international relations research agenda. By implication, this volume simultaneously constitutes an *international relations manifesto* which can relay to a wider historical sociology audience what some of the major international relations variants have to offer them, and demonstrate how international relations insight can enhance and reconfigure the study of historical sociology.

This opening chapter has two core objectives: the first part appraises mainstream international relations theory through a critical historical sociological lens, and reveals its ahistorical and asociological biases, while the second part lays out in summary form seven major theoretical approaches which are covered in this volume, all of which suggest ways to transcend or remedy prevailing modes of ahistoricism and asociologism in international relations. Steve Hobden's contribution to this introduction (chapter 2) then considers how and why mainstream international relations has been *re*constructed in the last fifty years along asociological and ahistorical lines – given his claim that before 1919, international relations comprised a corpus of knowledge which incorporated various disciplines, not least economics, history, sociology, law and moral philosophy. He ends by discussing the contribution that historical sociology can make to enhancing the study of international relations.

Revealing the 'chronofetishist' and 'tempocentric' foundations of mainstream international relations

There is little doubt that much, though clearly not all, of contemporary international relations is 'historophobic', in that it views historical analysis as superfluous, or exogenous, to the subject matter of the discipline (though as Steve Hobden shows in chapter 2, this has not *always* been the case in the history of the discipline). To the extent that contemporary mainstream international relations theorists have concerned themselves with history, they have generally employed what might be called an 'instrumentalist' view of history, where history is used not as a means to rethink the present, but as a quarry to be mined only in order to confirm theories of the present (as found especially in neorealism). As Michael Barnett puts it in his chapter, 'If history mattered at all it was as a field of data to be mined, for cases to be shoehorned in the pursuit of grand theory building, and for evidence of the cycles of history that realists used to mark historical time' (p. 100; also, Cox, 1986: 212). Or as Rosecrance declared, 'history is a laboratory in which our generalizations about international politics can be tested' (Rosecrance, 1973: 25).

By contrast, we argue for the employment of a 'temporally relativist' or 'constitutive' reading of history, in which theorists examine history not simply for its own sake or to tell us more about the past, nor simply as a means to confirm extant theorising of the present, but rather as a means to *rethink* theories and *problematise* the analysis of the present, and thereby to *reconfigure* the international relations research agenda. Ignoring history does not simply do an injustice to the *history* of the international system. Most significantly, it leads to a problematic view of the *present*. Seen through an historical sociological lens, mainstream international relations appears caught within two modes of ahistoricism and asociologism: what I shall call *chronofetishism* and *tempocentrism*.

The first mode of ahistoricism: 'chronofetishism'

The construction of the term *chronofetishism* – *not* to be confused with Powelson's (1994) term 'chronocentrism' – takes as its starting point Karl Marx's concept of 'fetishism'. In *Capital*, Marx argued that liberal political economists fall into the trap of fetishism when they argue that, for example, the commodity has an inherent value that is *autonomous* of class exploitation. In the process, the commodity is reified, and thus 'a definite social relation between men . . . assumes in their eyes, the fantastic form of a relation between things' (Marx, 1954: 77). Marx's 'scientific method' remedies 'commodity fetishism' by revealing the exploitative class relations by which the value of a particular commodity is determined. In the process, he shows that the commodity is not autonomous because it does not exist in a sphere that is independent of the relations of production (Marx, 1954: 76–87). More generally, he takes classical liberal political economists to task primarily on the grounds that in *reifying* capitalism as a phenomenon that operates according to its own self-constituting 'laws of supply and demand', and by thereby obscuring the contradictory class relations upon which capitalism is founded, they fall prey to the fetishist illusion that capitalism is 'natural', 'autonomous' and consequently 'eternal'. Marx's project in *Capital* was to remedy this fetishist illusion by uncovering the exploitative and transformative class processes that define capitalism, thereby revealing its unnatural and transient nature.

By extension, *chronofetishism*, the assumption that the present can adequately be explained only by examining the present (thereby bracketing or ignoring the past), gives rise to three illusions:

(1) *reification illusion*: where the present is effectively 'sealed off' from the past, making it appear as a *static, self-constituting, autonomous* and *reified* entity, thereby obscuring its historical socio-temporal context;
(2) *naturalisation illusion*: where the present is effectively *naturalised* on the basis that it emerged 'spontaneously' in accordance with 'natural' human imperatives, thereby obscuring the historical processes of social power, identity/social exclusion and norms that constitute the present;
(3) *immutability illusion*: where the present is *eternalised* because it is deemed to be natural and resistant to structural change, thereby obscuring the processes that reconstitute the present as an immanent order of change.

Table 1 reveals the essence of these two ahistorical modes, chronofetishism and tempocentrism, and juxtaposes them with the historical sociological *remedies* that this book is concerned to develop. We begin by revealing the problems with the three illusions of chronofetishism. The

Table 1. *Conceptualising the two dominant modes of ahistoricism in international relations*

Mode of ahistoricism	Resulting illusions (danger)	Historical sociological remedy (escape)
Chronofetishism	A mode of ahistoricism which leads to three illusions:	Employment of historical sociology to:
	(1) *Reification illusion* where the present is effectively 'sealed off' from the past, thereby obscuring its historical socio-temporal context, and making it appear as a *static, self-constituting, autonomous* and *reified* entity;	(1) Reveal the present as a *malleable construct* which is embedded in a historical context, thereby serving to unearth the processes of temporal continuity and discontinuity with previous social practices;
	(2) *Naturalisation illusion* where the present is effectively *naturalised* on the basis that it emerged 'spontaneously' in accordance with 'natural' human imperatives, thereby obscuring the historical processes of social power, identity/social exclusion and norms that constitute the present;	(2) Denaturalise the present and reveal that it emerged not in accordance with 'natural' human impulses but rather through processes of power, identity/social exclusion and norms;
	(3) *Immutability illusion* where the present is *eternalised* because it is deemed to be natural and resistant to structural change, thereby obscuring the processes that reconstitute the present as an immanent order of change.	(3) Reveal the present as constituted by transformative (*morphogenetic*) processes that continuously reconstitute present institutions and practices.
Tempocentrism	A mode of ahistoricism which leads to the:	To remedy tempocentrism, historical sociology:
	(4) *Isomorphic illusion* in which the 'naturalised' and 'reified' present is extrapolated backwards in time to present all historical systems as 'isomorphic' or 'homologous', resulting in the *failure to recognise the unique features* of the present (an *inverted* 'path dependency').	(4) Traces the fundamental *differences* between past and present international systems and institutions, to thereby *reveal the unique constitutive features of the present.*

'reification illusion' – the assumption that the present is autonomous and self-constituting – is problematic because it ignores the fact that no historical epoch has ever been static and entirely 'finished' or 'complete', but has been in the process of forming and re-forming. Historical sociological enquiry is able to remedy the 'reification illusion' by revealing the present as a *malleable construct* that is embedded within a specific socio-temporal context. The assumption that the present is autonomous and self-constituting is also a classic sign of the second chronofetishist illusion – the presumption that the present system is 'natural' and that it emerged *spontaneously* in accordance with 'natural' imperatives. This illusion is problematic because it necessarily obscures the manifold processes of social power, identity/social exclusion and norms, which constituted the present system. Thus, for example, Kenneth Waltz assumes that the international system emerged spontaneously through the unintended consequences of state interaction (Waltz, 1979: 91); and that the modern sovereign state is the highest form of political organisation, not least because an alternative world government 'would stifle liberty [and] become a terrible despotism' (Waltz, 1986: 341; 1979: 112). Liberals see in liberal capitalism and the modern democratic state the highest forms of economic and political expression, because they supposedly reflect the impulses of human nature – namely the inherent propensity to 'truck, barter and exchange one thing for another' (Adam Smith, 1937: 13).

Finally, the 'immutability illusion' – the notion that the present is immune or resistant to structural change and thereby 'eternalised' – is problematic because it obscures the *transformative* or 'morphogenetic' (Archer, 1982) processes that are immanent within the present order. Neorealism and liberalism both fall into this trap, though in different ways. Liberalism believes that with liberal capitalism and democracy, history has reached its terminus, with no fundamental change beyond the present being either possible or desirable (Fukuyama, 1992). Neorealism argues similarly that structural change within or beyond the present is impossible. Indeed, Waltz's theory 'contains only a reproductive logic, but no transformational logic' (Ruggie, 1986: 151), in that *systems maintenance* is fundamentally inscribed into the structure of Waltz's theory, given that it is logically impossible for one state to create a hierarchy under the 'balance of power' (Waltz, 1979: ch. 6; see also Hobson, 2000: 26–30). And ironically, Waltz's (1986: 340–1) reply to Ashley – that the balance of power has and always will continue to exist – merely confirms the conclusion that neorealism is, indeed, 'a *historicism of stasis*. It is a historicism that freezes the political institutions of the current world order', thereby ruling out the possibility of future change (Ashley, 1986: 289, 258, 290–1). Thus neorealism's ahistoricism is symptomatic of a 'problem-solving theory' that is distinguished from an historical sociological 'critical theory' (Cox, 1986). However, chronofetishism does not exist in isolation, and is deeply entwined with a second form of ahistoricism in international relations: what I call *tempocentrism*.

The second mode of ahistoricism: 'tempocentrism'

If chronofetishism leads to a 'sealing off' of the present such that it appears as an autonomous, natural, spontaneous and immutable entity, tempocentrism extrapolates this 'chronofetishised' present backwards through time such that *discontinuous* ruptures and *differences* between historical epochs and states systems are smoothed over and consequently obscured. In this way, history appears to be marked, or is regulated, by a regular tempo that beats according to the same, constant rhythm of the present (reified) system. This is in fact an *inverted* form of 'path dependency'. Tempocentrism is, in effect, a methodology in which theorists look at *history* through a 'chronofetishist lens'. In other words, in reconstructing all historical systems so as to conform to a reified and naturalised present, they tarnish all systems as homologous or 'isomorphic' (i.e., as having the same structure). In this way, the study of international relations takes on a 'transhistorical' quality.

It is *this* tempocentric manoeuvre which leads such theorists to look constantly for signs of the present in the past, and, in a type of self-fulfilling prophecy, come back and report that the past is indeed the same as the present. Thus, for example, the dominant theory of international relations – neorealism – assumes either that history is repetitive such that nothing ever changes because of the timeless presence of anarchy (Waltz, 1979), or that history takes on the form of repetitive and isomorphic 'great power/hegemonic' cycles, each phase of which is essentially identical, with the only difference being *which* great power is rising or declining – i.e., same play, different actors (Gilpin, 1981). In this way, neorealists assume that the 'superpower' contest between Athens and Sparta is equivalent to the recent cold war between the USA and the USSR; or that current US state behaviour is broadly equivalent to that of historical great powers such as sixteenth-century Spain, the seventeenth-century United Provinces (Netherlands), eighteenth-century France, or nineteenth-century Britain (Kennedy, 1988; cf. Gilpin, 1981). Moreover, neorealists assume that ancient imperialism is equivalent to that found in the nineteenth century (Waltz, 1979: ch. 2); or that all great-power wars are rooted in the same causes (Gilpin, 1981); or that European feudal heteronomy is broadly equivalent to the modern system and can be understood in similar ways (Fischer, 1992). At the most general level, neorealists tempocentrically conclude that 'the classic history of Thucydides is as meaningful a guide to the behavior of states today as when it was written in the fifth century BC' (Gilpin, 1981: 7), or that 'balance of power politics in much the form that we know it has been practiced over the millennia by many different types of political units, from ancient China and India, to the Greek and Italian city states, and unto our own day' (Waltz, 1986: 341). It is this 'trick' to represent all historical actors and systems as isomorphic or homologous that leads neorealists to conclude that world politics *must* always have been governed by the timeless and constant logic of anarchy, which thereby enables them to dismiss the utility of historical sociological enquiry (see Waltz, 1979: 43–9).

What is the matter with this view of international history that Rob Walker (1993) has labelled 'the theme of Gulliver'? Firstly, it presents the whole of international history as a static, monolithic entity that operates according to a constant and timeless logic, such that structural change becomes entirely obscured. The problem here is that this ignores the fact that there has not been one international system but many, all of which are quite different, and all of which are marked by different rhythms or tempos. But more importantly, the fundamental problem with tempocentrism is that in constructing states systems and actors as isomorphic throughout world-historical time, *the theorist fails to recognise the uniqueness of the present system and simultaneously obscures some of its most fundamental or constitutive features.* This 'tempocentric paradox' can be simply expressed: that in extrapolating a reified present back in time, the theorist not only does a disservice to the past, but, more importantly, does serious injustice to understanding the present. Thus mainstream international relations theory (as in neorealism and neoliberal institutionalism) takes for granted precisely those categories about the contemporary era that need to be problematised and explained. Historical sociology's prime mandate is to reveal and remedy the tempocentrism (as well as chronofetishism) of mainstream and conventional international relations theory. Thus, for example, when we show through historical sociological enquiry that the rivalry between Athens and Sparta is *not* equivalent to that between the USA and the USSR (not least because the former rivalry – unlike the latter – existed within a single international society), the problem becomes to refocus our explanation on the unique particularities of the Cold War. Or, when we show through historical sociological enquiry that all historical forms of imperialism have *not* been equivalent, not least because they have been embedded within different normative environments (R. Hall, 1999), we are forced to rethink the specific normative processes that inform the uniqueness of modern imperialism. Or when we show that European medieval heteronomy is very different to the modern Westphalian system (Hall and Kratochwil, 1993), again because of radically different normative settings, we are necessarily forced to rethink the unique normative constitutive features of the latter. Similarly, when we show through historical sociological enquiry that ancient historical states systems are not equivalent to the modern Westphalian system, either because of different class-based contexts (Rosenberg, 1994), or because of different moral purposes of the state (Reus-Smit, 1999), we are forced to rethink the various social processes which gave rise to, and constitute, the unique qualities of the modern system.

Tempocentrism is also fundamental to the neorealist theory of hegemonic stability. Thus when we show through historical sociological enquiry that Britain in the nineteenth century either had a very different foreign policy to that of the United States between 1945 and 1973, or was *not* actually a hegemon (Schroeder, 1994; Hobson, 1997: 199–204; Mann, 1993: ch. 8), it becomes apparent that hegemony is unique to one country (the United States) at one particular time in history. Here neorealists err by drawing out some of the basic features of US foreign policy, which are equated with hegemony as a generic phenomenon, and then, in typical tempocentric fashion, extrapolating this conception back in time to 'fit' the British case. Given also that Japan turns out to be a poor candidate for future hegemony, as most Japan specialists conclude (Inoguchi, 1988; Taira, 1993; Katzenstein, 1996a), we are left with only one example of a hegemon (at least within the neorealist canon), a conclusion which logically undermines this cyclical theory of hegemony. But the key point is that such tempocentrism not only does a disservice to understanding Britain in the nineteenth century, but also renders problematic our understanding of US hegemony in the twentieth century, as well as the question of a future hegemony. The problem then becomes *not* to analyse American *hegemony*, but to rethink the specific origins of *American* hegemony (Ruggie, 1993b, 1998b: ch. 4) – a project which requires historical sociological insight. Finally, when we show that the free trade regimes of the nineteenth and twentieth centuries were radically different from each other, so we need to rethink the specific and unique social processes that enabled the modern free trade regime (Hobson, this volume, pp. 78–80).

Tempocentrism is also found in neoliberal institutionalism and its theory of international regimes (e.g., Keohane, 1984). Neoliberals assume that states have fixed identities and interests; that they are rational egoists that seek to maximise their long-term utility gains, and that this can best be achieved when states harness themselves to co-operative norms that are embodied within state-constructed international regimes. While arguably there is much in the theory forwarded, nevertheless, it is not enough to assume that co-operation and international regimes are brought into play simply because of the timeless assumption that states are rational egoists. For if this assumption is correct, then why did multilateral economic institutions and international economic co-operation only come into existence in the nineteenth century (and only fully after 1945)? Put simply, *if* the rational egoistic sovereign state has existed since 1648 (a problematic assumption in itself), why did we have to wait at least two hundred years for such institutions to appear? Thus in typical tempocentric fashion, neoliberal institutionalism fails to recognise that international multilateral economic co-operation is *unique* to the late-modern era, which suggests that it cannot be explained as a simple function of rational state behaviour. Accordingly, neoliberalism not only does a disservice to understanding state behaviour prior to 1945, but also renders problematic our understanding of contemporary co-operative relations between states. The problem then becomes *not* to analyse multilateral *institutions*, but to rethink the origins of *multilateral* institutions and international economic co-operation – a project which can only be achieved through historical sociological analysis (cf. Reus-Smit, Barnett, and Hobson, ch. 3, this volume; also Ruggie, 1993, 1998b).

Finally we can present the formal definitions of chronofetishism and tempocentrism, which are entwined together, as follows. Chronofetishism is a mode of ahistoricism which conveys *a set of illusions that represent the present as an autonomous, natural, spontaneous and immutable system that is self-constituting and eternal, and which necessarily obscures the processes of power, identity/social exclusion and norms that gave rise to, and continuously reconstitute, the present as an immanent order of change.* Tempocentrism is a mode of ahistoricism which conveys *the illusion that all international systems are equivalent (isomorphic) and have been marked by the constant and regular tempo of a chronofetishised present, which paradoxically obscures some of the most fundamental constitutive features of the present international system.*

In sum, therefore, the main limitation with mainstream international relations is not simply that it problematically flattens out international *history* (tempocentrism), but that it problematically flattens or smooths out and thereby naturalises the *present* (chronofetishism). Accordingly, both modes of ahistoricism have effectively written the issue of 'change' off the international relations agenda altogether. Indeed neorealists, such as Gilpin and Waltz, do not even try and hide from their conclusion that 'the fundamental nature of international relations has not changed over the millennia. International relations continue to be a recurring struggle for wealth and power among independent actors in a state of anarchy' (Gilpin, 1981: 7, 230), or that, 'the texture of international politics remains highly constant, patterns recur, and events repeat themselves endlessly. The relations that prevail internationally seldom shift rapidly in type or quality. They are marked by a dismaying persistence' (Waltz, 1979: 66, 67; 1986: 341, 342–3). All in all, neorealists have effectively engaged in a fascinating conjuring trick, in which we have been fooled by an adept sleight-of-hand into believing in the naturalness of their totalised picture. Our task then is to reveal this sleight-of-hand and to overcome the illusions of ahistoricism that have duped us for too long. Reintroducing historical sociological enquiry, therefore, enables us to bring into focus the rocky and mountainous landscape of continuity, discontinuity and contingency that actually constitutes past and present international relations. This argument clearly presupposes a definition of historical sociology that has underpinned our analysis so far, but which can now be formally presented.

The extreme claim that history and sociology are incompatible (e.g., Goldthorpe, 1991), no less than the extreme claim that international history and international relations are incompatible (Sked, 1987) and occupy radically different worlds, is usually justified on the epistemologically spurious ground that *history* is founded upon the search for 'empiricist particularity' of the past, whilst *sociology* is based on theory and the quest for 'theoretical generalisations' of the present. It is 'spurious' because historians always implicitly make theoretically loaded assumptions about the world, based on their own experience in a particular time and place. To acknowledge this *should* be the first task of the historian – not just the sociologist (see especially Carr, 1961). As Hobden argues, what ultimately *links* history and sociology is the study of 'time': 'Social relations do not stand apart from time. All social interactions are affected by what has gone before, and in the understanding of the present the past cannot be avoided' (Hobden, 1998: 24; cf. Scholte, 1993: 7). The 'artificial divide' between the past and present that chronofetishism and tempocentrism create is artificial precisely because

The 'past' is . . . never really 'past' but continuously constitutive of the 'present', as a cumulatively and selectively reproduced ensemble of practices and ideas that 'channel' and impart directionality to ongoing human agency. The present, in other words, is what the past – as received and creatively interpreted by the present – has made it (Bryant, cited in Hobden, 1998: 24).

Thus we may define 'historical sociology', or what we term 'world sociology' (see chapter 13), as *a critical approach which refuses to treat the present as an autonomous entity outside of history, but insists on embedding it within a specific socio-temporal place, thereby offering sociological remedies to the ahistorical illusions that chronofetishism and tempocentrism produce.*

14   *John M. Hobson*

The extreme paradox here is that such a definition would be at fundamental odds with the more conventional definitions implicitly used by Skocpol, Tilly and other neo-Weberians working within historical sociology. This is because such writers reproduce the chronofetishist and tempocentric fallacies that are found in mainstream international relations (see Hobson, ch. 3, this volume), thereby denying the *raison d'être* of historical sociology in the first place. Accordingly, it should be clear that we are not simply transplanting an unproblematised historical sociological approach into the study of international relations. Instead, we have sought to reformulate the definition of historical sociology in order to historicise international relations; paradoxically, this leads to an approach that is no less critical of mainstream historical sociology. This provides one of the most compelling reasons why we believe historical sociologists working outside of international relations (no less than mainstream international relations scholars) *should* also engage in the project outlined in this volume if they are to enhance their own discipline.

The remainder of this section applies our historical sociological conception to reveal the tempocentric biases of the 'commonsense' assumption, widely held in international relations (best represented by neorealism), that the *anarchic* international system represents a single *distinct, autonomous and self-constituting* realm which comprises *sovereign* states (*like-units*) that are neatly *separated* by *distinct sovereign* borders – and simultaneously shows how historical sociology can remedy the problems that are contained therein. But before I do so, it is important to clarify one point here. For it might be argued that focusing on neorealism in such detail is a somewhat pointless task because neorealism is 'either past its hegemonic peak', or because it is only one of the mainstream theories that needs to be considered. I have three responses. First, pick up any issue of one of the leading international relations journals, *International Security*, and one would be hard-pressed *not* to find at least one realist contribution. Moreover, even if neorealism is past its 'hegemonic peak', it is impossible to pick up any of the leading international relations theory journals and *not* find neorealists constantly referred to, even if it is in the form of a critical debate. Second, my major task here is not simply to critique neorealism *per se*, but rather to use it as an example of tempocentrism in international relations theory, in order to show how historical sociological enquiry can transcend the limits of tempocentrism more generally.

The third, and possibly the most urgent reason why I choose to critique neorealism is because it is the Waltzian version that has done more than any other theory to mark out the borders of international relations so as explicitly to exclude and marginalise historical sociology from what constitutes 'real international relations' (see Waltz, 1979, chs. 2–5, esp. pp. 43–9). Indeed it has been the obsessive quest for scientific certainty, and a celebration of positivism which sees 'legitimate international relations enquiry' as defined *only* by the acquisition of objective knowledge, that prompted Waltz and others to find in international politics 'law-like patterns' of recurrence and continuity, patterns which could *not* be revealed through an historical sociological lens. In short, this quest for 'scientificity' necessarily dictated the exclusion or dismissal of historical sociology from the ever-narrowing borders of 'legitimate' international relations. And while not all mainstream international relations theorists are neorealists, it *is* clear that neoliberal institutionalists, and indeed many international relations scholars for that matter, have accepted the current positioning of the mainstream borders that *exclude* historical sociology from engaging in the 'legitimate' purposes and tasks of international relations. It is as if historical sociologists, according to mainstream international relations scholars, *can* be seen but must *not* be heard. I, therefore, see it as a first-order objective to undermine the popular belief that 'historical sociology is simply *not* international relations', if historical sociology is to have any success at all in gaining entry into what constitutes 'legitimate international relations enquiry'.

Problematising the notion of 'like-units' under anarchy

Waltz's fundamental claim is that international politics has never changed but is repetitive, in that the international has always been a realm of competition between political forms (units) (Waltz, 1979: 66, 67). He observes that the domestic aspects or identities of states cannot affect the international realm because all states (liberal or authoritarian, capitalist or communist), or all political units (empires, city-states or nation-states), behave *similarly* in the international system (i.e., conform to the logic of competitive survival). In order to explain 'continuity', Waltz sought to ignore or bracket the specific features and identities of the domestic realm. The units must *not* be included in a 'theory of international politics' (Waltz, 1979: ch. 5), because if they were, the 'continuity' aspect of international relations would necessarily give way to the notion of constant and immanent change (because the units themselves are constantly changing through time); 'if changes in international outcomes are linked directly to changes in actors, how can one account for similarities of [international] outcomes that persist or recur even as actors vary?' (Waltz, 1979: 65; 1986: 329). Rather, he argues, states are the pure product of anarchy. Anarchy (that is, a multistate system in which there is no external authority that stands above the sovereign states) *socialises* states into 'like-units' (by which he means that the political units all perform exactly the same survival function, and that they have a dual monopoly of the means of violence and rule such that no alternative or competing forms of domestic political authority exist). It should be noted that neo-liberals also implicitly view states as 'like-units'. But the key point here is that in creating a parsimonious 'systemic' theory which brackets (or ignores) the importance of domestic politics in the international system, Waltz explicitly *dismisses the relevance of sociological and historical sociological analysis* (Waltz, 1979: chs. 2–6, esp., pp. 43–9), precisely because such an approach would produce a picture of constant international change as opposed to continuity. In short, Waltz's whole theory, along with his efforts to marginalise historical sociology, rests on the assumption that states are 'like-units'. Demonstrating that such an assumption might be false or problematic would necessarily jeopardise his whole theory as well as his justification for the necessary exclusion of historical sociology from the 'legitimate' international relations research agenda.

One of the most striking insights of historical sociology is the point that the presence of *unlike* or *functionally differentiated* units (i.e., where there are competing sources of political authority at the domestic level) under anarchy has not only occurred in world history, but, above all, has taken precedence over the existence of 'like-units' for something like 99 per cent of world history (cf. Ruggie, 1983; Mann, 1986; Tilly, 1990; Buzan, Jones and Little, 1993; Spruyt, 1994). Such a point strikes at the very heart of Waltz's project, because it shows that the existence of 'like-units' is anomalous or exceptional. This has three major ramifications: first, that we urgently require a renewed focus on accounting for the *uniqueness* of modern 'like-units'; second, that anarchy cannot adequately explain their presence, given that anarchy has (at least according to Waltz) always existed in world history; and third, that only an historical sociological analysis can perform this sensitive task.

Problematising the notion of a 'distinct self-constituting' international realm

Historical sociology reveals as highly problematic the seemingly inno-cent claim that international relations can be understood by omitting the impact of the domestic realm. Historical sociologists in particular have shown that the domestic and international realms are thoroughly interpenetrated and mutually constituted. Societies and international so-cieties are not unitary but are 'constituted of multiple overlapping and intersecting socio-spatial networks of power' (Mann, 1986: 1; cf. Elias, 1978; Giddens, 1985; Runciman, 1989). This poses a major problem for

Waltzian neorealism because if neither the international nor the national are 'self-constituting entities', then the assumption of a separate discipline of international relations divorced from historical sociology cannot logically hold.

Problematising the sovereign spatial relations between units (spatial differentiation)

Historical sociological insight is also important in that it draws our attention to thinking about the varying historical forms of spatial relations that separate political units (i.e., *spatial differentiation*), which in turn requires us to theorise the specific *emergence* of modern sovereign borders – a point that Ruggie (1983) originally made. A major aspect of Ruggie's critique of neorealism was that systemic analysis is insensitive to changes in the spatial relations between the units. Drawing on historical sociological insight, he argued that under European heteronomy (800–1648), the feudal units were spatially arranged according to overlapping jurisdictions and overlapping loyalties. By contrast, the spatial relations between modern sovereign states have been strikingly different, and entail a radical jurisdictional and spatial separation between independent units. Though he did not put it as such, the most profound insight that Ruggie brought us in this article was the claim that Waltz committed the *tempocentric error*, since he mistakenly took the Westphalian moment as typical of inter-state spatial relations and then extrapolated it back in time to encompass all previous states systems. Waltz's theory leads to a problematic understanding of pre-modern international relations, in which non-sovereign conceptions of territoriality predominated (Anderson, 1974; Poggi, 1978), where loose boundaries rather than borders 'separated' societies (Giddens, 1985), and where fluid conceptions of political space often prevailed – e.g., nomadic migrations (Lattimore, 1962). More importantly though, because Waltz fails to treat inter-spatial relations between units as historically variable, he is thereby robbed of the capacity to explain the emergence of modern sovereign borders. Given that this is no small lacuna because the issue of sovereign borders remains a major one in contemporary international relations, this must constitute a serious flaw not just in neorealism but in all tempocentric international relations theory. As Ruggie put it, 'without the [historical sociological] concept of spatial differentiation . . . it is impossible to define the modern era in international politics – modes of [spatial] differentiation are the pivot in the epochal study of rule' (Ruggie, 1998b: 180, 193; cf. Agnew, 1994, 1999; Brenner, 1999). The issue here is not simply to point to the need for explaining different forms of spatial relations in history, but more importantly, to point out that Waltz is unable to explain one of the most fundamental aspects of the modern world – the existence of sovereign spatial relations between states.

Problematising anarchy as a 'differentiated' structure

Historical sociology problematises Waltz's view that 'international anarchy' (i.e., a system of competing sovereign states with no higher external authority) and international 'hierarchy' (e.g., empires, hegemonies), are mutually exclusive (Waltz, 1979: 114–16). Historical sociological insight reveals firstly that these categories are 'ideal-types', and have never existed in pure form; and secondly, that they are not mutually exclusive. Particular hierarchies (or what Martin Wight (1977) called 'suzerain states systems') – e.g., ancient Rome, imperial China, the Mongol and Habsburg empires – have *co-existed* at different times with other hierarchies as well as with decentralised anarchic multistate systems – e.g., warring-states China, ancient Greece, ancient India and the Italian city-state system. And within feudal Europe, although the continental system was anarchic, it was at all times cross-cut by various hierarchies (e.g., the papacy, the Holy Roman Empire and the Merovingian and Frankish empires, as well as the Mongolian and Habsburg empires). Moreover, this is no less true of the modern world, where hierarchies (e.g., Warsaw Pact, US hegemony/NATO, British and French empires, etc.) have co-existed under anarchy (see also Watson, 1992; Wendt and Friedheim, 1996; Ruggie, 1998b; Paul, 1999).

Analysing the different historical forms that international relations has taken in the past enables us critically to rethink the particular forms that it has taken in the last three hundred years. As we note in the subsequent discussion of Buzan and Little's 'structural realist' historical sociology, the key point here is that anarchy is not a pure self-constituting monolith but is itself *differentiated*, in that it almost always exists in conjunction with various cross-cutting subsystem hierarchies. Rather than imagining a contemporary world covered in a pure blanket of anarchy, historical sociology reveals it as one that comprises an extremely delicate mosaic or patchwork of intersecting anarchies and subsystem hierarchies. Accordingly, it should be the task of historical sociologists to tease out the various processes that create this continuously changing mosaic.

Problematising 'inter-systemic' and 'inter-societal' relations

Assuming the world to be a monolithic anarchy is problematic not least because it fails to recognise that there has not been just one international system throughout history, but many (as noted above). Having recognised this point, we should consider how their boundaries have contracted and expanded over time, both historically and contemporaneously. It is important to differentiate the boundaries of international *systems* (which are territorial) from those of international *societies* (which are moral). Thus in breaking with tempocentrism, historical sociology offers us new ways of thinking about and theorising 'inter-systemic' and 'inter-societal' relations, and enables us to begin charting the expansion and contraction of the territorial boundaries of international systems, and the moral boundaries of international societies, something which is raised in the works of various historical sociologists (e.g., Mann, 1986; Watson, 1992; Linklater, 1998, and this volume; Buzan and Little, 2000, and this volume).

So to sum up the arguments of this section: the view that the international is an anarchy comprising territorially demarcated sovereign states is less the product of common sense and more the result of an intellectual construction. Historical sociological insight reveals that mainstream international relations theorists have in effect taken a chronofetishist 'snapshot' of the present Westphalian system at a particular moment, from which its most basic features were extracted without regard to its specific historical setting, in order to derive a 'scientific' theory of international relations. This can only be problematic because the Westphalian 'moment' is *precisely* that: it is the temporal exception rather than the norm in international history. The next move by mainstream international relations theorists was to take this exceptional 'moment' and then tempocentrically extrapolate it back in time so as to tarnish *all* historical systems as isomorphic or homologous, thereby imposing an historically sanitised and totalised character to past and present international relations, and obscuring the significant differences and discontinuities between historical systems. Indeed, 'Waltz (mis)takes the Westphalian moment for the ontology of the international system' (Spruyt, 1998: 19). But it is also clear from the above discussion that this chronofetishised snapshot failed to pick up some of the most fundamental constitutive features of the present system, features that can only be brought into focus through a more sensitive historical sociological lens.

In short, historical sociological insight is significant not simply because it tells us new things about previous historical international systems. More importantly, it is significant because, firstly, it forces international relations theorists to move beyond chronofetishism and tempocentrism, and thereby problematise the most basic institutional, moral and spatial forms that constitute modern international relations; and, secondly, it provides new ways of theorising and explaining the emergence and development of the modern international system/society in its multiple dimensions. Thus our project necessarily entails a rejection of the mainstream project, which unwittingly seeks to impose a totalising logic of continuity and regularity upon a temporally protean past and present international relations. In this way then, there is clearly a great deal at stake in 'bringing historical sociology back into international relations' for the discipline as a whole.

Transcending chronofetishism and tempocentrism in international relations: seven major historical sociological approaches in international relations

I now turn to a discussion of the seven major historical sociological approaches that are covered in this volume. My task here is twofold: firstly, to provide an outline of what each of the theories looks like; and secondly, to show how each approach overcomes either chronofetishism or tempocentrism, or both. The chosen format is *not* meant to convey seven mutually exclusive approaches; nor does it convey *all* the various historical sociological approaches that are presently on offer within international relations – two of which are the English School and feminism. The omission of the former is partially made good by the fact that both Linklater and Buzan and Little explicitly draw on the English School. Unfortunately, we have not covered feminism. While this is regrettable, we do insist that a feminist approach would have a great deal to offer the historical sociological project outlined here.

Neo-Weberian historical sociology in international relations

Of all the historical sociological approaches on offer in international relations, the neo-Weberian is ironically one of the most famous, with references to Mann, Giddens, Skocpol and Tilly appearing frequently; 'ironically' because it is equally apparent that within the international relations community as a whole, there is as yet very little understanding of what neo-Weberianism comprises and above all, how it can be applied to international relations – Hobden (1998) is a notable exception. The approach has been summarised elsewhere through 'six principles', which amount to the fundamental commitments to ontological complexity (see Hobson, 1998a: 286–96) and an historicist approach.

In his chapter, John Hobson argues that there have been two waves of Weberian historical sociology within international relations: a 'first wave', which adopts a neorealist and reductionist theory of the state and international relations – found typically in Skocpol (1979), Collins (1986) and

Tilly (1990) – and a 'second wave', which seeks to develop a more complex or methodologically pluralist, *non*-realist approach. Hobson argues that the adoption of a neorealist definition of the international by first-wave Weberians necessarily leads them unwittingly to contradict the basic objectives that their explanatory model seeks to realise. It causes them to: 'kick the state back out'; produce a sociologically *reductionist* account of social change; and posit a distinct separation between the national and international realms. The deepest irony, though, is that in the process, they become incapable of overcoming chronofetishism and tempocentrism, and accordingly deny their commitment to *historical sociological* enquiry.

To solve these problems, Hobson calls for the need to develop a 'second-wave' Weberian historical sociology approach, which breaks with neorealism, and adopts a *non*-realist conception of both the state and the international. To achieve this, he argues for a *structurationist* approach, which notes that state–society complexes are agents that both constitute, and are constituted by, socio-domestic and international/global structures. Borrowing the phrase from Buzan and Little, he argues that we need a 'thick' conception of the international, and by extension, a thick conception of the state–society complex, which implies that international and domestic structures are co-constituted and are fundamentally embedded within a series of social relationships. This is necessary because it is the prevailing thin conceptions of the state and the international that have led to chronofetishism and tempocentrism. To develop and *illustrate* this model he draws on the case study of trade regime change in late-nineteenth-century Europe.

In essence, he begins by bracketing state–society agency and focuses on the international and domestic structural forces that pushed continental states to shift from relatively free trade back to tariff protectionism after 1877. In particular, all states faced fiscal crisis owing to the fact that the second military revolution increased the costs of war at the same time that economic depression led to a contraction of government revenues. Domestically, most states faced social pressures to move towards protectionism, mainly from their dominant classes. Weak states – those that were isolated from society and had low amounts of infrastructural power – chose to increase indirect taxes and, therefore, shifted to tariff protectionism (tariffs are an indirect tax). The strong British state – which was broadly embedded in both the working and dominant classes, and had high levels of infrastructural power – was able to avoid tariff protectionism because it could resort to the income tax. Accordingly it maintained free trade until the First World War. But, he argues, if we left it here, we would end up with a structuralist approach, in which states simply respond or conform to international and domestic structural constraints.

The second part of the argument brackets structure and focuses on the agency of state–society complexes. Here governments dipped into the domestic and international 'resource pools' in order to push through domestic reforms – reforms which had nothing to do with conforming to international structural requirements. Thus the German government dipped into the international economic realm and raised tariffs so that it could enhance its despotic power over the lower classes (as did the Russian government), as well as to enhance the power of the dominant Junker class. The British government, by contrast, maintained free trade and used this in order to push through the income tax to court the working classes, while simultaneously catering to the trading needs of the dominant classes. In sum, trade regime change was informed by a complex mixture of variables – domestic, national and international. And moreover, he argues, only an approach which focuses on structure *and* agency can provide a sufficient explanation of trade regime change.

Finally, this approach enables a break with prevailing chronofetishist and tempocentric theories of the rise of free trade after 1945. He argues that the mid-nineteenth-century free trade regime was different from the post-1945 regime, not least because the former was far less robust and far less 'free' than the latter. The differences are explained by the presence of two radically different constellations of social power forces, comprising international normative environments, international institutional architectures and the social embeddedness of the state–society complex. The earlier regime was based on a *neo-mercantilist* international norm, a *bilateral* international institutional architecture, and a *socially disembedded* state–society complex which, once the costs of government rose, turned immediately to tariffs to secure the required revenues. Accordingly, the regime was both weak and temporary. By contrast the post-1945 regime was based on an *embedded liberal* set of international norms, a *multilateral* international institutional architecture, and a *socially embedded* state–society complex which relied on the income tax and could therefore drop its earlier dependence on tariffs for fiscal revenues. Accordingly, the convergence of these three social power configurations enabled a much freer and more robust trade regime in the post-1945 era. In this way, he argues, only an historical sociological analysis of state–society relations that breaks with chronofetishism and tempocentrism can reveal the unique social forces that underpinned and enabled the seemingly 'natural' post-1945 free trade regime.

I include Martin Shaw's piece in this section because it draws on neo-Weberianism, even though it does not fit the pure label, given that he also seeks to draw on Marx. Critical of prevailing sociological models of globalisation, he argues that they exaggerate the importance of economic and, especially, technological forces, at the expense of the political and

military dimensions of globalisation. His argument begins with the claim
that '1945' represents the major discontinuity or historical turning point
in world development – one which witnessed a transition from a state system based on 'imperial nation-states' to one based on a single Western
state 'conglomerate', where the component states have pooled their 'monopolies of violence'. The Western states no longer confront each other
as potential military enemies but form one large internally pacified conglomerate, which has been territorially demarcated as such since 1945.
Its relative strength derives from its unrivalled economic and military resources as well as its strong authoritative resources. These authoritative
resources are based on the 'democratic revolution', which now defines
the principal axis of world politics – between a democratic Western state
conglomerate and a non-Western system of 'quasi-imperial patrimonial
states'. As a direct challenge to 'first-wave' Weberian historical sociology, Shaw claims that 'to try to understand "international" relations in
exclusively, or principally, geopolitical terms goes against much that has
been gained in the "new" international theorising of the last decade, and
much of what historical sociology is placed to offer' (p. 92). He goes on
to argue that *international* relations among Western states has now given
way to *internal* relations within the conglomerate, thereby fundamentally
breaking with chronofetishism by revealing the present system as open
to change. He simultaneously breaks with tempocentrism in so far as he
is able to delineate fundamental breaks or discontinuities between traditional and modern international relations.

Shaw argues that the case study of revolution provides a useful means
for rethinking international relations (cf. Halliday, 1994, 1999). Halliday
has analysed the international forces that led to domestic revolution,
which then led back to inter-state conflict (i.e., an international–national–
international chain). Shaw extends this approach by effectively conceptualising a set of transnational linkages that flow across global society.
Specifically, he notes a linkage between global revolution, democratic
revolution and genocidal war. The democratic revolution is radically different from previous notions of revolution in so far as it: represents the end
of the linkage between centralised revolutionary parties and the seizure
of political power; creates a link with universal standards of democracy
and human rights; and establishes a link with the state-building activities
of oppressed minorities. This has two ramifications for global politics: it
strengthens the international bureaucracy of the UN system, and it enables the expansion of the Western state, which is increasingly involved
in humanitarian intervention in the old imperial-patrimonial states. This
enables him to locate a fundamental change in the mode of warfare.

Following Mary Kaldor, he argues that modern warfare can no longer
be understood as a 'socially neutral' means of resolving issues between

states (as in traditional *realpolitik*), but is fundamentally based on the internal conflicts that emanate within the old patrimonial states. These conflicts appear as ethnic in nature, but are in fact political conflicts between patrimonial elites that are seeking to suppress democratic (or counter-revolutionary) movements, often through genocide within their own countries. As these local conflicts spread across the old patrimonial world, so they draw in the Western state, in turn promoting the coherence of the conglomerate as well as enhancing the bureaucratic layer of the UN. In this way, he adapts Halliday's argument and shows how global democratic revolutionary norms impact upon the populations of the patrimonial states, which then engage in the struggle for reform domestically. As the patrimonial elites fight back with genocide, so the Western state and the UN become involved in warfare. Thus the dialectic of international war and domestic social revolution continues but in an historically new form, which not only changes the mode of warfare, but fundamentally enhances the emerging supranational political structures that emerged after 1945.

Constructivist historical sociology in international relations

As with Weberian historical sociology, constructivism began life within sociology, but has in the last decade diffused across into international relations. While there are a variety of constructivist approaches (see Price and Reus-Smit, 1998; Hobson, 2000: ch. 5), I begin by setting out four general principles that lie at the base of constructivism, and then consider how our constructivist contributors develop an historical sociology of international relations.

(1)   *The primacy of ideational factors.* Constructivists argue that mainstream international relations theory is excessively materialist (or 'rationalist'), and fails to capture the autonomy of norms that guide and shape state behaviour. In their parlance, norms are 'constitutive' rather than simply 'regulatory'.

(2)   *Agent interests are derived from identity-construction, which is constituted in the course of social interaction.* Rationalism views agent preferences as unproblematic – that they are exogenously formed prior to social interaction. Rather than beginning with an inherent portfolio of interests which agents seek to maximise on the international stage through an 'instrumental rationality', constructivists insist that state interests are derived from agents' identity, which is in turn derived by the process of 'normative socialisation'. Michael Barnett and Chris Reus-Smit both argue that constructivists are inherently structurationist: that constructivists 'are just

as concerned with the role of agents' practices in the production and re-production of social structures, as they are with the way those structures shape agents' identies and interests (Reus-Smit, p. 132).

(3) *Communicative action and moral norms specify 'appropriate' behaviour.* Actors tend to follow behaviour that is deemed to be morally appropriate or legitimate. As Reus-Smit points out, in those instances in which agents pursue behaviour that does not comply with these moral norms, so they will have to justify their behaviour. And they justify their behaviour by appealing to established codes of social conduct in the 'linguistic court of appeal'. The upshot of this is that justifying behaviour in terms of moral norm compliance acts as a constraining force upon actor behaviour. Failure to comply is punished by 'shame' and, at the extreme, by sanctions or even war.

(4) *The importance of historical international change.* Agent identities are highly malleable and change as normative structures change. Because identities change as normative and moral structures change, so the process of international change becomes a fundamental aspect of the constructivist project. It is mainly at this point that constructivism overlaps with historical sociology, because by charting changes in actor behaviour, constructivists examine the changes in norms through historical time and how these impact differently upon inter-state relations (see especially, Hall and Kratochwil, 1993; Ferguson and Mansbach, 1996; R. Hall, 1999; Reus-Smit, 1999). And as Michael Barnett argues in his chapter, constructivism overlaps with historical sociology in so far as it: seeks to recover the roots of social constructs over time; examines the role that individual acts and events play in producing international change; and notes the path-dependency associated with the impact of previous historical events. More specifically, he argues, constructivism shares with Weberian historical sociology the desire to: overcome mono-causal theory; examine the direction of historical change; chart the changing social properties that structure social interaction; and engage in case-based research especially through the comparative method.

Concerning the fourth point, our two constructivist contributors between them pose an interesting conundrum. Barnett argues that while there is much potential overlap between constructivism and historical sociology, it remains largely unexplored at present. The reason for this, he argues, concerns the specific moment of constructivism's birth within international relations. In seeking to gain 'disciplinary legitimacy', constructivists had to take on neoliberalism and neorealism, both of which are, as we noted above, 'historophobic'. In meeting them on their own grounds, many (though clearly not all) constructivists have tended to focus on rethinking the present. By contrast Reus-Smit argues that constructivism is inherently historical sociological (though paradoxically, Barnett would not disagree). As he puts it, 'norms change over time, making historical process and change central constructivist concerns'. Either way though, the central questions to be answered here are: how does constructivism develop the historical research agenda within international relations; and how does constructivism overcome chronofetishism and tempocentrism?

Michael Barnett argues that there are at least three possible research areas that constructivists should develop in order to advance historical sociology in international relations: first, the need to develop better analyses of state–society relations (an area that, he argues, Marxist and Weberian historical sociologists have pursued for a long time); second, the need to examine political economy issues – which constructivists, he argues, have hitherto largely conceded to rationalist approaches (but see Burch and Denemark, 1997); and third, the need to consider the overlap between state-formation, bureaucratisation and international organisations (IOs). The second part of his chapter develops this third area in some detail. Here he draws on Max Weber's account of bureaucracy and uses it to demonstrate the autonomy and importance of IOs within contemporary global society. In this analysis, Barnett draws close to what I have called an 'international society-centric' constructivist approach (Hobson, 2000: ch. 5), which focuses primarily on the importance of international norms and international organisations in the shaping of state identities, interests and policies.

Barnett begins by noting Weber's four defining criteria of modern bureaucratic organisation: hierarchy, continuity of functions, impersonality of procedures, and specialist knowledge or expertise of officials. The key point that he makes concerns the power or autonomy that bureaucracies derive from these norms. Following Weber (1978), he argues that bureaucratisation introduces new forms of *authority* – specifically 'rational-legal' authority – which modernity views as 'legitimate' and 'good'. Independence is also generated by the procedural form that bureaucratic organisation entails. Thus, first, bureaucrats have technical and specialist knowledge which generates considerable 'authority'. Second, bureaucratic power is 'cloaked power': it paradoxically emerges through the discourse of rationality, impartiality and objectivity. Third, bureaucracies are not neutral regulatory institutions, which enable actors to overcome co-ordination problems; they also instruct actors as to what their 'proper' goals and activities should be. From here, Barnett suggests that bureaucratic norms empower IOs in the international realm. As he puts it, 'IOs have a distinct [bureaucratic] organisational culture, [their] officials have autonomy and [they] can act without the permission of states, and in opposition to state interests' (p. 113). Thus IOs gain authority through their role as experts, working within a so-called neutral, apolitical and technocratic environment. IOs do not simply solve co-ordination problems that confront states, but also wield authoritative power, which enables them to specify the normatively desirable means and ends for such problems to be solved. This enables him to overcome the chronofetishist 'naturalist illusion', firstly, by showing how international bureaucracies are not apolitical and neutral, but are fundamentally 'implicated in power politics' and, secondly, by showing how IOs are transforming the present international realm. He also provides a way of overcoming the tempocentric 'isomorphic illusion' by demonstrating a radical discontinuity between present and past world politics in terms of the emergence of IOs and new patterns of authority relations.

One of the most interesting linkages between the constructivist analyses of Barnett and Reus-Smit concerns their treatment of Max Weber's classic definition of the state: 'A compulsory political organization with continuous operations ... will be called a "state" insofar as its administrative staff successfully upholds the claim to the monopoly of the legitimate use of physical force [violence] in the enforcement of its order' (Weber, 1978: 54, 56; Weber 1948: 78). Reus-Smit, in particular, takes neo-Weberians to task for their materialist reading of Weber's theory of the state, and seeks rather to emphasise the constructivist dimension of the theory: namely, that part which emphasises 'legitimacy' and 'authority'. He notes that there are at least two cues for a constructivist theory to be found in the works of Max Weber – that his theory of the state emphasises legitimacy and that Weber's 'switchman metaphor' is suggestive of the role that ideas can play in international change (Weber, 1948: 280; Weber, 1926: 347–8). Nevertheless, he concludes that in the end, both Weber and neo-Weberianism fall short of producing a full 'history with ideas', because ideas are treated only as 'intervening', rather than 'full', independent, variables. However, though such a claim is forcefully and well argued, it glosses over some constructivist strands found in the works of Mann (also Hobson, this volume, pp. 78–80). Nevertheless, it would be entirely fair to conclude that neo-Weberians need to draw out the constructivist strand more fully. Either way though, Reus-Smit seeks to explicitly resuscitate the constructivist cue in Weber's work, in order better to account for both epochal change and changing international institutional architectures. Here he places prime focus on how domestic conceptions of the moral purpose of the state affect the conduct of international relations.

He begins by arguing that the common equation of the birth of the modern international system with the emergence of sovereignty in 1648 is problematic for three main reasons: first, sovereignty is not the only aspect of the modern system, but is one of three core principles that define the modern – the other two being a 'hegemonic conception of the moral purpose of the state' and a 'norm of procedural justice'. Second, sovereignty itself needs to be problematised given that its meaning changes through time. And third, while sovereignty existed from the fifteenth century to the early nineteenth century, the period saw two different conceptions of sovereignty at different times. Moreover, the core features of the modern international institutional architecture – contractual international law and multilateralism – were not established until the mid-nineteenth century. As Reus-Smit puts it, 'Why did the paired institutions of contractual international law and multilateralism – which together provide the basic structure of governance in the modern international system – not take off until after the age of revolutions?' (p. 135).

In order to rethink epochal change, Reus-Smit proposes two new conceptions of change: first, 'purposive change', which involves a redefinition of the moral purpose of the state, in turn leading to shifts in the meaning of sovereignty and procedural justice; and second, 'configurative change', which entails a shift in the moral purpose of the state, as well as a shift in the spatial configuration of international politics – or what Ruggie (1983) describes as 'systems change'. The period between 1555 and 1815 was an example of configurative change, in which the moral purpose of the state changed and the spatial configuration of inter-state politics shifted. But the key point is that the new system was *not* modern: states enjoyed 'dynastic' sovereignty, which implied an 'authoritative' conception of procedural justice, where 'the standards of right and wrong were dictated ... by a supreme authority – God in the first instance, monarchs by deputation' (Reus-Smit, p. 138). Here law was 'law as command'. And because international law came to reflect this reconceptualisation of the moral purpose of the state, it came to be understood as an expression of God's law, as opposed to one based on reciprocally binding contracts between sovereigns. This, he argues, explains why modern multilateralism did *not* emerge under dynastic sovereignty.

The most important shift in international politics came not in 1648 as is conventionally thought, but *after* 1789, when the new principles associated with the French Revolution led to a 'purposive change' – to new conceptions of sovereignty and procedural justice. Only after 1789 did the fundamental institutional aspects of the modern system emerge. The moral purpose of the state was redefined by new *individualist* norms, based around a broader conception of citizenship rights. This in turn affected international law and procedural justice, such that the former came to express the notion of reciprocal accord (in which new domestic conceptions of the general will were internationalised into contractual international law), and the latter took the form of multilateralism. Accordingly, multilateralism took off in the nineteenth century.

In sum, Reus-Smit produces an important contribution to an historical sociology of international relations, by linking moral changes in domestic state behaviour to changes in international law and forms of international procedural justice. He is able to break with chronofetishism by denaturalising the present as well as by tracing its historical origins, and simultaneously breaks with tempocentrism by revealing the present system as fundamentally different to that of the past.

World systems historical sociology in international relations

Most international relations theorists associate world systems theory with Immanuel Wallerstein. What this misses is that in the last decade, world systems theory has progressed into a new form which shares some commonalities with Wallerstein, but also makes some radical departures. To capture the differences, I refer to *classical* world systems theory (associated with the likes of Immanuel Wallerstein and Samir Amin), and *neoclassical* world systems theory (associated with the recent work of André Gunder Frank, Barry Gills and others) (for a full discussion, see Hobson, 2000: ch. 4). Wallerstein's approach is well known in international relations, though for the most part, he is most closely associated with his theory of *dependency* (known as the 'layer cake model'). International relations scholars, however, are much less familiar with his historical sociological approach.

Wallerstein's historical sociology advocates a strong break between the modern world system and the pre-modern, where the former is based on a world-economy founded on the 'law of ceaseless accumulation', and the latter was based on world empires and a 'tributary mode of production' (Wallerstein, 1974: 15; Amin, 1996; Wallerstein, 1996). By contrast, neoclassical world systems theorists do away with the 'great discontinuity' and the related assumption of historical 'dichotomies', and in their place posit, in Gills's words, a 'continuity thesis'. Arguably (though Gills denies this), the approach tends to repeat the tempocentric mistake that mainstream international relations theory makes, since the past is made to look the same as the present. Such writers insist that the rise of the West did not occur because of the rise of a modern world system/economy *after* 1500;

it was merely the latest phase or shift *within the pre-existent world system* (see the contributions in Frank and Gills, 1996). As Frank puts it, 'the world system was not born in 1500; it did not arise in Europe; and it is not distinctively capitalist' (Frank, 1996: 202). In strict contrast, they trace it back some 5,000 years to 3500 BC – although Abu-Lughod (1989) traces it back to AD 1250. Thus there has been not many, but only one world system, which has existed for 5,000 years and has been governed by the timeless and regular beat of a series of about ten 500-year 'long-wave cycles'.

The key point here is that in positing a 'continuity problematic', Gills seeks to make a series of adjustments to some of the familiar concepts that are employed by most Western social scientists. In claiming that capitalism has been around for some five millennia, *neoclassical* world system theory effectively suggests that the 'pre-modern' needs to be economically upgraded, while the modern needs to be economically downgraded. Or as Barry Gills puts it in his chapter here, 'In general we have tended to view the "pre-modern" as being too primitive, and the "modern" as being rather too modern' (p. 143). The dismissal of the '1500 discontinuity' necessarily requires us to do away with the prevailing dichotomous concepts of developmental history: between 'feudalism and capitalism', 'free and unfree labour' (Marx), '*oikos* and bureaucratic capitalism', 'merchant capitalism and rational capitalism' (Weber), or '*gemeinschaft* and *gesellschaft*' (Toennies). Smoothing out these differences necessarily requires a rethink of these fundamental 'dual' categories that have long dominated historical sociology. This is one of the major tasks that preoccupies Gills in his chapter in this volume.

Because the relations of distribution rather than the relations of production were central for Wallerstein, he was able to argue that since 1600, the world economy has been capitalist, even though the social relations of production across the world system took on a variety of forms – of free and unfree labour. Gills applies a similar logic but effectively extrapolates it back to 3500 BC. Thus he argues that free and unfree labour, as well as '*oikos* and capital', have *always* co-existed in a dialectical relationship. Moreover, he argues that even in the contemporary world system, a variety of forms of social relations continue to exist; so much so that he argues that slavery has been instrumental in the rise of the modern phase of the world system, and that it is even now re-emerging in large parts of the world.

Even if Gills's approach does not fully succeed in overcoming tempocentrism, I believe that he is partially correct to point out that capitalism is not entirely new and unique to the modern West, and that Eurasia rather than solely Europe was the creator of modern capitalism. And in this respect his approach most definitely overcomes chronofetishism in so far as he is able to problematise the 'orientalist' assumptions of much of the developmental theory literature.

Critical historical materialist historical sociology in international relations

A fourth major historical sociological approach which has recently emerged in international relations is that of critical theory. Though critical theory is a complex body of thought with many different variants, what unites all critical theorists is a rejection of what Cox (1986) calls 'problem-solving theory'. Rather than search for ways to manage the present system as smoothly as possible, critical theory is not only *critical* of present structures and institutions, but also *emancipatory* in that it seeks to find, and make possible the construction of, a new society – in both the domestic and international realms – that is free of social exclusion (Cox, 1986). Two of the leading writers in this field are Robert Cox and Andrew Linklater, who develop complementary but ultimately different approaches. This volume displays both variants, with Linklater setting out his own version (discussed in the next section), and A. Claire Cutler setting out a version which leans heavily on Cox's Gramscian theory. It is worth noting that Gramscian analysis has been utilised by a growing number of scholars within both international relations and international political economy, and within an historical sociological context (see, especially, Murphy, 1994).

Cutler's central task is to rethink the role of international law and to show how it has played a vital constitutive role in the determination of economic social relations. She begins by claiming that the study of international law in international relations is in 'crisis' – a crisis that originates with the tendency of mainstream international relations and international law theory to utilise a state-centric and ahistorical 'instrumental' framework. Such mainstream approaches are 'instrumental' because they posit international law to be a mere instrument of states, to be used, or neglected, in the furtherance of states' goals. And they are simultaneously ahistorical because they focus only on 'positive' international law (which is determined by states) and necessarily obscure the degree to which 'customary' international law empowers a range of non-state actors, which challenge the statist orthodoxy. Cutler's *remedy* for the chronofetishist and tempocentric illusions with which international law is understood within the mainstream, rests on the theme of a dialectical process that constitutes international law, which is intimately connected with reconceiving international law as praxis. This dialectical process begins with the formulation of formal positive law, created by and for states, but which necessarily gives voice to anti-statist non-state actors which harness potentially emancipatory and liberating practices. And praxis embodies the notion that law (traditionally assigned to the 'superstructure') can come to constitute social relations and simultaneously enable the contestation of the power of the dominant hegemonic bloc by the marginalised.

In developing her preferred critical historical materialist approach, Cutler begins by rejecting 'crude' (or 'vulgar') Marxist materialism, which operationalises the traditional 'base–superstructure' model (outlined in Marx, 1976). In this model the 'independent' base, comprising the class struggle within the 'mode of production' (i.e., the social relations of production), determines the form and function of the 'dependent' superstructure (i.e., everything that lies outside of the mode of production – in this case, international law). In consigning state behaviour and international law to the superstructure, such a 'vulgar' Marxist approach views them as 'epiphenomenal' (i.e., wholly determined by the class struggle), and accordingly denies such 'superstructural elements' any effectivity as an historical-social force. In turn, because Cutler's prime objective is to restore the role of international law as a social force that does not simply reflect class imperatives, but also constitutes the social relations of production, she necessarily seeks to find a critical alternative to the traditional base–superstructure model. In this task, she joins the majority of neo-Marxists whose dissatisfaction with this model is aptly conveyed in Ellen Wood's words: 'The base/superstructure model has always been more trouble than it is worth. Although Marx himself used it very rarely . . . it has been made to bear a theoretical weight far beyond its limited capacities' (Wood, 1995: 49).

Her solution to this is to go beyond the famous 'relative autonomy of the state' approach of the French structuralist school (which still in fact operationalises a base–superstructure model), and effectively to *collapse* the distinction between the base and superstructure altogether, thereby in effect positing international law as constitutive of the base. In the process, she draws from two main currents of neo-Marxism which have invoked this solution to the problem of the base–superstructure model, namely Gramscian theory (Gramsci, 1971; Cox, 1986) and Political Marxism (e.g., Thompson, 1975; Wood, 1995) – the latter finding its 'international relations voice' in the work of Rosenberg (1994). She draws on Gramsci's notion of hegemony, in order to reveal the 'mechanisms by which laws become internalised in the consciousness of people', which enables her to then consider how 'we might begin to theorise law as an effective agent in history' (p. 197). This also enables her to consider the ways in which 'counter-hegemonic' forces pursue their various eman- cipatory political projects. Thus she is able to reveal the emancipatory processes that remain obscured by mainstream chronofetishist analyses of international law.

In breaking with chronofetishism, she seeks to allow a plethora of hid- den voices to be heard, not least those of women and indigenous peoples as well as those of the working class. More generally, her critical analy- sis enables the theorist to examine the ways in which various aspects of international law have 'historically operated to exclude marginalised and repressed peoples and developing countries by favouring existing positive law over potentially destabilising, if not revolutionary, customary law' (p. 199). By breaking with the rigidity of traditional Marxist approaches and simultaneously conceiving international law as informed by dialec- tics and praxis, she is thereby able to reveal the counter-hegemonic forces that are presently destabilising the international order. Moreover, her ap- proach also breaks with tempocentrism in so far as she is able to reveal fundamental differences in the constitution of international law over time, something which she develops elsewhere (Cutler, forthcoming).

Critical historical sociology of international relations

All versions of critical historical sociology are especially strong both in their ability to overcome tempocentrism, by revealing the radical breaks between the past and present, and in their ability to overcome chronofe- tishism by denaturalising existing structures and institutions, and thereby revealing the present as an immanent order of change. Echoing Cox's clarion call, Linklater begins his recent book *The Transformation of Polit- ical Community* by arguing that 'social investigation reveals that present structures are not natural and permanent but have a history and are likely to be succeeded by different arrangements in the future. Identifying the seeds of future existing social orders is a key feature of [historical] socio- logical enquiry' (Linklater, 1998: 3). Unlike critical Marxists such as Cox and Cutler, Linklater does not advocate revolution and the overthrow of the mode of production as the means of achieving the universal society, ultimately because he sees the problem of 'social exclusion' as something which cannot be reduced only to class factors or the mode of produc- tion. Instead he emphasises the importance of 'praxeology', which refers to the process of 'reflecting on the moral resources within existing social arrangements which political actors can harness for radical purposes. It is preoccupied not with issues of strategy and tactics but with revealing that new forms of political community are immanent within existing forms of life and anticipated by their moral reserves' (Linklater, 1998: 5).

In particular, Linklater's normative praxeology advocates a 'triple trans-formation' of political community which comprises the need to reduce material inequality, the need to ensure respect for difference (especially across different cultures as well as between the sexes and among income groups) and, finally, the need to ensure the advance of an ethical uni-versalism, which means transcending the effects of the modern state's particularistic or 'totalising' project – a concept which he borrows from Corrigan and Sayer (1985). He is centrally concerned with the process by which states construct the identity of their societies, which are de-fined negatively against 'foreign others'. Linklater is able to overcome tempocentrism in so far as he posits a discontinuity between the past and present by showing that modern states create *particularistic* definitions of identity, as opposed to the more *universalist* notions that ancient states relied on. Following Mann (1986), he argues that ancient states had in-sufficient power resources to be able to create highly exclusively defined societies, and accordingly tended to rely on universalist ideologies. By contrast, the modern state is very effective at achieving high levels of ex-clusion (i.e., totalising projects), owing to its high levels of infrastructural and surveillance powers (a position which is not altogether different from Carr's (1951) concept of the 'socialised nation'). But it is a central as-pect of his argument that while the modern state has been able to initiate highly particularistic 'totalising projects', these have, nevertheless, been resisted by social movements. And it is social resistance that creates the possibility of the emergence of what he calls a 'universal communica-tion community', which could ultimately transcend the 'totalising' state. Herein lies the central contradiction or 'paradox' of the modern state (Linklater, 1998: 146–61): that the totalising state, to paraphrase Marx, creates the seeds of its own destruction. This is also enabled by the pro-cess of globalisation, which has served to greatly enlarge the moral and sociological horizons of peoples across global society (Linklater, 1998: 155), thereby providing a growing counter-measure to particularism.

His concept of the universal communication community draws on Habermas's concept of moral learning, in which the creation of *dialogic communities* presents the best opportunity for the reconstruction of inter-national society. A dialogic community is one in which the systematically excluded enter into dialogue about the ways in which social practices harm their interests; and it is one in which individuals are equal and free to decide the principles of inclusion and exclusion which regulate their lives (Linklater, 1998: 176). Drawing on the arguments of the English School, he argues that within contemporary Europe, there is evidence of what Hedley Bull (1966b; see also Wheeler, 1992) called a 'solidarist' international society – which resists the exclusion of individuals, minority nations and indigenous peoples from the protection of international law (Linklater, 1998: 168). This community enables the transcendence of particularistic forms of exclusion by widening the boundaries of communication and by enabling a redress of injustices suffered, especially through human rights violations. These strong co-operative international norms provide a launching pad for the transition to a post-Westphalian society, in which the principles of sovereignty, territoriality and national citizenship come to an end, to be replaced by a universal communication community. In this way, Linklater breaks with the chronofetishist 'immutability illusion' in that he is able to envisage change beyond the present system.

In his chapter in this volume, Linklater complements and builds upon the arguments of his recent book by setting out to develop a 'critical historical sociology of transnational harm'. Transnational harm is defined in the generic sense as 'injury caused by the state, or non-state actors, or forms of social organisation to the members of another society or societies', and is differentiated from *international* harm which is harm that states do to other states. He also analyses *concrete* harm (which has predominated throughout most of world history), in which particular societies *intentionally* impose harm on those deemed to be 'different' and 'inferior', and contemporary *abstract* harm, which is unintentionally diffused across boundaries, principally through universal modes of production and exchange. Abstract harm is especially significant in that it throws up possibilities of creating new cosmopolitan political organisations, which can in turn reduce such harm. How, then, is this incorporated into an historical sociological approach to international relations?

Linklater's critical historical sociology approach charts the construction of 'harm conventions', which refer to the *cultural* configuration of bounded communities, 'and particularly [to] that area of the moral code which sets out what can and cannot be done to outsiders', and how these conventions *differ* among societies and across civilisations through historical time (thereby offering a remedy for tempocentrism). In particular he shows how, in the modern world, abstract harm is increasingly replacing concrete harm. Thus a central task for a critical historical sociology of international relations 'is to reflect on the world-historical significance of the changing relationship between concrete and abstract transnational harm' (pp. 179–80). Moreover, he argues that perhaps *the* central concern for such an approach is to ask whether the present international system can establish a 'universal communications community', and thereby finally abolish all forms of exclusion and oppression. This is a question which he answers in the affirmative (simultaneously enabling him to break with the chronofetishist 'immutability illusion').

Postmodern historical sociology in international relations

In his chapter, Steve Smith provocatively argues that mainstream historical sociology is statist and realist on the epistemological grounds that it is 'causal' rather than interpretivist, materialist rather than idealist, and utilises an 'outsider' rather than an 'insider' account (i.e., is positivist). Accordingly, he sees it as either part or potentially part of (i.e., able to speak directly to) mainstream international relations theory (i.e., neorealism and neoliberalism). In its place he advocates a postmodern approach, derived largely though not exclusively from Foucault, which he views as a radical alternative to mainstream historical sociology. Ultimately his message is not nihilistic (in the sense that he does not see all historical sociology as inadequate) – and he argues that a postmodern historical sociology is not only possible but also the only desirable alternative to mainstream international relations theory. In the following discussion I do not intend to evaluate his critique of mainstream historical sociology (this is reserved for chapter 13, pp. 272–4). But I shall take a different stance concerning postmodernism's contribution to the historical sociological project. In essence, while he sees it as a radical alternative to mainstream historical sociology, I see it as but one variant of the overall project, and one, therefore, that complements all the others. I do not accept his separation of postmodernism (i.e., reflectivism) on the one hand from mainstream historical sociology on the other; rather, I see all the variants as placed along a continuum (at one end of which is a materialist/outsider account and at the other is an idealist/insider account).

Smith offers us the basic structure of his preferred Foucauldian approach, but accepts that he has not applied it to producing an actual historical sociology of international relations. In order to produce such a picture, I shall draw on Smith's discussion but illustrate it with the arguments made by various postmodernists such as Richard Price and Cynthia Weber. In my opinion, postmodernism offers us one of the most interesting, and dare I say more important, historical sociology variants, in large part because it offers such a powerful means to overcome or remedy the problems of chronofetishism and tempocentrism. And although I see constructivism and postmodernism as complementary historical sociological variants (as Smith does), in that they are both 'idealist' and operationalise 'insider' accounts, nevertheless, there are in my view some crucial differences, most notably the way they deal with power. Constructivists have (perhaps overly) concerned themselves with denying rationalist premises, and in the process have tended to downplay, and at times altogether deny, the role of power. For constructivists, norms are in no way an effect of power; rather, norms guide and channel actors' identities and hence interests. For postmodernists, while ideas do very much shape agents (as in constructivism), it is also the case that all norms and knowledge itself embody power relations, and that revealing the 'relations of domination' that underpin ideas is a fundamental aspect of their historical sociological approach. This is why they (as opposed to Wendt, 1999) fundamentally reject the 'positivist' assumption of the fact/value distinction.

As Smith argues, one of the central aspects of postmodern historical sociology is its emphasis on the *genealogical method*, which among other things reveals that there is no coherent story or explanation that is waiting to be uncovered, and it seeks to reveal the system of rules that proceed from domination, and how the successful have managed to appropriate these rules. For Foucault 'effective history' introduces discontinuities and seeks to destabilise and deprive 'the self of the reassuring stability of life and nature' (Foucault, cited in Smith, p. 241). One of the criticisms made by various contributors, notably Smith, Reus-Smit and Barnett, is that modern neo-Weberians have neglected or 'betrayed' Max Weber's sociology of legitimacy. Though they tend to downplay the constructivist insight in some neo-Weberian scholarship (e.g., Giddens, 1984; Mann, 1986, 1993; Hobson, ch.3, this volume), nevertheless, I would argue that Weber's legacy has, ironically, been avidly taken up by constructivist and, especially, postmodern historical sociologists, who accord prime attention to the issue of legitimacy.

One important application of this approach concerns the study of sovereignty (Walker, 1993; Bartelson, 1995; C. Weber, 1995). Postmodernists (like constructivists) see sovereignty not as a material phenomenon, which has a meaning that is fixed once and for all (as rationalists assume), but as a social construct whose meaning constantly changes through time (see, especially, Biersteker and Weber, 1996). Postmodernists, however, place particular emphasis on the process of statecraft (the means by which states craft the appearance of domestic legitimacy). Specifically, statecraft, or 'writing the state', refers to a process by which states forge the appearance of a unified domestic political community which they can then claim to legitimately represent through sovereignty – what Weber (1995) calls the 'logic of representation'. This process leads the state to create an arbitrary distinction or separation between the so-called domestic 'good life' and the international 'war of all against all'. By creating the appearance of a threatening 'other', the state is better able to unify the domestic political community (Ashley, 1989; Walker, 1993: ch. 8; Bartelson, 1995: 83–4; C. Weber, 1995: ch. 1). This involves creating a false distinction between 'self' and 'other'. That is, states tend to create the appearance of a *threatening* 'other', against which the 'self' is defined negatively. But because this domestic community is constantly fracturing, so sovereignty constantly fractures. Accordingly, the state must be constantly rewritten, a process through which new ethical bases for the social construction of sovereignty are found. Above all, statecraft requires states to intervene and 'discipline' other 'deviant' states – that is, states whose mode of representation does not equate with that of the disciplinary state and which, therefore, creates a crisis of representation in the disciplinary state (because they offer a potentially attractive alternative). Where, though, is the link with historical sociology?

Rather than black-box sovereignty as an effect of state power and treat it as static if not eternal, postmodernists reveal its contested nature as the site of social struggles, and as something which is made and remade through time. Cynthia Weber (1995), for example, shows how in the last two hundred years, states have engaged in warfare in order to discipline other 'deviant' states. Drawing on Foucault, she chooses three case studies, in which the mode of disciplinary intervention was variously the 'sign', the 'mark' and the 'trace'. And in each case, states came to redefine their mode of sovereignty in order to overcome their crisis of representation. A complementary account to this can be found in Roxanne Doty's historical sociological analysis of the changing identity of the British nation before and after 1945 (Doty, 1996). Such accounts immediately break with tempocentrism, and reveal that the genealogy of sovereignty or the nation is marked by radical discontinuities through historical time, and is the product of social and ethical processes connected with identity formation and legitimacy. And sovereignty (as well as the nation) both reflects *and* constitutes changes in the identity of states and simultaneously leads to changes in the international sphere.

Finally, one of the most interesting examples of this approach is found in Richard Price's *The Chemical Weapons Taboo* (Price, 1997). He shows how the chemical weapons taboo is a social construct that reflects the relations of domination through which the West maintains its superiority over the Third World. Its historical sociological cutting edge derives from the fact that he is able to show how moral interpretations inform the construction of military technological taboos, and he is able to show in rich detail that this process is one that is full of contingencies and discontinuities. Echoing Steve Smith, he insists that such contingencies cannot be revealed by essentialist, materialist and deductive theoretical modes of reasoning, but can only be brought to light by a rejection of causal explanatory theory in favour of an approach that seeks to understand the meaning of discursive practices (Price, 1997: ch. 1). And, of course, the postmodern approach is especially strong in its ability to overcome chronofetishism, given that its prime rationale is to deconstruct and denaturalise international relations – past and present – and to reimagine possible alternative futures. Paradoxically, therefore, postmodernism does not, in my view, transcend 'mainstream historical sociology' as Smith contends, but provides a complementary variant – and one which very powerfully succeeds in remedying tempocentrism and chronofetishism.

Structural realist historical sociology in international relations

The seventh approach contained in this volume – 'structural realism' – emerged at the beginning of the 1990s, making its first appearance in the seminal *The Logic of Anarchy* (Buzan, Jones and Little, 1993), but has been taken further by Buzan and Little (2000, and this volume). Like Weberian historical sociology and critical theory, structural realism is highly eclectic. It draws not just from Waltzian neorealism, but also from a range of other approaches, such as constructivism and the English School. For this reason, the label 'structural realism' is somewhat problematic given that the approach is neither purely neorealist nor structuralist, and should, therefore, *not* be confused with Waltz's 'structural neorealism'. Waltz's theory developed out of his observation that throughout world history, international politics has been governed by *continuity*. It was this 'continuity problematic' that led him to generate a parsimonious theory which explicitly sought to omit the influence of the units, and thereby make the purely defined international political structure ontologically primitive – what Buzan and Little call a 'thin conception' of the international structure. By contrast, their preferred 'structural realism' develops out of the observation that international politics has taken on radically *different* forms over the millennia. Thus by developing a 'thick conception' of the international structure (Buzan, Jones and Little, 1993: 13–14), they are able to break with Waltz's tempocentrism. In this section, I begin with some of the key aspects of the approach that was originally presented in *The Logic of Anarchy*, before proceeding to consider how the approach has been developed in their most recent work (as presented in their chapter in this volume).

In general, their approach develops through a 'creative dialogue' with Waltz. The basic claim is that Waltzian neorealism is not so much wrong, as unnecessarily parsimonious (i.e., narrow) and static in its conception of the international system (Buzan, Jones and Little, 1993: 6, 42). They begin by reconsidering the relationship of the units to the international political structure. Building on the insight of Ruggie (1983), they suggest four possible combinations, or configurations, of the relationship between the units and the international structure (Buzan, Jones and Little, 1993: 39):

- Type 1 system: hierarchy and like-units
- Type 2 system: anarchy and like-units
- Type 3 system: hierarchy and unlike-units
- Type 4 system: anarchy and unlike-units.

For Waltz, types 1 and 4 can logically never exist, since hierarchy would create unlike-units, and anarchy, like-units. Thus 'Because [Waltz] puts too much emphasis on sovereign states, and too little on governing, Waltz's theory is simply unable to deal with type 4 systems' (Buzan, Jones and Little, 1993: 42). The central question then becomes: how can we explain the persistence of unlike-units over sustained periods of historical time? In large part, the construction of structural realism occurred in order to explain this anomaly in Waltz's theory. To achieve this, they sought to develop an ontologically complex theory of the international system. Such a 'thick' conception embodies three main aspects: first, the international system is *sectorally differentiated* between the economic, cultural and political-military realms; second, unit-level forces are constitutive of the international system; and third, the international comprises *interaction capacity* (the degrees of contact between states), *process* (the types of interaction such as warfare, trade, etc.) and *structure* (the principles through which the units are arranged and how that affects their behaviour) (Buzan, Jones and Little, 1993: chs. 3–4; Buzan and Little, this volume). Unlike units persisted in medieval Europe because the domestic arenas were too weak and generated insufficient 'interaction capacity' to enable the socialising logic of anarchy from cutting in (Buzan, Jones and Little, 1993: 43, 74–5). The Greek city-states did *not* conform to the logic of anarchy and remained functionally differentiated because the nobility, in seeking to preserve their domestic power position, was able to block the necessary militarily adaptive reforms (reforms that would have undermined this class's social power position). Moreover, the balance of power also failed, thereby leading to the demise of the whole states system (Buzan, Jones and Little, 1993: 121–5, 144–7).

In their most recent work, they use this thick conception to somewhat new research ends. *The Logic of Anarchy* was principally concerned with explaining, firstly, the persistence of unlike-units over time and, secondly, why the balance of power and state adaptability to the logic of anarchy has not always prevailed. By contrast, their new work is mainly concerned with charting the evolution and central characteristics of different international systems in world history. A thin conception of the international system leads to tempocentrism (or what they refer to as simply 'ahistoricism'), because it necessarily obscures different international systems through time. Naturally, therefore, their thick conception brings a range of systems back into focus.

They suggest that world history has witnessed three basic types of international system: first, the primitive 'pre-international system', which comprises mainly socio-cultural interactions and no significant military-political interaction; second, a less primitive 'economic international system', which embodies economic and socio-cultural interactions but no significant military-political interaction; and finally, the most developed, a 'full international system', in which all types of interaction occur. Within each of these international systems, unlike-units have existed. Only in the full international system do like-units exist, though crucially, they argue, these often co-exist alongside unlike-units (thus returning us to the discussion above). Moreover, in contrast to Waltz, they argue that inter-unit behaviour is not simply *mechanically* governed (through laws of governance as in Waltz), but is also *socially constructed* through norms and accepted rules of co-existence. Thus to understand inter-unit behaviour, they insist on the supplementation of Waltzian analysis with insight from the English School, spliced with constructivism. Finally, they suggest that the history of the international system can be traced as far back as 3500 BC, with the emergence of the Sumerian city-state system (the first 'full' system), though a range of less complete systems were in evidence for many thousands of years prior to this – an analysis that is examined in considerable detail in their recent book (Buzan and Little, 2000). In sum, such an historical sociological analysis enables them to break both with chronofetishism, not least by showing the complex origins of the present which cannot be explained by orthodox Eurocentrism, and with tempocentrism by revealing historical discontinuities between international systems.

This concludes the discussion of the seven major approaches. It now remains to contextualise the role of historical sociology within the discipline of international relations and in the process understand why we are calling not simply for an 'historical sociological turn' but for an 'historical sociological *re*-turn', or why we are looking to 'bringing historical sociology *back* into international relations'.

2 Historical sociology: back to the future of international relations?

Stephen Hobden

Introduction

This chapter provides a selective overview of the development of international theory, with particular respect to the way that theorists have thought about and made use of history and sociology. The aim is to provide a context for the other chapters in this book . The intention is to show that thinking about history and sociology within international relations is not a new phenomenon, and in fact is a long and distinguished tradition. Mainstream theories of international relations are frequently criticised for being ahistorical and lacking a sociological context. However, I would argue that, looking back over the development of international relations theorising, both history and sociology have played a significant part. History and sociology both have a 'past' in the discipline and, in my view, both have a future. This is a view shared by my co-authors, though as will be seen, there are a variety of ways in which this future could be manifested.

Historical approaches in particular have been important in the study of international relations. The chapter examines a selection of work by international relations theorists, and asks how they have thought about and employed history. It describes how, with the behavioural revolution in the United States, a move to ahistorical approaches occurred. However, in the theoretical diversity that marks contemporary international relations there is a small, but growing, trend towards historical and sociological approaches in the study of global processes. The overall aim of this book is to analyse and encourage such developments, and to argue that a return to the inclusion of a multi-disciplinary approach would be a positive step for the discipline.

I would like to express extra special thanks to Tim Dunne for all the help he gave me in getting this chapter started and for sharing with me his extensive knowledge of the English School. I would also like to thank John Hobson and Nick Wheeler for their incisive and extremely useful comments on earlier, and very partial, drafts. My thanks also go to all the participants at the Aberystwyth conference and the reviewers from Cambridge University Press for their comments. All errors, misinterpretations and over-generalisations are mine entirely.

The chapter should be read in the context of two sets of issues. The first concerns my personal view about the way the study of international relations can best be advanced. The purpose of the book is to advance a *manifesto* calling for the development of a specific way of thinking about global issues. The second set concerns the promotion, in the other chapters of this book, of a range of ideas about how this way of thinking about the world could be developed. Underlying these different strands is a set of key questions.

With regard to my personal view of the most fruitful direction for the discipline to follow, the following three very closely interrelated assumptions underlie the argument of the chapter.

(1)   The study of international relations is not best served through the pursuit of monocausal explanations. Mainstream international relations theory has become reductionist in the sense of relying on one element of explanation alone (see Hobden, 1998: 182). To contradict Morgenthau (1985: 13), politics is *not* an autonomous realm, but needs to be thought about in relation to a number of other social processes. All the authors in this book share the view that a multi-causal account provides the best way of understanding global processes.

(2)   A logical extension to the previous point is that the discipline of international relations is not self-standing. The emergence of disciplines in the university system during the eighteenth and nineteenth centuries made sense in terms of breaking knowledge up into more manageable portions, and in terms of the bureaucracy of universities. However, this practice of separating disciplines has served to obscure the totality of the social world. The discipline of international relations not only needs to draw upon a number of disciplines, in particular history, sociology, economics, philosophy and law, but should also actively promote 'inter-disciplinarity'.

(3)   The divide that has emerged between the analysis of international politics and that of domestic politics (seen at its apotheosis in Waltz's neorealism) is deeply problematic. As Michael Mann has argued, societies are not unitary, but rather 'are constituted of multiple overlapping and intersecting sociospatial networks of power' (1986: 1). The so-called 'domestic' and 'international' realms are not entities that can be analysed in isolation, but are part of one social world, which needs to be examined as a whole. The terms 'domestic' and 'international' are fundamentally misleading, as they obscure the 'overlapping and intersecting sociospatial networks of power' to which Mann refers. Both suggest a division of the social world that none of the authors in this book would accept. A starting point might be to argue that phenomena that are considered to be 'domestic' or 'international' are co-constitutive. However, it is the

character of these processes of co-constitution that should be the focus of study.

The second set of issues refer to the questions that underlie the contributions to this volume.

(1)   What does the study of international relations involve? How can our knowledge of international processes be best advanced? These questions, of course, relate directly to the points made above. Are we in a position to say what we are studying when we talk about international relations, and what are the best ways of achieving an understanding of these processes?

(2)   What is historical sociology? What do approaches to the study of international relations that are historical and sociological look like? What can an approach to studying the social world that is historical and sociological contribute to our knowledge of global processes?

(3)   How can the disciplines of international relations and historical sociology inform each other? Is there an area of overlap between the two disciplines? If so, what are the issues that are being studied there?

(4)   What would the agendas for a global historical sociology look like? All the contributions to this volume share the characteristic that they are not only concerned with exploring the theoretical aspects of the study of the world. They are also involved in developing theoretical tools to understand specific global issues.

It is my view that elements of work being done in historical sociology and international relations are moving in the same direction and are asking the same questions. For example, both are concerned with thinking about the character of the state – its pasts, presents and futures. Both are concerned with thinking about the way that states interact. Historical sociology has paid particular interest to historicising the state – an area that international relations scholars have sadly neglected. A key contribution from historical sociology is to perceive the state as one social actor amongst many, thus providing a route away from the state-centric approaches of much international relations. Both are concerned with the social forces and actors operating globally, and it is in this area, perhaps, that international relations can assist historical sociology.

In the previous chapter John Hobson assessed in greater depth the benefits to be gained from a closer engagement by international relations theorists with historical sociology. This chapter aims to give a background context for thinking about history and sociology in international relations. The purpose of this book is to promote a dialogue between scholars of historical sociology and of international relations. The intention is that the product of this dialogue will help to promote the development of approaches to the study of international relations along the lines pre-scribed above (concerning my personal view of the most fruitful di-rection for the discipline to follow). This chapter makes the argument that historical and sociological elements have been central to much think-ing in international relations in the past. My view is that not only are we now witnessing a renaissance in such approaches, but also that the study of global politics based in history and sociology provides the best hope of understanding the contemporary world and its problems.

Such an approach to analysing global processes is not straightforward. Such a theoretical enterprise celebrates the virtues of 'complexity' rather than 'parsimony' (as John Hobson has already noted). This chapter of-fers no answers to the problems of complexity that such an undertaking demands, nor does it aim to provide a particular route map for the kind of project that the authors included in this volume have in mind. How-ever, if international theory is to emerge that can understand the rapidly changing world that we inhabit, then, in my view, these are the kinds of issues that we need to address.

Institutional beginnings

I noted above that the division of disciplines began in the eighteenth and nineteenth centuries. This occurred primarily because of the realisation of the complexity of the social world, and the resultant need to implement some kind of division of labour. Perhaps then, if we wish to depict the dominant strand of international relations theorising as mono-causal, cut off from its related disciplines and built on an unsustainable divide be-tween the 'domestic' and the 'international', we should equate this strand with the establishment of the first department of international relations. In the wake of the First World War, Lord Davies endowed the first chair of international politics at Aberystwyth. For the first time, international processes were to be studied in and of themselves, and not as an adjunct to history, politics or law. Davies endowed the first chair in international *politics*, not in international *relations* nor in international *law*. Davies could therefore perhaps be held responsible for setting international relations apart from its cognate disciplines and for bringing about its concentration on politics rather than encouraging it to develop as a multi-disciplinary undertaking. However, we cannot blame Davies for the directions that the discipline has subsequently taken. It is likely that he would not have approved of many of the avenues that the discipline has explored. In-deed, he was firmly of the view that the new chair should promote an inter-disciplinary study of the subject (Booth, 1996: 328). Zimmern, the first holder of the chair, did have such a multi-disciplinary background.

Trained in the classics at Oxford, his first book was an analysis of the Greek commonwealth. His first lectureship, at the London School of Economics, was in sociology (Rich, 1995: 80). For Zimmern, 'The study of international relations extends from the natural sciences at one end to moral philosophy', and 'from the academic point of view, international relations is clearly not a subject in the ordinary sense of the word' (quoted in Schmidt, 1998: 156). E. H. Carr, whose appointment and subsequent work resulted in Davies's disillusion with the project, was first and foremost a historian (see Dunne, 1998: ch. 2).

Although Davies's role in any history of the discipline is significant, the study of international relations did not begin in Aberystwyth. The Department marked the establishment of the first institutional site for the discipline, but it did not mark the beginning of the study of international processes. People have been writing about the character and history of relations between different communities probably for as long as writing, and what could be viewed as separate communities, have existed. Thucydides' history of the Peloponnesian War, of course, is the classic text of the European tradition, but examples could be found from other eras and other parts of the world.

Following Wight (1966a: 19–20), thinking about international relations in the European tradition can be subdivided as follows:

- *World order theorists*. These include writers such as Erasmus, Sully, Campanella, Crucé and Penn who were concerned with trying to find ways of reducing the destructive levels of warfare in Europe. They were primarily concerned with the development of schemes that would promote the peaceful negotiation of differences between communities.
- *The Machiavellians*. These writers, such as Meinecke, Ranke and Hintze, drawing their inspiration in particular from Machiavelli and Thucydides, developed the notion of the *Machtstaat* – the view of the state as being primarily outward orientated and concerned with maximising its own power, in particular through warfare.
- *The philosophers of history and politics*. These writers, such as Rousseau, Bentham, Burke and Kant, were concerned with the development of philosophical ideas about the character of politics and the processes underlying the courses of history. In particular the 'Romantic Historians' attempted to develop an approach to history which transcended the narration of events and attempted to analyse underlying structures.

Hence at the start of the twentieth century, there was a very rich tradition of thought about international relations from which the fledgling discipline could draw. Schmidt (1998) stresses the significance of the international law tradition, particularly in the United States. Traditional accounts of the discipline's history stress the role of writers in the world order and *Machtstaat* traditions. However, I would argue that there has been a consistent element of writing that has sought to analyse the underlying structures of history, either through a comparative approach, or through a rationalist account.

History and international relations theory

Since 1919 there has always been an important and significant element of traditional history within the discipline.[1] By this I mean 'diplomatic history', the close and detailed study of the interactions at the personal and political level between the representatives of states. This has co-existed with the uses (and perhaps abuses) of history by international theorists. Here I concentrate on the latter of these two approaches to the study of history. In international theory, the use of history has taken two forms. Primarily history has been used as a deductive source. History has been used as a repository of facts, from which either theorists' own theories could be validated, or other people's theories discounted. Less frequently, history has been employed as an inductive source. History has been used to develop comparative analyses and as a way of thinking about the development of international processes and institutions.

During the inter-war years the prime aim of the new discipline was the development of thinking, drawing on the international law tradition, that sought to find ways of bolstering the League of Nations, maintaining peace and encouraging disarmament. This work was a continuation and development of world order theory, which over the previous millennium had been considering the same sort of questions and discussing what kinds of institutions could best deliver international peace. As such, this work had primarily legal (considering, in particular, issues of sovereignty) and institutional (looking at the development of historical and contemporary international institutions) foci. Much of this work considered the ethical and legal basis of the state. Harold Laski (discussed in Schmidt, 1998: 164–6), for example, rejected the view that the state should be considered as the sovereign actor, with unrestricted powers over its citizens. He suggested rather that communities had a plurality of social organisations. States were just one of a number of legal/political organisations which could make a claim for the loyalty of civilians. Individuals, he argued, had the right to refuse to conform with orders that conflicted with their abilities to be moral and productive citizens.

---

[1] 'Traditional' here is in no way intended as a slight.

Other work examined the development of international institutions. Zimmern wrote his *magnum opus* during the 1930s on the League of Nations. Zimmern, a great supporter of the League, viewed its establishment as a major transformation in the way that international politics would be organised. Somewhere between a superstate and a multilateral alliance, the League could lead us down the road to peaceful international relations. Even so, for Zimmern the League was essentially a piece of machinery, the effectiveness of which would depend on the ways in which, and the purposes for which, states and state leaders employed it.

Hence in the first phase of the development of the discipline, the primary focus was on the development of theory regarding international law, sovereignty, state and analyses of international organisations – particularly with regard to the role of the League of Nations. Discussions and the analysis of history were primarily relegated to a secondary role related to these two undertakings. Historical analysis became more central to international theory with the increasing significance of realist thought.

Carr's *The Twenty Years' Crisis* was an analysis of the inter-war period, but was primarily intended as a polemical essay aimed at universal or utopian thought. Carr's work is seen as the first major statement of a 'realist' position, though whether the development of realism within international relations would have been to his liking is at the very least debatable. But it is perhaps more with Morgenthau's work that we primarily associate the realist or 'classical realist' position.

Morgenthau certainly did have a theory of history. For him, there was a continuity in international politics founded on the constancy that he perceived in human nature. 'Human nature, in which the laws of politics have their roots, has not changed since the classical philosophies of China, India, and Greece endeavoured to discover these laws' (Morgenthau, 1985: 4). For Morgenthau, the constancy of human selfishness and a desire for power enabled him to argue that the realm of international politics was one marked by the existence of 'perennial forces'. The basis of these perennial forces was that 'man responds to social situations with repetitive patterns' (Morgenthau, 1985: 7). It was necessary to work with these forces rather than attempt to change them. This persistence of certain social processes founded on the constancy of human nature permitted Morgenthau to argue that international politics was marked by consistent patterns of behaviour. It also allowed Morgenthau to 'black box' the state, as Singer (1961: 81) argued. As human nature is a constant, all state leaders can be expected to act in a similar and consistent way. The social and political organisation of a particular community will not have an effect on the way in which foreign policy is organised. This patterned and recurring character allows the analyst to predict behaviour. As long as state leaders followed their 'interest defined in terms of power', then a balance of power would emerge. The balance of power, for Morgenthau, 'is indeed a perennial element of all pluralistic societies' (Morgenthau, 1985: 11).

Morgenthau not only had a theory of history, he also used history extensively to back up his explanation of the world. Extremely knowledgeable about European history of the eighteenth and nineteenth centuries, he drew many examples from this period in order to support his theoretical position. Morgenthau worked deductively, seeking to find evidence to support his approach to analysing world politics. At the same time, he had a theory of history, seeing it as a constantly repeating cycle, and it was this element of repetition which enabled him to make the claim that his approach to global politics was a scientific one. Yet there is a tension here between the Morgenthau of the 'perennial forces' and the rich historical sociological Morgenthau noted by other writers (see Hobson, 2000: ch. 2). The classical realists, in practice, were much closer to a multi-disciplinary approach, but in the epistemological revolution of the post-war United States sought the legitimation that a claim to a scientific approach gave them. The 1940s and early 1950s were the heyday of this classical approach to the analysis of world politics – an underlying view of history as cyclical and a rich use of history as an underlying source of narrative to validate the theoretical arguments.

However, the period of classical realist dominance was comparatively short-lived. In the United States all the social sciences were swept by the behaviouralist revolution in the period after the Second World War, and international relations was no exception. Morgenthau's attempts to show that his approach to the study of international relations was scientific were, in part, a reaction to changes in the prevalent view of the way in which the social world should be studied. The behaviouralist approach stressed a strict empiricism, and had little room for historical speculation. As Brown notes, 'the intellectual climate of the 1950s and 1960s was unaccommodating to virtually all variants of political philosophy' (Brown, 1992: 8). The work of the classical realists was criticised for its reliance on the concept of 'human nature', a variable that was not quantifiable (Hollis and Smith, 1991: 29).

As in the rest of the social sciences the behaviouralist revolution had an enormous impact on the study of international relations. This impact led to the development of two main approaches to the study of the discipline: the assembly of vast databases of knowledge, for example Singer's 'Correlates of War' programme, and the introduction of systems-based theories, found for example in the work of Morton Kaplan (1957). The behaviouralist approach also encouraged a division between analysis at the domestic and at the international levels. Discussing his book *Systems and Process in International Politics*, Kaplan noted that 'structural features chosen to classify national actors are quite gross ... even these gross characteristics of national actors are far removed from their historical complexity' (Kaplan, 1961: 8). Such a division between domestic and international became almost codified when Singer (1961) posed the level-of-analysis problem. Singer was concerned that behaviouralist approaches to studying international relations were not making the rapid progress that had been expected. His explanation for this was that researchers were not taking account of different levels of analysis when collecting data. 'We have roamed', he noted, 'up and down the ladder of organizational complexity with remarkable abandon' (Singer, 1961: 78). His view was that it is problematic to combine data from different levels of analysis. This was because different levels introduce different biases into the analysis. For example, analysis at the systems level gives more weight to conformity in international politics, whilst the national level over-emphasises differences between communities. Singer's view was that because of the bias that different levels introduced, it was not possible to collect data at more than one level. 'There *is* this preliminary conceptual issue and ... it must be temporarily resolved prior to any given research undertaking' (Singer, 1961: 90).

Hence the behavioural revolution had at least two significant impacts on the international relations discipline. First, it marked a move away from approaches to understanding international relations using historical examples as a source for confirmation of theory. Behaviouralists were much more concerned to examine variables that could be quantified and aggregated. Historical accounts are not amenable to such a procedure.[2] Second, and for different reasons from those of the classical realists, behaviouralist approaches assumed a division between different levels of analysis, and hence a division between the analysis of the domestic and international realms. The two realms were regarded as autonomous. Not only was an understanding of the links between different levels unnecessary, it was positively unhelpful.

Not that the behaviouralist approach swept the board without opposition. The most sustained attack on this approach came from the other side of the Atlantic. We will look further at the 'English School' in a moment, but Hedley Bull, one of the school's most significant contributors (though an Australian) was responsible for the most sustained critique of the behaviouralist approach. In 'International Theory: The Case for a Classical Approach', Bull argued vehemently against the new

---

[2] That is to say, unless they were codifiable. For example, the Correlates of War programme operated by collecting data on length of wars, number of participants, level of battle deaths, and so on.

scientific approaches to the study of international relations.[3] His view was that 'if we confine ourselves to strict standards of verification and proof there is very little of significance that can be said about international relations' (Bull, 1966a: 361). In other words the attempt to apply strict standards of scientific method to the complexity of the social world was, for Bull, not an appropriate or useful means of study. 'The distinctive methods and aspirations these theorists have brought to the subject are leading them down a false path,' Bull concluded, 'and to all appeals to follow them down it we should remain resolutely deaf' (Bull, 1966a: 377).

History and sociology in the English School

Amongst the members of the 'English School' there has been a continued commitment to the careful analysis of history. And of course a key element of the School was the analysis of state relations within a 'society'. As Butterfield and Wight note in their introduction to *Diplomatic Investigations*, a collection of papers from the early years of the British Committee, in comparison to scholars of international relations in the United States, British writers 'have probably been more concerned with the historical than the contemporary, with the normative than the scientific, with the philosophical than the methodological, with principles than policy' (Butterfield and Wight, 1966: 12).

This contrast between US and British approaches has also been noted by Christopher Hill:

Both sides, of course, categorize international relations as a social science, but whereas the tone of much American work is undoubtedly positivist, most British scholars define 'science' in the classical sense, as something involving a systematic but broad pursuit of knowledge along many parallel paths: analytical, legal, philosophical – and historical (Hill, 1985: 130).

Martin Wight was perhaps the most historically minded of the English School writers. His background was in history and before entering academia he had worked as a secondary school teacher of the subject. His perhaps most famous contribution to thinking about international relations theorising, 'Why is There no International Theory?', was very much a call for the use of historical methodology for the understanding of international relations. Noting the weakness of the development of a political theory of international relations, he argued that the job could be

---

[3] A rather ironic title for, as Brown remarks, Bull's article 'was rather more effective as the case *against* behavioralism than as a case *for* anything' (Brown 1992: 9).

done more effectively through the study of international history:

Historical Literature at the same time does the same job – the job of offering a coherent structure of hypotheses that will provide a common explanation of phenomena; but it does the job with more judiciousness and modesty, and with closer attention to the record of international experience. So one might venture tentatively to put forward the equation: Politics: International Politics = Political Theory: Historical Interpretation (Wight, 1966a: 32–3).

Hence for Wight, historical analysis provided the key to the understanding of international politics in the same way that political theory provided the means for the study of domestic politics. Significantly, in the index to the volume where the article is reprinted, 'history' is subindexed as 'the true international theory' (Butterfield and Wight, 1966: 220), although Wight does not use this phrase in his piece.

Unfortunately, very little of Wight's work was published during his lifetime (Dunne, 1998: 48–9). However, he was responsible for one of the great works of comparative historical analysis with *Systems of States*, a collection of papers previously presented to the British Committee. Hedley Bull assembled these after Wight's death into book form. In this work, comparisons were made of several systems of states, and in particular the Greek and modern systems. This led him to draw out specific commonalities between state systems (Wight, 1977: ch. 1).

Others in the English School were also wedded to a similar approach to the study of international relations. Bull's argument for a classical approach to the study of international relations has already been discussed. Paradoxically, given his commitment to a 'classical approach', Bull's work *The Anarchical Society* is perhaps one of the least historically informed works of the English School canon. However, it is the work that develops the sociological aspect of the English School to the highest degree. The analysis of rules and norms that affect international behaviour is the distinctive feature of the English School approach. Other works within this tradition attempt to combine the sociological element with a more significantly historically informed approach. Adam Watson, for example, produced a work of comparative history of state systems with *The Evolution of International Society*. In a similar way to Wight this was a comparative study of the development of state systems. His study involved an examination of the various systems that led to the creation of the European nation-state system. The significant thing about Watson's study was that he developed the idea of society to include a spectrum of various forms to describe the relationships between the members of the system, and the notion of a pendulum-like swing between one type of state system and another.

A comparative historical approach was also employed by Bull and Watson for their edited volume *The Expansion of International Society*. This work, rather than a comparison of state systems, was an analysis of the way in which the European state system was diffused throughout the globe. For Bull and Watson the use of a comparative historical approach was essential: 'we certainly hold that our subject can be understood only in historical perspective' (Bull and Watson, 1984: 9). The work of Bull and Watson would seem to confirm Wight's comment that 'international society . . . can be properly described only in historical and sociological depth' (Wight, 1966b: 96).

The development of ahistorical international relations

In the United States, despite the vehemence of the Bull assault on be-haviouralism, it was this approach that remained the central theme of much international relations theorising through the 1950s and 1960s. The late 1960s and 1970s saw the emergence of a different approach to the analysis of world politics – 'transnationalism' (see, in particular, Keohane and Nye, 1971). Located in the political and economic crises of the United States of that period, it marked a considerably different ontology and methodology. Transnationalists questioned the dominant role of the state, and argued that it was necessary to include an analysis of other actors (e.g., transnational corporations and revolutionary groups). In other words the study of other actors apart from states was necessary for an understanding of world politics. For these writers a divide between domestic and international was not appropriate. Hence the transnationalist approach was an important attempt to transcend the theoretical split between domestic and international. However, this was in a primarily *ahistorical* context. Such writers were primarily concerned with analysing contemporary events without considering the historical developments that had led to them.

An ahistorical approach also marked the return of a realist approach to dominance in international relations theory. Waltz's neorealism perhaps marked the most extreme version of an abstract theory of international politics that sought to isolate the analysis of international processes from any kind of domestic influence. As with the classical realists, Waltz argued that there is a timeless characteristic to global politics. He noted that 'the texture of international politics remains highly constant, patterns recur, and events repeat themselves endlessly' (Waltz, 1979: 66). In order to explain this continuity in world politics, Waltz argued that it was necessary to adopt a systemic approach. This systemic approach would focus on the structures of international politics. In order to isolate those forces operating internationally, Waltz argued that it was necessary to abstract from the analysis the features of domestic systems. Any theory that failed to do this would be 'reductionist':

Definitions of structure must leave aside, or abstract from, the characteristics of units, their behaviour, and their interactions. Why must those obviously important matters be omitted? They must be omitted so that we can distinguish between variables at the level of the units and variables at the level of the system (Waltz, 1979: 79).

Waltz was seeking to develop a theory that stood outside of history. For him, states and their interactions had a timeless quality. There was no historical development of states or their ways of interaction. Of the three main elements to his theory, only one has an element of historical variability. The deep structure for Waltz is anarchy. This is as compared with domestic political systems, where the ordering principle is 'hierarchical'. For Waltz, anarchy is the absence of government. This leads him to assume that states' prime aim will be to survive. As there is no higher body to which states can appeal for assistance they are forced to be self-regarding when it comes to issues of survival. For Waltz, anarchy has been a consistent and unchanging feature of world politics, and this element of constancy in the deep structure of politics enables him to develop a theory that stands outside history.

His second element of structure is the character of states. Anarchy in the international system dictates that all states must fulfil the same functions – they are 'functionally undifferentiated'. For Waltz (1979: 96), a state 'decides for itself how it will cope with internal and external problems'. In the anarchical condition of the international system all states can only, in the end, rely on themselves for their survival. As all states have to fulfil the same functions, this means that the character of the units can be dropped from the definition of structure. Hence Waltz is not interested in the possible historical development of states, or in considering the possibility that different states could have different characteristics and paths of development. For him, states exist outside of an historical context.

It is only at the third level of structure that any element of change is incorporated. This is the level of the distribution of capabilities. Here Waltz is concerned with the distribution of power across the system, not the capabilities of individual states. 'Although capabilities are attributes of units, the distribution of capabilities across units is not. The distribution of capabilities is not a unit attribute, but rather a system-wide concept' (Waltz, 1979: 98). It is power relative to other states that is important, not the absolute level of power of the individual states. The distribution of power is obviously a very important factor in the character of the system at any one time. It determines the type of system which is operating at any time, but is also the only element where Waltz can envision change. The previous two components are comparatively stable. Any change in those would mean a complete change to the system, and the only change that Waltz can envision is from anarchy to hierarchy, with the emergence of a world government. Waltz, for example, does not see the emergence of functionally differentiated states or the possibility of the inclusion of other actors. This would involve a change *of* system. Changes in the distribution of power result merely in changes *in* the system.

Waltz's neorealism, then, is perhaps the antithesis of the type of international relations theory discussed at the start of this chapter: it is monocausal – only concerned with political power; the only element of change can be through a variation in the distribution of capabilities; it tries to establish the study of international relations as something distinct from the study of other areas of the social world – in particular, history; and it envisages a distinct dichotomy between the domestic and the international.

It is easy to see why such an approach to the study of international relations was popular during the Cold War, when structures did seem to be unchanging. However, this concentration on 'unchanging' structures misled international relations theorists into ignoring the significant elements of change occurring at a global level. These developments ultimately led to the end of the Cold War. Additionally in the post-Cold War world, international politics is marked much more by change than by continuity. At the start of the twenty-first century change and transformation seem to be the dominant features of global politics. As Tilly has observed, 'right now the international system is undergoing one of those deep mutations' (1992: 187–8). This transformation not only has the impact of altering relations between states but also the character of politics within states. What is needed now is an approach to global politics that is capable of studying change, and in particular incorporates other actors and examines the interrelations between domestic and international, an approach that in effect allows us to completely reconceptualise these categories.

Thus, looking at the development of international relations theory up to the early 1980s, when neorealism emerged as the nearest thing to a paradigmatic consensus, the extent to which historical and sociological approaches have been employed has fluctuated. Before the setting up of the Department of International Politics at Aberystwyth there was a tradition of the study of international relations primarily making use of historical approaches, for example through the works of Hintze, Ranke and Weber. In the initial phase of the discipline there was an emphasis on

legal issues and the relationship between states and international organisations. During this period the large-scale historical approaches were less
significant. Most of the classical realists came from an academic background in the study of history, with a particular concentration on the
study of nineteenth-century Europe. These writers were caught in a bind
between their historical approach and their views (based on conceptions
of human nature) of essential continuities in global politics. Despite the
attempts of the classical realists to create a scientific foundation for their
work, the behavioural revolution marked a change of direction, with the
emphasis on measurement and quantification. Although the behaviouralists were happy to draw on past events their concern was not with historical processes. History was not a database to be mined as a source of
illustrative material nor as the basis of an inductive approach. Such a lack
of concern with historical processes also marked Waltz's neorealism. This
theoretical approach aimed to predict the behaviour of states under different forms of an anarchical international system. It was not concerned
with an analysis of the development of its key units, states, nor with how
change *of* the system could occur (i.e., from anarchy to hierarchy). This
lack of a theory of change resulted in its failure either to predict, or to be
able to give an account of, the major change in international relations in
the last fifty years – the end of the Cold War.

Through the late 1980s and early 1990s the dominance of neorealist
theorising within international relations started to decline. This can be
explained as a combination of:

(1) paradigmatic breakdown, as more and more international phenomena could not be explained within its framework, and
(2) the development of other theoretical approaches.

As a result the past decade has seen the emergence of a number of new
pathways to the analysis of international processes. Amongst these is an
increasing interest in historical approaches. This could perhaps be called
an 'historical turn'. However, given the great significance that historical
approaches have played at various times in the discipline's development,
an 'historical *re*turn' might be a more appropriate term.

Much of the credit for this development can be given to writers of
historical sociology. From 1979 onwards, writers such as Wallerstein,
Skocpol, Tilly and Mann started to develop analyses of the social world
that were asking questions about the development of the state and the
character of international relations. Pushing against the domestic society
focus of sociology, writers such as these became increasingly interested
in global and inter-state processes. Wallerstein, for example, started his
academic career as a student of African sociology. He found, though, that

he was unable to explain the continuation of widespread poverty in Africa without an analysis of a global economic structure of power (Wallerstein, 1974: ch. 1). Skocpol's background in 1960s politics led her to consider a much wider frame of sociological analysis (Skocpol, 1988). In particular, historical sociologists sought to analyse the domestic and international as part of one social system. As such, their work provided challenges to both sociology and international relations. The historical element in their work allied them with international relations theorists such as those of the English School. Given this concurrence of interests between historical sociology and international relations it is not surprising that writers within the latter discipline started to take notice. Halliday (1987), Jarvis (1989), Linklater (1990) and Hobson (1994) first highlighted this work for an international relations audience.

Since Halliday's 'Second Agenda' article there has been a flourishing of work within international relations, either drawing directly on the work of historical sociologists, or which could be described as having a historical and sociological character (Hobden, 1998: 189–93). One of the purposes of this volume is to provide a sampler of some of the work that is on offer within this field, and to encourage the wider exploration of this literature. This approach to the study of international relations is not monolithic, and as John Hobson outlines in his introductory chapter, this work has a number of significant and distinctive strands (this volume, ch. 1). Yet there is more that links the international relations scholars working within an historical sociological framework than divides them (this volume, ch. 13). One key element that unites the contributors is a commitment to a multi-disciplinary approach. As such, they are continuing a tradition which, although at times obscured, has been central to thinking about international relations throughout the history of the discipline.

Conclusion: looking both backwards and forwards

Departments of international relations should be the inevitable homes of those people who think that we cannot understand the social world without an understanding of global processes. Those who seek to understand the dynamics of global social change, inequalities between different parts of the world, social injustices and the potentials for progressive social change have often found that a global perspective is needed. The message of the contributors to this volume is that these processes need to be understood in a world-historical social context. As such, departments of international relations should be the homes of historians, sociologists, philosophers, anthropologists and lawyers who have an interest in examining these dynamics. The founders of the discipline clearly had such a purpose in mind. As the first section of this chapter indicated, all were committed to a multi-disciplinary approach. This volume, together with other research within an historical sociological framework, suggests that in many ways international relations is seriously re-engaging with such a multi-disciplinary account of global politics. Our intention is to promote such a re-engagement.

This chapter suggests that such a re-engagement is not a novel undertaking, but that history and sociology have provided a foundation for the study of global relations both prior to, and since, 1919. Our call for the development of such approaches finds an echo in a 1959 article by Stanley Hoffmann. In that article he provided a critique of realist approaches to the study of international relations, and of the search for law-like understandings pursued by the behavioural school. Instead, he advocated an historical sociological approach. The central problem with realism, Hoffmann argued, was that it viewed global relations as unchanging: 'realist analysis fails because it sees the world as a static field in which power relations reproduce themselves in timeless monotony' (Hoffmann, 1959: 350). Similarly, the search for law-like statements based on the accumulation of data would not lead to an understanding of global politics. Instead, 'the best we can achieve in our discipline is the statement of trends' (Hoffmann, 1959: 357). The way of achieving such a statement of trends, Hoffmann argued, was to 'proceed *inductively* and, before . . . [reaching] any conclusions about trends manifest throughout history, . . . [to] resort to systematic historical research' (Hoffmann, 1959: 367).

Hoffmann's call has remained unanswered for too long. After his article the study of international relations in the United States moved in precisely the opposite direction, away from history, and away from an inductive approach. With the main exception of the English School, an approach to the study of international politics as envisioned by Hoffmann was not seriously considered until the late 1980s and early 1990s. The evidence of this volume is that there is now a critical mass of scholars who are seeking to develop a more historically and sociologically informed approach to the study of international relations.

That such a critical mass should emerge at the current time is, perhaps, not surprising. The world around us appears to be undergoing a fundamental transformation. The existing tools that we have been using seem not to be able to provide us with the insights needed to understand the character of the changes that we are witnessing. In such a time of transformation an analysis of change is desperately required. An approach rooted in history and sociology can provide an understanding of the global transformations occurring. Based on the contributions to the current volume, and other work taking place within this field, there is plenty of evidence that Hoffmann's message is now being heard.

This, of course, is the purpose of this volume – to lay out the major historical sociological approaches in international relations on the menu for choice; to assess the contribution to the understanding of global politics from historical sociology; to evaluate the current work being undertaken by international relations scholars that has an historical and sociological perspective; and to consider the future for such an approach within the discipline. I would argue that, taking into consideration the work displayed in this volume, all four of these purposes are rich with potential. Work done by historical sociologists provides a rich framework for thinking about international politics. Additionally, taken together, their contributions provide a sizeable body of empirical work for international relations scholars to draw upon. The contributions to this volume from international relations specialists indicate that adopting a multi-disciplinary approach provides a powerful tool for the analysis of global issues. Such approaches also indicate that the potential research agenda for such a project is very wide indeed, an issue that chapter 13 considers.

An overall conclusion to this chapter would be that the future for an historical sociological approach to the study of international relations is full of possibilities. However, such an approach is not new to the study of international relations. The argument of this chapter is that it was there from the initiation of the discipline, and has always remained part of the study of global processes, even if at times a somewhat marginalised one. The contributors to this volume are, therefore, *not* seeking a radical reorienting of the discipline, but *are* suggesting a return to the discipline's founding commitment to multi-disciplinarity. In this way, our volume is *not* asking the discipline to deny its *raison d'être*, but that it should go *back to the future* of international relations, by 'bringing historical sociology *back* in'.

Part II

Historical sociologies of international relations

3 The two waves of Weberian historical sociology in international relations

John M. Hobson

Trading places: neo-Weberian historical sociology and neorealist international relations theory

Since 1979, neo-Weberian historical sociology has implicitly been moving towards the discipline of international relations, in so far as it has sought to 'bring the state back in', to 'bring the international back in', and to develop an 'integrationist' theory which focuses on the complex linkages between the subnational, national and international realms. Although many neo-Weberians have promoted such ideas (e.g., Tilly, 1975a, 1975b; Bendix, 1978; Elias, 1978; Poggi, 1978; Collins, 1986; Mann, 1986; Runciman, 1989; Weiss and Hobson, 1995), it was Theda Skocpol who most famously brought much of this to the academic world's attention (Skocpol, 1979, 1985). This linkage was reinforced by the fact that many neo-Weberians saw in neorealism a theory that could complement and enhance their own – see the explicit and positive allusions to realism in Skocpol (1979: 31) and Collins (1986: ch. 7). For such writers working within sociology, (neo)realism appears to be an attractive theory because it *seems* to satisfy the objectives of neo-Weberian sociology in so far as it: *seems* to take the state seriously; emphasises geopolitics and refuses to 'reduce' the state to the mode of production; and *appears* to offer the potential for an integrationist approach, given its ability to bring the international back in.

Paradoxically, on the 'other' side of the border, many international relations scholars have become increasingly critical, since the early 1980s, of international relations theory's hitherto dominant paradigm – neorealism. Now is truly the time of neorealism's long winter of discontent. It is neorealism's *lack* of a theory of the state, its *inability* to explain structural change, and its *inability* to focus on the complex set of linkages between the subnational, national and international realms, that has in part led to

I would particularly like to thank Steve Hobden for his insightful thoughts on various drafts of this chapter, and, more generally, the various participants at the Aberystwyth conference for their comments. Of course, I accept full responsibility for the arguments (and any errors) made.

this rising discontent. And *most* paradoxically, in order to overcome these limitations, some international relations scholars have specifically turned to Weberian historical sociology in order to find a way out of the current crisis of international relations theory (e.g., Halliday, 1987, 1994; Jarvis 1989; Hobson, 1997, 1998a, 2000: ch. 6; M. Hall, 1998, 1999; Hobden 1998; Seabrooke, 2001). Here it is sometimes assumed that Weberian historical sociology can overcome each of these deficiencies in neorealism. But the problem here is that neo-Weberians within sociology looked (wittingly or unwittingly) to neorealism to solve the problems within their own discipline, at the same time as international relations scholars looked to Weberian historical sociology to go beyond the limitations of mainstream international relations theory (especially neorealism).

Thus while neo-Weberianism *promises* to go beyond neorealism, much of it in fact perfectly replicates neorealism. Indeed, there is a rising ground swell of opinion which not unreasonably asserts that Weberian historical sociology is, in effect, little more than a 'realist wolf dressed up in sociological sheep's clothing' (Yalvaç, 1991: 94; Scholte, 1993: 23, 96, 101–2, 112; Spruyt, 1994; Little, 1994: 9–10; Fuat Keyman 1997: ch. 3; Halperin, 1998); or, put differently, that Weberian historical sociology represents a form of 'sociological realism'. Hence the paradox: that Weberian historical sociology simply traded places with neorealism and accordingly failed to realise its own promise, thus providing a cul-de-sac for both neo-Weberian historical sociologists and their counterparts working within international relations.

Two questions present themselves here: first, is not the neorealist tendency found in these neo-Weberian writings an inevitable symptom of Max Weber's realist approach to the state and international relations? Second, does this accordingly mean that Weberian historical sociology has nothing to offer international relations other than to reinforce neorealist orthodoxy? While not wishing to elaborate on this point here, it is my belief that Max Weber's theory of the state and international relations was decidedly non-realist and had much in common with the English School – even if his analysis *augments* rather than simply mirrors the English School (see Hobson and Seabrooke, 2001). There is, therefore, nothing inevitable about the neorealism of neo-Weberianism. In this chapter, I shall argue that there are two waves of Weberian historical sociology in international relations. Thus while the 'first wave', typified by Skocpol and Tilly, perfectly reproduces the neorealist theory of the state and international relations, I argue that there is now emerging a 'second wave' of Weberian historical sociology, which is decidedly *non*-realist and provides an avenue out of the current impasse in international relations theory (see also Hobson, 1997, 1998a, 1998b, 2000: chs. 6 and 7). This has been the central goal of my work in the last five years, but I suggest that it can also be found, albeit implicitly, in the work of Michael Mann (1986, 1993); for an elaboration on Mann's non-realist approach, see Hobson (2000: 198–203).

It is my central argument that it is essential to develop a *non-realist* Weberian historical sociology of the state and international relations, because failure to do so leads to an approach which necessarily contradicts the fundamental theoretical objectives upon which neo-Weberianism is founded. How so? In terms of Skocpol's criteria of what constitutes an 'adequate' theoretical approach, neorealism, or 'sociological realism', suffers three basic shortcomings that Skocpol sees in liberalism and Marxism, in that firstly it 'kicks the state back out' precisely because it embodies a *reductionist theory of the state* and denies it 'international agential power' (to be defined shortly); secondly, it operationalises a *reductionist base–superstructure model* (where international outcomes are reduced to the requirements and dictates of the international 'structure'); and thirdly, it succeeds in 'bringing the international back in' but fails to produce the sort of *integrationist theory* that neo-Weberians seek precisely because it 'kicks society back out'. Most importantly though, neorealism is ahistorical and reproduces the twin problems of chronofetishism and tempocentrism (see Hobson, this volume, pp. 5–13). Thus if we are to fulfil the criteria required for an adequate historical sociological theory as laid out by Skocpol and others (Skocpol, 1979; Giddens, 1984; Collins, 1986: ch.1; Mann, 1986: ch. 1; Runciman, 1989; Hobson, 1998a), we need to cut the Gordian knot that has hitherto tied neorealism and first-wave Weberian historical sociology together, and create a theoretical base that can provide a solution or remedy for chronofetishism and tempocentrism. Paradoxically, in the process, we can return to a more faithful reading of Max Weber from one that has been distorted by neo-Weberians and international relations theorists alike (Hobson and Seabrooke, 2001).

This chapter has five main parts. The first part lays out an alternative schema for understanding 'state autonomy' to that found in the conventional literature. The second part then extracts the core of the neorealist approach, which is then used to show how first-wave Weberian historical sociology reproduces neorealist logic (in the third part). The next part proceeds to develop a non-realist second-wave Weberian historical sociology, which is drawn from my own writings and is, I argue, able to satisfy the criteria laid down by Skocpol and others as to what constitutes an adequate historical sociological theory of the state and international relations. The final part shows how my second-wave approach overcomes the twin problems of chronofetishism and tempocentrism.

66   *John M. Hobson*

Two faces of agential state power: domestic and international agential state power

In order to tease out the theories of the state utilised by neorealists and Weberians, I suggest that we need to relocate theory within the *agent–structure problematic*. When international relations scholars (as well as sociologists and comparative political scientists) think of state power, they usually equate it with what I call *domestic agential state power*: 'the ability of a state to construct state policy and shape the domestic realm free of domestic structural constraints or non-state actor influence' (Hobson, 2000: ch. 1; cf. Skocpol, 1985: 9). The second form of state agential power is one that has been largely ignored by international relations scholars, as well as sociologists and others – namely the *international agential power* of the state: 'the ability of the state to construct policy and shape the international realm free of international structural constraints or international non-state actor influence' (Hobson, 2000: chs. 1 and 7). Here I suggest that there are three broad levels of international agential power. High international agential power refers to the ability of the state not simply to shape the international realm free of international structural constraints, but also to mitigate inter-state competition and to solve the 'collective action problem' – as in liberalism and constructivism (Hobson, 2000: chs. 3, 5). Moderate international agential power refers to the ability of the state to shape the international realm free of international structural constraints, but falls short of the levels required to create a peaceful international realm and overcome inter-state competition – as in post-structuralism and Marxism (Hobson, 2000: chs. 4, 5).

The basic argument of this chapter is that neorealism and first-wave Weberian historical sociology reify international structure and accordingly deny the state or state–society complex any degree of international agential power. By contrast, second-wave Weberian historical sociology produces a structurationist theory of the state and international relations in which states and state–society complexes have agency to shape, and are simultaneously shaped by, the international system. In order to reveal the neorealist limitations of first-wave Weberian historical sociology, it is necessary to begin by drawing out the basic features of neorealism.

The neorealist theory of the state and international relations: 'kicking the state back out'

Waltz and the 'passive-adaptive' state

Waltzian neorealism is often thought of as *the* theory that ascribes the state with power and autonomy in world politics. Though according the state high levels of domestic agential power, Waltzian neorealism, nevertheless, denies the state any degree of international agential power and has no theory of the state (see Waltz, 1986: 339–40). This sociologically reductionist theory of the state forms the rational kernel of his overall theory, as outlined in *Theory of International Politics* (Waltz, 1979). How and why is this the case?

Waltz was fundamentally concerned to deny the use of historical sociology when constructing a 'theory of international politics', and sought instead to define a theory in terms of its ability to explain 'continuity' (see especially Waltz, 1979: 43–9). By continuity, he meant that international relations has always remained the same (Waltz, 1979: 66) – that international relations has always comprised conflict between political units, whether these be empires, city-states or nation-states. Put differently, the international has always been a 'realm of necessity and violence'. To explain this *uniformity* of international outcomes, Waltz began by rejecting what he confusingly calls 'reductionist' theory (which seeks to explain the international realm in terms of its units or component parts). National-level variables had to be bracketed (ignored) because they are always changing, and yet the international realm has never changed (Waltz, 1979: 65). Rather than focus on actors or agents, Waltz chose to focus on the international political *structure*. The key point is that this sole explanatory variable had to be defined by excluding unit-force (i.e., state, state–society) variables. How was this achieved?

Waltz argues that the international political structure has three tiers, though, crucially, the second tier drops out. The first tier refers to the *ordering principle of anarchy* (in which there is no world authority that stands above individual states), where the lack of a world government means that there is nothing to prevent states from preying upon each other, which in turn prompts states to pursue individual policies of 'self-help'. Moreover, because of the third tier – the *distribution of state capabilities* – it is inevitable that under anarchy, the strong states will both threaten the weak states as well as challenge the other rival strong states in order to move up the great power ladder, so all states must follow 'self-help'. The key to understanding his theory of the state lies with his treatment of the second tier – the *character of the units* (i.e., states).

For Waltz, all states are functionally alike (like-units) and are differentiated only in terms of capability. Why? They are alike because they are socialised by the international system – a system which requires all states to emulate each other. Failure to emulate the successful practices of the leading states makes states vulnerable to potential attack, because it leads to a widened *relative power gap* between the strong and the weak. Accordingly, over time, all states emulate the successful practices of the great powers so as to narrow the relative power gap between themselves and the leading powers, thereby diminishing their vulnerability (see Waltz, 1979: 127–8). In the process, all states come to functionally converge, developing centralised governments with a monopoly of the means of violence. Note, however, that Waltz does *not* say that all states will always emulate; merely, that if they do not (for whatever reason), they will decline, become vulnerable and perhaps even become extinct (Waltz, 1979: 92, 118, 128). The key point for Waltz is that because states do not *functionally* vary, they cannot constitute independent variables. And so we arrive at Waltz's 'approach' to the state.

As is well known within international relations, the paradox of Waltzian neorealism is that while it is allegedly 'state-centric', it in fact has *no* theory of the state, given that domestic factors play no role in shaping the international system. A more accurate way of putting this is to say that Waltzian neorealism is *not* state-centric but is (international) *structure-centric*. Thus Waltz argues that states have no international agential power either to shape the international structure or to overcome its constraining logic. In short, for Waltz the state has little real choice but to 'passively adapt' (i.e., conform) to the military survival requirements dictated by the international political structure. This embodies a 'thin' conception of the state, firstly, because it derives the state from an exogenous structure and, secondly, because the state is separated from its domestic social space. The notion that the state is embedded within a network of social forces within or without society is fundamentally rejected. However, while first-wave Weberian historical sociology replicates much of Waltz's schema (albeit unwittingly), I shall argue that Skocpol in fact perfectly reproduces the 'modified neorealist' approach found in the works of Gilpin. It is therefore important very briefly to consider this variant on Waltzian neorealism.

Modified neorealism and the passive-adaptive state

Although Gilpin does open up the black box of the state, he still fails, I argue, to grant the state international agential power, because, as for Waltz, the international structure constitutes the primary independent variable in his theory. Gilpin reproduces Waltzian logic because his central argument, found in *U.S. Power and the Multinational Corporation* (Gilpin, 1975) and *War and Change in World Politics* (Gilpin, 1981), seeks to explain the rise and decline of great powers in terms of the theory of the military-adaptive state. Gilpin's most basic claim is that the adaptive states (i.e., those that can emulate the successful practices of the leading or most innovative states) rise to the top of the system; conversely, those that are maladaptive sink to the bottom. This is precisely equivalent to Waltz's argument where he claims that, 'To say that "the [international] structure selects" means simply that those who conform to accepted and successful practices more often rise to the top and are likelier to stay there . . . The game one has to win is defined by the structure that determines the kind of player who is likely to prosper' (Waltz, 1979: 92). The key point is that states must adapt or conform to the international political structure. It is true that Gilpin opens up the black box of the state, but the key point is that social forces are viewed only as intervening variables (and as such are under-theorised). How so?

Gilpin's theory of the rise and decline of great powers argues that states naturally seek to expand their power base against others, and will continue to do so until they come up against what might be called *domestic fetters*. In particular, Gilpin specifies two interrelated domestic variables: domestic agential state power and domestic social fetters. Thus he argues that when a state's domestic agential power (or institutional autonomy) is low and the strength of domestic fetters is high, the state encounters limits to adapting or conforming to anarchy. In particular, to remain internationally competitive, a state must continuously adapt and transform its domestic economic structure, not least by harnessing the latest technological innovation. If not, the locus of economic innovation shifts away to the more adaptive states, which then rise to the top, leading to the relative decline of the maladaptive great power (Gilpin, 1981: 160–2, 175–82). Gilpin also focuses on those domestic fetters which impede a state's ability to extract sufficient tax, upon which its military power ultimately rests. Thus because the majority of the population prefers to spend its money on higher private and/or public welfare consumption, the amount of taxation that can be allocated to military expenditures is reduced (Gilpin, 1981: 96–103, 163–5). The key point is that if the state has only low domestic agential power, it will be unable to overcome these domestic fetters that block its continued international expansion, leading to the decline of a great power and an expansion of its more adaptive rivals – see, for example, Gilpin's discussion of the decline of British and American hegemony after 1873 and 1973 respectively (Gilpin, 1975: 88–97, ch. 7).

In the end, Gilpin, like Waltz, drops the second tier and, therefore, fails to accord the state any international agential power. How so? While he does indeed specify domestic forces (unlike Waltz), nevertheless, they have no real agency. They are merely *intervening* variables. That is, domestic variables are only salient to the extent that they promote or hinder a state's ability to conform to the primary logic of the international political structure. They affect a state's ability to conform, but they do not constitute independent variables which define state behaviour; that is left to anarchy. This reproduces Waltz's 'thin' conception of the state, since strong social forces do not empower the state. Only when the state is autonomous of domestic forces can it successfully adapt to the international political structure. As in Waltz, states that *can* conform to the international political structure will rise in the inter-state system; those that *cannot* (for whatever reason) will decline.

In sum, Gilpin is able to tell us *why* it is that *particular* states rise and *particular* states decline (a story that Waltz is not interested in telling). That is, he adds empirical sensitivity and specificity, or particularity, to Waltz's general position. But the international structure is still accorded primacy, and the state must adapt or conform to its constraining requirements or suffer the consequences (i.e., defeat in war, decline or extinction). In other words, the state is fundamentally denied agential power to shape the international system. It remains a passive victim of the international structure's imperatives.

First-wave Weberian historical sociology and the neorealist theory of change: 'kicking the state back out' and 'denying historical sociology'

Now that we have laid out the basic neorealist framework, we can turn to consider how (first-wave) Weberian historical sociology reproduces neorealist logic. To illustrate this, I draw on Theda Skocpol's (1979) analysis of social revolutions. I shall argue that it merely reproduces a pure neorealist logic. The paradox here is that while Skocpol herself passionately argues that social scientists must 'bring the state back in', I will argue that in characteristic neorealist fashion, Skocpol ends up by 'kicking the state back out', because she reduces it to the international political structure. Thus for Skocpol, states have no real choice but to conform to the survival imperatives of the international structure, because failure to do so leads to defeat in war and subsequent revolution. In general, though, Skocpol perfectly reproduces Gilpin's logic. Skocpol implicitly emphasises the centrality of international anarchy and the uneven distribution of capabilities (Waltz's first and third tiers of the international political structure), but, in line with Gilpin, supplements this with a set of 'intervening' domestic variables. These comprise varying domestic agential state power (i.e., varying institutional state autonomy), and internal *social fetters* – either the power of dominant agrarian classes *vis-à-vis* the state or the agrarian nature of the economy. Skocpol's basic claim is that in order to conform to the international political structure, states must enjoy high domestic agential power (institutional autonomy) to allow them to push through economic and fiscal reforms against resistance put up by the various domestic fetters. Failure to overcome these domestic fetters is punished through defeat in war and subsequent social revolution. Thus in both France and China, powerful noble dominant classes blocked the state's attempts to increase taxation and to implement modernising reforms, both of which were designed to enhance the military power base of the state. These reforms were blocked because both states had insufficient domestic agential power or autonomy to overcome these powerful internal blockages or fetters. Because these 'proto-bureaucratic' states were inadequately centralised, they were unable to collect taxes directly from the provinces, and accordingly had no choice but to rely on the nobles to collect them on their behalf, even though about 50 per cent of the takings were never passed on to the state. Accordingly, fiscal crisis set in, thereby undermining these states' ability to adequately compete internationally (since warfare required high amounts of taxation). In turn, military breakdown or exhaustion led on to social revolution, in France in 1789 and in China in 1911.

In Russia, the main social fetter was the backwardness of the agrarian economy, which impeded the state's military capacity. Here the low domestic agential power (institutional autonomy) of the state prevented it from implementing modernising economic reforms sufficient to enhance its military power base (Skocpol, 1979: 85–9). Skocpol argues, in classic neorealist fashion, that, in contrast to Prussia and Japan, 'the sluggishness of Russian agriculture after the (1861) emancipation fettered tsarist attempts to adapt imperial Russia to the exigencies of the modernizing European states system' (Skocpol, 1979: 109). Accordingly, the maladaptive state was defeated in 1905 (by Japan), and subsequent military exhaustion during the First World War was punished by social revolution in 1917. By contrast, Prussia and Japan did not succumb to either defeat in war or domestic social revolution, because they enjoyed high domestic agential state power and were highly adaptive. Thus both Prussia and Japan 'adapted speedily and smoothly to international [military] exigencies through reforms instituted from above by autocratic political authorities' (Skocpol, 1979: 110). Moreover, she concludes that France, Russia and China 'endured revolutionary political crises because agrarian structures impinged upon autocratic and proto-bureaucratic state organisations in ways that blocked or fettered monarchical initiatives in coping with escalating international military competition in a world undergoing uneven transformation by capitalism' (Skocpol, 1979: 99, also 50, 110, 285–6).

What then of Skocpol's historical sociology of social change? Undoubtedly the greatest irony here is that in reproducing neorealist logic, Skocpol unwittingly *denies* the rationale for historical sociology in the first place.

Because I have discussed the various sources and aspects of ahistoricism (chronofetishism and tempocentrism) in neorealism in my introductory chapter, I will not repeat them here (see pp. 5–13). Suffice it to say that Skocpol's approach similarly suffers from chronofetishism because she unwittingly reproduces Waltz's argument that anarchy reproduces itself and, therefore, that international structural change is not possible. For Skocpol, although maladaptive states are selected out for punishment in the inter-state system through defeat in war, subsequent revolution leads ultimately to a stronger state apparatus, which enables that state to remain competitive within the international system, thereby unintentionally reproducing the anarchic system of states: 'the new state organisations forged during the Revolutions were more centralized and rationalized than those of the Old Regime. Hence they were more potent within society and more powerful and autonomous over and against competitors [i.e., states] within the international states system' (Skocpol, 1979: 161–2, and ch. 4). And her argument is fundamentally tempocentric because each social revolution that she analyses is broadly equivalent (i.e., where she falls prey to the *isomorphic illusion*). The different cases are conceived of as isomorphic in that it is always the maladaptive states (those that cannot overcome strong domestic social fetters) that are punished, firstly by military exhaustion/defeat in war and, secondly, by subsequent social revolution. There is simply no notion that there are different international and domestic social forces/processes at work in different times and places which underpin the outbreak of social revolutions.

What then of Skocpol's 'theory' of the state and international relations? It should be evident by now that because Skocpol relies heavily on Waltz's overall approach, and similarly reifies the international structure, she unwittingly denies the possibility of a 'theory of the state'. How so? Firstly, with regard to the (European) international political structure, she states that it was one 'in which no one imperial state controlled the entire territory of Europe and her overseas conquests' (Skocpol, 1979: 20–1). This is equivalent to Waltz's first tier of the international political structure – the ordering principle of anarchy – because the international realm appears as a 'realm of (military) necessity' in which states must adapt through competition and emulation if they are to survive. Indeed, whenever she discusses inter-state relations, these are always, without exception, understood as conflictual. Secondly, power differentiation, or the uneven distribution of military capacity among states (Waltz's third tier), is implicitly invoked as a central aspect of her whole approach, because it was the fundamental military challenge that the stronger states made to the weaker states that led to their defeat in war and subsequent social revolution.

But the crucial question is: does the state (the second tier) drop out as an agent in the international realm (as it does for Waltz and Gilpin)? Put differently: does Skocpol succeed in 'bringing the state back in', as she claims to have done (thereby implying a non-realist theory of the state)? I argue that while, unlike Waltz, she opens up the black box of state and state–society relations, she does so in a way that is entirely congruent with Gilpin's 'modified neorealism'. As with Gilpin, a state's domestic agential power or autonomy, as well as state–society relations, are *intervening variables*; they are only salient in her analysis to the extent that they affect the state's ability to conform to the primary logic of anarchy and military competition. Thus high domestic agential power or institutional autonomy promotes international adaptability; low domestic autonomy creates international maladaptability. That is, states and states' domestic autonomy are reduced to the 'primitive' structure of anarchy. Social forces do not define state behaviour; that is left to the anarchic political system. For Skocpol, as for Waltz, 'The game one has to win is defined by the [anarchic] structure that determines the kind of player who is likely to prosper' (Waltz, 1979: 92, 128). Thus despite all the talk about state autonomy and state–society relations, reflected especially in the first part of her definition of the state (see Skocpol 1979: 32), the state is reduced to the logic of the international political structure. Accordingly, Skocpol produces a 'thin' conception of the state, and paradoxically, as in Waltz, offers us no *theory* of the state. It was surely not for nothing that Skocpol (1979: 31) ironically, though correctly, described her theory of the state as '(neo)realist', even if she was unaware of the fatal ramifications this would have for her impassioned plea to 'bring the state back in'. Thus in the end, Skocpol unwittingly 'kicked the state back out'.

'Second-wave' Weberian historical sociology: 'bringing historical sociology and states/societies/international society back in'

Thus far I have argued that first-wave neo-Weberians, as do neorealists, reify the international political structure, and deny the state and the state–society complex any international agential power. In the process, this has paradoxically led neo-Weberians to deny the rationale for historical sociology. In this section, I argue that if we *are* serious about producing an *historical sociology* of international relations that is free from ahistoricism, we need to grant the state and state–society complex international agential power and move away from structuralist tempocentrism. Only in this way can we realise the central objectives of Weberian historical sociology that went unfulfilled in the first wave.

Here I argue that the key to producing an adequate Weberian historical sociology requires that we adopt a structurationist approach that accords a rough balance between the state's international agential capacity, on the one hand, and domestic/international/global structures, on the other. This entails what Buzan and Little (this volume, ch. 10) call a 'thick' conception of the international system (i.e., one which does not reduce the international to the prime logic of anarchy, and one which envisages the *social* dimension of the international realm). But a thick conception of the international system/society is of little use if it is not integrated with a thick conception of the state, the development of which constitutes one of the central aims of this chapter.

Beyond structuralism and agent-centrism: state–society relations and the international

In developing a structurationist approach I seek to provide a synthesis of state agency/state–society agency and structure by bringing the *partially* autonomous state back in *alongside* the *partially* autonomous structures of the domestic economy, the world economy, domestic and international normative environments and the international state system. Here I emphasise the *co-constitution* of state and society as well as state and international society. Is this manoeuvre merely equivalent to taking the various bits of each theory – class or domestic interest groups (Marxism and liberalism respectively), international state system (neorealism), capitalist world economy (world systems theory) and domestic/international normative structures (constructivism) – and pasting them together in some sort of arbitrary grand synthesis? This is not the case because bringing in more variables requires a *major ontological reconfiguration* of the nature of the agents and power structures. Not only do the different power and spatial realms mutually entwine and become *partially* autonomous rather than absolutely autonomous, but also 'structures' are no longer simply conceived as anthropomorphic and 'all-constraining' in nature.

Two key insights are basic to the structurationist approach developed in this section. First, we need to reject the common tendency to view state agential power in binary 'either/or' terms, such that high state agential power implies weak social or non-state actor power, and low state agential power implies strong social power. By adopting an inclusive 'both/and' approach, I suggest that state agential power is enhanced when the state co-operates with, and embeds itself in, strong social power. Paradoxically, low agential power derives from an 'isolation' from domestic and international social forces. Adding in a social dimension to theorising state agential capacity is a vital aspect of my thick conception of the state. Second, by applying this 'both/and' logic, we can (re)view the nature of structures (both domestic as well as international and global) as *double-edged*, such that they 'enable' as well as 'constrain' states. In this thick conception, international, global and national 'structures' are now viewed as 'realms of opportunity' as well as 'realms of constraint'. In this way, domestic, international and global society partially constrain states, requiring them to adapt to their logic. Moreover, we need to recognise that domestic and international structures are also *social* in nature and help construct the identity and behaviour of states – as constructivists argue (I integrate this into my model in the next section). But domestic, international and global structures also become *partial resource pools* into which states-as-agents dip in order to push through reforms in the different realms. And it deserves emphasising that failing to grant states international agential power necessarily leads to a structuralist approach, which denies the benefits of structurationism. Combining these insights produces the basis of a structurationist approach, in which states and state–society complexes come to constitute international/global society while simultaneously being shaped by these structures and processes.

To illustrate this approach, I draw from my analysis made in *The Wealth of States* (Hobson, 1997). There I used the example of the shift from free trade to tariff protectionism in the late nineteenth century, in order to develop such a 'structurationist' approach to the state and international relations (for a summary, see Hobson, 2000: 203–13, 223–35). The argument begins with one fundamental claim: that tariffs went up in the late nineteenth century firstly because states required more tax revenues and, secondly, because states sought to shift their domestic revenue bases, in part for various domestic reasons. This argument becomes understandable once we recognise that tariffs are a form of taxation, specifically an *indirect tax*.

We begin by noting that various constraints and imperatives emanating within the international system brought on fiscal crisis in many European states (i.e., the rising costs of warfare and the decline of tax revenues due to the international economic depression after 1873). In this sense then, the international political system and international economy acted as 'realms of constraint', to which states had to adapt, with continental European states resorting to tariff protectionism to fund the fiscal revenue gap. Moreover, as I argue in the next section, the international normative environment, based on neo-mercantilist norms, also constituted the identity of the agents (i.e., states), pushing them towards tariff protectionism. The next part of the argument emphasises (the differing degrees of) state agential power and how the domestic and international realms are also 'resource pools' (i.e., 'realms of opportunity'). I argue that states had different degrees of *governing capacity* (i.e., domestic agential power); that is, they were endowed with different abilities to govern. For example, the British state had generally high governing capacity which enabled it to shift to income taxation and, therefore, to avoid raising indirect taxes and tariffs (thereby maintaining free trade). Conversely, Germany and Russia had low levels of governing capacity, leading them to rely on regressive indirect taxes and, therefore, to revert to tariff protectionism. This entails a thick conception of the state. What, then, does a thick conception of governing capacity comprise?

A thick conception requires noting the complex institutional and, above all, social properties of state agential power. Traditional definitions of domestic state autonomy equate it with the power to construct policy *against* the interests of domestic groupings (see Krasner, 1978; Skocpol, 1979, 1985). But I argue that state governing capacity is enhanced *precisely when the state co-operates and negotiates with a broad array of social forces*. Conversely, when a state is isolated from society and seeks to repress social forces, its governing capacity is greatly diminished. This can be understood when comparing the trade policies of Britain and Russia.

The Russian government chose tariffs firstly because the state lacked sufficient penetrative or infrastructural power to collect the income tax (given its surprisingly weak bureaucratic capacity). But the most important component of state agential power derives from the degree to which it is embedded within the broad networks of social power within society. The Tsarist state sought to repress *all* social groupings, and accordingly chose regressive indirect taxes (which hurt the peasantry and working classes), while simultaneously initiating a 'schizophrenic' tariff policy which ultimately hurt the producer classes (for full details, see Hobson, 1997: ch. 4). Accordingly, the state became increasingly isolated from society and paradoxically, in the process, its overall governing capacity was greatly diminished *vis-à-vis* the British state (not least because indirect taxes provided a low fiscal yield). In contrast to Britain's domestic disembedded liberal norms, Russia was shaped by 'disembedded mercantilist' norms, which prompted it to intervene in the economy in a way that enabled it to remain socially isolated or disembedded.

By contrast, the British state had a very strong fiscal-bureaucratic capacity, which was an important prerequisite for raising the income tax. Most importantly, the British state enjoyed deep levels of social embeddedness, in that it was broadly embedded not only in the dominant economic classes, but also in the subordinate classes and in the domestic liberal norms of society. It sought to co-operate with both groupings in its choice of tax policy. Thus it kept the dominant classes onside by maintaining free trade, while simultaneously keeping the working classes onside by raising income tax on the upper income groups. In the process this enhanced the state's overall fiscal capacity, given that the income tax is highly productive. Moreover, the domestic norms of 'disembedded liberalism' prevailed, thereby constructing the state's identity around the notion of minimalist government and free trade.

Sketching a structurationist theory of the constitutive state and international relations

So how does this all relate to the structurationist approach that I specified at the beginning of this section? First, I note that international and global structures are *double-edged* – they both constrain and enable states. So I showed that fiscal crisis in the late-nineteenth century was in part determined by the imperatives of the inter-state system (i.e., rising fiscal costs of warfare) and the international economy (i.e., reduced fiscal revenues). In this sense the international structure constrained states and pushed them to adapt (as in neorealist structuralism). But in this thick conception, the international system was also in part a resource pool into which states dipped, not only to resolve fiscal-military crisis, but also *to push through domestic reforms that were not connected to international imperatives* (as discussed above).

The second point of departure is the central claim of this section: that states had varying international agential power (depending on their levels of domestic agential power), which in turn shaped their actions and policies *vis-à-vis* trade policy. In other words, in this thick conception, a nation-state's internal social and normative properties and agential power are crucial to the determination of international trade regime change. Put differently, this suggests that Waltz's second tier – the character of the units – must not drop out but should stay in; and that a *theory of the state* is crucial to understanding international relations. Thus the British state enjoyed high international agential power in the early twentieth century, precisely because it had high domestic agential capacity, given that it was deeply embedded in a broad range of domestic and normative social forces. This enabled it to shift to the income tax and maintain the international co-operative policy of free trade. Conversely, the German and Russian states had only low governing capacity – they were relatively isolated from domestic social forces – and, within a domestic neomercantilist normative environment, chose to rely on regressive indirect taxes and tariffs. In turn they had only moderate international agential power in that they chose to defect from co-operative trade relations by returning to tariff protectionism.

Bringing historical sociology back into Weberian historical sociology: beyond chronofetishism and tempocentrism

How then does my approach remedy the problems of chronofetishism and tempocentrism that pervade first-wave Weberian historical sociology and neorealism (defined on p. 12 of this volume)? I seek to overcome chronofetishism in the first instance by noting the point that free trade is neither natural nor inevitable. Given that free trade has existed for a mere 10–15 per cent of the years between 1600 and 2000 (almost all of which occurred in the post-1945 era), such an historical anomaly urgently requires historical sociological analysis. Moreover, free trade is *not*, as liberals assume, the outcome of spontaneous and natural impulses associated with human nature, nor is it the inevitable consequence of hegemony (British or American). Rather, trade regimes owe their emergence to a *constellation* of three uniquely configured social power forces: normative environments (domestic and international), international institutional architectures and a specific type of state–society complex. Moreover, my approach also enables us to break with tempocentrism, which pervades the dominant approaches that seek to explain the emergence of free trade after 1945. Neorealism and neoliberalism, in particular, assume that the two great periods of free trade – the mid-nineteenth century and the post-1945 era – are isomorphic, and can be explained through reference to the same causal factors. I noted in my introductory chapter that neoliberalism tempocentrically extrapolates the assumption of state egoism back to explain the outbreak of free trade in the nineteenth century. And I also noted that neorealism explains both periods through reference to hegemony (British and American), where hegemony itself is seen in isomorphic terms (see pp. 11–12). My historical sociological approach reveals firstly that both periods were in no way isomorphic. The nineteenth-century regime was not particularly free (see also Stein, 1984), and, most significantly, it lasted a mere seventeen years at most. By contrast, the post-1945 regime has been generally much freer and, above all, has been sustained over a significant time period (and is intensifying further under the WTO). Why the differences? Put differently, how can my approach overcome the chronofetishism and tempocentrism of neorealism and neoliberalism?

Returning to the point made above, the differences in the nineteenth- and twentieth-century free trade regimes can be explained by reference to the constellation of three uniquely configured social power forces. Firstly, the *international normative environments* were very different. The post-1945 regime was in the first instance dependent upon the international norm of 'embedded liberalism' (in which it was deemed 'economically appropriate' for states to intervene in the domestic economy but *not* to intervene in the international economy), while in more recent years, the free trade regime has begun to intensify further under the international norm of 'disembedded liberalism' (in which it is deemed 'economically appropriate' for states *not* to intervene in either the domestic or international economies). These norms significantly contributed to the onset and deepening of the post-1945 free trade regime. Conversely, neither of these international norms existed in the nineteenth century (though Britain embodied a *domestic* set of disembedded liberal norms, which helps explain its unilateral free trade stance). By contrast, the nineteenth-century international norms were based on 'neo-mercantilism', in which it was deemed 'appropriate' for states to intervene in the international economy in order to shore up the state's national military power base. Thus when the costs of government rose after 1873, states very quickly resorted back to tariff protection to secure the necessary fiscal revenues.

The second social power force comprises the *international institutional architectures*, which have been radically different in the two periods. The post-1945 regime has been successful in part because of the GATT structure and more recently the WTO (particularly because both architectures have been embedded with pro-free trade international norms). Here the key point is that such an architecture has been founded on *multilateralism*, which has proved to be highly effective in bringing states together to accept freer trade. By contrast, no equivalent to this existed in the nineteenth century, in which the architecture was primarily *bilateral*. Free trade was dependent upon individual states signing bilateral treaties to secure lower tariffs (though such an architecture gave a cursory nod to multilateralism in the shape of the Most Favoured Nations Clause). Accordingly, there was no overarching framework to draw all states together to pursue freer trade in a sustained way.

The third, and perhaps most important, factor is the nature of the *state–society complex*. The post-1945 state–society complex has proved highly conducive to free trade, in contrast to that of the mid-nineteenth century. The post-1945 regime was only possible in the first instance because the prevailing state–society complex within international society was based on a highly co-operative set of relations between state and society. That is, because the state was broadly 'socially embedded', it was able to shift to the income tax, thereby enabling it to break its dependence up to that time on indirect taxes and protectionist tariffs. Thus in addition to Ruggie's (1998b: ch. 2) insight that the post-1945 free trade regime was dependent upon the 'compromise of embedded liberalism', we also have to recognise that this compromise itself was only possible with the rise of *socially embedded* states, which in turn enabled the raising of the income tax. By contrast, in the mid-nineteenth century, states were relatively isolated from the majority of social forces at the domestic level. Being unable to collect sufficient amounts of income tax, they turned to regressive and repressive indirect taxes, i.e., protectionism (Hobson, 1997: 19–20, 145–7, 210–11, 245–6, 247–8). Thus while there is evidence that states moved towards *freer* trade after 1860, this tentative move was abruptly terminated when the fiscal costs of government increased rapidly after 1873, thereby prompting most European states (bar Britain) to shift back to indirect taxes and hence tariff protectionism.

While I would not wish to reduce the international institutional architecture and the international normative environments to the primacy of state–society complexes, nevertheless, I would argue that both the post-1945 multilateral institutions and normative frameworks can *in part* be explained by the presence of socially embedded state–society complexes (i.e., where the socially embedded state–society complex was internationalised into the institutional and normative international frameworks). However, I conclude that these three social power forces are mutually embedded in each other and cannot, therefore, be treated in isolation of each other, nor ultimately be reduced to one of their component parts. In this way, I suggest, second-wave Weberian historical sociology is able to remedy the chronofetishism and tempocentrism associated with mainstream international relations theory as well as first-wave Weberian historical sociology. And I would add here that this analysis also answers, at least to some extent, Reus-Smit's critique of my so-called 'rationalist' approach (Reus-Smit, this volume, pp. 126–9).

Conclusion: bringing second-wave Weberian historical sociology into international relations

This chapter agrees with the various critics of Weberian historical sociology that much of it reproduces neorealist logic, which in turn leads Weberians and Weberian-inspired international relations scholars into a theoretical cul-de-sac. By extension, I have argued that, ultimately, the main problem in trading places with neorealism has been that the first wave has denied its commitment to an historical sociological approach. By contrast, my second-wave approach is able to remedy chronofetishism and tempocentrism because it rejects *ahistorical* state-centrism and international structuralism, and seeks to situate the 'partially' autonomous state alongside, and in mutual interaction with, 'partially' autonomous domestic and international social and normative structures as well as non-state actors. In short, only by adopting a thick conception of the state and the international system can we move beyond first-wave Weberian historical sociology in order to realise Weberianism's basic tenets as a genuinely historical sociological approach.

4   Globality and historical sociology: state, revolution and war revisited

Martin Shaw

Our social world is in rapid transformation, and the traditions of the social sciences are struggling to keep pace with the change. International relations, a late arrival, has found itself locked into a particularly narrow definition of its object, as the study of the relations of states in international systems.[1] This intellectual framework owed much of its force, moreover, to the particular historical conjuncture of the Cold War. As the latter has faded, an intellectual ferment has developed in international studies, in which international political economy has become an increasingly distinct field, Marxist and critical theory have become more influential, and feminist approaches have emerged (almost two decades after they had begun to influence other social sciences).

To a visitor (as I was a few years ago) from planet sociology, international relations had some of the charm of a 1950s theme park, where questions long since thrown up – and seemingly answered in other fields – were popping up as novelties. However, there was a reason for my visits: the big historical questions – world order, state development, war and peace – did at least have a place in international studies. In sociology, once the excitements of the 1960s had died down, these macro-concerns, although treated by major figures like Theda Skocpol (1979), Anthony Giddens (1985) and Michael Mann (1986, 1993), became curiously marginal to the vast, fragmented empirical underbelly of the subject.

Moreover, although globalisation began to be discussed at the cultural end of sociological theory – and once again it was Giddens who pushed the question into the heart of the field – there was a curious disconnection between the new 'global' discourse and the macro-historical sociologies of power. This disjunction was even manifest between these two phases of Giddens's own work: the theoretical and historical connections between

---

[1] The concept of international system is unavoidable, and indeed I long ago argued that a problem of Marxist theory was its failure to develop such a concept (Shaw, 1984). However, it is not in itself an adequate problematic for international relations as a field. Hence, I do not find the failure of historical sociologists to develop 'thick' concepts of such systems a strong basis for a critique, as argued by Stephen Hobden (Hobden, 1999).

his mid 1980s theory of the nation-state (Giddens, 1985) and his early 1990s work on global change and modernity (Giddens 1990, 1991) have not been tightly drawn. Other major historical sociologists gave little attention to globality, or where they did so, tended to be sceptical about the significance of contemporary transformations (Mann, 1997).

My own work in the 1980s had been concerned with a particular subset of historical sociological concerns, the sociology of war (Shaw, 1984b, 1988; Shaw and Creighton, 1987).[2] War was central to the work of the well-known historical sociologists but they often operated, I argued, with inadequate theories of its development.[3] Like many others, I found myself revising my ideas to make sense of the dissolution of the Cold War order in 1989–91 (Shaw, 1991). As I attempted to relate the new debate about 'globalisation' to the theoretical perspectives of an historical sociology of the state, I found my work entering more and more into international relations (Shaw, 1994). Although at first I tended to emphasise the sociological limitations of international debates, increasingly I saw the problem as double-sided. Sociology had not only failed to develop an adequate theory of the international, but its account of the new globality was also limited by its neglect of the political and military dimensions of contemporary historical change.

In approaching the contribution of historical sociology to contemporary international debates, my starting point is therefore one of dual critique. We cannot take the categories of international relations as givens, searching for instance for more sociological explanations of traditional international realities: I have argued that this is a weakness of John Hobson's proposal (Hobson, 1998a, 1998b; Shaw, 1998). The rupture of traditional international relations, expressed in James Rosenau's argument for 'post-international' concepts and many others' embracing of the idea of 'global' transformations, is for real. This is not, of course, to deny the importance of grasping the continuities: in accounting for the present, obviously we must not throw out of the window our accumulated historical understanding – indeed, specifying contemporary change requires precise models of past developments. It is, however, to argue that we acknowledge the radical disjunctures of the present, that we investigate the nature of contemporary historical change and make the evaluation of its significance a central historical task.

By the same token, however, we cannot simply take over the given tradition of historical sociology as a basis for contemporary international or

---

[2] The sociology of war is distinguished from the related field of military sociology that concerns itself primarily with the evolution of military organisations.

[3] See, for example, my critique of Giddens's, *The Nation-State and Violence* (Shaw, 1989).

global understanding. Historical sociology has greatly enriched our grasp of international processes, but most important work has been located in the earlier periods of modernity, in which the national–international duality was first entrenched – not the present, in which it is being transformed. There remains a real danger, as international critics first noted more than a decade ago, that an historical sociological approach will reinforce outdated realist approaches to international relations, just as critical international scholars are moving beyond them.

This understanding of the problems of existing historical sociology, as well as of the contemporary possibilities of the approach, leads me to be cautious about definitions that tend towards closure. As C. Wright Mills argued, the sociological imagination is intrinsically historical (Wright Mills, 1970). I want to defend this understanding as a common inheritance of sociology, and not allow it to be defined as the prerogative of one particular school. Marxist as well as Weberian, and indeed other, approaches will have contributions to make. Marx's central contribution to historical sociological thought is the principle of historical specificity.[4] Its value is enhanced if we understand it in ways more complex than his own – periodising in terms of political- as well as production-relations, for example. The emancipatory thrust of Marx's social theory also remains a powerful impetus, even if we now interpret this in broader terms than those of proletarian revolution. Similarly the idea that social groups may become collective actors in their own emancipation is a fundamental insight, even if the contribution of social movements is now partially de-linked from the role of the working class.

It is true that the most fruitful contributions to historical sociology have come, in recent decades, from writers already mentioned (and others, including contributors to this book) whose main reference point is Weber rather than Marx. These contributions have incorporated, however, some of these insights of Marx, even as they have transcended a Marxist position. The lessons of Marx that I have instanced may be useful correctives to any tendency in Weberian historical sociology towards transhistorical categories or generalisations, towards abstract structuralism, or towards neglect of the emancipatory questions which are central to understanding contemporary world changes.

The approach in this chapter reflects this broader conception of historical sociology. I also start from some of the achievements of recent Weber-inspired writers who have escaped from the constrictions of the Marxist approach. However, I propose to develop their insights in the context of a broad understanding of a sociological approach, which also

---

[4] For an elegant exposition, see Korsch (1963).

sees in some international relations literature a broadly sociological perspective. In order to develop an historical sociological international and
global understanding in this period of political and intellectual flux, we
need an open conception of theoretical tradition and method.

The problem of global transformation

The central historical sociological problems that this chapter seeks to
clarify are the nature of contemporary 'global' transformation and its
meaning for international relations. My starting point is that globality is
poorly understood in sociology and international relations alike. Most
'globalisation' literature fails to define 'global'. Globalisation is grasped
as a spatial, or time-spatial development, in which social relations are
simultaneously stretched and intensified. There is a tendency to reduce
globality to technical changes, particularly in the character of communications. Its social and political contents are neglected – seen as consequences or implications of the core globalising processes, not as central
to the meaning of globality itself.[5]

There is an unhelpful kind of sociologism, and even technological determinism, not only in the sociological but in the international relations
literature. According to many accounts, changes in technology, the economy and culture are 'undermining' the state. This sort of argument invites
the necessary, but insufficient, riposte that the nation-state is far from
impotent – as Linda Weiss has suggested, its 'powerlessness' is a 'myth'
(Weiss, 1998).[6] A long line of international theorists, criticising the traditional 'realist' ideas of the discipline, has developed parallel arguments.
According to the pioneering 'pluralists', Robert Keohane and Joseph Nye,
the salience of military power decreased with the growth of 'complex interdependence' among advanced economies (Keohane and Nye, 1977).
According to Rosenau and Czempiel, what is developing is 'governance
without government' (Rosenau and Czempiel, 1992). According to the
radical liberal Richard Falk, we are moving into 'a post-statist world order' (Falk, 1997: 125).

This tendency is reinforced by the inevitable economism and sociologism of Marxist-inspired accounts. According to Robert Cox, there
is an 'internationalisation of the state', but only in the sense that nation-
states are adapting to international capital (Cox, 1987, 253–65). Stephen
Gill interestingly identified an emerging 'trilateral' hegemony of North
American, Western European and Japanese capital (Gill, 1990). My

---

[5] I have developed this argument further in Shaw (1999a).
[6] See also Hirst and Thompson (1996).

Sussex colleague, Kees van der Pijl, has explored the unity of the 'heart-land' of capital at the level of class relations, in the emergence of a 'transatlantic ruling class' and the 'cadre class' (van der Pijl, 1984, 1994).

I have argued that the common failing of the whole international relations critique of realism is that it bypasses the serious examination of the state and the state system, thus not meeting head-on the realist conception of the state (Shaw, 1999b).[7] Their 'emancipatory' political perspectives place excessive reliance on the potential of social movements, civil society and class forces, and underestimate the potential of reformist mobilisation of the resources of state power.

Of course, there have been interesting developments from within a broadly realist (or 'neo-realist') framework of analysis. The work of Barry Buzan and Richard Little, represented elsewhere in this volume, is a good example of this strand. Here, however, we have the opposite problem – that although the historical evolution of states systems is seriously problematised, the sociological contextualisation is thin. States systems do not appear in their character as one kind of network of social power, but as *the* enduring structural form of power, which may be organised around military or economic foci.

This re-historicised realism reproduces the other side of the dilemma of international relations in the era of global transformation: if we are not to remove states and states systems from the centre of our gaze, we must reassert their continuity into the present. A similar problem presents itself with a 'geopoliticist' historical sociology: the reconfigurations of state power in the contemporary period are merely new forms of empire. While these kinds of continuity are not unimportant, the interesting question is precisely the novelty of state and state-system formations in the global era. Whether we trace world-systems back a mere five hundred years, or many thousands as Barry Gills proposes in his chapter, the one thing that it is not easy to see as unchanging is the form of political power.

The common assumption that globalisation is economically driven has led to a misleading historical debate. On the one hand, those like Kenneth Ohmae who are impressed by the expansion of the world market at the end of the twentieth century, and argue that the state is newly undermined, assert the novelty of contemporary global change (Ohmae, 1995). On the other, those like Roland Robertson who recall half a millennium (or more) of world market development see globalisation as a long historical process (Robertson, 1992).

[7] A parallel argument is made from a Marxist point of view in a study by my Sussex colleague Justin Rosenberg (1994).

It seems more apposite to contend that, while there has been a long growth of market relations on a world scale, the really significant ruptures in social development – which have determined much of the pace of market expansion – have been the results of political and military upheavals. What happened in Russia after 1917 was not a spontaneous demise of markets, but a political movement, accelerated after Stalin's 'revolution from above' in 1929, towards a command economy. What has happened since 1989 is not a spontaneous surge towards the market resulting from the growth of information technology, but a political upheaval erupting from a major crisis in state power.

My proposal is, therefore, that we take the social relations and forms of state power as the starting point for understanding global change. In doing so, we need to make a radical break with the dominant ways of thinking in international relations. The more historical approaches in international relations – especially the English School from the work of my Sussex predecessor, Martin Wight (1977), to much recent analysis – are certainly far more interesting than their structuralist counterparts.

There is, however, a common problem, which is exacerbated by the tendency to see international systems in terms of norms as well as power. This is the tendency to give excessive weight to the juridical definition of the state. For much of the field, states are defined by a particular legal attribute – sovereignty – and international relations are conducted principally between units that possess it. I do not wish to deny the great significance of these legal relations. However, an historical sociological approach will necessarily, and properly, see them as embedded in messy, complex organisations of power, embroiled in equally complex social struggles. The characters of these organisations and relations in the present period are highly distinctive, in a way that none of the strands of international relations, nor actually existing historical sociology, has fully recognised. A principal task of historical sociology today is to explore the uniqueness of these changes, by placing them in the most relevant larger historical narratives. I intend to use the remainder of this chapter to show, in outline, how the interlocking narratives of state, revolution, war and genocide might be transformed to account for contemporary globality.

The global transformation of state relations and forms

States are best defined in Michael Mann's terms, as organisations of power which radiate from centres, make rules, mobilise legitimacy and project force (Mann, 1993: 55). They are not necessarily, however, *simple* territorial monopolists of violence, as Max Weber has generally been understood to mean. States came to approximate this model, to become – as Giddens put it – 'bordered power containers', under certain historical conditions, namely the consolidation of the imperial nation-state, especially in the late nineteenth and early twentieth centuries. The heyday of this historical form, the period of the world wars with its economic autarchy and total ideological mobilisation, appears in retrospect as the historical exception, not the rule. Societies were not closed entities before the twentieth century, and they are not as we enter the twenty-first. Even the great European empires, which appeared to be self-sufficient world orders (so that earlier globalisation was serial rather than singular), permitted considerable cross-fertilisation especially at the elite level.

The idea of 'the' state, with 'its' discrete national society, is therefore transient. The normal question is what, in the flux of world-wide social relations, constitute more or less distinct – if always complexly overlapping – societies, cultures and states. Defining distinct 'states' is, moreover, different from defining societies or cultures (which I do not have space to discuss here). What defines a distinct centre of state power, in relation to other centres, is not merely its international legal status or the rule-making aspect considered in isolation, but a more or less autonomous capacity for the organisation and projection of violence.

In these terms, we can see the historic transition of the mid-twentieth century – the outcome of the Second World War – as the replacement of rival, autonomous imperial nation-states in Western Europe and Japan, by powerful post-imperial national entities which were nevertheless deeply dependent on the United States. This was an utterly crucial historical change and, considered in isolation, probably a more important one than that of 1989–91. Most of the major nation-state-empires of the previous century, the centres between which two world wars had been fought, ceased to be fully autonomous centres of state power.

We should see this dramatic result as confirmed and increased by the process of the Cold War. The apparently lower salience of military issues, which Keohane and Nye noted, was not the result of interdependence; rather dramatically new military conditions, in which a Western bloc confronted its Soviet rival, was the cause of interdependence. These new military relations were also, of course, what produced the lower visibility of military questions in the relations of state entities within the West. A whole academic industry, which considers contemporary states as juridical and economic units and neglects the common military structure of the West, has been built on the failure to grasp this transformation. From this point of view, what matters is the competition within the West – thus according to Philip Cerny (1990), the contemporary state is a 'competition state' – rather than the larger framework.

From these contingent historical results developed deep structural change. In essentials there emerged a new common centre of state power, through three kinds of major institutional development: pan-Western military, political and economic organisations; the political-economic integration of Western Europe; and the embryonically global political organisations of the United Nations system. The latter was, of course, the most problematic, since it embraced other clearly independent centres of state power – not only the Soviet bloc, but the disparate and increasingly numerous states of the Third World. Nevertheless, it was important as a legitimation framework, and to the extent that it was able to cohere, reinforced the unification of the West.

For even during the Cold War, despite the appearance – and in military terms, the reality – of competition between two more or less equal blocs, the West was already not only the most powerful but also the dominant world bloc. And although Western dominance was always in important senses American dominance, van der Pijl, Gill and others are right to suggest the maturation of a broader, 'transatlantic' or 'trilateral' Western hegemony. Indeed, by focusing on the relations and forms of state power, rather than class or economic relations, we can see that Western world hegemony was based on structural change within the West.

The significance of these Cold War developments has been put into sharp relief since 1989. Contrary to the expectations of those in the 1970s like Ernest Mandel (1970), who saw a contest of 'Europe versus America', and Mary Kaldor (1979), who wrote of the 'disintegration of the West', the West has held together. Fierce economic rivalries are managed within common institutions (like the World Trade Organisation); they do not lead to deep political rifts, let alone anything approaching war. The end of the Cold War has led to war and instability on the periphery of Europe, as John Mearsheimer (1990) predicted, but more striking is the way that the centre has held, not just within Europe but across the Atlantic. Not only has the West failed to fall apart, but its essential common interests have been confirmed, its common framework enhanced. Both are increasingly globally projected. Everything suggests that here we have a major structural development.

The contemporary West can be seen, therefore, as an increasingly integrated, comprehensively institutionalised, international 'conglomerate' of state power. Even the most powerful national state centres – including the United States – are increasingly constrained by their involvement in this bloc of power. Of course, it is important to emphasise that there are considerable structural tensions within the West. The American, and to some extent the Japanese, model (and ideology) emphasises the supremacy of the national state, whereas internationalisation is integral to contemporary European state development (and ideology). Following this, Europe and America have different relations with the global layer of state. The character of formal pan-Western institutions is still limited. Political legitimacy is still heavily mediated through national democracy, and as yet there are few direct international manifestations of democracy (although the European Parliament is increasingly seen as a model with wider applicability).

These contradictions all contribute to the instability of the Western state. We must not assume that its unity is irreversible; but it is unlikely to be reversed in the near future. Clearly both the unity and the stability of the West depend on the complex, often unpredictable tests of its global projection of state power. The paradox of the West is that it possesses unparalleled resources, but even so, finds even relatively small political conflicts difficult to manage. Although internally very strong in comparison to any of its rivals, its global power projection has weak legitimacy. The strength of the Western state lies partly in its completely unrivalled economic and military resources. Although in absolute terms, the major non-Western centres of state power, such as Russia, China, India, Brazil and Indonesia, have considerable resources by comparison with the unified West, each is chronically weak. The West's strength, moreover, does not rest merely on its financial resources or military capabilities. It rests on the development of its authoritative resources. The major non-Western states, and many of the lesser but still powerful centres, such as those of the Middle East, represent still largely unreconstructed concentrations. These powerful states are still essentially 'quasi-imperial nation-states' and reproduce, albeit in varied forms, the nation-state-empires of the West before 1945.

Table 2 contrasts the main characteristics of state power in the West and in the major non-Western centres. Of course there is great variation among those states that more or less fit the latter type, but the contrast between major non-Western states and the West is sufficiently stark to make it a useful one. It would obviously be possible to expand this table, to include the new, small centres of state power produced by state fragmentation, weaker 'quasi-states', etc., or to distinguish within the non-Western category. Partly for reasons of space, I shall not expand on these sorts of refinements to my categories.

However, there are also analytical reasons for this focus. The new polarity between an expanded, internationalised, democratised, wealthy West and the major non-Western centres which, while populous, are often fragmenting, nationalistic, authoritarian and relatively poor, constitutes more than the new version of the old geopolitical international system. It also places inter-state relations at the centre of explosive socio-political

Table 2 *Characteristics of the Western and major non-Western states at the end of the twentieth century*

	Western state	Major non-Western states
Military internationalisation	A relatively cohesive and enduring bloc of military power, centred on NATO but including other alliances (notably with Japan), which has survived the end of the Cold War and is held together by the challenges to its common interests in the new world situation; has clearly gone beyond simple alliances of national entities.	Survival, or even development, of the historic national monopoly of violence, and the pursuit of state interests including to the point of inter- and intra-state war.
Economic internationalisation	An increasingly complex institutionalised framework of pan-Western political-economic organisations through which the West manages its common interests in the world economy.	Weak integration into Western-led world political-economic organisations.
Internationalisation of law	A framework of internationalised law and regulation through which national jurisdictions are harmonised, and transnational mobility by corporations and individuals is made possible.	Weak involvement in the internationalisation of law and regulation.
Regional internationalisation	The highly developed formal internationalisation of the pivotal European region, in which formal and substantive democratisation is increasingly reinforced, and in which significant elements of internationalised citizenship are developing.	Weak, superficial internationalisation at best; persistence of major regional rivalries, including in military and even nuclear forms.
Relation to global institutions	Ambivalent (especially in USA), but increasingly utilising UN system to legitimise its world-wide hegemony, and supporting extensions of international law, economic management and political and military intervention.	Ambivalent, but tending to be suspicious of Western-led international innovations; utilising UN system in negative sense, to restrain West and inhibit international authority impinging on national prerogatives.

Table 2 (*cont.*)

	Western state	Major non-Western states
Democratisation	Political democracy normalised within West, and increasingly deeply rooted, reinforced by internationalisation; also promoted outside West, to a growing extent.	Authoritarian or semi-authoritarian regimes and weak (or in some cases virtually no) democratisation, in which formal electoral democracy (if it exists) is often crudely manipulated by elites; political and social freedoms are weakly recognised and enforced.
Social inequality and welfare	Despite large socio-economic inequalities, some combination of state and private welfare systems which supports the majority of the population.	Large socio-economic inequalities, with inadequate or no social welfare systems, and coercion of both urban and rural society.
National and ethnic conflict	Increasingly multi-ethnic societies with relatively sophisticated mechanisms for managing national and ethnic conflicts, so that these are contained without the enormous disruptive potential which they have had in the past and continue to have outside the West.	Multinational societies in which the relations between states and peripheral, minority and indigenous groups are quasi-imperial: these groups have little protection; national or ethnic conflicts are often violent and these are 'managed' with fairly crude coercion.
Media and propensity to war	Expanded media spheres which sensitise publics to military violence and make the management of conflict problematic for state power.	Only partially open media in which the abilities of state elites to manage news and opinion and fight wars is greater than in the West, but not unlimited.

conflicts, as we have seen over the last decade. To try to understand 'international' relations in exclusively, or principally, geopolitical terms goes against much that has been gained in the 'new' international theorising of the last decade, and much of what historical sociology is placed to offer. We now understand fairly well that inter-state relations do not exist in a world apart from the rest of world politics.

Much of what is conventionally understood as inter-state, or international, in fact constitutes the internal politics of the Western state-conglomerate. The old division between domestic and international has manifestly been transformed. This is nowhere truer than in the European Union, where all kinds of economic, social and legal questions are now subject to Union-level processes. However, on the geopolitical model itself, it is also true of relations between America and Europe (not to mention Japan and Australasia): as the wars of the 1990s – from the Gulf to Kosovo – have shown, the West functions as a single military actor. The West can be regarded as a single state-conglomerate because its component national legal entities have pooled their 'monopolies of violence'. They are no longer seriously capable of producing war among themselves, and have institutionalised their common military (as well as economic and political) interests in manifold, mutually reinforcing ways – which partly emphasise the division between them and the rest of the world.

There is a more fundamental reason, though, for insisting that interstate relations should not be understood apart from other aspects of world politics. This is that precisely those 'international' relations between separate 'centres' of state power (as I have defined these) are completely implicated in important relations of state and society. Of course, this is not, in itself, a new discovery. Sociologically minded international scholars like Fred Halliday have long insisted on this, and notably on a dialectic of domestic revolt and international conflict.[8] Hobson (1998a) sees the exploration of this process as a major contribution of historical sociology to international relations, and my own studies have emphasised these relations in the context of total war (Shaw, 1998).

What seems to me to be new are the particular kinds of linkages between national and international, social movements and war, that are now developing. The 'global' character of world politics is determined not merely by the impact of technological, economic and cultural globalisation, but by the way in which common global issues, centred on the same problems of state power, are coming to be the substance of both international and societal politics. I intend, therefore, to explore the nature of globality further in the context of the contemporary characters of revolution and war.

Global revolution and genocidal war

It was Marx who perceptively remarked that all previous revolutions had 'perfected this [state] machine instead of smashing it' (Marx, 1950: 301). Although he implied that the proletarian revolution would be different, his axiom has never applied more completely than to the revolutions made in the name of Marx's own doctrine. The proletarian revolution in

---

[8] For a recent statement, see Halliday (1999 and this volume, ch. 12).

Russia led – through civil-war militarist centralisation and the subsequent consolidation of the Stalinist elite – to the totalitarian state. The militarised national-liberationist revolution led, especially in China, to a similar end.

Fifty years after the victory of the latter – and ten years after the fall of Soviet communism – we can see that their legacies of authoritarian state power are among the most serious problems of world order. Of course, varieties of authoritarianism are much more widespread; they exist among post-colonial elites in Western-inclined, as well as communist or ex-communist, states. Even in major post-imperial states like India, where the state was built up through much more peaceful mass politics, and with democratic electoral forms, elites still wield arbitrary power against the rural poor and minorities.

In recent decades, the idea of proletarian revolution has declined once again after its brief revival in the late 1960s and early 1970s. More importantly, we have seen the growing political bankruptcy of the national-liberationist revolutionary tradition, and shifts from armed struggle to mass politics, and a new trend towards negotiated settlements, most successfully in the case of the African National Congress in South Africa. The other major case of this kind, the Palestine Liberation Organisation's *détente* with Israel, has been more problematic, and even the minor examples, such as the Irish Republican Army and the Basque separatist movement, ETA, have been inconclusive. Nevertheless, the trend is clear, at least within the West, and in states like Israel and South Africa that are closely linked to it.

These transformations within the national-liberationist revolutionary tradition are symptomatic of a larger transformation in the pattern of revolution. The main 'revolutionary' tradition of our times, challenging especially the authoritarian non-Western states of all kinds, is the democratic revolution. From the uprisings against Soviet rule in East Germany, Hungary and Poland in the 1950s, through the 1968 movement that challenged state power in all three sectors of the Cold War world, to Polish Solidarity and the successful 1989 revolutions, there is a clear thread. These movements that played a major part in the decline of the Soviet state-bloc were always linked to democratic social movements in the West. The final decade of the Cold War began with mass protests on the streets of Western European capitals, and ended with those on the streets of Eastern European cities.

The real 'revolution in the revolution' was not Che Guevara's updating of Maoist guerrilla tactics, but the transformation of democracy into a popular cause which threatens to sweep away the Cuban and Chinese communist states together with their Soviet counterparts. The significance of this revolution, however, is that its appeal extends across the non-Western world, with powerful ramifications within the West as well. Since 1989, major national upheavals have taken place from the Philippines to South Africa, South Korea to Indonesia, not to mention the defeated movement in China itself.

The democratic revolution involves a triple transformation of the character of revolution. First, it abandons the link of revolution with the centralised revolutionary party or grouping aiming to use the popular process to seize power for itself. Because democracy is by definition a plural project, democratic revolution does not put the revolutionaries into power in a simple manner. Of course, in a case like South Africa, the party of change may succeed in hegemonising subsequent politics, but this seems to be the exception – where a national-liberation party has successfully transformed itself into a democratic majority. Elsewhere, however, popular democratic movements have paved the way for new or regrouped elites to compete for popular support.

Second, since the democratic revolution played a crucial part in the demise of the Cold War system, it has increasingly become a globalist movement. Everywhere, democratic change appeals not merely to national ideals but to universal standards of democracy and human rights. For the subjects of the more extreme authoritarian regimes, and for national minorities everywhere, the appeal to universal values – and to legitimate global institutions – is an unavoidable strategic as well as ideological choice.

Third, in this sense the democratic revolution, too, is linked to state-building. It is linked, first, to the creation of new mini-nation states of oppressed minorities. However, these states are rarely viable without international support. The democratic revolution is therefore intimately connected to two wider processes of state-building. On the one hand, it leads to the strengthening of the global layer of state, the international bureaucracies of the United Nations system. (And it is worth noting here that one of the weaknesses of Michael Barnett's interesting semi-'constructivist' chapter (this volume) on international bureaucracies is that he does not define clearly enough the situation in which these organisations are being developed.) On the other, it leads to the practical expansion of the Western state, either directly (as in the NATO occupation of Kosovo) or indirectly (when the West provides the core of a UN force as in East Timor).

The processes through which this occurs are connected to two further transformations, of counter-revolution and of war. State elites in authoritarian states, threatened by combinations of democratic reform and national minority movements, are increasingly tempted towards violent coercion as means of refashioning their rule. What are all too often still described in both sociology and international relations, naively if not culpably, as 'ethnic conflicts' are actually counter-revolutionary wars. The post-Yugoslav wars of the 1990s can be traced to Slobodan Milosevic's coup in 1989, which abolished legitimate institutions in the Serbian province of Kosovo. The Timor crisis of 1999 can be traced to the Indonesian army's invasion to suppress local autonomy in the wake of Portuguese withdrawal in 1974.

The transformations of war can be connected, therefore, to these changes in political conflict world-wide. One of the most important contributions of historical sociology is that it shows that warfare should not be understood as a socially neutral means of resolving issues between states – as international relations has generally assumed. On the contrary, warfare is a central process and a complex structural force of modern society – entrenched in, transforming and transformed with the social relations and forms of state power. The question which is raised today is what kind of mode of warfare accompanies the development of the Western and global state, the crisis of the authoritarian, quasi-imperial nation-state – not to mention the 'failures' of many state entities and institutions in Africa and elsewhere?

The answer given by Mary Kaldor (1999) is that these are 'new wars', characterised by state breakdown, a parasitic political economy, 'ethnic cleansing', privatised forces and international humanitarian intervention. However, her model understates the continuities in modern warfare. On the one hand, war still involves major centres of state power, such as Iraq, Serbia, Russia and the West itself. Conflicts between such centres and between them and society are interlinked, as they were in earlier periods. On the other hand, what is distinctive is that genocide has developed from being a secondary form of violence, in the period of classic total war, to the principal mode in many conflicts of the global era.

The concept of genocide is a problematic one. The international convention clearly suggests that it is the intentional destruction, 'in whole or in part', of an 'ethnic, national or religious group' (Orentlicher, 1999: 154). As an historical sociological concept, it is not clear that there is any good basis for excluding other kinds of groups, such as political or social groups (which were left out so as not to implicate Stalin's Russia). Certainly, the mass extermination carried out by the Khmer Rouge is widely (and validly) regarded as genocide, not because of the killing of ethnic minorities, but because of the deliberate destruction of an entire population, including specified social as well as national groups.

The question of intentionality or deliberation also raises critical questions. It arises not only where the destruction of a group is an end in itself, as with the Nazis, but also where it is an intended consequence of a larger goal, as in the American use of the atomic bomb to defeat Japan. E. P. Thompson's use of 'exterminism' rather than 'genocide' for the consequences of nuclear annihilation is an attempt to distinguish here (Thompson, 1982), but it is not clear that it is useful. Since our 'genus' is humankind, not a national or any other group, the use of 'genocide' to refer to the intended destruction of any human group seems reasonable. Likewise, that there is a clear spectrum from partial killing to the total extermination of a group means that we should regard genocide as a process that can be more or less complete. It makes sense to see certain practices as 'genocidal' where there is clearly the potential for the destruction of a group.

In this sense, 'new wars' are (to a large extent) the practice of genocide, relabelled by the perpetrators as 'ethnic cleansing'.[9] The new genocidal wars are the work of states like Iraq, Serbia and Indonesia, but also Russia, as well as of smaller state centres, para-statal forces and private armies. The genocidal character of war is critical to its significance for world politics and global state-building. Not only do the victims and their political representatives have little choice but to appeal to legitimate global institutions and the *de facto* power of the West, but the Western state no longer has the excuse of the Cold War to ignore inconvenient protests, and it is faced with enhanced media capabilities to project victims' suffering dramatically into the homes of its electoral base.

As I have shown in my detailed study of the Kurdish crisis in 1991, the major precedent for the Western military interventions of the late 1990s, local wars are reproduced as 'global crises', which call for global political responses (Shaw, 1996). Such crises are leading to major extensions of the global layer of state power: the prevalence of globally legitimated Western military forces in zones of crisis, the development of international criminal tribunals and the new International Criminal Court, and the UN-brokered humanitarian relief operations on which numerous vulnerable populations depend.

Conclusions

Globality, from an historical sociological point of view, is therefore the result of a very specific historical transformation. At the beginning of the twenty-first century (which historically we might date from 1989–91 – the end of Eric Hobsbawm's 'short twentieth century' (Hobsbawm, 1994)), the combination of the 'global-democratic revolution' with the new balance of power between Western and non-Western states is creating a new stage in world order. It is these shifts which give political meaning to the more familiar phenomena of globalisation – the communications revolution, etc.

[9] I have explored this issue further in Shaw (1999c).

The novelty of global change can be debated, and ultimately the counter-position of continuity and change is a sterile argument in which neither side can claim a conclusive victory. Which side of the case we emphasise depends on our purposes. Clearly, there are echoes of empire in the new Western hegemony. However, if we choose to press this continuity, we shall need to explain the difference between the old and the new 'imperialisms'. From the point of view of the principal victims of the new wars and other struggles of the global-democratic revolution, Western interventions are repeatedly called for, and when they take place, welcomed. In this context, the critique of the 'imperialism of human rights' is just as paradoxical as the phenomenon itself (New Left Review, 1999). Where a neo-Weberian geopolitical orthodoxy coincides with this kind of Marxist critique, there is reason to question whether it is sufficiently historically sensitive.

Similarly, the dialectic of international war and social revolution remains important – but has more than its form changed? That revolution takes the form of the demand for reform, which often leads to local war in the form of genocide, which in turn provokes the development of globally legitimate authority, and is a different kind of process from that previously observed in historical sociological work. This is true in the important sense that it leads to increasing transcendence of the historical orthodoxies of international practice, which have stressed the sovereignty of discrete centres of state power. This is not unimportant to the practice of either states or other social groups.

From this perspective, the contribution of historical sociology to international relations is not to negate the new global agenda, but to provide it with a theoretical perspective on state development and socio-political change. This opens up a rich area of research. How far can we regard the unprecedented forms of state development, in the conjunction of the Western state-conglomerate and the global layer of state power, as the basis for a 'global state'? Will the conflicts and wars produced by the explosive combination of global-democratic revolution and the transformation of quasi-imperial authoritarian states continue to stimulate this development – or will they create such pressures that the global state will fall apart before it is consolidated in any meaningful sense?

These questions can be seen, from some perspectives, as new forms of old dilemmas of world order. In the social practice of international relations they are, however, radical issues that demand new answers. To answer them seems to me an important task of the growing historical sociological school in the field.

5 Historical sociology and constructivism: an estranged past, a federated future?

Michael Barnett

Introduction

Historical sociology and constructivist international relations theory have much in common, not that scholars from either camp know or advertise it. This chapter provides an assessment of their common roots and mutual detachments, begins to suggest one way that traditional historical sociological concerns might be productively employed to generate new insights into the character of international politics and in ways that are quite congenial to constructivism, and speculates about their possible future. The chapter is organised accordingly. I begin by surveying the common social theoretic commitments of historical sociology and constructivism, and suggest that constructivists have exempted historical sociology from their merciless appropriation of various parts of the sociological canon *only* because of the disciplinary context in which constructivism came of age.

The next section challenges constructivists to correct this sin of omission. To demonstrate the payoff for doing so, I suggest how the state formation and bureaucratisation literatures can generate new understandings regarding the dynamics behind, and consequences of, IO-building and global bureaucratisation. Doing so has both the empirical payoff of exploring some unmapped features of global politics, and the important theoretical implication of forcing both constructivists and historical sociologists to consider how international relations scholars should carve up global space, examine the interactions that exist within and between states and non-state actors within and between those spaces, and consider the dynamics of international political change.

The past

There have been no shortage of 'turns' in international relations theory over the last decade. Of them all, however, the 'sociological' and the 'historical' turns have been the most influential. The sociological turn represents a rebellion by international relations scholars against the economistic reasoning that has come to dominate the field over the last two decades. This reasoning is most starkly represented by Kenneth Waltz's claim that anarchy is akin to markets and that states are comparable to firms, and is abundantly present in the logic of various neo-utilitarian theories. Many international relations scholars quickly embraced economic models because their supposed properties can be applied to a breathtaking range of phenomena. No more. Baulking at *homo economicus* and images of society that are atomistic and devoid of cultural content, many international relations theorists have turned to *homo sociologicus* and images of society that are culturally and thickly constituted. The field is now in the throes of a sociological revolution.

The 'historical' turn has been less widely noted, but has been no less important in shaping the field.[1] The decided preference for abstract, systemic models that could generate timeless laws pertaining to inter-state interactions, made international relations theory intentionally insensitive to historical matters. If history mattered at all, it was as a field of data to be mined, for cases to be shoehorned in the pursuit of grand theory-building, and for evidence of the cycles of history that realists used to mark historical time. Some members of the discipline were more clearly guilty of this anti-historical bias than were others – systems theorists were wilfully uninterested in history while those in the English School always exhibited an historical disposition – but the overall profile gave credence to the old joke, 'scratch a bad historian, find a political scientist'. Over the last decade, however, international relations theorists have exhibited a new appreciation for historical analysis, for the *path-dependent* character of international change, and for the different forms of international politics. This development is partially understood as a response to the unsatisfactory explanatory character of abstract model-building that purposefully purged any temporal dimension. Yet unquestionably, contemporary events were a central factor behind this historical turn. The end of the Cold War triggered a profession-wide search into the past for some glimmer of the possible futures. And 'globalisation' led to a debate about whether the quality and character of the states system is undergoing a fundamental transformation, which, in turn, provoked scholars to look for alternative organising principles and global arrangements. Uncertainty shakes even the most law-abiding scholar.

Constructivist international relations theory embodies both turns, which helps to explain its rather rapid and remarkable rise to prominence

---

[1] However, see Hobden (1998: ch. 1); Ferguson and Mansbach (1996); and the symposium on 'History and Theory' in *International Security* (1997). For a good summary of the historical turn, see McDonald (1996).

in the discipline. At the outset it is important to note what constructivism is and is not. Constructivism is less a theory with well-developed hypotheses than it is a bundle of social theoretic commitments and concerns, including the attempt to understand: how agents and structures are involved in a process of mutual creation and reproduction; how actors' interaction is constrained and shaped by that structure; and how their very interaction serves to either reproduce or transform that structure (Onuf, 1989; Katzenstein, 1996b; Adler, 1997; Wendt, 1999). These commitments and concerns derive largely from sociological thought, and constructivists have wielded a sociological stick with great success in their jousts with a card-carrying neo-utilitarian mainstream. Constructivists, however, have been less attentive to historiographical issues than they probably should be. Nevertheless, they embody markings of the historical turn as they have attempted to: recover the roots of social constructs and categories of action by tracing the knowledgeable activities of culturally inscribed but strategic actors, and the sometimes accidental turns that underlie and define historical processes; demonstrate how the normative structures that are taken as given were socially constructed and exhibit regional and longitudinal variation; trace the role that individual acts and events play in producing international change; and subscribe to Charles Tilly's (1981) dictum that the time at which things happen and the sequence in which they happen will shape what happens.

Given constructivism's sociological and historical disposition, it is somewhat surprising that these scholars have been relatively inattentive to historical sociology.[2] After all, constructivism's social theoretic commitments are virtually identical to those of historical sociology. Historical sociologists were rebelling against what they saw as a neglect of either the time dimension of social life, or the changing character of social properties that structure social interaction and the direction of historical change (Smith, 1991: 3). Belittling the walls that divided history and sociology, sociologists were interested in the historicity of social structures, how these social structures winnowed the process of historical change and how events and particular acts could be transformative moments; and historians were increasingly drawn to the general properties of social structures that embedded and shaped particular events.

Historical sociology and constructivism, therefore, have much in common. Both were rebelling against similar silences in their respective disciplines and arguing in favour of rather similar developments. At the ontological level they were calling for a greater awareness of the relationship between agency and structure, for considering how the actions of subjects

---

[2] An important exception is R. Hall (1999).

constitute a social world that, in turn, creates the possibility conditions for their actions (Thompson, 1978; Anderson, 1980; Abrams, 1982; Wendt, 1987). At the epistemological level they were arguing against the monomaniacal search for a master causal variable, in favour of both the *multi-causal* character of grand outcomes, and equafinality. At the methodological level both groups demonstrated a clear preference for case-based research, comparative methods and counterfactual analysis (Skocpol, 1985; Katzenstein, 1996b).

Given all these shared traits, why did constructivism not more fully avail itself of historical sociology in the social theoretic frameworks it advanced, and in its search for disciplinary respectability? Much is owed to constructivism's birth and development at a particular disciplinary/historical moment. Constructivism waged two, related, struggles for recognition and disciplinary legitimacy, which significantly shaped what literatures it was likely to draw on for theoretical and empirical inspiration and protection, and thus what it became. The first struggle was against the neo-utilitarians; that is, neorealism and neoliberal institutionalism. In order to convince these scholars that constructivists' work should be read and taken seriously, constructivists took aim at critical silences of these established theories in order to demonstrate constructivism's value-added nature. Several themes quickly emerged: the desire to unpack the content and origins of state interests, a matter that neo-utilitarians took as exogenous for methodological and theoretical reasons; how norms are not merely 'regulative' but also *constitutive*, and thus can shape state identities, interests and rationalities; and how global order and global change must include reference to normative structures.

Although several disciplines in the social sciences and the humanities were making comparable claims regarding identities, the relationship between structure and agency, and social order, constructivists borrowed heavily from sociological theory for several reasons. Sociology was readily digestible by political scientists (the transaction costs are lower, for instance, than going to anthropology). Sociology was unmistakably part of the social sciences and thus could not be as easily dismissed by the mainstream on the grounds that it was not social science (as could be and was the case with anthropology and other disciplines in the humanities). And the scholars that informed many of constructivism's theoretical claims, including Max Weber, Emile Durkheim and George Herbert Mead, had already greatly influenced other parts of political science. These and other sociological patron saints offered sophisticated and rigorous theoretical statements concerning, in John Ruggie's (1998a) words, 'how the world hangs together' – statements that were able successfully to challenge prevailing theories.

Constructivists also laboured to differentiate themselves from post-modernism and to convince the mainstream that they were committed to 'science'. At first, mainstream theorists dismissively labelled constructivism as 'anti-science' – a remarkable claim that only served to highlight how quaint was much of the discipline's conception of social science (Keohane, 1988; Mearsheimer, 1995a). Accordingly, constructivists worked to widen and modernise the concept of social science and to differentiate their position from postmodern approaches. To those in the mainstream, constructivists hammered home how their differences were around ontology and not epistemology, and over time their relations got better. To those on their epistemological left, from whom they had derived considerable intellectual insights, constructivists were increasingly drawing boundary lines over the 'science question', and over time their relations grew increasingly testy (Neuman, 1996; Adler, 1997; Campbell, 1998; Price and Reus-Smit, 1998; Wendt, 1999).

This brief disciplinary history begins to explain why constructivists did not form a transdisciplinary alliance with historical sociology. At the substantive level, constructivists and historical sociologists took aim at different phenomena. Neorealism's 'war problem' and neoliberal institutionalism's 'co-operation problem' helped to define the agenda of international relations theory. To establish constructivism's 'value-added' impact, scholars began demonstrating how certain omitted 'variables' – including the failure to treat interests and identities as endogenous and malleable – provided competing and superior explanations for *systemic* outcomes that they judged as 'important', including how global norms shape patterns of inter-state politics, the onset of war, alliance behaviour, arms racing, Great Power transformation, and the like. For their part, historical sociologists were taking aim at *domestic* and *societal*-level phenomena that their respective disciplines judged as important, including industrialisation, democratisation, capitalism, bureaucratisation, state formation, social inequality, class conflict and revolution (Smith, 1991: 4–5). This is not to say that constructivists (and other international relations scholars) were oblivious to historical sociology; those interested in the origins of the state system and sovereignty drew heavily from historical sociologists like Charles Tilly and Michael Mann (Ruggie, 1983; Spruyt, 1994; R. Hall, 1999). Still, there was relatively little substantive overlap between historical sociology and constructivism.

A second reason why constructivists did not draw from historical sociology has to do with the sociological theories that informed their arguments. Constructivists were attempting to demonstrate that the substantive issues that defined the scholarly agenda of international relations could be better informed by sociological than by economic models. Accordingly, they went to those sociological models that could provide theoretical and methodological leverage over the normative basis of global politics – Weber, Durkheim and Mead were exploited for that very end. Historical sociologists, on the other hand, were more significantly influenced by the Marx–Weber debate on various macro-historical outcomes; accordingly, their arguments tended to be rooted in the disputed relationship between the political economy, class structure and class conflict, and the state. Their different substantive concerns, not surprisingly, led them to different parts of the sociological menu; constructivists were drawn to sociological theorists who spoke directly to questions of social and political organisation, while historical sociologists were more inclined to draw from those who engaged economic categories. Historical sociologists and constructivists might be comforted to know that they derive considerable inspiration from the same body of water, but ultimately they were drinking from different streams.

Enough of the past; what of the future? Should constructivists make amends for their past oversights and now more fully consider the value of historical sociology? This partly depends, of course, on what one imagines to be (or should be) constructivism's research agenda. Among the various agenda items, which include the relationship between rational choice and constructivist approaches (Katzenstein, Keohane and Krasner, 1998), and a second generation of norms-based research (Finnemore and Sikkink, 1998), constructivists and historical sociologists are most likely to find common ground on issues pertaining to global transformation and governance, including a growing awareness that non-state actors shape important outcomes in world politics (Keck and Sikkink, 1998), the changing organisational basis of world politics (Boli and Thomas, 1999), and how the observed (though rarely empirically validated) density of transnational networks interfaces with, and is structurally situated alongside, the states system.

Historical sociology might contribute to the constructivist agenda in various ways, though I want to identify two possibilities that revolve around matters of global organisation and transformation – the first I mention only in passing; the second I develop at length. Constructivism has been oblivious to production categories, an oversight that historical sociologists would say is not simply unfortunate but probably grievous. There are three reasons why constructivists would do well to correct this omission. First, constructivists have incorporated domestic variables in either an *ad hoc* way or by reference to institutional theories. But historical sociologists have developed highly rigorous theories of state–society relations, oftentimes rooted in sophisticated understandings of the dynamic and variable relationship between class-based organisation and mobilisation, state structure and state policy. To my knowledge, card-carrying constructivists have not availed themselves of these state–society and non-reductionist models, though they might with great payoff (and, as they do so, they should wrestle with Gramscian approaches). Second, constructivists have largely conceded the political economy field to neo-utilitarian theorists (but see Muppidi, 1999). Not only is this a huge mistake for practical and substantive reasons, but it also unintentionally reproduces an anachronistic view of the state where 'high politics' is virtually autonomous from 'low politics'. Third, historical sociologists have wrestled with the relationship between production and ideational categories in ways that have successfully avoided charges of economic reductionism, and that have forwarded cultural categories in sophisticated ways (Sewell, 1996). As constructivists take aim at political economy, they are likely to engage the very themes historical sociology has already confronted and so would do well to examine its findings.

State formation, bureaucratisation and international organisations

In this section I explore how the literatures on state formation and bureaucratisation might provide insights into how international organisations are increasingly authoritative actors in global politics. Historical sociologists have contributed greatly to our understanding of state formation, which can be generically understood as those processes that lead to the centralisation of political power over a well-defined continuous territory, and with a monopoly of the means of coercion. Initial research into the process of state formation attempted to identify and isolate primary forces and categories. These efforts can be grouped roughly into the following: (1) geopolitical analyses, which highlighted the competitive logic of the states system and the place of the state within that system; (2) world-system analyses, which focused on the logic of an (emergent) capitalist world-economy and the place of the state within that world-economy; (3) capitalist dynamics and class conflict, which advanced the logic of, and contradictions in, productive systems and economic modes of production; and (4) statist analyses, which identified semi-autonomous political changes that produce governability crises and threats to political power for the ruling elite (Tilly, 1994: 3). The initial search for a modal process, a master variable and a mono-causal explanation has yielded to a greater awareness of the vagaries and complex compounds that have produced the outcomes under investigation, of how the same variable can lead to highly differentiated outcomes, and of equafinality. There are many paths towards state formation.

A central feature of state formation is bureaucratisation – that is, the means by which the state administers, monitors and regulates society, and extracts revenues from it. The modern bureaucracy is defined by four central features (Beetham, 1996: 9–12). It exhibits *hierarchy*, for each official has a clearly defined sphere of competence within a division of labour and is answerable to superiors; *continuity*, where the office constitutes a full-time salary structure that offers the prospect of regular advancement; *impersonality*, where the work is conducted according to prescribed rules and operating procedures that eliminate arbitrary and politicised influences; and *expertise*, where officials are selected according to merit, are trained for their function, and control access to knowledge stored in files. The modern bureaucratic form is distinguished by the breaking down of problems into manageable and repetitive tasks that are the domain of a particular office, with the tasks being co-ordinated under a hierarchical command.

These are the very qualities and traits that led Weber to characterise modern bureaucracies as more efficient relative to other systems of administration or organisation and reflective of the rationalisation processes that were unfolding.[3]

Bureaucracy exemplified 'rationality'... because it involved control on the basis of knowledge; because it clearly defined spheres of competence; because it operated according to intellectually analyzable rules; because of the calculability of its operation; finally, because technically it was capable of the highest level of achievement (Beetham, 1985: 69).

Bureaucracies, in Weber's view, are a grand achievement in that they depoliticise and depersonalise decision-making, and subject decisions to well-established rules. Decisions, therefore, are made on the basis of technical knowledge and on the knowledge of files and the possession of information. Decision-making procedures informed by these qualities define a rationalised organisation, one that can deliver precision, stability, discipline and reliability.

Modern bureaucratisation also introduced a new form of authority, *rational-legal* authority, that modernity views as particularly legitimate and good. In contrast to earlier forms of authority that were invested in a leader, legitimate modern authority is invested in legalities, procedures and rules, and thus rendered impersonal. This authority is 'rational' in that it deploys socially recognised relevant knowledge to create rules that help determine the means that should be selected to pursue already identified ends. A bureaucracy's authority also derives from specialised

---

[3] For statements by Weber and his interpreters, see Weber (1948, 1978), Mouzelis (1967) and Beetham (1996).

knowledge that is technical, originating from training and profession-
alised criteria and control over information that is not immediately available to other actors. According to Weber (1948: 299),

... in legal authority, submission does not rest upon the belief and devotion to
charismatically gifted persons . . . or upon piety towards a personal lord and master
who is defined by an ordered tradition . . . Rather submission under legal authority
is based upon an *impersonal* bond to the generally defined and functional 'duty
of office.' The official duty – like the corresponding right to exercise authority:
the 'jurisdictional competency' – is fixed by *rationally established* norms, by enactments, decrees, and regulations in such a manner that the legitimacy of the
authority becomes the legality of the general rule, which is purposely thought out,
enacted, and announced with formal correctness.

Bureaucracies are to provide an efficient response to the increasingly
complex demands of modern life in a stable, predictable and non-violent
way. They are technically superior because they bring precision, knowledge and continuity to increasingly complex social tasks (Weber, 1978:
973). And their embodiment of rationality is why people are willing to
confer authority on bureaucracies.

Several important and related points must be noted regarding bureaucratic authority. First, this form of authority also generates the bureaucracy's independence and autonomy. As occupiers of bureaucratic roles,
as possessors of technical knowledge, as guardians of the files and as the
'experts' in their domain, bureaucrats have considerable autonomy, independence and discretion. Weber stressed that while technical rationality
might enable the bureaucracy to be more efficient in carrying out the directives of politicians, its own claim to authoritative knowledge and control over information enabled it to exceed its implementing and advising
role and to become autonomous from its creators and can come to dominate the societies it was created to serve (Weber, 1948: 233; Beetham,
1985: 74–5). Bureaucracies, in this fundamental respect, can be both a
tool and an independent authority. As agents of principals, they merely
carry out the directives and implement the decisions of others. As an
authority in their own right, they can be expected to have independence
and autonomy.

Second, authority, as Weber reminds us in his discussion of domination, is tied to power, and bureaucratic authority is no different.[4] But
bureaucratic power is power that is cloaked, owing to the discourse of

---

[4] Weber (1978). Others, however, argue that authority is less about domination *per se* and
more about actors that are given a presumptive right to speak and to act because of
their position or standing. The claim is that some actors, because of their standing in the
community and polity, and the roles that they occupy, are given the right to speak; see
Lincoln (1994).

rationality, objectivity and technical knowledge. Said otherwise, bureaucratic power is partially contingent on a particular presentation of 'self': as impersonal, technocratic and neutral – as *not* exercising power, but instead, as serving others; the presentation and acceptance of these claims is critical not only to their legitimacy and authority but also to their power (Ferguson, 1990; Fisher, 1997; Shore and Wright, 1997).

Third, while the discourse of objectivity, rationality and technical knowledge that surrounds the bureaucracy suggests an absence of values, in fact these are values in and of themselves, and the bureaucracy is generally involved in transmitting other values as well. According to Weber (1948: 199), the technical rationality of bureaucracy that legitimates it could be a myth: 'Behind the functional purposes [of bureaucracy], of course, "ideas of culture-values" usually stand.' These may not be particularly endearing values. Weber, for instance, worried that the bureaucracy was creating a society that was as calculating as itself. Bureaucracies, moreover, often exercise power in repressive ways, in the name of general rules because rules are their *raison d'être*. And while bureaucratic and legal authority must be tied to community standards and prior cultural beliefs, bureaucrats are notorious for using these community-linked rules to generate or mask their own indifference and to assert their own particularistic and bureaucratic interests (Herzfeld, 1993; Beetham, 1996: 13–15).

Fourth, bureaucratic authority is intended to help pursue various societal goals, but bureaucracies not only co-ordinate the activities of their members, they also instruct them as to what their proper goals and activities should be. There are two key aspects here. One is that authorities help to determine when there exists a co-ordination problem, which has clear connections to the function of bureaucratic activities (Raz, 1990: 6–11). There are various sorts of 'games' in social life, and only some of them can be properly defined as co-ordination games. It is not immediately apparent, however, when actors are in a game of co-ordination or in some other game. Authorities help 'to get people to realize that they are confronting a coordination problem' (Raz, 1990: 9). There are potentially many different institutional forms available to solve co-ordination problems, some of which are viewed as more efficient and normatively desirable than others, but many of which are desired not because of evidence of their efficiency and technical prowess but rather because of their symbolic legitimacy (Meyer and Rowan, 1983). Authorities help to constitute and construct the social world.

In general, Weber and others have chronicled the rise of the modern bureaucratic form. This form has several features that distinguish it from previous bureaucratic forms and make it a normatively desirable and more efficient mechanism of administration and governance. The rational-legal qualities that make the modern bureaucratic form desirable also generate its authority and make people willing to submit to it, which, in turn, provides the basis for its autonomy and independence. Bureaucracies might use this independence and authority to carry out dutifully the decisions and desires of their principals, but perhaps not. Authority cannot be divorced from issues of power and domination. Thus the bureaucratic discourse and the very presentation of 'self' as 'technical', 'rational' and 'objective' is actually fostered by the bureaucracy's discursive power.

What forces have led to the global isomorphism of the modern bureaucracy? Expectedly, theories of bureaucratisation closely parallel theories of state formation. Chris Dandeker (1990: 3–6) usefully identifies three broad dynamics. The first locates bureaucratisation as deriving from capitalism and class conflict. Most readily identified with Marxist theory, the argument is that bureaucratisation is a functional response to class struggles, and a strategic means by which one class reproduces its power over another class. Various bureaucratic developments – from the development of the welfare state to the establishment of new forms of governmental surveillance – can be linked to the imperatives of capitalism.

A second theme sees bureaucratisation as a direct response to the technical exigencies of industrialisation and a growing division of labour. These theories of industrial society, with their roots in social theorists such as Comte, Spencer and Durkheim, see bureaucratisation as a necessary 'administrative response to the technical imperatives of a structurally differentiated society'. In contrast to Marxist accounts that situate the bureaucracy in broader class and power struggles, these theorists claim that bureaucratic development enables society to achieve its collective goals in a more conflict-free way through various functional responses, including: the creation of uniform currencies, measures, weights and codes of conduct as a way to standardise the environment and to lower transaction costs in order to further trade and commercial activities; the performance of important duties of state, including policing and information exchange, that might even promote the conditions for civil society; and the establishment of various monitoring and enforcement mechanisms that help individuals and societal groups overcome co-operation and co-ordination problems.

Finally, war-making and the competitive states system contributed to the development of the modern bureaucratic state. Bureaucracy was the real winner in war. Various scholars have contributed to this view, including Machiavelli, Hintze, Elias, Mann and Giddens, all noting that in order to mobilise men, extract revenue and organise the war economy, the state's bureaucracy expanded exponentially during war-time and rarely

dissipated after war termination. The functional and logistical requirements of modern war necessitated a modern bureaucracy, and those states
that were able to develop such a bureaucracy had a decisive advantage
over those states that did not. States have responded to various domestic
and international challenges by establishing and augmenting their bureaucratic infrastructure. The modern bureaucratic form proved decisive
in these various political battles, class struggles, and in meeting technical
and industrial demands.

International organisations

These observations regarding state formation and bureaucratisation
provide considerable leverage for thinking about the causes and consequences of international organisation-building (IO-building henceforth).
There are surprisingly few statistical analyses of the pattern of IO-building, though scholars have implicitly used the categories of industrialisation, capitalism and class conflict, and inter-state conflict to organise
the forces behind IO-building.[5] But first, let us note some general observations regarding the pattern of IO-building. Over the past century
the number of international organisations has shot up exponentially. In
1860 there were five IOs and only one international non-governmental
organisation (INGO). By 1940 those numbers had grown to 61 IOs and
477 INGOs. By 1996 they stood at 260 IOs and 5,472 INGOs (Shanks,
Jacobson and Kaplan, 1996; Union of International Associations, 1996).
There have been distinct waves of institution-building, largely corresponding to times of war and economic developments. A growth spurt at
the close of the nineteenth century introduced many of the more technically oriented IOs that were designed to overcome collective action and
co-ordination problems. The end of World War I and the development
of the League of Nations witnessed a new round of creating international
organisations that were to manage many of the transboundary problems,
population movements and externalities associated with the crumbling
of the multinational empires and the rise of national states. The end of
World War II inaugurated a new round; many of the institutions created
then famously dealt with various security, economic and human rights
issues. Not only are there more IOs, but they are involved in more activities than ever before. We are keenly aware of the activities of international
organisations in co-ordinating relations between states. But perhaps more
impressive is that they are increasingly engaged in domestic governance,

---

[5] For a statistical analysis, see Cupitt, Whitlock and Whitlock (1996). For broad historical
overviews of the pattern of IO-building, see Groom (1988) and Murphy (1994).

including democratisation, domestic security and local economic activities – all matters that used to be the prerogative of national states but are
increasingly being shared with, or assisted by, IOs. This is an increasingly
bureaucratised world.

How did we get here? The broad categories used by historical sociologists to explain domestic bureaucratisation provide insight into the processes that have contributed to international bureaucratisation. Global
economic expansion and industrialisation certainly have played a role.
This argument, in fact, represents a core claim of neoliberal institutionalism. In its view, states seek to develop international institutions and
organisations as functional responses to the presence of, and the desire
for, increasing exchanges between states (Krasner, 1983). In order to take
advantage of these exchanges (rather than be taken advantage by them),
states will establish international institutions in order to define better the
rules of the game and codes of conduct, to monitor state and non-state
action and thus to minimise the fear of cheating, and to identify possible sanctions and penalties for when such violations occur. In a slightly
different way, Craig Murphy (1994) also has argued a strong linkage between the phases and expansion of industrialisation and the supply of
international organisations.

Class conflict and production approaches to IOs advance the view that
they are functional responses to, and an ideological coating for, transnational capitalism's reproductive and expansionary requirements. Most
prominent here is the 'Italian School'. Drawing on the work of Antonio
Gramsci, Stephen Gill (1993), Craig Murphy (1994), Robert Cox (1996)
and others have examined how transnational capitalism generates various
sorts of contradictions and demands that are ameliorated through institutions and organisations at the domestic and at the global level. These
IOs cannot be strictly 'read off' the economic structure, for an independent role is given to various intellectual movements, ideas and political
forces. In addition to these Gramscian approaches, some scholars have
used world systems theory to consider the changing role of IOs (Hawdon,
1996).

The final explanation for IO-building derives from war. Here the great
experiments in regional and global governance – namely the Concert of
Europe, the League of Nations and the United Nations – are assembled in
response to Great Power wars.[6] The post-Cold War world is no different
except in one important respect: rather than attempting to augment and
institutionalise the international community's ability to limit inter-state

---

[6] Note, however, that more IOs are being established by other IOs (Shanks, Jacobson and
Kaplan, 1996).

war, now various organisations are impressively pushing to tackle *intra-state* wars, in order to help states navigate the transition from civil war to civil society. This new orientation has led to an explosion of peacekeeping and peacebuilding activities by international and regional organisations over the last ten years. Global industrialisation, capitalism and security are important drivers of international bureaucratisation, and suggest how IOs represent functional and instrumental responses by states to preserve their interests in the face of various environmental demands.

Anthony Giddens (1985: 261–5), one of the few historical sociologists to have written directly on the subject of international bureaucratisation, similarly argues that states have addressed challenges to their sovereignty by developing international organisations.[7] Giddens might be surprised to learn that his observations and claims are consistent with neoliberal institutionalism and neorealism in three important ways. First, neither Giddens nor these theories give much autonomy to IOs. In their view, states establish IOs to further their immediate and long-term interests, and, therefore, IO practices can be easily and immediately traced back to state preferences. To understand what IOs do requires looking at what states tell them to do. Speaking counterfactually, had states not developed these international organisations they would have been beset by various contradictions and unresolvable challenges – and if states did not like what IOs were doing, they would simply pull the plug on them. A second shared trait is that their reductionist approach to IOs denies to them any independent effects on world politics. This is not terribly surprising: once IOs are denied agency it becomes theoretically impossible to attribute causal standing to them. Third, these authors seem to be interested in the effects of IOs only to the extent that they shape state practices and interests. Perhaps IOs are shaping other elements of global politics, but if they were, we would not know about them.

International organisations as bureaucracies

However empirically plausible these observations might be, they do not exhaust the possible roles, practices and effects of international organisa-tions. IOs are not simply passive mechanisms and hand-maidens of states; rather, they can be creative, energetic and independent entities that have agential properties. Studies of an impressive range of international organ-isations – including the EU (Ross, 1995; Pollack, 1997), the UNHCR (Kennedy, 1986), the World Bank (Nelson, 1995; Wade, 1996), the IMF

---

[7] This claim is echoed from various corners of the international relations discipline, and particularly by those influenced by the English School.

(Feldstein, 1998) and the UN Department of Peacekeeping Operations (Human Rights Watch, 1999) – document how IOs have a distinct organisational culture, how IO officials have autonomy and how IOs can act without the permission of states, and in opposition to state interests. Not only are IOs engaged in activities that are not always favoured or authorised by states, but they also are shaping the constitutive character of world politics (Barnett and Finnemore, 1999). There is nothing accidental or unintended about this role. Officials in IOs often insist that part of their mission is to spread, inculcate and enforce global values and norms. Those involved in peacekeeping operations exclaim that they are trying to 'save failed states' by injecting them with a liberal architecture (Paris, 1997). Those in the OSCE are quite candid about trying to spread Western values and norms to the former Eastern bloc (Adler, 1998). These examples strongly suggest the need for a social theoretic framework and conceptualisation of organisations and bureaucracies that allows for – indeed, enables us to see – the possibility that IOs can be independent actors that have the capacity to transform the constitution of global politics.

Weberian approaches to bureaucratisation can do just that.[8] To begin, IOs might have a source of authority that derives from their rational-legal character. Mainstream theories of IOs see their authority as delegated authority; whatever authority that is possessed by IOs is contingent upon the say-so of states.[9] Weberian approaches to bureaucratisation, however, note how particular organisational forms can have an authority of their own; what is true of modern, domestic bureaucracies might be equally true of modern, international bureaucracies. The UN Department of Peacekeeping Operations, the UNHCR, the IMF, the World Bank and myriad other IOs, are all conferred tremendous authority because of their status as experts that derives from credentials, training and experience. To be sure, other state and non-state actors claim expertise over shared issue areas. But those in IOs have an important advantage over these rivals: IO officials are able to couple their expertise to claims of 'neutrality' and an 'apolitical' technocratic decision-making style that denies to them the possession of power or a political motive. In short, IOs have authority in global politics and the ability to shape international public policy because of their 'expertise', and our acceptance of their presentation of 'self' as apolitical and technocratic.

Second, once we recognise that IOs have an independent basis of authority in world politics, then it becomes easier to imagine that they are

---

[8] This section draws heavily from Barnett and Finnemore (1998, 1999).
[9] Although in other ways very consistent with this analysis, Boli's (1999: 282) sociological institutionalist approach makes the exact same claim regarding the delegated authority of IOs.

more than simply the hand-maidens of states, and have a 'relative' autonomy from states. The crucial point is that IOs can have 'relative autonomy'. IO autonomy has at least two sources.[10] The first, already noted,
is its authority and legitimacy. The second is the degree of resource independence. This is a point on which state theorists and organisational
theorists agree. State theorists observe how the relative autonomy of the
state increases when the state's resource base is independent of the dominant classes. Organisational theorists make comparable claims, hypoth-
esising that the less dependent the organisation is on the environment for
its resource base, the more autonomous it becomes. These arguments
can be used to understand IO autonomy: IOs are more likely to be autonomous the more they are resource-independent. Which resources are
key? Drawing from organisational theory, Barnett and Finnemore (1998)
identify the centrality of knowledge and material resources; the more the
organisation has an independent basis of information and revenue, the
more autonomous it will be, and vice versa. In this view, for instance,
the World Bank is likely to have more autonomy from states than is the
UNHCR, because the former has a relatively independent source of funds
and its own research and analysis units, while the latter is dependent
on voluntary contributions and has relatively little information-gathering
and analysis capacity.[11]

The third issue concerns what IOs do with that autonomy and authority. The standard view is that IOs represent a functional and technocratic response to an increasingly complex world that demands greater
co-ordination among a diverse array of actors and their activities in order
to further their shared interests. In this view, international bureaucracies,
as authorities, help actors (namely states) to overcome their collective
action problems and to regulate their activities in a Pareto-superior way.
But IOs as authorities also have another side: they are actively promoting
which institutional forms are the most normatively desirable and efficient
for solving these co-ordination games. To define the proper and legitimate
means and ends of states and non-state actors is to be implicated in power
politics.

IOs are the new missionaries in world politics. Although they rou-
tinely claim that they are value-neutral, objective and apolitical, in fact
IOs are actively preaching that specific political and economic institutions are the most efficient and normatively desirable. Consider how IOs
present themselves as acting for all of humanity and for transnational goals
of progress, development, human autonomy and freedom and security.

---

[10] For an additional possibility derived from the public choice literature, see Snidal (1996).
[11] For other statements concerning the conditions under which IOs are likely to be autonomous, see Cox (1996: 317–48) and Moravcsik (1999).

To further those aspirations of the global community, IOs unabashedly promote some institutional forms as the most preferred (Boli, 1999). The UN system has converged around the desirability of democracy and markets – liberal values and norms – as the 'best' form of domestic governance, and the form that is most likely to generate international peace and security. Peacekeeping and peacebuilding operations are exemplars here. Attempts to 'save failed states' have required a nearly unprecedented degree of IO intervention, in the hope that by transferring various liberal norms to the local context, these states will become stable and responsible members of international society. UN peacekeeping and peacebuilding activities stand alongside those of myriad other IOs, whose ends are remarkably similar and cannot be strictly or easily derived from state demands.

In general, IOs are intervening in local affairs to help regulate what already exists and to help constitute something new. Not infrequently, their expertise and technical knowledge represents a bridgehead that they quickly establish, which is then used to expand their control over an increasing area of social, political and economic life. And they are employing that authority not simply to help regulate and co-ordinate already existing activities, but also to alter the domestic topography in ways that make it more consistent with already existing and legitimated (Western) models of political, economic and social organisation.

This growing presence of IOs need not imply that local and state authorities are undermined. International relations theory tends to operate with a zero-sum view of authority: there is a finite amount of authority, and if the authority of some actors is increasing, then the authority of other actors must be decreasing. This zero-sum myopia fails to recognise that authoritative activities can have 'additive' rather than subtractive properties. Sometimes this additive property is by design. The UN employs its authority to reinforce rather than diminish the authority of local and state agents. IOs, for instance, have been involved in strengthening the autonomy and capacity of grassroots and indigenous movements. These movements, in turn, are using the legitimacy provided by IOs to strengthen their authority over certain realms. Many UN peacekeeping interventions are intended to strengthen local authorities precisely because of the view of the global community that these authorities are in a state of disrepair. Accordingly, their peacebuilding and post-conflict reconstruction activities tend to be directed at rebuilding the state's infrastructural power and limiting its despotic power. And even when IOs are not necessarily operating with the goal of expanding state power, their own failures and follies might lead to that very outcome. James Ferguson (1990) provocatively suggests that World Bank development failures must be treated as a success in a particular way: they have strengthened the power, control and authority of the state over local actors.

We need to move away from zero-sum conceptions of authority in order to imagine the various ways in which different authority structures interact and combine to produce different constellations of authority. IOs have a refractive property as they are creating a space for non-state actors to organise, produce their own authority and challenge state activities, as well as change the character of global culture. IOs are intervening in ways that are intended to bolster state capacities and increase their governance and control over society. States are turning to, and strengthening, IOs as a way of handling domestic challenges to state authority and control over society. In this way, global bureaucratisation and state formation can be mutually reinforcing, and can create spaces where new sets of actors interact according to new legitimation and organising principles.

For constructivists and historical sociologists that have exhibited a statist bias, these are rather radical implications. The state-centrism found in international relations has been aptly summarised by John Agnew's (1994) observation that international relations scholars have been ensnared by the 'territorial trap'. This territorial trap has several defining features: (1) the world is carved up into mutually exclusive territorial states; (2) states are assumed to have authority over their political space, and there is no authority above the state; (3) the rigid domestic/foreign distinction generates what R. B. J. Walker (1993) has called an 'inside/outside' image of global politics. The consequences of this myopia are that international relations theorists have a difficult time conceptualising space as anything but territorial, or seeing how actors are nested in different organisational arrangements that generate different patterns of interactions within and across these spaces.

While constructivism and historical sociology have been defined, in their different ways and for different reasons, by a state-centrism, scholars from both camps, nevertheless, are demonstrating the ability to think 'outside the (statist) box'. Constructivist international relations need not be statist because there is nothing in the ontology or social theoretic framework that demands it. That several of its most famous formulations are state-centric should be viewed as an artefact of disciplinary battles, and not an ontological property or commitment of constructivism (Katzenstein, 1996b; Wendt, 1999). Recently, however, constructivists have ventured away from a focus on the changing pattern of inter-state relations and towards global governance issues more broadly defined. The increasingly prominent literatures on NGOs (Smith, Chatfield and Pagnucco, 1997; Price, 1998), epistemic communities (Adler and Haas,

1992) and transnational movements (Keck and Sikkink, 1998) are highly attentive to how these actors are able to operate at different 'levels', and with different power resources, to shape the character of global politics. Historical sociology also exhibits its own state-centrism, though here the pathogen is not the anarchy *problematique* that haunts the discipline of international relations but rather a 'societal' bias that defines the discipline of sociology. Historical sociology, like much of sociology, famously sees the outer possibility of society as demarcated and delineated by the territorial boundaries of the state. Consequently, historical sociologists have tended to introduce systemic variables and transnational forces in an *ad hoc* and unsatisfactory way, and typically only when these forces influence domestic outcomes. Nevertheless, state-centrism is not a necessary property of historical sociology, and those international relations scholars who are interested in historical sociology need not employ only its state-centric versions (despite the common charge that a Weberian-oriented historical sociology leads to a neorealist or state-centric position).[12]

But some historical sociologists are developing *non*-state-centric understandings of global politics that should interest constructivist scholars. Specifically, various historical sociologists are seeing society as existing at the transnational and global levels; are departing from the international/national duality; and are examining the actors that populate that global society, the authority that they possess, and how their intensifying dynamics and linkages are serving to transform the constitutive character of global politics (Albrow, 1996; Shaw, 1998). Consider Michael Mann's (1997) recent statements. Mann's modified network approach identifies the possibility of several, analytically distinct, spaces of interaction, the organisational forms those interactions produce, and the different resources and powers that those organisations possess. Specifically and briefly, he argues that there are five 'socio-spatial' networks: a local (subnational) network; a national (state) network; an international (geopolitical) network; a transnational (macro-regional) network; and a global network. These different networks are populated by different actors that possess different resources and (implicitly) interact according to different organising principles. Mann reminds international relations scholars that while the contemporary international system gives significant advantages to states, there are other ways in which the playing field is levelled; that

---

[12] It should be clear, however, that my position is that there is nothing inherent in Weberian theorising that necessarily leads to state-centrism; compare Hobson (1998a and this volume, ch. 3), and Reus-Smit (this volume). Rather, the state-centrism associated with historical sociology should be attributed to the theoretical statements that have been drawn from its vast reservoir to understand international politics; there exist alternative approaches in Weber and historical sociology that challenge that state-centrism.

there are also normative forces that constrain state actors; and that the states system does not define global politics or preclude non-state actors from bringing about historical change.

The sorts of questions that these historical sociological approaches raise are exactly those that constructivists are now addressing. First, can we discern historical variations in the causal importance of these different networks for the outcomes under investigation? While we have been fairly successful at demonstrating a range of empirical anomalies and new patterns, we have been less successful in presenting rigorous explanations for those outcomes (Albrow, 1996; Armstrong, 1998; Clark, 1998; Shaw, 1998, and Shaw, this volume). How would we go about substantiating and documenting the nature of the connections between these spaces, how they have changed over time, and how actors are able to cross them in various ways to shape outcomes? Second, how should we conceptualise the nested and structured relationship of these different networks? Are they ontologically independent? Or are they mutually constitutive? How should we think about the relationship between these different spaces/levels, and the reproductive practices and transformative capacities of actors at all these different spaces? International relations theorists, like all scholars, face the daunting task of trying to discern how to study connections that exist at different levels, sites and political spaces (Hollis and Smith, 1990; Onuf, 1995; Keck and Sikkink, 1998; Latham, Kassimer and Callaghy, forthcoming). Third, what sorts of resources and powers do actors have in these different spaces, and how do they employ these powers to shape outcomes? Mann recognises that there exist different sources of power, deriving from ideological, economic, military and political organisational forms. These different power resources combine in different ways at different historical moments, and the challenge is to tease out the source that might be dominant, the relationship between these different sources of power, and how these different sources of power consolidate into different social relationships both at a particular historical moment and in comparison to other epochs. Constructivist scholars have been confronting a rather similar set of challenges.

How should we carve up global space, conceptualise the actors, power resources, and organisational forms that populate that space, and imagine the historically variable configurations that exist? Scholars from historical sociology and constructivism (and others) have begun to outline answers to these questions. So far they have demonstrated an impressive ability both to identify the weaknesses and empirical anomalies of extant theories, and to derive new concepts, categories and typologies that can theorise about contemporary international political change, and situate the contemporary moment in historical perspective. But concepts, categories and typologies are only a first step and are no substitute for the careful theory-building, hypothesis-testing and construction of research designs that will be necessary for convincingly substantiating their theoretical and empirical claims.

Conclusion

Although in many ways they launched from the same theoretical banks and have been drifting towards the same horizon, historical sociologists and constructivists have been gazing in different directions because of their different disciplinary contexts. There are good reasons for both groups to show greater awareness of each other's presence. The vast menu of historical sociology can provide a detailed, rigorous and provocative examination of various outcomes at the global level. As I have suggested, historical sociological claims regarding state formation processes and bureaucratisation potentially provide key insights into the dynamics behind IO-building and the consequences of global bureaucratisation. Furthermore, Weberian approaches to bureaucratisation have radical implications for how we think about IOs as increasingly authoritative actors in global politics, as well as their capacity to restructure and constitute the global polity.

One of the challenges that lies ahead for both constructivists and historical sociologists is to break away from the 'territorial trap' and to carve up global space in new ways. On this point, historical sociologists and constructivists find themselves drifting (unknowingly) in remarkably comparable directions. A little awareness of each other might have dramatic payoffs. Constructivists might avail themselves of the important methodological and theoretical approaches offered by network-inspired work in order to generate more historically nuanced, but analytically rigorous, studies and claims. Historical sociologists, for their part, might profit from the theoretically impressive and detailed work done by constructivists to document the conditions under which these often noted changes are in fact taking place.

6 The idea of history and history with ideas

Christian Reus-Smit

For the best part of two decades, rationalist modes of theorising have dominated the field of international relations. Neorealists and neoliberals, working from sparse assumptions about states as 'defensive positionalists' or 'rational egoists', have championed the development of abstract, deductive theories of international relations. The 'atemporal structuralism' of these approaches has not gone unanswered, though. From the outset, critical theorists and postmodernists have challenged the privileging of ahistorical structural theory and abstract, economistic models of rationality over historical interpretation and socially embedded conceptions of human agency. Neorealism and neoliberalism, they argue, have replaced historical process with stasis, historical practice with structural determinism, and the creativity of politics with structurally bounded economic action. One of the principal consequences of this has been the inability of theorists in both schools to understand international change; in particular, to explain the rise of the system of sovereign states itself, or to comprehend its transformation. Condemning rationalist theories for their failure to explain the very world they presuppose, critics have advocated the pursuit of a critical theory of international relations that 'does not take institutions and social and power relations for granted but calls them into question by concerning itself with their origins and how and whether they might be in the process of changing' (Cox, 1986: 208; cf. Linklater, this volume).

It was in this context that calls were first heard for the development of an historical sociology of international relations. Inspired by developments within sociology, which entailed a rediscovery of history and the resurrection of the concept of the state, Fred Halliday, Tony Jarvis, Andrew Linklater and others argued that the time had come for international relations scholars to place the state under the microscope, to produce an historically informed 'fit between societies, states and geopolitics' (Halliday, 1987; Jarvis, 1989: 291; Linklater, 1990). Instead of treating the state as conceptually and historically unproblematic, they sought to distinguish the state from society, and to understand the complex social forces which operated at the domestic and international levels to shape the nature and practices of states. If this path were not taken, they insisted, 'International Relations scholars will increasingly be left out of the subject matter which was once their sole claim but which is now enthusiastically taken up by others' (Jarvis, 1989: 291). Fortunately their calls have not gone unheeded, and there is now an emergent body of literature in the historical sociology of international relations (Cox, 1987; Rosenberg, 1994; Shaw, 1994; Hobson, 1997). Neo-Weberians have assumed some prominence in this burgeoning literature, taking the lead in specifying what an historical sociology of international relations should look like (Hobson, 1998a).

Important though the neo-Weberian contribution has been, it exhibits a subterranean rationalism and materialism that handicaps the development of an heuristically powerful historical sociology of international relations. Despite their stated commitment to multi-causality, neo-Weberian authors end up privileging the forces of capitalism, industrialism and military competition over non-material factors such as culture, identity, ideas and values. An underlying rationalism, the assumed ubiquity of the will to power, and the identification of ideology with pre-modern politics, further conspire to marginalise ideational forces. If this enriched our understanding of international relations it would be entirely warranted, but much of international life is simply incomprehensible from these standpoints. Issues as fundamental as the nature and implications of sovereignty and the institutional architectures of international societies are inexplicable without reference to culture, identity and norms. Ideational factors such as these give meaning to material structures and processes and define actors' identities and interests.

This chapter makes the case for a constructivist turn in the historical sociology of international relations. My purpose is not to deny the importance of rationality or material forces in history, but to argue that rationality is historically and culturally contingent, and to follow Marshall Sahlins in arguing that 'material effects depend on their cultural encompassment' (Sahlins, 1976: 194). After considering in greater detail the vision of historical sociology of international relations outlined by Halliday, Jarvis, Hobson and others, I examine how this vision has been translated into analytical practice, demonstrating how a professed commitment to multi-causality has transmuted into rationalism and materialism. Once the explanatory limitations of such approaches have been shown, I outline the theoretical foundations of an alternative, constructivist historical sociology. The final section of the chapter demonstrates the heuristic power of such an approach, by revisiting the question of epochal change in international society, and the relationship between ideational transformations and the institutional architecture of international relations.

The vision

Reconceptualising and retheorising the sovereign state has been central to the development of an historical sociology of international relations. The conventional view of the state as a unitary actor, constituted only by the competitive dynamics of the international system, has been condemned as theoretically impoverished and empirically unhelpful. This 'totality' understanding of the state (Halliday, 1994b: 78–84), which conflates state and government and state and nation, which denies connections between the domestic and international and which attributes all causal significance to the balance of military power between states, obscures the complex interconnections between states and social forces, the mutually constitutive relationship between the domestic and the international and the multiple factors that shape state structures and interests. The challenge, proponents of historical sociology argue, is to reconceive the state and to problematise, not occlude, these complexities. In short, international relations needs a theory of the state – one that highlights relations between states, societies and geopolitics (Jarvis, 1989).

Three ideas have come to form the foundations of historical sociology in international relations. The first concerns the autonomy of the state. The state is understood, not as a singularly purposive territorial unit, encompassing harmoniously ordered authorities, institutions and population, but as a distinctive coercive and administrative institution, characterised by its own capacities and interests (Halliday, 1994b: 84–93; Hobson, 1998a: 289–95). This definition begs multiple questions – such as the socio-political location of the state, the status of the state as both an institution and an actor, and, if the former, the attribution of agency and interests to an institution – but it has the virtue of opening up state–society relations to investigation, permitting an analysis of the state's impact on society and the role of social forces in the constitution of the state. The second idea concerns the world systemic nature of social forces. While historical sociologists usually retain the notion of domestic and international realms, so as to specify the role of the state in the constitution of domestic society, the impact of the international on the domestic, and the contribution of international factors to the autonomy of the state, they see these as dimensions and products of a single, unified social order, comprising mutually interdependent domestic, international and transnational social, economic and political forces (Hobson, 1998a). The third idea concerns the principle of 'multi-causality'.

Following the lead of sociologists, historical sociologists in international relations have rejected reductionist explanations, insisting 'that social and political change can only be understood through the interaction of multiple forces, none of which can be reduced to a single essence' (Hobson, 1998a: 287). Theories that privilege a sole cause – such as the logic of anarchy or the logic of capitalism – are abandoned in favour of multicausal explanations, that seek to capture the interaction between diverse social forces, most often of ideological, economic, political and military forms.

Rationalism and materialism ascendant

After the austere theorising of the 1980s, calls for an historical sociology of international relations that opened up the black box of the state, and that recognised the causal significance of diverse social forces, were refreshing indeed. Even more refreshing was the apparent willingness of historical sociologists to move beyond the standard litany of material causes, most notably military competition and capitalism, and to credit 'fuzzy' variables, such as ideology, with explanatory power. While they disagree at times about how many social forces should be woven into their theoretical models, ideology almost always features. Sadly the rhetoric of multi-causality surrounding the theoretical debut of historical sociology, both outside and within international relations, has been betrayed at the level of theoretical specification and analytical application. Neo-Weberians speak loudly about the virtues of multi-causality, and yet their rationalist understanding of human behaviour occludes the role of ideas in identity and interest formation, leaving material forces dominant and interests reduced to a ubiquitous will to power.

Neo-Weberian rationalism

Given the varied and subtle nature of Max Weber's writings, it is not surprising that neo-Weberians profess a commitment to multi-causal explanation. Crucial here are the cues Weber provides for the incorporation of non-material variables such as ideas. His definition of the state represents one of the most celebrated of these cues. The state, he writes, 'is a human community that (successfully) claims the *monopoly of the legitimate use of physical force* within a given territory' (Weber, 1948: 78). This has often been construed in strictly materialist terms – that simply having a monopoly on physical force is sufficient; but for Weber, the notion of legitimacy is central. 'The state', he insists, 'is considered the sole source of the "right" to use violence' (Weber, 1948: 78). In using the term 'considered', Weber grants 'belief' central importance, and in emphasising the rightful control of violence, he ties the authority of the state to social consent and sanction. The second, and equally celebrated, cue is provided by Weber's 'switchmen' metaphor: 'the "world images" that have been created by "ideas" have, like switchmen, determined the tracks along which action has been pushed by the dynamic of interest' (Weber, 1948: 280). Ideas, for Weber, thus play a crucial role in shaping social and political action, channelling the pursuit of interests in distinctive ways – ways not explicable with sole reference to material causes.

On close inspection, however, these cues highlight the importance of ideational forces while simultaneously circumscribing their causal significance. The emphasis on legitimacy and state power draws attention to the importance of consent as well as coercion, to the moral standing of the state as much as its material capacity to enforce compliance. And while the state's ability to deliver certain material goods, such as physical security and economic welfare, is clearly essential to ensuring such consent, it is not sufficient. Historically, a much wider spectrum of values have conditioned the legitimacy of states, values ranging from monarchical right to the protection of the inalienable rights of individuals. Weber's stress on legitimacy is thus an invitation to explore the foundational role of ideas in undergirding the sovereign state. The switchmen metaphor, however, severely impedes such exploration, as well as more general exploration of the social importance of culture, ideas and norms. The metaphor is inherently rationalist. 'Interests' are the engines that propel 'action' along the 'tracks', with ideas acting as intervening 'switchmen' to determine the tracks travelled. Ideational forces are not constitutive of interests; they merely condition the strategic pursuit of interests, making some roads to interest satisfaction appear, at least to the actors concerned, more efficient, desirable or feasible. The whole imagery of switchmen and tracks is one of constraint and direction, not constitution and inspiration.

Unfortunately, Weber's invitation to explore the constitutive role of ideas – particularly the role of ideas in sustaining the legitimacy of the state – has not been taken up by contemporary neo-Weberian historical sociologists. Instead, the rationalism of the switchmen metaphor dominates. Nowhere is this more apparent than in Michael Mann's voluminous writings. At first glance, Mann's commitment to the principle of multi-causality appears unquestionable. Because there is no such thing as a unitary society, he argues, 'social relations cannot be reduced "ultimately", "in the last instance", to some property of it – like the "mode of production", or the "cultural" or "normative system", or the "form of military organization"' (Mann, 1986: 1). Mann proceeds to formulate a 'model of organized power' that seeks to incorporate not one, two or three sources of social power, but four: ideological, economic, military and political.

His underlying model of human behaviour, however, unnecessarily impedes his appreciation of the role of ideational forces in social and political life. Embracing the language of rational choice theory, Mann portrays humans as 'restless, purposive, and rational, striving to increase their enjoyment of the good things of life and capable of choosing and pursuing appropriate means for doing so' (Mann, 1986: 4). Contrasting his project with 'motivational' theories, he disavows any interest in the origin of human preferences. This does not mean that he considers such preferences unimportant: goals, interests and desires, he insists, provide 'the forward drive that enough humans possess to give them a dynamism wherever they dwell' (Mann, 1986: 5). His theory is concerned, though, with means not ends, with the resources available for preference satisfaction, not with preferences themselves (Mann, 1986: 6). Within this model of human behaviour, the role of ideas in the constitution of human interests is explicitly bracketed, confining ideational factors to the realm of means. Ideology, though privileged as one of the four sources of social power, does not feature as a determinant of actors' identities or interests, only as a power resource. Mann acknowledges that 'concepts' and 'categories' give 'meaning' to our 'sense perceptions', but he is only interested in how 'collective and distributive power can be wielded by those who monopolize a claim to meaning' (Mann, 1986: 22). He also acknowledges the importance of social norms in facilitating social co-operation, but again he is concerned with how monopolising norms provides a 'route to power'. Finally, he recognises the centrality of aesthetic/ritual practices, yet only because a 'distinctive power is conveyed through song, dance, visual art forms, and rituals' (Mann, 1986: 23).

Despite this bracketing of interest formation, Mann's theory requires some conception of human interest to give motion to his image of social and political life. But in the absence of a richer exploration of the role of ideational factors in constituting actors' preferences, Mann is left with nothing more than a ubiquitous will to power. He denies that power is 'an original human goal', but argues that since 'it is a powerful means to other goals, it will be sought for itself. It is an *emergent* need' (Mann, 1986: 6). The net effect is that he ends up in precisely the same position as Hans Morgenthau, with 'the concept of interest defined in terms of power' (Morgenthau, 1985: 5). Morgenthau sees states pursuing a wide range of goals, but he, like Mann, is interested in means not ends, particularly the means provided by power: 'Whatever the ultimate aims of international politics, power is always the immediate aim' (Morgenthau, 1985: 31). In seeking to defend neo-Weberian historical sociology from the accusation that it is simply reheated realism, Hobson and others have successfully argued that their conception of the state is radically different from that of neorealists (Hobson, 1998a: 291–5). They have not, however, addressed the striking similarity between their conception of interest and power and that deployed by classical realists, a similarity that is hardly surprising given the intellectual debt Morgenthau owed Weber. It bears further reflection, though. Morgenthau reduces interest to power to gain greater explanatory purchase, believing that it 'infuses rational order into the subject matter of politics, and thus makes the theoretical understanding of politics possible' (Morgenthau, 1985: 5). That this move actually obscures more than it reveals has been shown time and time again, with a wide range of scholars demonstrating that actors occupying similar structural positions can have diverse interests, which produce diverse actions – actions that are not explicable in terms of a homogeneous will to power.

The subterranean rationalism of Mann's work is echoed by neo-Weberian historical sociologists of international relations. Again, their commitment to multi-causality appears unquestionable. In Hobson's words, the 'approach insists that social and political change can only be understood through the interaction of multiple forces, none of which can be reduced to a single essence' (Hobson, 1998a: 287). Yet when one turns to their analytical frameworks and empirical investigations, ideational factors are noticeably absent. Hobson's analysis of tariff protectionism prior to the First World War is instructive here. At neither the level of interest formation nor that of strategic interaction do ideas, norms or culture play any role. Hobson insists that states have interests, that these are principally of a fiscal, military, economic and social nature, and that they cannot be reduced to the interests of dominant classes (Hobson, 1997: 11–12, 56–7, 242–4). Curiously, though, he provides only the barest theory of state interests. Just as Waltz attributes a basic survival motive to states, Hobson argues that 'Supplying finance and achieving fiscal sovereignty is the first prerogative of states' (Hobson, 1997: 32). Without denying that this is an important state objective, it is worth noting that it is upheld as a universal state interest, varying neither historically nor across types of state. Furthermore, Hobson gives this universal interest a single cause – the exigencies of military competition under fluctuating international economic conditions (Hobson, 1998a: 299). In contrast to Waltz, though, Hobson argues that states respond to the geofiscal imperatives of the international system in different ways, some raising tariffs, others seeking revenue through income taxes. The domestic structure and capacity of the state is crucial here, not its cultural context, social or corporate identity or ideological orientation. Nor are there any ideational forces operating at the international level to condition state policies. In sum, whatever the explanatory merits of Hobson's schema, it is entirely rationalist, providing only a thin material/structural account of state interests, and ignoring even a 'switchman' role for ideas in interest satisfaction.

The limits of history without ideas

Showing that neo-Weberian historical sociology is inherently rationalist, and that it privileges material over ideational forces, does not itself damn the neo-Weberian project, even if it does expose a gap between the rhetoric of multi-causality and scholarly practice. If rationalist assumptions about human behaviour and emphasis on the role of select material forces are heuristically powerful, then it may well be justified. It is questionable, though, whether neo-Weberian historical sociology carries such heuristic power, at least in its application to international relations. Its limitations become apparent if we unravel the logic of Hobson's argument about trade regimes.

In responding to the geofiscal imperatives of the international system, Hobson contends, states of the late-nineteenth and early-twentieth centuries adopted different policies. Those with strong domestic capacities, measured by degree of concentration, infrastructural reach and level of state (embedded) autonomy, favoured free trade and income tax, while those with weak domestic capacities preferred protectionism and indirect taxes. So long as state capacity remained low across most of Europe, movement towards an international free trade regime was near impossible. As state capacities across the international system grew, however, the desirability and viability of such a regime increased, ultimately resulting in the post-1945 GATT regime. Rejecting arguments that attribute GATT to American hegemony, Hobson claims 'that the existence of GATT was only possible in the first place because of the income tax, which in turn was only made possible through strong state capacity' (Hobson, 1998a: 303; Hobson, 1997: 210–11). And against neoliberal arguments about the persistence of institutional co-operation 'after hegemony', he claims that continued high levels of state capacity have been crucial. Nowhere does he deny GATT's contribution to lowering tariff levels among developed countries, but he repeatedly insists that 'the basis of the GATT was made possible only by the prior existence of the income tax' (Hobson, 1997: 211). Hobson thus presents a modified second-image argument. While international geofiscal imperatives loom large in the nineteenth century as the principal determinants of state interests, by the second half of the twentieth century those interests are taken as given, and international institutional developments are tied to the convergence of domestic structural conditions.

That a connection exists between state capacity, preferred taxation options and predilections towards free trade or protectionism is convincingly argued by Hobson. But the connection he then draws between such factors and the development of international institutions, such as GATT, is less plausible. At best he identifies a permissive condition, a domestic structural characteristic in the absence of which states could not possibly entertain a particular international policy objective, in this case free trade. The existence of this condition – the gradual increase in state capacities across the developed world, and the concomitant shift towards income taxation – cannot explain why growing state interest in free trade was translated into the development of multilateral regulatory institutions after 1945. Although we have grown accustomed to the coincidence of the two, there is no straightforward functional connection between free trade and multilateralism, and Hobson certainly goes no further than anyone else in demonstrating one. Lisa Martin has shown that at an abstract rational level, there is no way to explain why the United States or any other states chose multilateral forms of international economic management, and her own appeal to the structural condition of hegemony under conditions of bipolarity has been successfully critiqued by John Ruggie, who shows a clear US preference for multilateralism well before the emergence of Cold War structural conditions (Martin, 1993; Ruggie, 1993b). The fact is that the pursuit of free trade through GATT was but one expression of a wider process of multilateral institutional construction which dates back to the middle of the nineteenth century – a process that Christopher Hill describes as 'the most striking line in the evolution in diplomacy' (Hill, 1991: 90).

Explaining the development of international economic institutions is not Hobson's central project. Yet his failure to establish a connection between a predilection to free trade and multilateralism is indicative of a more general lacuna in neo-Weberian historical sociology – its failure to recognise, let alone explain, the institutional dimension of international relations. The 'international' is understood purely in material terms, consisting solely of military competition between states and developments in the international capitalist economy. Missing altogether is the web of intersubjective understandings that give the 'international' a truly social dimension. At a minimum, this web consists of three tiers of institutions: international regimes, such as GATT and the NPT; fundamental institutions, or basic institutional practices, such as multilateralism and international law; and constitutional values, such as sovereignty. None of these institutions features in the analytical schema proffered by neo-Weberian historical sociologists, within or outside of international relations. Nor can that schema explain such institutions. A connection between domestic state capacity and international institutional formations is yet to be established, and appeals to international geopolitical or economic conditions go no further to explain such formations (Reus-Smit, 1999).

This lacuna undermines the neo-Weberian historical sociology of international relations in two ways. First, it leaves a significant dimension of the global political landscape unacknowledged and unexplained. Neo-Weberians have done much to reveal the state as an historically contingent political formation, a quasi-autonomous administrative agency, the product of interacting military and economic forces. While this distinguishes them from ahistorical neorealists, their neglect of international institutions, at whatever level of international society, leaves them closer to Waltz and his followers than to just about any other school of international relations scholarship. Second, their failure to address the institutional dimension of international life detracts from the central project of neo-Weberian historical sociology – that of understanding the sovereign state as an historically situated and variable political formation. As both neoliberals and constructivists have demonstrated, formal and informal international institutions play a key role in constituting the social identity of the state, in shaping domestic state structures and institutions, in teaching states their interests and in mediating the pursuit of those interests.

A constructivist turn

Drawing on the insights of critical social theory and postmodernism, constructivists seek to develop a social theory of international relations, a theory that treats actors and action as inherently social, as the products of institutionally grounded identities and normatively sanctioned repertoires of conduct (Adler, 1997; Checkel, 1998; Hopf, 1998; Price and Reus-Smit, 1998). Such identities and repertoires are in turn considered the products of the knowledgeable practices of social agents, the actions of which are essential to the production and reproduction of social structures. For constructivists, therefore, sovereignty is a social institution, a complex of norms governing the distribution and exercise of power and authority, which ordains the state with a particular 'sovereign' identity, and which licenses certain forms of internal and external conduct. Because the norms that comprise the institution of sovereignty are the outcomes of social practices, both of states and other actors, they vary over time, making historical process and change central constructivist concerns. Not surprisingly, the development of constructivist international theory has been accompanied by a growing body of constructivist history, an historical genre that has evolved parallel to neo-Weberian historical sociology in international relations, but which moves beyond the rationalism of that perspective, to examine the role of ideational forces in the social construction of sovereign states and the definition of rightful state action (Ruggie, 1993c; Thomson, 1994; Weber, 1995; Hall, 1997; Bukovansky, 1997; Reus-Smit, 1999).

An idealist philosophy of history

While constructivist historical sociologists acknowledge the role that material forces play in conditioning human behaviour, they embrace a distinctly 'idealist' philosophy of history. Not idealist in the traditional form, criticised by Carr and others for its teleological faith in human progress and peace through law, but idealist in the sense that intersubjective ideas, norms and values are considered important determinants of actors' identities, interests and actions. It is a philosophy of history that Carr himself endorsed when he wrote that 'History cannot be written unless the historian can achieve some kind of contact with the mind of those about whom he is writing' (1961: 24), and that Heeren, the nineteenth-century international historian, upheld when stating that to understand 'the ruling ideas of each age, and exhibit the particular maxims arising from them, will be the first requisite of the historian' (1829). Such a philosophy of history is justified, constructivists contend, on both social theoretic and explanatory grounds, resonating as it does with an established body of social and cultural theory, and explicating important aspects of international life obscured or misunderstood by other perspectives.

The constructivist philosophy of history is informed by four interrelated theoretical assumptions. First, to the extent that social structures shape individual and collective human action, ideational structures are considered just as important as material structures. Ideational structures are intersubjective ideas, norms and values that enable human agents to describe, explain, and attach meaning to, the physical world, their social universe and their own status and actions. The fact that they are intersubjective, that they reside in the collective consciousness and not just in the individual psyche, gives them their structural quality, their capacity to constitute and constrain agents and action. Such structures include religious and scientific cosmologies and world-views, the three tiers of international institutions mentioned above, and the whole gamut of intersubjective beliefs that circulate globally to condition legitimate individual and collective agency and action, domestically, internationally and transnationally. Constructivists stress the importance of such structures for two reasons: ideational structures condition how actors interpret the material conditions of their existence, and they define actors' social identities and interests. With regard to the first of these, Alexander Wendt notes that the distribution of military power has no meaning independent of the ideational structures in which it is embedded: 'U.S. military power has a different significance for Canada than for Cuba, despite their similar "structural" positions' (Wendt, 1992: 397).

Anticipated above, the second theoretical assumption informing the constructivist philosophy of history is that ideational structures shape actors' social identities. We have seen that rationalists treat ideas as switchmen – variables that mediate between interests and actions. Constructivists argue that ideas also operate at a much deeper level, at the constitutive level where actors learn who they are, and where they learn the social identities that enable them to function in a world of complex social processes and practices (Wendt and Duvall, 1989: 60). The role of ideational structures in the definition of state identities is nowhere more apparent than in the membership norms of international society – norms which operate at both systemic and regional levels. During the nineteenth century, a constitutionalist 'standard of civilisation' came to define the self-identity of European states, and was used to determine which non-European polities would be admitted to the select club of sovereign states (Gong, 1984; Adas, 1989). Similarly, a distinctive set of liberal political and economic norms now define the self-identity of member-states of the European Union, norms which also define the criteria by which Eastern European states are granted or declined membership.

The third theoretical assumption informing the constructivist view of history is that actors' social identities inform their interests. Rationalists treat interests as exogenous to social interaction, as though actors are, in some classic liberal sense, sources of their own conceptions of the good. Actors are assumed to enter social relations with a pre-existing repertoire of relatively stable preferences, and society is reduced to a strategic domain, a realm of competition and co-operation among rational egoists. Constructivists, in contrast, see interests as endogenous to social interaction, as the products of socially constituted identities. Just as ideational structures socialise actors to assume certain social identities, those identities carry with them certain associated interests (Wendt, 1992: 398). The 1999 military intervention in Kosovo clearly illustrates this point. That NATO member-states have interests at stake in Kosovo is undeniable, but it is impossible to understand those interests without reference to their identity as liberal-democratic states, and without some understanding of the responsibilities that such an identity is believed to entail.

The final theoretical assumption informing constructivist history is that structures and agents are mutually constitutive. The preceding discussion might suggest that constructivists are structuralists – that they see a one-way path of constitution running from intersubjective ideas to identities, to interests, to actions. Certainly Wendt's recent writings, which posit a 'supervening' relationship between structures and agents, lend credence to such an interpretation (Wendt, 1995, 1996), as do constructivist studies that emphasise the importance of social norms in shaping state behaviour. This having been said, most constructivists are *structurationists*, not structuralists. They are just as concerned with the role of agents' practices in the production and reproduction of social structures, as they are with the way those structures shape agents' identities and interests. To ignore this role is not only to ignore an undeniable ontological reality – that without practices structures would simply cease to exist – but also to ignore the only source of social change: if everything is structurally determined, how does anything change? The wealth of constructivist research on the impact of intersubjective norms on state behaviour has thus been matched by explorations into the social construction of those norms, whether they be deep constitutive norms of sovereignty, or issue-specific norms, such as the taboo against the use of chemical weapons (Thomson, 1994; Price, 1997). Returning to the example of Kosovo, constructivists are not just interested in how the liberal-democratic identity of NATO states defines their interests and actions, but in how the practice of military intervention for humanitarian purposes reinforces or undermines the intersubjective foundations of that social identity, both within the community of NATO states and within the wider international community.

By what mechanisms do ideational phenomena affect the behaviour of actors, both individual and collective? Constructivists emphasise three such mechanisms: imagination, communication and constraint. With regard to the first of these, intersubjective ideas, norms and principles define actors' expectations – what they consider necessary and possible, both in a practical and an ethical sense. Rationalists imagine a world in which actors, equipped with a universal sense of rational calculation, pursue their interests in the most efficient and effective manner possible, given the environmental constraints they encounter. For constructivists, the universal rational actor is a myth. Historically and culturally contingent beliefs define how actors understand themselves, and who they think they are not only affects their interests but also the means they entertain to realise those interests. Prior to the Wars of the Spanish Succession (1701–13), European monarchs believed that they were God's lieutenants on earth, that the extent of their rule was determined by the reach of the family tree, not by rigidly demarcated territorial boundaries, and that they had the right to pursue their paternal rights through war. Modern liberal democracies hold that the state is only legitimate to the extent that it expresses and protects the interests and rights of its citizens; that states which severely violate those interests and rights forfeit their right to non-intervention; and that in the most extreme situations, military coercion is justified. In each case, the social identities of the states in question have scripted their behaviour, to such an extent that absolutist monarchs would find the liberal-democratic script incomprehensible, and liberal democracies would find the behaviour prescribed by the absolutist script unimaginable.

Ideational phenomena also shape behaviour through processes of communicative action. This is especially true of ideas with normative content, of the norms, rules and principles that define some forms of conduct as legitimate and others illegitimate. These ideas provide the basic framework for successful social and political action, as they provide actors with a socially sanctioned language to describe and justify their choices, projects and actions. For constructivists, most human action is rule-governed, in the sense that 'it becomes understandable against the background of norms embodied in conventions and rules which give meaning to action' (Kratochwil, 1989: 11). This is most palpable in situations of controversy, when an individual's conduct is considered questionable (why did he or she act?), or when collective action is required (how should we act?). In both cases, the existing panoply of social norms provides the linguistic court of appeal. The individual under scrutiny seeks to justify his or her behaviour with references to established codes of conduct or moral imperatives, or members of a collectivity debate alternative courses of action with reference not only to practicalities but also to prescribed norms of conduct (Heller, 1987: 239). For an individual, failure to justify an action may lead to nothing more than embarrassment, but in international relations a state's inability to justify internal or external actions may lead to the withdrawal of recognition, economic sanctions or even military intervention, particularly if its actions transgress the prevailing terms of legitimate statehood.

Through the first of the above mechanisms, ideas structure the imaginations of actors; through the second, they structure the communicative processes that surround action. Both rely on 'belief' to translate ideas into action: in the former, the belief of an individual actor in his or her own identity and values; in the latter, the belief of all discursive participants in the meta-norms structuring communicative action. Under the final mechanism, ideas shape behaviour through constraint not belief. Constructivists are directly at odds with realists here. Recall

Morgenthau's claim that ideology has no independent political salience: 'the true nature of the policy is concealed by ideological justifications and rationalizations' (Morgenthau, 1985: 101). This not only clashes with the constructivist arguments canvassed above, but is challenged by two further constructivist claims. First, the very appeal to intersubjective values to rationalise behaviour is testimony to the existence and power of such values: if they had no normative standing or persuasive capacity they would make useless rationalisations. Second, justifying behaviour with reference to a particular set of intersubjective values immediately places a constraint on that behaviour (Skinner, 1978: xii). Even if NATO countries did not believe in the humanitarian values they invoked to justify their military intervention in Kosovo, those values gave them only a limited sphere of action. Their conduct of the campaign could not be seen to violate the principles of either international humanitarian law or *jus in bello*, and the intervention had to deliver a settlement broadly consistent with the values invoked. Anything less, and the domestic and international support needed to sustain the campaign would crumble.

Epochal change and institutional architecture

The discipline of international relations has so long been preoccupied with stasis, continuity and repetition, that it lacks the conceptual and theoretical apparatus to think sensibly about transformation (Ruggie, 1983). This conceptual and theoretical retardation is reflected in two assumptions that presently handicap discussions of international change. First, there is the assumption that epochal change is necessarily associated with the rise and decline of sovereignty. Whether it is seen as an attribute of the state or an institution of international society, most international relations scholars treat sovereignty as an unquestioned given of the present international system. And to the extent that they think about large-scale change in that system, it is in terms of the rise or decline of the sovereign order. This equation of epochal change with the fate of sovereignty is reflected in the prevailing conception of systems change, which is commonly defined as a shift from a system based on sovereignty to one based on some other organising principle (Waltz, 1979: 70). Second, there is the assumption that the forces driving change are essentially material. While some emphasise the importance of capitalism, most scholars emphasise war-fighting and the struggle for material power. Not only has the rise of the sovereign order been attributed to warlordism among European monarchs and princes, but systemic changes within that order have been understood almost exclusively in terms of shifts in the military and economic balance of power between states (Krasner, 1993).

These two assumptions do not provide an adequate conceptual or theoretical framework for either describing or explaining epochal international change. Simply pointing to the rise of sovereignty tells us nothing about the nature of the sovereign order in question, and material factors alone cannot explain the nature of the order. For traditional international relations scholars, such issues never arise, as sovereign orders are all assumed to be the same – anarchy is said to produce 'like-politics' in all systems of sovereign states. Yet using the rise and decline of sovereignty as the sole marker of epochal change, and placing all one's explanatory eggs in the material basket, leaves several puzzles about the modern international system unanswered. Foremost here is the institutional puzzle. If the advent of sovereignty between the fifteenth and seventeenth centuries marks the birth of our present system of sovereign states, why did the institutional architecture of that system not arise until the middle of the nineteenth century? Why did the paired institutions of contractual international law and multilateralism – which together provide the basic structure of governance in the modern international system – not take off until after the age of revolutions?

   In one of the few systematic studies of the emergence of this institutional order, Ruggie concludes that 'while numerous descriptions of this "move to institutions" exist, I know of no good explanations in the literature of why states should have wanted to complicate their lives in this manner' (Ruggie, 1993b: 24). Functionalist arguments, such as Martin's, that see multilateralism as a rational solution to the co-operation problems faced by states are confounded by the problem of multiple equilibria – the fact that historically states have confronted several equally efficient institutional solutions means that there is no way to explain, at an abstract rational level, why multilateralism was chosen over other options. Explanations that tie multilateralism to US hegemony are equally unsatisfactory, as the rise of such institutions predates Pax Americana by at least one hundred years, and in other historical systems of sovereign states, hegemons have pursued different institutional strategies. One could appeal to the functional requirements of capitalism to explain the rise of multilateralism, but such arguments would have difficulty escaping the pitfalls of *post hoc* reasoning, and would be confounded by the fact that multilateral principles were first upheld and institutionally enshrined in the security realm, not the economic. There is always the argument that the very complexity of the modern international system demands multilateral institutions, yet the international system of the nineteenth century was not especially complex, with relatively few states addressing co-operation problems in relatively few issue areas. Finally, Ruggie's own explanation, which posits a functional connection between the stabilisation of territorial property rights and the development of multilateral institutions, is contradicted by the absence of such institutions in the crucial period of stabilisation, 1555–1815 (Reus-Smit, 1999).

The constructivist philosophy of history outlined in the preceding section provides a more fruitful conception of international change than the conventional rationalist and materialist narrative of sovereignty – one that offers greater insights into the nature of particular sovereign orders, especially their varied institutional characteristics. Such an approach requires that we look more closely at the normative structure of the international system, at how this affects the social identity of the state, and what implications this has for institutional rationality. Constructivists usually assume that the normative structure of the international system is synonymous with the institution of sovereignty – that the organising principle of sovereignty, and sovereignty alone, forms the normative bedrock of the society of states. I have argued elsewhere that this greatly understates the complexity of that structure, and that the normative foundations of international systems should be seen to comprise not one, but three elements: a hegemonic conception of the moral purpose of the state, an organising principle of sovereignty and a norm of procedural justice (Reus-Smit, 1999).

This model brings Weber's emphasis on the legitimacy of the state to the fore, as the concept of the moral purpose of the state refers to prevailing intersubjective beliefs about what constitutes a legitimate state. These ideas give sovereignty meaning in a particular historical context, providing the basic language for justifying the state as a political institution and for establishing the bounds of rightful state action, internally and externally. Ideas about the moral purpose of the state also inform norms of procedural justice. One of the principal functions of the sovereign state is to solve co-operation problems between its constituents, and it follows that ideas about legitimate statehood always entail associated beliefs about the procedures 'good' states employ, domestically and internationally, to address such problems. Together these values form the deep 'constitutional structure' of international societies, but their content is always historically contingent, and thus varies from one system of sovereign states to another. Most importantly for our purposes, as norms of procedural justice change, so too does institutional rationality, leading states in different historical contexts to embrace different institutional solutions to their co-operation problems.

This framework enables us to formulate a more nuanced understanding of epochal international change. If the constitutional structures outlined above define and shape the nature of international systems, then changes in the meta-values that comprise those structures must be important determinants and markers of systems change. By embracing a more complex understanding of the normative foundations of international systems, we are freed from the prevailing conceptual and theoretical framework of extremes, which conceives systems change only in terms of the existence or absence of the organising principle of sovereignty. More specifically, it enables us to distinguish between two different forms of systems change: *purposive* change and *configurative* change. Purposive change involves a redefinition of the moral purpose of the state, leading to shifts in the meaning of sovereignty and procedural justice. It involves a change in the values that are used to justify the organisation of political life into centralised, autonomous political units. Configurative change entails not only a shift in the moral purpose of the state, but also a change in the organising principle governing the distribution of power and authority. It involves a change in the principles that determine the spatial configuration of politics, as well as in the moral language used to justify the spatial order. The transition from medieval heteronomy to absolutist sovereignty, so insightfully illuminated by Ruggie, represents precisely such a configurative change (Ruggie, 1983).

This understanding of epochal change enables us to solve the institutional puzzle of the modern international system – the emergence of the fundamental institutions of contractual international law and multilateralism only after the age of revolutions. From the perspective outlined above, the period from the fifteenth century to the present encapsulates not one but two international systems: the absolutist system of states that expired with the demise of the nineteenth-century Concert of Europe, and the modern system that emerged in its wake. The basic organising principle of sovereignty persisted across both systems, but a profound purposive transformation occurred after the French Revolution, in which the underlying moral purpose of the state and the associated norm of procedural justice were fundamentally reconceived. In the language of constructivism, the normative structure of the international system changed, altering the social identity of the sovereign state and the prevailing form of institutional rationality, prompting the construction of an entirely new institutional architecture.

The sovereign states that emerged in Europe after the Peace of Augsburg (1555) were decidedly pre-modern. The transnational authority of the Roman Catholic Church had been rejected, but Christianity still provided the basic ideological resources for the constitution of political identities and the legitimation of systems of rule. The moral purpose of the new sovereign state was defined as the preservation of a divinely ordained, rigidly hierarchical social order, and to fulfil this purpose, monarchs were ordained with supreme authority. In the words of Jean Domat, a leading French jurist in the reign of Louis XIV, it is 'necessary that a head [sovereign] coerce and rule the body of society and maintain order among those who should give the public the benefit of the different contributions that their stations require of them' (quoted in Church, 1969: 76). This rationale for the sovereignty of dynastic states implied an authoritative conception of procedural justice. The standards of right and wrong conduct that were to regulate co-operation and conflict between the subjects of the state were not to be negotiated or legislated by those subjects or their representatives, but were to be dictated by a supreme authority: God in the first instance, monarchs by deputation. This was reflected in the prevailing conception of law as command. 'The word law', Jean Bodin argues, 'signifies the right of command of that person, or those persons, who have absolute authority over all the rest without exception, save only the lawgiver himself' (Bodin, 1967: 43).

This idea of procedural justice filtered into relations between absolutist states and profoundly affected the institutional development (or underdevelopment) of the new international system. Because law was understood as the command of a supreme authority, and because no stable hierarchy existed among 'God's lieutenants', international law was understood as an expression of God's law and natural law, not of reciprocally binding contracts between sovereigns. And without the institution of contractual international law, no incentive existed for the development of multilateralism, correctly defined as the co-ordination of the 'behavior of three or more states on the basis of generalized principles of conduct' (Ruggie, 1993b: 11). We see, therefore, that 'naturalist' international law resided primarily in the writings of legal publicists, the interpreters of God's law and natural law, and that the major international settlements that stabilised territorial property rights between absolutist states – the Peace of Westphalia (1648) and the Peace of Utrecht (1713) – bear little evidence of multilateralism, constituting, as they do, complex aggregations of bilateral agreements (Reus-Smit, 1999: 87–121).

During the eighteenth century, revolutionary changes in thought and practice undermined the ideological and material foundations of dynastic rule. Following shifts in scientific thought, political and economic theorists abandoned holistic conceptions of society, championing instead new ideas of political and economic individualism. The impact of these ideas was profound, with political individualism fuelling the American and French revolutions, and economic individualism providing the ideological resources for the Industrial Revolution. In the ensuing fifty years, Europe was torn by protracted conflict over the terms of legitimate rule, compounded by the economically induced dislocation of traditional patterns of social organisation and affiliation. By the middle of the nineteenth century a new set of constitutional meta-values was emerging, the rise of which signalled the birth of modern international society. The moral purpose of the state was increasingly tied to the expression of the interests of the citizenry and the protection of their civil and political rights. As the French Declaration on the Rights of Man and Citizen declared, 'The aim of every political association is the preservation of natural and inalienable rights of man; these rights are liberty, property, and resistance to oppression.'

This *raison d'être* of the state entailed a new principle of procedural justice – legislative justice. This principle prescribed two precepts of rule determination: that only those subject to the rules, or their representatives, have the right to define them; and that the rules of society must apply equally to all citizens, in all like cases. Encapsulating this idea of law as reciprocal accord, the French Declaration states that 'law is the expression of the general will; all citizens have the right to concur personally, or through their representatives, in its formation; it must be the same for all, whether it protects or punishes'. Once these constitutional ideas had altered the terms of governance within the major European states, a transition which was well in train by the second half of the nineteenth century, they began to structure institutional developments at the international level. Reflected most dramatically in the Hague Conferences of 1899 and 1907, the idea of law as reciprocal accord informed the rapid development of contractual international law, and the principle of participatory governance that this implied, prompted the equally rapid development of multilateralism. In the period 1815 to 1914, European states concluded 817 multilateral treaties, a seven-fold increase on the number concluded between 1648 and 1814 (Mostecky, 1965; Hill 1991; Murphy, 1994).

Conclusion

If history was once integral to the study of international relations, and somewhere along the way was pushed to the margins by crude behaviouralism, then the development of an historical sociology of international relations promises to return it to centre stage (see Hobden, this volume). Furthermore, the attempt to refine international history by applying the insights of social theory, promises to inject greater system and rigour into a field too long mired in diplomatic storytelling. Yet the neo-Weberian variety of historical sociology that has come to prominence is hamstrung by its own theoretical commitments. As we have seen, Weber has been read in a distinctly rationalist way. Humans have been portrayed as rational egoists, their interests have been treated as exogenous to social interaction, ideas have been relegated to the role of intervening switch-men, power has assumed the status of a universal interest, and material forces have been privileged. Those cues in Weber that point to the importance of legitimacy in framing agency and action have been largely ignored, even though those cues are to be found in his very definition of the state. Whatever the explanatory merits of existing neo-Weberian scholarship – and I would not wish to deny them – its heuristic power is unnecessarily impeded by this rationalist orientation. In particular, not only has the institutional dimension of international life no place in neo-Weberian theory, it cannot be explained by that theory.

This chapter has made the case for a constructivist turn in the historical sociology of international relations. Such a turn would involve four departures from neo-Weberian historical sociology as it presently stands. First, it would involve re-emphasising ideational structures, as they provide the lenses through which actors interpret the material conditions of their lives, and the language through which they describe themselves and justify their actions. Second, it would involve treating individual and collective actors as inherently social, as deeply constituted by the social universe in which they live and act, as having their very identities shaped by the ideational structures of the prevailing social order. Third, it would involve treating actors' interests as endogenous to social interaction, as defined through processes of social learning and role enactment. And fourth, it would involve placing greater analytical emphasis on the way in which actors' practices produce and reproduce the ideational conditions of their lives. These departures would not only bring the institutional dimension of international life to the fore, but would enable the development of an historical sociology that can explain that dimension.

7 World system analysis, historical sociology and international relations: the difference a hyphen makes

Barry K. Gills

> The ceaseless quest of the modern historians looking for the 'origins'
> and roots of capitalism is not much better than the alchemist's search
> for the philosopher's stone that transforms base metal into gold.
>
> (Chaudhuri, 1990: 84)

Prolegomenon: 'The difference a hyphen makes'

In so far as there has been a 'world system' in world economic history, it has (always) been predominantly 'capitalist'. The world system, in fact, is not a creation merely of trade, but of 'capital accumulation'. Capital accumulation has existed on a 'world scale' for several millennia, not several centuries. It is this central contention that constitutes the basis of the 'continuity thesis' (Gills, 1996), the starting point for world system analysis of 'capital and power in the processes of world history' (Gills, 1995) and of the changing relationship between the world economy and the inter-state system(s).

World system analysis differs from the Wallersteinian world-system analysis (Wallerstein, 1974, 1980, 1989) in a number of highly significant ways. These differences are discussed in detail elsewhere (Gills and Frank, 1990; 1992; Wallerstein, 1992, 1995, 1996; Gills, 1995; Frank and Gills, 1996), but the essence of the disagreement surrounds the contrasting interpretations given to the notion 'ceaseless accumulation', which to Wallerstein is the *differentia specifica* of *modern* capitalism, whilst to Frank and me, it is in fact a *constant* feature of the world system. This disagreement is fundamental and leads us to very different understandings and analysis of the historical origins and development of 'capitalism' or capitalist practice in world history, of the origins and development of the world system itself (e.g., 'five hundred years or five thousand?'), and to a radically different sense of what a 'transition' to capitalism might be in world historical terms and particularly of the role of Europe within it. The most significant changes and ruptures in world history are consequently viewed quite differently, being less focused on the idea of the 'transition to capitalism' (especially as uniquely European) and more concerned with the long 'global history' of capital and the shifting locus of capital accumulation and power over space and time (i.e., the 'hegemonic transition').

Thus, the basic difference between this approach and that of Wallerstein hinges on the difference that a hyphen makes. As Wallerstein put it in a reply to Frank and Gills, '[t]hey speak of a "world system". I speak of "world-systems". I use a hyphen; they do not. I use the plural; they do not' (Wallerstein, 1996: 294). Speaking for myself, whereas Wallerstein sees only one 'historical capitalism', I see many. While there have indeed been plural 'world-systems' (that eventually fused into one 'world system'), this process has involved both continuity and discontinuity, with significant change over historical time occurring in the technological and social relations governing material life, the development of the 'technics' of power organisation, and the locus of capital accumulation and its hierarchical organisation.

Introduction

It is of the utmost importance in conducting world historical research that we first identify a clear question to guide our search for knowledge and understanding.[1] I will pursue the following central question: what is the role of *capital* in world history, i.e., how have the practices and the process of capital accumulation influenced the course of world history? In answering this question, it is imperative that we investigate the relationship between *capital* and power throughout world history.

This chapter attempts to develop conceptual tools and an analytical template that will help us understand the impact of capital accumulation throughout world economic and social history. It is likewise an attempt to build both a theory, and an empirical investigation, of the world system and its development over a period of several thousand years. Moreover, the theory and the template are intended to be applied to comparative analysis of two world historical systems: the Eurasian system and the pre-Columbian Americas, prior to their fusion after 1492. By combining a structuralist analysis (of world system dynamics) with a critical approach to political economy (in the tradition of economics as moral philosophy), the goal is to contribute to a humanocentric account of 'global history' (Frank and Gills, 1996), and to further the 'historicisation' of international political economy (Amoore *et al.*, 2000).

---

[1] I owe this insightful admonition to William H. McNeill, in private conversation, Colebrook, Conn., July 1997.

Conventional understandings of world economic and social history emphasise a linear pattern characterised by 'stages' of development, in which the 'rise of the market' and of 'capitalism' are slow and 'late' developments. Capital accumulation is deemed to be important only in fairly recent history and, at most, for the past few centuries. The framework presented here, however, argues for a non-linear perspective which rejects the conventional dichotomy between 'capitalist' and 'pre-capitalist' stages in world economic history. Instead, it explores the thesis that capital accumulation has played a continuous role throughout world economic history which has influenced the ways states and societies have evolved and interacted.

In general we have tended to view the 'pre-modern' as being too primitive, and the 'modern' as being rather too modern (Ekholm and Friedman, 1982). The antidote to the conventional approach is to emphasise the notion of the *dialectic* in world history. The *dialectic of forms*, as a method, attempts to understand the nature of the perpetual co-existence of contending economic forms (including capital), and the historical tensions among these contending forms throughout world history. Therefore, the governing processes of world history are to be viewed as being neither strictly linear nor cyclical, but rather, as perennial and dialectical. Two historical tensions are the subject of the analysis:

* capital versus *oikos*
* free versus unfree labour.

(Note that I have not included 'state(s) versus market(s)', a dichotomy I do not accept.) The relationships between the 'contending forms' are analysed as *world historical processes* and not merely as static comparisons of category concepts. As discussed below, long-term processes of social change of central interest here are the historically recurrent patterns of 'capitalisation' versus 'de-capitalisation', 'commercialisation' versus 'de-commercialisation', 'commodification' versus 'de-commodification' and the relationship of these patterns to 'hegemonic transitions', 'cycles of hegemony' and 'centre shifts' in the inter-state system. These patterns are investigated in relation to world systemic conditions of general 'equilibrium' and 'dis-equilibrium'; or put another way, between the systemic conditions that are associated historically with periods of prosperity or expansion and those which are associated with crisis, contraction or 'entropy'. Such 'world system cycles', each of several centuries duration, stretch back several millennia (Gills and Frank, 1992).

There are three important analytical premises on which this historical (international political economy) framework depends: no formal analytical separation of politics from economics; no necessary separation between the 'domestic' and the 'international'; and no strict separation between past, present and future (Gills, 2001). This allows us to view 'the state' not only as a type of political power, but also as an economic 'form' in itself, and intrinsic to the 'economic system'. Furthermore, 'capital' is understood as being not purely an economic 'form' but a type of social power. Capital accumulation is understood to be embedded in the economic and political frameworks of individual states as well as of systems of states and empires. Capital accumulation takes place in symbiosis with the working of state power at these various levels. Therefore, states, empires and inter-state systems and their historical rhythms and institutions are as intrinsic to world economic history as the economic 'forms' themselves. Thus, 'international relations' constitutes the larger framework within which world economic history is best understood (cf. Buzan and Little, 2000 and this volume). Finally, power itself must always be analysed from a critical perspective, not as a mere quantity; this requires a critical social theory of power, in both its economic and political aspects.

'Capital', 'capitalist class' and 'capitalism(s)': disentangling definitions

The goal of this analysis is to study the (entire world) history of 'capital', the social power of the 'capitalist class', and 'historical capitalism(s)'. There is much to be gained in terms of analytical precision and clarity, however, by making distinctions among the concepts 'capital', 'the capitalist class' and 'capitalism'. Adam Smith, like other early political economists, used the term 'capital' to mean merely 'stock' or the goods in inventory (Smith, 1937). Marx, being concerned to critique 'bourgeois' political economy, used the term 'capital' to denote not a thing but a social relation, i.e., the (exploitative) power of the owner of the means of production to command labour power and extract surplus value from it (Bottomore, 1991). Weber (apparently following Aristotle) defined 'capital' as private acquisitive capital (*Erwerbskapital*), used to acquire profit in an exchange economy.

I will define 'capital' as a social relation, rooted in private property, operating through the use of money and commodity production and exchange, in command of labour power and seeking profit through an (exploitative) transfer of value. As a form of social power, 'capital' commands labour power. As a social relation it involves the transfer of value from labour to the holder of capital. By seeking profit (and its realisation in monetary form), it is inextricably connected not only to the exchange relations of a commodified economy, but also to the unceasing quest for the increase of capital, or its 'accumulation'. In effect, there can be no capital without capital accumulation. In economic terms it is a condition of capital accumulation that the producer be separated from the consumer and that values be expressed in the setting of relative prices. It is central to my argument that capital and capital accumulation be recognised as having existed from quite early in world economic history and thereafter having played a continuous and important, or even 'governing', role (in terms of its 'logic') in the creation, and development, of the world economy and the world system. Therefore, long-distance commerce (and capital's role in it) has played a key role in shaping the world system for several millennia. This must be the case as 'inter-regional or long-distance trade cannot by definition function without capital, money, and prices' (Chaudhuri, 1985: 203). Thus, the analysis starts from the position that many local economies, even in 'the remote historical past', have had 'an exchange economy based on division of labour and the implied condition of capital accumulation' (Chaudhuri, 1985: 203). However, it is long-distance exchange (which separates producer and consumer over both geographical space and real time) which perhaps most encourages the development of 'a more advanced circuit of capital' (Chaudhuri, 1985: 203). To argue for the centrality of capital accumulation in world economic history is not, however, to insist that it is all a history of 'capita*lism*'. On the other hand, in contrast to either conventional economic history or Wallersteinian world-system analysis, capital accumulation in the ancient and medieval periods (of both Occident and Orient) should not be relegated to a residual category such as 'proto-capitalist' or, worse still, 'pre-capitalist'.

It is useful to re-examine the historical origins of 'capital' and disentangle this from historical 'capitalism'. What is capital? I begin the answer to this central question with the proposition that 'capital' originates in an *urban* context. Thus, the places and times of the origins of 'capital' tend to coincide with those of urbanism, i.e., within an economic situation already at a fairly high level of technological and organisational sophistication; a context of social stratification and hierarchical class relations; and an authority structure in which 'the state' and a ruling class has emerged. The division of labour and specialisation must be at a well-developed level, and commodity production and exchange exist at both local and long-distance scales. A complex system of economic accounting and a formal 'value complex' make capital and its accumulation possible, and this is facilitated by the emergence of money (though not necessarily on a metallic standard).

Thus, the origins of 'capital', 'the state' and 'civilisation' (defined as the culture of living in cities) are parallel developments. Moreover, the origins of civilisation, the state and capital in urban centres should not be understood as having occurred 'first' in some pristine case, such as Sumeria, and then having spread, but rather to have developed more or less simultaneously (allowing for unevenness) across a much larger economic nexus in Eurasia from the late Neolithic onwards. That is, the embryonic world system (long-distance exchange and the gradual development of the division of labour, with settlement growth and differentiation) gave rise to the first fully developed 'cities', to 'capital' and possibly to 'the state' as well. Therefore, capital accumulation in world history is situated within a continuous *city-centred* nexus of trade and production, which has never existed independently of an 'international' or inter-state system framework. They are truly 'co-constitutive'.

Why 'capital accumulation'? While we should reject the urge to posit a fixed or essentialist theory of unchanging human nature in order to explain the psychological origins of capital accumulation, certain characteristics of human psychology, nevertheless, are implicated in the emergence of 'capital' and its historical associations with wealth, power and social status. The 'accumulation complex' is a profound aspect of human social history, expressed in innumerable individual life histories, and deeply rooted in economic and political history. It deserves serious investigation.[2]

The underlying material basis of 'capital' is, simply put, the storing of a surplus. Surplus only becomes 'capital', however, through a particular kind of conversion, one which requires a formal 'value complex', in which not only goods but also human labour become measurable quantities subject to purchase. Capital is therefore Janus-faced, being a means both of 'wealth creation' and of human exploitation. The conversion of the surplus into values requires the careful measurement not only of quantities (and qualities) of goods, but of human labour also. Thus, the social conversion of surplus into 'abstract wealth' and 'capital' depends in the first instance upon the development of sophisticated methods of accounting (Schmandt-Besserat, 1992). Complex accounting systems facilitate the manipulation of the surplus to definable ends, including productive, consumptive and reproductive ones. Complex accounting systems (including writing and numerical systems) are an indication of the emergence of a formal value complex. Such a value complex is a *sine qua non* of 'capital' and its accumulation.

The control of economic surplus is a fundamental form of social power in all human societies. Marx rightly believed that all historical social

[2] I undertake this investigation in my forthcoming work, *Capital and Power: A Global History*.

systems could be studied and compared on the basis of how the surplus was produced and distributed. In terms of class position, capital is
an instance not only of the commodification of goods and labour, but
also of 'invidious comparison' between human beings (Veblen, 1994).
The social reproduction of a 'leisure class', i.e., a class elevated above
manual labour, is a deeply embedded pattern of human history and an
intrinsic aspect of capital accumulation (though 'capital' is not the exclusive means to this end). In Smith's classical political economy, man was
'rich or poor depending on the amount of labour that he can command
or afford to purchase' (Speigel, 1991: 248).

The emergence of capital is associated with the 'privatisation' of control over surplus and the command of labour power. Thus, the origins
of capital occur in tandem with certain types of class formation, which
must include a private propertied class. Capital is therefore always a class
position and associated with a 'capitalist class'. In this regard, Max Weber
(1978) provides a useful catalogue of the 'positively privileged property
classes' and their historical counterpart, the 'negatively privileged property classes' (e.g., labourers and debtors). However, whereas Marx ties
capital to wage-labour, capital is in fact not restricted to free wage-labour.
Capital utilises many forms of value, including both free and unfree ones.
There is no necessary incompatibility of capital or capitalism even with
the most severe forms of slavery. The history of 'primitive accumulation'
in early modern capitalism illustrates this point clearly.

Once we accept the existence of capital, and with it of a capitalist
class, from very early in world economic history, our understanding of
the origins and development of historical capitalism(s) is changed as well.
Looking for the historical origins of 'capitalism', as opposed to 'capital',
is usually done by trying to identify a point in national or world economic
history when capitalist social relations become overwhelmingly dominant
in the economic system. For some, such as Braudel, this point comes as
early as the thirteenth century in Europe; for others, like Wallerstein, it
occurs in the 'long sixteenth century'; still others reserve the transformation for the time of the great 'industrial revolution' of the late-eigh-
teenth and the nineteenth centuries. Moreover, this threshold of 'historical capitalism' is understood in Wallersteinian world-system theory, as
well as in many standard liberal and modernisation accounts of economic
development, to be co-terminous with the origins of the world-system
or world-economy itself, which radiated outwards from newly capitalist
Europe.

Conventionally, the first 'bourgeois revolution' occurred in England
and the Netherlands in the course of the sixteenth and seventeenth centuries, in which world commerce strengthened a bourgeoisie composed of

bankers, ship-owners, merchants and manufacturers, and where 'capital-ist agriculture' first reigned. Certainly, these were states that were charac-terised by a new dedication to the almost unbridled pursuit of commercial profit on a world scale. However, to propose that these were the original 'bourgeois' economies is to ignore earlier manifestations (even in Europe, such as Italian capitalism) in an excessively Eurocentric view.

I certainly do not suggest that all of world economic history is sim-ply (unchanging) 'capitalism'. Following Weber, I argue for instances of 'ancient capitalism', 'medieval capitalism' and 'modern capitalism', in-sisting that each instance has distinctive characteristics (Weber, 1976). It would be a serious methodological error to insist that the conditions of modern (industrial and finance) capitalism must first exist in order for us to acknowledge any form of 'historical capitalism' whatsoever in the pre-modern eras. Moreover, I am certainly not simply extrapolating present world economic conditions back through time. I am, however, rejecting the idea that 'capital' and 'capitalism' are uniquely modern. By smash-ing this false dichotomy between capitalist and pre-capitalist 'stages' of world economic history, we can shatter the conventional (and Waller-steinian) Eurocentric interpretation of 'historical capitalism', which in-sists that Europe alone created capitalism and thus the world-system also.

The 'continuity thesis' suggests capital accumulation has played an im-portant role in both Occidental and non-Occidental history from ancient times onwards, including during the presumably 'feudal' medieval cen-turies. The prevalence of capitalist practices in the local, regional and world commerce of medieval Islam, and in the Hindu and Confucian zones of Asia is an historical reality that should be vigorously reinves-tigated, laying to rest the ghost of Marx's misformulated 'Asiatic mode of production' (Abu-Lughod, 1989; Chaudhuri, 1990; Frank and Gills, 1996; Goody, 1996; Frank, 1998). Rather than being backward and stag-nant, the medieval economies of Asia were often the 'engine room' of Eurasia's world economic system, to which much of Europe (outside Italy and Flanders) was a mere peripheral and 'backward' appendage. Such a perspective is crucial to an overdue rectification of our under-standing of the relative contributions of 'East' and 'West' (or Asia and Europe) to the history of capitalism in particular, and to world history in general (Hodgson, 1974, 1993; Lombard, 1975; Frank, 1998).

But chasing the phantom of 'capitalism' in world history would prove to be an illusion. What is more important is to try to understand the real role of 'capital' and capital accumulation in world economic history, though there may or may not be sufficient evidence to designate entire social formations as 'capitalism'. Understanding the social power of the capitalist class is a more realistic goal. As I have suggested, where there is 'capital', there is also a capitalist class, whether in the ancient, medieval or modern periods of world history. Conventional understandings of economic history, whether liberal or Marxist, have tended to consider so-called 'merchant classes' as being pre-capitalist and therefore quite different from a proper capitalist class. The ubiquitous 'merchants' of world history are rarely if ever referred to by scholars as 'capitalists', though in many, if not all, cases that is exactly what they were. This conventional, and in my opinion false, view relies on the assumption that the merchant classes were separated from the sphere of production, i.e., operated exclusively in the sphere of circulation. However, historical evidence exists to suggest that such a strict separation between production and circulation is not accurate. So-called 'merchants' typically operated in a network of interlocking spheres of capital, encompassing the production, commodity circulation and credit spheres. If this is the more common model of historical capitalist practice, the ancient and medieval 'merchant classes', whether Oriental or Occidental, represent the *capitalist class* of those periods and places. As Weber suggests: 'All over the world, for several millennia, the characteristic forms of the capitalist employment of wealth have been state-provisioning, tax-farming, the financing of colonies, the establishment of great plantations, trade, and money lending' (Weber, 1978: 614). Mogens Larsen (1967) has demonstrated that joint capital(ist) enterprises flourished in the second millennium BCE in Assyria and Anatolia. The noted Sumerologist Samuel Noah Kramer (1959) insisted that the third millennium BCE city of Lagash was a 'mixed' economy, 'partly socialistic and state-controlled, and partly capitalistic and free'. Capital is certainly old, if not ubiquitous.

Oriental versus Occidental historical capitalism(s)

Even when we trace the progress of the arts and sciences, notwithstanding the pains which the nations of the west have bestowed in cultivating such pursuits and conferring upon them, as it were, an impress of their own, we find ourselves uniformly recalled to the east as the place of their origin . . . Europe has no production which Asia has not; and most of those which she possesses in common with the latter are inferior (Heeren, 1833: 2–3).

Conventional wisdom tells us that 'capitalism' as an economic system was entirely a modern invention of European origin, which was later diffused to non-Europeans by trade, investment, colonialism and conquest. However, as I have already argued, 'capital' itself was an ancient, Eastern invention rather than a modern Western and European innovation. We can find support for this hypothesis in Weber, who argued, in discussing late medieval European capitalist practices relating to credit, that 'the forms themselves have perhaps a common Oriental (probably Babylonian) origin, and their influence on the Occident was mediated through Hellenistic and Byzantine sources' (Weber, 1978: 613).

Therefore, rather than interpreting world economic history as a case of Western capitalism versus Asian non-capitalism, it would be more correct to start from the assumption that there have been capitalist practices in both regions for a very long time indeed. However, the level of 'capitalisation', 'commodification' and 'commercialisation' in the economy has fluctuated in both regions over time, and this has influenced their position relative to each other. These fluctuations need to be empirically compared, but in a way that understands the rhythms of both Europe and Asia within the same world systemic context, which includes the mutuality of influence among the two major regions of Eurasia (McNeill, 1963; Curtin, 1984; Abu-Lughod, 1989; Hodgson, 1993; Bentley, 1993; Frank and Gills, 1996; Goody, 1996; Denemark *et al.*, 2000).

Even if 'historical capitalism' may have an Asiatic origin, there are important historical variations of capitalist practices between (teacher?) Orient and (pupil?) Occident. A key issue here is the nature of 'the firm', i.e., variations of type among joint capital ventures, partnerships and family enterprises, and their different institutional characters. Weber (1978: 379) held that the separation of the household from the workshop was known in both Occident and Orient, and was the typical system in Islamic cities. Likewise, the development of the 'firm' from a family name existed in China, and joint liability of the family stood behind the debts of the individual. Weber traced the roots of private commercial capitalistic enterprise (initially as *ad hoc* arrangements for long-distance trade) to Babylonian partnerships.

For Weber the crucial distinction between Occidental and Oriental enterprise rests in 'the separation of household and business for accounting and legal purposes, and the development of a suitable body of laws, such as the commercial register, elimination of dependence of the association and the firm upon the family, separate property of the private firm or limited partnership, and appropriate laws on bankruptcy' (Weber, 1978: 379). This distinctive contractual character of Western firms relates to the separation of private from commercial accounting. Therefore, 'The capitalist enterprise, created by the household which eventually retreats from it, thus is related from the very beginning to the "bureau" and the now obvious bureaucratisation of the private economy' (Weber, 1978: 379). Needless to say, we are still debating the relative merits of variations of the capitalist firm, its social and legal underpinnings and regulation, especially between Oriental and Occidental 'models' of capitalism. To Weber, and many who still follow him, it is these specific legal conventions that are the characteristic *uniquely* Occidental development (and source of superiority).

Rather than a false historical comparison between Western capitalist and Eastern non-capitalist economic practices, what emerges is a need for objective analysis of the distinctions between Eastern and Western *institutional variants* of capitalist practices. It follows from this premise that a serious enquiry into the history of capital must include a consideration of the extent to which these variants are culturally influenced and to what extent this matters. The question therefore arises of the relationship between religious systems, social institutions and ideology and historical capitalism(s) – a question of the utmost centrality and purpose, and which is, to some degree, another way of enquiring into the spiritual or moral aspects of political economy and their bearing on what we like to call 'civilisation' or 'culture' and even human progress.

Clearly, non-Western social systems and ideational forms are not necessarily incompatible with capitalist practices. On the contrary, capitalist relations have existed and even flourished within Islamic, Hindu and Confucian frameworks, to name but a few. Both Weber and Tawney, in their famous studies of this general problem, were concerned to investigate the idea that certain types of religious attitudes, particularly Northern European Protestantism, might be more conducive to capitalist practices than others. Chaudhuri's (1985) work certainly attests to the vitality of capitalist practices in the Indian Ocean during the medieval and early modern periods within both Muslim and Hindu religious frameworks. Rodinson's (1974) analysis of Islam and capitalism rejects the idea that Islam was incompatible with capitalism or was responsible for the relative backwardness of the Muslim world in the modern era. Rodinson's interpretation stands in sharp contrast to the usual (mis?)reading of Weber on Islam, which views Islam as being on the whole an impediment to modern capitalist development (Turner, 1974). To be fair, however, Weber was more concerned about the institutional impediments to the emergence of a Western-style bourgeoisie in Islamic social systems, such as patrimonialism, than he was about intrinsic religious obstacles to any form of capitalism. Jack Goody (1996) has argued that there were no deep impediments that were structural, such as differences in rationality, that prevented the oscillation of power between East and West, but rather only more immediate contingent ones. David Landes (1998) has recently tried to revive 'orientalist' prejudices within this debate, by arguing that both Islamic and Chinese thought-systems were inhospitable to modern development, in contrast to the superiority of the Judaeo-Christian tradition. Jim Blaut (1992: 366) considers the presumption of rationality as the cause of Western superiority to be the supreme example of Eurocentrism in historical thinking. Recently, revisionist authors have rejected the inherent incompatibility of Confucian values with capitalism, rediscovering 'Confucian capitalism' as a dynamic and competitive historical variant in the contemporary world. Interestingly, they note its familistic and network-oriented organisational approach to enterprise and credit. Samir Amin (1988: 84) has argued that many religious or social-ideational frameworks, including Christianity, Islam and Confucianism, may function as ideologies of capitalism.

Indeed, the spirit of acquisitiveness that animates capitalist practices was to be found widely dispersed in both the ancient and medieval world, across both Occident and Orient. Weber sums up the point best: '... the ancient and medieval business temper... typical of all genuine traders, whether small businessmen or large-scale moneylenders, in Antiquity, the Far East, India, the Mediterranean littoral area, and the Occident of the Middle Ages: [is] the will and the wit to employ mercilessly every chance of profit, "for the sake of profit to ride through Hell even if it singes the sails"' (Weber, 1978: 614).

In conclusion, therefore, recognising the common existence of capitalist practices in East and West for much of world history allows us to reassess completely the overarching dynamic of the world system and the capital accumulation process on a world scale. This is the intention of world system theory: to reveal the common rhythms, the competition and rivalry, and the mutual influence among all the zones of the world economy over a period of several millennia, without prejudice as to cultural or religious orientation, but with an objective structural emphasis on the process of capital accumulation on the world scale and the real patterns of this process, both in terms of the 'long cycles' of world economic expansion and contraction, and the 'centre shifts' between rival economic and political power centres.

Capital versus *oikos*

I identify the historical tension between 'capital' and '*oikos*' (two perennial 'forms' of economic organisation) as a key theme of world history. The pairing of these two 'forms' (i.e., abstract types or categories into which many specific or concrete historical examples may be fitted or organised analytically) implies an antagonism and not just a mere juxtaposition for purposes of comparison. Their antagonism is deep-rooted. Capital has an innate antagonism to communal property, and to its social ethos. Capital by its very nature does not easily co-exist with communal forms of property nor with 'reciprocity' as a norm governing exchange relations in society. Capital is fundamentally based on private property and commodified exchange relations, and on the acquisitive spirit (or the *appetitus divitiarum infinitus* – the unbridled indulgence of the acquisitive spirit), which generates a specific species of asymmetrical relationships between both individuals and classes.

The opposition between capital and *oikos* is, therefore, based on their different uses of property and labour in pursuit of the production and extraction of surplus. This antagonism has existed from the earliest emergence of these two forms in world history and has persisted until the present era. It is even possible that capital's first emergence was associated with the dissolution of original *oikos* forms, such as the redistributive temple and palace economies, or the self-sufficient or manorial household economy. Their antagonism generates not only conflict or tension between the forms themselves, but also a class conflict. The inter-elite class conflict between the capitalist class and the landed or 'feudal' classes is a constant feature throughout world history. The state is a terrain of this contest and is pulled in both directions. Moreover, these conflicts spill over into, and involve, class conflict between the elite, propertied classes and the common or labouring classes. The tension between these contending forms is also implicated in another great conflict of human history, that between 'civilisation' and 'barbarism' and the unrelenting expansionist tendency of the former. The 'free' tribal areas of the world have, for the past several millennia, been inexorably 'incorporated' into the ever-expanding purview of civilisation and the world system, with its hierarchical class relations. Trade, colonisation and conquest have ever been key levers in this long and bloody encounter between cultures based on radically different social ecologies and organising principles (Wolf, 1982; Josephy, 1995; Wilson, 1998)

Karl Rodbertus first developed the concept of the '*oikos* economy', and, more importantly, the idea of its dominance throughout ancient economic history, which has been widely accepted. Thus, the conventional (and Eurocentric) view of world history teaches us that in the medieval era there was a ubiquity of the manor (and the guild) and a paucity of capital. Karl Bucher regarded the *oikos* as one of the 'stages' in his grand historical developmental scheme. Gordon Childe (1942) analysed the role of the royal (or palace) and manorial (household) estates in Bronze Age Near Eastern economic history, which he regarded (from an underconsumptionist perspective) as a constraint upon economic development because of the concentration of the surplus among a narrow elite.

For Weber (1978: 379, 381), the *oikos* is a variant of the development of the undifferentiated or unified household, which combines 'household', 'workshop' and 'office'. It is 'the authoritarian household of a prince, manorial lord, or patrician. Its dominant motive is not capitalistic acquisition but the lord's organised want satisfaction in kind.' Weber complicates the definition, however, by allowing that the lord of the *oikos* may use 'any means, including large-scale trade', and 'market-oriented enterprises' may even be 'attached to it' (Weber, 1978: 379, 381). Nevertheless, the 'utilisation of property' is decisive for the *oikos* lord, 'not capital investment'. Above a fairly low level of technological development, it is worth noting that the *oikos* is 'rarely a purely collective natural economy, for it can exist purely only if it permanently eliminates all exchange' and aims at autarky or self-sufficiency (Weber, 1978: 381).

Overall, a key characteristic of the *oikos* is its tendency to make use of dependent, household-tied or unfree labour, rather than 'free' or commodified wage labour. Weber refers to the tendency of the *oikos* to use 'an apparatus of house-dependent labor' and 'personally unfree labor', which can be highly specialised, but which produces all of the goods and services which the lord requires, often using raw materials from the lord's land, with his own workshops producing all other materials. Other services are provided by attached servants, officials, priests and warriors. The *oikos* form is therefore associated with family, kinship, household and the state (or royal household), emphasising inter-personal mutual obligations and tied labour. Therefore, normally, transfers of value in the *oikos* sphere are analytically outside the category of capital. Certain types of the transfer of value, however, can and should be treated under the category of the *oikos* form. These include, for example, taxation paid to the state (whether in kind, cash or labour), tithes paid to the church (in kind, cash or labour), rents or dues paid to the lord of a manorial household estate (via cash, kind or labour services) and 'gifts' given under a variety of obligations in inter-personal relations, both public and private in nature.

These associations of capital and *oikos* with contrasting types of labour and value transfer bring us to the theme of 'free' versus 'unfree' labour in world economic history (discussed further below). It would be misleading, however, to assume a strict or absolute opposition in which *oikos* always equals unfree labour and capital always equals free labour. The real situation is far more complex. Historically, although *oikos* units (e.g., of the paradigmatic 'high feudalism' of medieval Norman-Frankish Europe) did maintain servants and workers wholly dependent on the lord's household, implying that 'autarkic utilization of labor' existed, the normal case was one in which only a part of the unfree workforce was completely tied to their household (Weber, 1978: 382). Capital, on the other hand, given its proclivity to production of commodities for exchange, does indeed utilise free labour; however, it also utilises unfree labour, including slavery, for the same purpose, and perhaps more profitably. Weber calls this practice 'capitalist utilization of unfree labor' and cites examples of the use of unfree workers for production for the market, ranging from ancient Carthaginian estates to Russian landlords' use of serfs in their factories. According to Weber, given the *oikos* unit's use of market-oriented production, 'there is a scale of imperceptible transitions between the two modes of economic orientation, and often also a more or less rapid transformation from one into the other' (Weber, 1978: 381).

At no point is either form, capital or *oikos*, entirely eliminated from economic history. A complete reversion to the *oikos* form, if possible, would mean the end of capital and capital accumulation, an idea implicit in Marx's 'eschatology'. The possibility of the historical elimination of capital accumulation was central to the idea of world revolution and communism in the twentieth century. The 'end of history' was actually the end of capital. Communist society was to be achieved via expropriation of all private property and the planned management of all resources (by the state) on behalf of the entire society. In previous eras of history also, the ideal society of dissenting or 'anti-hegemonic' social movements often included a return or reversion to *oikos* forms and either the complete elimination or severe curtailing of capital. In contemporary liberal economic orthodoxy and particularly in the idea of 'globalisation', there is an implicit notion of a very different 'end of history', in which perhaps the *oikos* form is eliminated and all economic life is organised via the 'free market', private enterprise and capital accumulation.

Finally, in terms of 'long cycles', the 'dialectic of forms' between capital and *oikos* (and by association between free and unfree labour) takes the form of an oscillation, fluctuation or historical tension between the tendency towards greater commercialisation, commodification and capitalisation of the economy and its opposite tendency towards greater de-commercialisation, de-commodification, and de-capitalisation. In this opposition, greater 'capitalisation', or the rising prevalence of capital, is associated with elaboration of the division of labour, specialisation, commerce and monetisation, and usually with greater urbanisation. These economic forces bear a direct relation to changes in state formation and the emergence of sophisticated, centralised and bureaucratised forms of state power. *Oikos* predominance, by contrast, is associated with reversion to 'natural economy' and thus with de-monetisation, de-commercialisation, de-commodification and de-capitalisation. These economic processes are associated with concomitant political processes, involving different modes of organisation, such as less centralised and bureau-cratic state organisation, and de-centralised or fragmented political authority.

Free versus unfree labour

'Free versus unfree labour' should not be understood as a clear linear progression in world history, but rather as a perennial dialectical tension. Moreover, this historical dialectic of 'free versus unfree labour' is a central aspect of world economic history. Its patterns should, therefore, be sys-tematically investigated in relation to changing configurations of power, and in particular to the historical dialectic of forms of 'capital versus *oikos*' and to the 'long cycles' of expansion and contraction, capitalisation and de-capitalisation, and equilibrium and crisis.

The definitions of the categories 'free' and 'unfree' labour depend on the juridical, social relational and institutional aspects governing the re-lations of transfer of labour value. The key element in distinguishing the forms and understanding their nuances is the socio-legal relations sur-rounding each concrete historical instance. Such socio-legal conditions of labour delineate the conditions of servitude, or obligation, on the one hand, and the legal provisions for protection of the person from (ex-treme) exploitation, on the other. The free labour category requires a definition whereby the person is separated legally, and in practice, from his/her labour power, which is why it can be associated with the 'free wage'. In the case of unfree labour, the person is not completely sepa-rated from his/her own labour power. Henry Brooks Adams (1895) dis-cussed Roman civilisation in terms of the great importance of law that was deliberately crafted by the Roman upper classes to favour the in-terests of (money) capital – it was explicitly designed to convert (free) debtors into (unfree) slaves. Mary Frances Cusack (1995: 144) con-trasted this 'cruel severity of the law of the insolvent debtors', character-istic of Roman practice, to the 'milder and more equitable arrangements' of Celtic law and practices, as embodied in the Brehon Code. 'By the Roman enactments, the person of the debtor was at the mercy of his creditor, who might sell him for a slave... The Celt allowed only the seizure of goods, and even this was under regulations most favourable to the debtor.'

Just as we have noted that there are variants of the 'enterprise' in the history of capital, likewise there are myriad and often quite complex vari-ants of labour forms in the ancient, medieval and modern periods. De Ste. Croix (1981: 53) recognises three primary forms of surplus extraction:

wages, coerced labour and rent. These basic forms are not always pure and separate, and often occur in complex combinations. The rule is that choice of form and variant of labour ultimately depends on what yields the highest returns to capital under prevailing economic conditions. Weber notes that the incipient combinations based on the possession of raw materials, as found in Athenian *ergasterion*, was further developed in the Hellenistic period (especially in Alexandria) and up to early Islamic times. The utilisation of unfree craftsmen, or specialised skilled workers, was common as a source of rent throughout antiquity in both Orient and Occident, during the medieval period, and into early modern times until the emancipation of the Russian serf (in 1861). The arrangement whereby the master leaves it to the trained slave to work on their own account in exchange for a rent is known from ancient Babylonian times (*mandaku*), through the classical period (Greek: *apophora*) to medieval European (German: *Halssteuer*) and early modern times (Russian: *obrok*). In other variants, the owner may provide workshop equipment (*peculiam*) and working capital (*merx peculiaris*). In fact, 'Historically, we find all imaginable transitions from almost total mobility to complete regimentation in barracks' (Weber, 1978: 383).

Hereditary unfree labour allows the 'full exploitation of labor power', but the decision by the master as to whether to use his unfree labour either as a workforce or as a source of rent 'depends above all on what yields most to him in a given situation' (Weber, 1978: 382). Hereditary unfree labour was not for the most part employed in centralised enterprises, but surrendered 'only part of their work capacity to the master', paying him a kind of 'fixed tax' (rent) in kind or money. The reproduction of 'barrack slaves' requires continual fresh supplies of slaves (from wars, raids or purchase) and low food costs, whereas hereditary-attached peasants and their families can pay a money rent only when local markets are available (to dispose of their surplus production), this availability being, in turn, dependent on some level of urban development. Under conditions where this was low and export of crops was the only avenue to fully exploit the harvest (as in Germany, the European East and the 'black earth' area of Russia in the nineteenth century), then the forced labour of peasants was the only way to make money (Weber, 1978: 382).

We should be especially wary of the idea of a straight-line progression in world history in regard to the form of labour, i.e., the idea of the gradual 'liberation' or 'emancipation' of labour, progressing from extremely unfree 'slavery' in the ancient period, through somewhat less unfree 'serfdom' in medieval times, to the final realisation of universal 'free' labour in the modern era of global capitalism. Actually, the institution of slavery has been a constant feature of world economic history from ancient, through medieval, and into recent times (Thomas, 1998). We know that the expansion of 'capital' is not exclusively associated with the expansion of free labour. In the case of the florescence of capitalist practices in the Occident both in the ancient Hellenistic/Roman period and (some 1,500 years later) in early modern Europe (the time of the 'primitive accumulation' of capital), there was an unmistakable and close association between the expansion of capitalist practices and slavery. The pivotal role of the slave trade (Williams, 1964; Thomas, 1998) and slave labour in the origins of 'modern capitalism' on a world scale tells us that no linear trend in the emancipation of labour is associated with capital in world history. Slavery is once again on the increase in the contemporary world economy, in areas ranging from Eastern European and Southeast Asian sex trades to the bonded child labour in India and plantation labour in West Africa.

The fundamental reason that the expansion of capital and the emergence of 'historical capitalism' is not associated exclusively with the 'emancipation' of labour resides in the very nature of 'capital' itself, which thrives on an increase in the rate of exploitation. This tendency to seek an increase in the rate of exploitation of labour is simply the underlying logic of capital as a social relation, i.e., to extract surplus value and to accumulate a profit. This quest for an increase in the 'rate of profit' affects industrial wage labour (e.g., via the immiseration of the proletariat, denounced by Marx as an inherent tendency of capital accumulation, or more recently via the 'flexibilisation' of labour and the global mobility of capital in search of lower labour costs), and leads to the proliferation of slavery (Thomas, 1998) and the drive to establish (neo)colonial forms of subjugation.

Therefore, class struggles between labour (both free and unfree) and capital are an intrinsic element in the history of capital and its role in world economic history, whether we are speaking of ancient, medieval or modern capital.

The upshot of all this is that we must pay very close attention to how the changes in forms of labour are related to wider social, political and systemic conditions in world economic history, and particularly to the 'long cycles' or 'pulsations' (oscillations that are not truly 'cyclical', but recurrent or repetitive in pattern) – such as 'capitalisation' versus 'de-capitalisation', and expansion versus crisis or 'entropy' – in world economic history. It may be most important when reconsidering the 'transitions' to examine why the conditions of capital accumulation changed when and where they did. The particular focus on European experience has generated an image of history wherein unfree labour became associated with economic backwardness or 'feudalism', and free labour, with progress and 'capitalism'.

World historical patterns

As Chaudhuri says, the real question is not about defining *capitalism* or seeking its origins, since *capital* and capitalist practices have been a consistent part of world economic- and social-history. The real significance of a thorough re-examination of the role of capital in world history is in judging its systemic social effects: economically, politically, ideologically and culturally. In particular, the relationship of capital's expansion to world systemic patterns must be a central analytical issue for international political economy, and the fertile meeting place of historical sociology and international relations.

As Weber observed, 'again and again we find that it is precisely in the periods of "justice and order" – equivalent of course to periods of economic stability – that there occurred a swift decline of *capitalism*' (Weber, 1976: 66). It is perhaps the greatest peculiarity of the West, and its particular modern variant of historical capitalism, that it gave so much freedom to capital to exploit labour and to threaten the larger economic system with disequilibrium. World system history, or 'global history', can be seen as a perpetual social contestation between the impetus to allow capital to expand unrestrained, and the impetus to constrain predatory capitalism and protect labour and society from its depredations. The current debate over the relationship between globalisation and global capitalism might benefit from such a world historical perspective.

Rather than interpreting world economic history as a linear series of stages, in which there was one and only one 'transition to capitalism', I suggest that there have been successive waves of capitalisation, and that there have been likewise recurrent phases of de-capitalisation. A de-capitalisation phase is associated with a decline in the prevalence of capital, and therefore, a relative increase in the prevalence of the *oikos* forms. A capitalisation phase, on the other hand, is associated with an increase in the prevalence of capital, usually at the expense of *oikos* forms. This implies changing levels of commodity production, exchange, commercialisation and monetisation of the economic system in each phase. These long-term processes are understood to be not only recurrent but also not geographically confined to Europe. Capitalisation, understood in this way, supersedes the idea of a single historical 'transition to capitalism' which took place only in early modern Europe. Likewise, 'de-capitalisation' or 'feudalisation' is understood in a way that supersedes the idea of a single historic transition or 'passage' from the slave society of late antiquity to the serfdom of medieval feudal society in Europe (Anderson, 1974). Finally, in regard to these centuries-long patterns of change, we can reassess in what sense they represent economic retrogression or progression and how this is related to changing forms of class structure and political power at state and inter-state level.

The historic retrogression we call the Dark Ages in Western Europe is only one example of many historical cases of economic or systemic 'entropy'. The decline and fragmentation of bureaucratic states and empires is part of the rhythm of history. The centralised (and bureaucratic) state, and its reliance on a monetised revenue system, acts as a social dissolvent of 'feudal' or aristocratic social power and as a facilitator of commercialisation, commodification and capitalisation. However, following S. N. Eisenstadt, over-exploitation of the revenue base by the state depletes the 'flexible resources' necessary to the centralised state's existence, giving rise to a counter-tendency of the 'aristocratisation' of the state, which undermines the bureaucratic order. These patterns push the system towards disintegration and economic retrogression to 'simpler, patrimonial, or at most feudal, units' (Eisenstadt, 1963). In my view, 'feudalisation' is not a mode of production experienced at a stage of development in a linear evolutionary sequence, but rather an aspect of the 'entropy' phase in the 'hegemonic cycle' experienced by virtually all empires or civilisations in history. This can also be modelled as patterns of the 'centralisation and decentralisation of accumulation'. Michael Mann identifies the 'core of world-historical development' as the dialectic between two variants of power configuration: 'empires of domination' and 'multi-power-actor civilisations' (Mann, 1986).

To summarise: if we begin from the assumption of the continuous presence of capital and of capitalist social relations in economic history, we can look for the historic 'ebb and flow' of capital and the process of capital accumulation, both 'locally' and at the world scale. This provides a framework through which to assess the 'progression and retrogression' of economic and political history as judged by the levels of 'capitalisation' versus ' de-capitalisation' – the latter being another way of understanding or expressing 'feudalisation' as an aspect of 'entropy' (Gills, 1993). It is these fluctuations in the level of historic capitalisation and de-capitalisation, and their attendant social and political forms, that we must attempt to understand or explain.

Class conflict must therefore be a central aspect of the study of such world historical patterns. This may occur in the form of 'class struggles and revolutions', whether between creditors and debtors or between capitalists and workers (including slaves and tenants), and does not necessarily aim at 'a change of the economic system', but rather at 'a redistribution of wealth' (Weber, 1978: 303–4). It is in the political and class struggles that we can closely examine the social power aspects of 'the dialectic of forms', in the contestation between capital and *oikos*, and in the changing role and status of labour and capital in world history. Therefore, the 'dual dialectic' of world history involves the relationship between the dialectic of 'capital versus *oikos*' and 'free versus unfree labour'. These dialectics, I argue, are at the heart of the 'rise and fall' of patterns of states in world history. Above all, we must abandon the idea of the single transition, in favour of the idea of multiple transitions in space and time, in a dialectical rather than a linear pattern. This implies fundamentally re-examining our ideas concerning the nature of progression and retrogression in world history and adopting a model in which 'cyclical' patterns of 'organisation' versus 'entropy' play a greater explanatory or heuristic role.[3] Current social contestations surrounding 'globalisation', both its causes and consequences, can be better historically grounded and understood though a dialectical global history perspective. Are we in a period of (Quigleyian) expansion of world civilisation and global capitalism, or a period of (Gillsian) entropy and 'implosion'? Will the ever deepening crisis of global polarisation engendered by the expansion of capital over the past thirty years be resolved by yet further 'freedom' via the 'free market' enjoyed by capital, or by concerted social action, spanning the globe, to impose controls on capital that restrain its unbridled expansion? The future of humanity may, as history teaches us, depend on the answer we give to this question.

[3] I am very grateful to Robert W. Cox for his comments on this chapter and for encouraging me in correspondence to emphasise my model of 'organisation versus entropy' as a cyclical pattern and heuristic device for understanding world history.

8 Towards a critical historical sociology of transnational harm

Andrew Linklater

This chapter employs the notion of cross-border or transnational harm to lay the foundations of a larger project which supports recent efforts to bridge the gulf between historical sociology and international relations. A central aim is to develop a conceptual framework which will at some later date yield useful comparisons and contrasts between different international systems. A more specific objective is to place contemporary efforts to protect human beings from unnecessary suffering and harm in comparative perspective.

Transnational harm refers to injury which the state, or non-state actors, or forms of social organisation do to the members of other societies. Harm raises important ethical issues in world politics, although concern with transnational harm has not been central to political thought throughout the history of international relations, and may not have featured prominently, or at all, in many earlier epochs. Support for this last observation is found in the statement that popular thinking in Ancient Greece was 'pervaded by the assumption that one should help one's friends and harm one's enemies' (Blundell, 1989: 26), and in the contention that few writers on the Ancient World 'have ever denied (and no Greek would have done so) that in warfare one has an obligation to inflict maximum damage on the enemy while producing maximum advantage for one's own side' (Blundell, 1989: 52).[1] Modern political communities appear to differ from those societies in crucial respects. A recent work has maintained that modern societies would be repelled by the forms of cruelty which were common in the Roman Empire and widespread throughout the Ancient World (Finer, 1997: 440).

The ethical problem of transnational harm may be a recent development, but just how recent is the intriguing question. Reflecting wider social attitudes, many of the seventeenth- and eighteenth-century international lawyers believed that states should avoid causing harm to each

I am grateful to Hidemi Suganami, Chris Phillipson, Ed Page, Michael Redclift and the conference participants for their comments on an earlier draft of this chapter.
[1] For different emphases, see Bauslaugh (1991) and Hanson (1998).

162

other. An example is Pufendorf (1927, 42:1) who argued that the principle that 'no-one should injure another' should be an 'absolute' in the society of states just as it had been in the original state of nature. Other quotations could easily be compiled, noting parallel sentiments in earlier times, but the more demanding task is to understand how far societies have made a moral concern with transnational harm one of their organising principles. In this context, it is worth asking whether any document prior to the Declaration of the Rights of Man and the Citizen made harm central to the constitutive principles of society.[2] The fact though that the Declaration focused on the harm which citizens do to each other, and on the injuries that states cause their own citizens, rather than on the harm states do to each other, raises the question of whether transnational harm has only become a profoundly important moral issue in more recent times.[3]

An additional question is whether moderns have progressed beyond the ancients in making the ethics of harm a central theme in their politics or simply display their cruelty in different ways.[4] This matter raises issues which lie outside the scope of this chapter. Suffice it to note that the moral question of transnational harm is important in the recent history of the modern system of states – possibly more so than in earlier times, although more research is required to ascertain whether this is the case. The key point is that there are intriguing comparisons to make and important contrasts to draw between the modern states system and earlier inter-societal systems. Understanding what has changed, and what has remained the same, is the main ambition of a sociology of transnational harm.

The chapter is in three parts. The first locates the research project which is outlined here in the wider literature on historical sociology and international relations. The second part considers some of the central conceptual issues in the sociology of transnational harm, while the final part raises a fundamental question about modernity which is of particular importance for the sociology of harm. This is whether the dominant forms of harm in international history have been reduced significantly, at least in relations between the most affluent core members of the world-system,

[2] Article 5 of the Declaration stated that 'legislation is entitled to forbid only those actions which are harmful to society', while Article 4 defined liberty as 'the capacity to do anything that does no harm to others' (see Finer, 1997: 1539).
[3] It is important to note here the long tradition of thought on the subject of 'non-combatant community' which becomes a key matter for international law in the Enlightenment (Thakur and Malley, 1999).
[4] The reference is to Foucault's claim that 'humanity does not gradually progress' to a condition of 'universal reciprocity' but 'proceeds from domination to domination'. See Rabinow (1986: 85).

or whether they have simply been reconfigured in the most recent phase of globalisation.

Beyond state-centric historical sociology

Leading efforts to develop links between historical sociology and international relations have made the state central to social and political inquiry. In sociology, the state and war have not always been at the heart of the analysis – hence the project of 'bringing the state back in' (Evans, Rueschemeyer and Skocpol, 1985). In international relations, the state has always been fundamental, although attempts to determine what the field can learn from historical sociologists are a recent trend. Efforts to reclaim the state for social theory have removed some barriers between sociology and international relations which blocked the development of a more comprehensive understanding of history and politics. The framework of analysis which will be developed in this chapter recognises the need for forms of historical sociology in which the state is central, but it differs from earlier approaches which have largely focused on the interplay between society, state, geopolitics and war. In this chapter the focus is on the moral and cultural dimensions of political communities, and particularly on that area of the moral code which specifies the forms of harm which are either permitted or prohibited in relations with foreigners. Borrowing from Walzer's (1980) work on war, I call this part of the moral code, the harm convention.

To explain how the present approach differs from other perspectives, it is useful to distinguish among three ways in which the state has been analysed in historical sociology. First, over the last two decades, sociologists such as Skocpol (1979), Giddens (1985), Mann (1986) and Tilly (1990) have argued that nationalism, the territorial state and war have been neglected by mainstream sociology and Marxism. Their argument has been that social structures and social change cannot be understood without placing societies in their geopolitical context. Each writer argued that elements of classical realism should be more central to sociological investigation without treating this perspective uncritically. Giddens (1985), for example, noted that realism was as guilty as Marxism of proposing a single-logic explanation of history and politics – and unlike Marxism it lacked a commitment to critical theory.

The emergence of neorealism led to a second form of state-centric historical sociology in the study of international relations. Waltz (1979) argued that neorealism superseded other perspectives because it explained why international politics have not changed across the millennia. His emphasis was on continuity rather than change (which is central to the historical sociologists mentioned earlier). In an important critique of neo-realism, Ruggie (1983) argued that it was unable to explain one of the great revolutions in international relations, the shift from medieval to modern international society. In a rejoinder, Fischer (1992) replied that geopolitical continuities were more significant than the differences between the types of political association found in the two historical periods. Although the nature of political community changed as the modern world replaced the medieval era, international anarchy persisted, compelling human collectivities to adopt the politics of self-help with respect to security and survival.

The debate has been joined in more recent times by those who argue that neorealism is flawed precisely because it thinks that all states systems are variations on eternal themes (Rosenberg, 1994; Reus-Smit, 1999). The appearance of structural realism is crucial in this regard. Influenced by neorealism, structural realism takes far greater account of international political change, including the evolution of different forms of political association and diverse types of exchange and interaction (Buzan and Little, 1994, 2000). There are similarities between this approach and the broad movement within sociology mentioned earlier, but the primary aim is to develop the realist contribution to international relations theory. This approach is the third form of state-centric historical sociology to emerge in recent years.[5]

State-centric historical sociology is a major development in the social sciences, and its influence will be evident in the rest of this discussion with its focus on the nature of bounded communities. But as previously noted, the emphasis of this chapter is not on state power, military organisation and war-fighting capabilities but on the moral and cultural forces which shape harm conventions in different international systems. States are as important for this approach as they are for other branches of historical sociology. This is because they remain the principal rule-makers in international society and retain an unusual capacity to regulate the pace of international legal change notwithstanding the growing importance of non-state organisations. In particular, states have an unrivalled ability to decide whether or not the society of states will introduce robust cosmopolitan harm conventions – conventions which are designed to protect peoples everywhere from unnecessary harm.

Conceptions of the moral rights against and duties to the rest of humanity are at the centre of this approach to political communities. What is critical is whether the moral boundaries of community are drawn in such

---

[5] Buzan and Little's interest in contributing to, and drawing from, the English School further distinguishes this approach from the other perspectives which have been mentioned.

a way that harm to outsiders is a way of life, whether they are constructed around the conviction that there are obligations to minimise suffering to outsiders, or whether they are shaped by a strong conviction that the state and international society should strive to reduce transnational harm. Put differently, the central concern is what separate societies regard as permissible in their dealings with outsiders, what they regard as optional and what they think is absolutely proscribed.

This is not to suggest that the social sciences in general are guilty of neglecting these issues. Many perspectives are relevant to the analysis of harm conventions even though their centres of gravity may lie elsewhere. An important task therefore is to bring together their most valuable features. In this brief overview, it may be useful to comment on the most salient characteristics of three distinctive approaches.

The first is the 'English School' of international relations, and especially Wight's pathbreaking work on the sociology of states systems (Wight, 1977). Developing a theme which was present in the writings of thinkers such as Grotius and Kant, Wight maintained that three different communities make claims upon political actors in all international societies. They are the state, the society of states and the cosmopolitan community of humankind.[6] Having made these distinctions, Wight raised the important sociological question of how states create order between themselves and how far different international orders have succeeded in supporting cosmopolitan arrangements which are not concerned with order between states but with justice for individuals.

This approach is relevant to the development of a sociology of harm in two important respects. First, as noted earlier, the institutions that comprise a society of states are designed to reduce the harm that states do to each other. Developing these institutions is no small achievement but it is also interesting to ask how far international societies have created cosmopolitan conventions which are designed to reduce harm to individuals and non-state communities such as minority nations and indigenous peoples. For the most part, the English School has been concerned with order and the control of harm in relations between states, but its members have also focused on the question of justice and on the prospects for an international society which is designed to alleviate the suffering of individuals (see Donelan 1990; Wheeler, 2000). The relationship between order and justice in international systems should be a central theme in the sociology of transnational harm.

---

[6] Wight's classification is mirrored in Mann's more recent discussion of the triple power network in Ancient Greece (Mann, 1986: ch. 7).

An additional point concerns the relationship between dialogue and harm. The English School claims that all societies of states have developed arrangements for facilitating dialogue between states. An intriguing question which is suggested by the approach is how far the modern society of states has extended the commitment to dialogue both horizontally and vertically – horizontally by admitting new societies into the diplomatic community, vertically by extending the right of participation in that community to individuals and non-state actors so that they can also protest against actual or potential injury and distress. Implicit in the approach is the question of how far the society of states can develop forms of dialogue through which individuals and non-state actors, as well as national states, can create harm conventions which protect the interests of all. As noted elsewhere, this is the point at which the English School contributes to an analysis of the prospects for a universal communication community as envisaged by Habermas's discourse ethics (Linklater, 1998).

The comparative-sociological perspective which is associated with Weber's writings and which was extended in several major essays by Benjamin Nelson is a second approach which is relevant to a sociology of transnational harm. In 'Religious Views of the World' Weber (1948: 329) argued that 'two elemental principles' were dominant in the early religions: 'the dualism of in-group and out-group morality', and the belief in the principle, 'as you do unto me, I shall do unto you'. Reciprocity in morals only applied in relations between insiders: it did not extend to relations with outsider groups. Weber (1948: 330) added that the 'ethically rationalised religions' such as Christianity and Islam moved dramatically in 'the direction of a universalist brotherhood, which [went] beyond all barriers of societal associations' so that care (*caritas*) was shown to the enemy. Those world religions overcame the limitations of earlier moralities and defended harm conventions which were considered to embrace the whole human race.

Nelson argued that Weber focused on the evolution of these solidarities *within* the major world civilisations; a further task was to inquire into whether and how cosmopolitan sentiments had developed in relations *between* civilisations. Nelson posed the questions of how far different civilisations have been prepared to treat outsiders as equals within universal 'communities of discourse' and whether this commitment seems likely to become stronger in contemporary international relations (Nelson, 1974). There is a clear parallel here with the analysis of the expansion of international society that is to be found in the English School (Bull and Watson, 1984). However, the comparative study of civilisations as developed by Weber and Nelson is a distinctive source of ideas and insights for a study of the development of global frameworks of communication which are designed to reduce or eradicate suffering caused by transnational harm.

It is possible to analyse these dynamics of world politics without subscribing to the agenda of critical theory, although the English School analysis of international society and Nelson's comparative study of civilisations both regard dialogue as a positive value in relations between human collectivities. The importance of dialogue is the starting point for a third approach which contributes to the study of transnational harm, namely Habermas's account of the structure of moral codes. Habermas has claimed that the most advanced moral perspectives insist that political decisions lack legitimacy unless they have the consent of all who stand to be affected by them – unless they have, from the vantage-point of this chapter, the consent of all who may be harmed by them. In the context of globalisation, this constituency may include the whole human race and cannot be narrowly confined to those who have special rights and duties as members of the same society. Studies of cosmopolitan democracy have asked how this normative commitment can be realised in practice (Held, 1995; Archibugi, Held and Kohler, 1999). These critical perspectives are a third strand of thought contributing to the sociological project outlined in this chapter. Along with the others surveyed, they enlarge the province of the sociology of international relations by shifting the analysis from the relationship between state-building, social structures and geopolitical rivalry to the moral and cultural forces which underpin efforts to reduce unnecessary suffering experienced by the individual members of the human race.

Conceptual issues

Before proceeding further, it is essential to clarify the meaning of the notion of transnational harm. The *Oxford English Dictionary* defines harm as 'evil (physical or otherwise) as done to or suffered by some person or thing: hurt, injury, damage, mischief'. The effects of harm include 'grief, sorrow, pain, trouble, distress, affliction'. The *OED* defines 'transnational' as 'extending or having interests extending beyond national bounds or frontiers as in the case of a transnational company'.[7] The international lawyer, Philip Jessup (1956: 2), popularised this term in his work on 'transnational law', which is the 'law which regulates actions or events

---

[7] Norman Angell may have been the first to coin the term when he wrote that 'much of Europe lives by virtue of an international, or more correctly, a transnational economy'. See the entry for 'transnational' in the *Oxford English Dictionary*.

that transcend national frontiers', in contrast to international law, which is the law which regulates relations between states.[8]

This distinction between international and transnational relations has been used elsewhere in the literature in response to the latest phase of capitalist globalisation and in connection with increasing global inequalities of power and wealth. De-Shalit (1998: 693n2) has distinguished between 'transnational exploitation', which is 'exploitative exchange that takes place between bodies and individuals in different societies', and 'international exploitation', which is 'exploitative exchange that takes place between states'. In an essay on global distributive justice, O'Neill (1991) separates transnational justice, which is justice between the individual members of world society, from international justice, which is justice between states. In the same spirit, it is possible to distinguish between international harm – harm between states – and transnational harm – harm or injury which spreads across national boundaries causing suffering and distress to the individual members of society.

This is not a distinction to press too far because, for the greater part of world history, the harm that states do to each other has been a principal source of the harm that has been inflicted on the individual members of other societies. The distinction between international and transnational harm had greatest utility under conditions in which states had a limited ability to project their military power into the heartland of other societies. In these circumstances, international harm occurred as rival political communities tried to frustrate each other's strategic ambitions. There may not have been an intention to harm the individual members of other societies although, invariably, attempts to harm states, for example by frustrating their strategic objectives, harm individuals by exposing them to fear and insecurity. The 'industrialisation of war' increased the prospects for transnational harm since states acquired greater global reach (Giddens, 1985). Increasingly, the desire to harm other states involved military policies which caused harm to civilian populations, whether deliberate or not. That is not to say that the distinction between international and transnational harm lost all utility. The principle of non-combatant immunity exists because states believe that while it may be legitimate to

---

[8] It is also worth noting Aron's comment that 'international systems are the inter-state aspect of the society to which the populations, subject to distinct sovereignties, belong. Hellenic society or European society in the fifth century BC or in the twentieth century AD are realities, that we shall call transnational, rather than inter- or supranational.' For Aron (1966: 105), commercial exchange, international migration and shared beliefs, amongst other things, were indicators of the existence of a transnational society larger than the society of states and comprising more than the realm of geopolitical interaction. Similar indices were emphasised by Keohane and Nye (1971) in their writings on transnational relations and world politics.

harm each other in war, it is not legitimate to cause unnecessary suffering to their respective civilian populations.[9] Although it is impossible to separate these two phenomena, states continue to distinguish between international and transnational harm in their diplomatic language.

The rise of the state's capacity to project its power into the heartland of other societies requires a distinction between two types of transnational harm. The first is limited transnational harm in which states cause unintended 'collateral damage' to civilian populations in war. Members of the just war tradition have argued that injury of this kind is justified as long as it is unintended and in proportion to military objectives. A second type is indiscriminate transnational harm in which, as in the case of strategic bombing in the Second World War, states deliberately target non-combatants with the aim of destroying civilian morale. Forms of indiscriminate harm in the modern era have posed novel questions about how harm can be minimised in the context of the new military technology.

The fact that international harm has declined in some parts of the world while transnational harm is increasing is a further reason for separating the two concepts. In regions such as Western Europe, citizens are not made insecure by the threatening behaviour of neighbouring states. Feelings of insecurity are more likely to result from the operation of global market forces which create economic uncertainty and the danger of unemployment. In parts of the Third World, citizens may feel more threatened by their state's decision to co-operate with firms to import waste products which can endanger health than by the danger of inter-state warfare.[10] There is little doubt, however, that international harm – and specifically war and conquest – has been the main source of transnational harm for most of human history. The revolution in transnational harm is also the result of the globalisation of capitalist relations of production and exchange. This is the form of harm which seems certain to increase in the next phase of world history. In the modern period, the industrialisation of war and capitalist globalisation have encouraged the development of a sense of moral responsibility for the most vulnerable members of world society, just as the growing interconnectedness of the

---

[9] It may be useful to recall Rousseau's claim that 'now that the state of nature is abolished among us, war no longer exists between individuals'. In short, war takes place between states: 'so true is this, that a subject who, taking literally the terms of a declaration of war, would wish . . . to attack the Prince's enemies would be punished or at least should be' (Rousseau, 1970: 178). Another way of expressing this is to say that there is a distinction between war and murder, and that actions which are permissible in war do not excuse murderous acts on the part of individual citizens. A leading exponent of this line of argument argues that military personnel do not have the right to kill prisoners of war, nor do the latter have the right to kill their captors (Walzer, 1970: ch. 7).

[10] On state decisions to 'export' land to firms which move hazardous waste from the more affluent societies, see De-Shalit (1998: 717).

human species during the Enlightenment stimulated the development of cosmopolitan orientations; but many would argue that these moral sentiments have never been, or will ever be, strong enough to alter the course of global capitalism.

These last few observations lead to a further distinction between types of transnational harm. The important distinction is between concrete and abstract transnational harm.[11] Concrete harm is harm that actors intend to do to designated others. As suggested earlier, the dominant form of transnational harm in international history has been one in which particular societies have deliberately set out to harm others deemed unworthy of equal respect. Concrete harm remains important in the contemporary world, as outbreaks of ethnic violence remind us. In the case of abstract harm, agents do not intend harm to others; rather, harm is spread across national frontiers in an unintended and haphazard fashion by the operation of global relations of production and exchange and by the process of industrialisation which has caused environmental damage which human beings were not aware of until recently.[12] This is the kind of harm which grew in importance with the universalisation of social and economic relations during the age of European conquest and which has become increasingly important since the rise of global industrialisation. To put this another way, for most of international history harm has been *exported* from one society to another, the intention being to injure specific others, but in recent history harm is increasingly *transmitted* across boundaries – often unintentionally – by global market forces and industrial modes of production.[13]

[11] This distinction is modelled on Hegel's distinction between concrete and abstract labour. In the case of concrete labour, individuals satisfy their needs directly; with abstract labour, they do so indirectly as participants within a complex division of labour. With the former, the actions of individuals have tangible and predictable results, but with the latter, actions have diffuse and unintended consequences because they enter into a larger stream of social relations which actors do not control. Abstract transnational harm is an instance of what Marx called the condition of alienation.

[12] Put another way, agents are not the only form of transnational harm, and structures play their own part. Financial markets are an example since they lead to currency speculation and devaluations in other societies, with harmful consequences for citizens. Clearly there are agents here – currency speculators in particular – who are the immediate cause of harm. However, such agents come and go, but transnational harm survives as long as the relevant structures endure. Agents are the immediate, and structures the deeper, source of harm.

[13] The Chernobyl effect, for instance, was not the result of one state's wish to harm outsiders, although the possibility of external injury presumably did not escape those who introduced this technology. The same is true of market forces which cause transnational harm in the form of poverty and unemployment in various parts of the world. The fact that particular groups of human beings will continue to be harmed by these forces is perfectly predictable, but it is a moot point whether those who support market economies do so with the intention of causing harm to particular groups of human beings. It may be more important to refer to indifference to the harm suffered by others.

It is useful to connect these concerns with the study of international society. The desire to regulate international harm is the main reason why states form a society, in which various institutions such as diplomacy and international law preserve order among themselves, as opposed to a system characterised by geopolitical competition and the permanent danger of war (Bull, 1977). Rising levels of indiscriminate transnational harm created pressures to weave cosmopolitan harm conventions into the society of states. The most important examples have been the development of the humanitarian law of war from the time of the Nuremberg tribunals and the creation of international law which prohibits genocide. The industrialisation of war, which has made such developments necessary, is part of a much larger revolution in world history which has exposed increasing numbers of human beings to forms of harm which originate outside their respective communities. There is no doubt that the growing export of hazards and the strength of corporate power in the most recent phase of globalisation have been accompanied by powerful arguments in support of an ethic of responsibility for the vulnerable members of world society (Shue, 1981). Whether the growth of abstract transnational harm will lead to bolder efforts to embed cosmopolitan values in international society is the intriguing question. These matters have not been central to the study of international society. But they were central to Marx's thought, which regarded rising levels of abstract harm as symptomatic of a new phase of world history, and they have remained vital to the Marxist tradition.

It is well known that Marx believed that the rise of abstract transnational harm was the creative force which would lead to the institutionalisation of the highest cosmopolitan visions of the age. He argued that ruling classes had become more reflexive as they struggled to assess the consequences of distant events and developments – a necessity if they were to flourish, or survive, with intensifying global competition. Subordinate classes were forced to develop a global perspective, albeit for different reasons. Counteracting the forces of capitalist exploitation required transnational class struggle. This latter development was made easier by the emergence of the 'age of equalisation' (Scheler, quoted in De-Shalit, 1998: 421) in which ethnic, racial and other particularisms were losing much of their earlier importance as foundational principles of social life. Marx argued that these badges of identity lost their traditional significance as subordinate peoples everywhere shared the same experience of exposure to the world market. His conviction was that the dominant forms of transnational harm in the modern world would not be anchored in hierarchical conceptions of gender, race and ethnicity as much as they had been in the past. Capitalist globalisation tilted the axis from concrete to abstract transnational harm, emphatically and irreversibly in Marx's view.[14]

This was an astute reading of the character of capitalist modernity even though Marx was wrong that higher levels of abstract transnational harm would mean that more free and universalistic social relations would replace the particularisms of nation, state, religion and race. The First World War forced Marxists to reconsider Marx's view that concrete international harm was gradually disappearing, although the main theorists of nationalism and imperialism believed that conflict was a function of monopoly capitalism and no more than a temporary digression from the more fundamental transnational class struggle.

Over the last five decades, various forms of Marxism have developed an account of the harms that are inherent in a capitalist world economy. More attention should be paid to what these accounts mean for the study of international society. We have noted how the rise of indiscriminate transnational harm has led to changes in the normative structure of international society. The central question posed by the development of more abstract forms of harm is whether international society will make significant progress in dealing with the social consequences of the more abstract forms of harm caused by the expansion of capitalist globalisation. It is whether cosmopolitan harm conventions will be developed that protect individuals everywhere from the scourge of capitalism as well as the ordeal of war. Pressures exist to create robust systems of cosmopolitan national and international law which protect vulnerable peoples not only from the effects of nationalism and statebuilding, geopolitics and war, but also from the harms associated with capitalist globalisation. But serious doubts remain as to whether international society will take serious measures to deal with the effects of abstract harm.

Marxist analyses of the relationship between capitalism and the state, and between the global economy and the international states system, do not encourage optimism. States are locked into a neoliberal economic system which has damaging consequences for the most vulnerable members of humanity and for the environment. Powerful economic elites look to states to create political environments which reduce their vulnerability to turmoil and unrest. Linkages between states and corporations export harm and hazards to societies in the Third World (see De-Shalit, 1998). On this account, the globalisation of capitalist social and economic relations does not suggest that international society is poised to introduce

---

[14] More detailed consideration of these points involves an analysis of the idea of the global risk society. For further discussion about these issues, see Beck (1992).

cosmopolitan harm conventions which protect individuals from the phenomenon of abstract transnational harm.

Some will point to the dangers of anthropocentrism in this formulation. They will argue that international society needs to be modified to prevent harm not only to human beings but to non-human species and to the natural world. The *OED* definition of harm supports consideration of this broadened agenda because it defines harm as evil that can be suffered by persons or 'things'. This is not the place to consider the significance of various developments in environmental ethics for the normative analysis of international society. Suffice it to say that opportunities to harm things were limited prior to global industrialisation, whereas, in the modern world, damage to the global environment might be regarded as a quintessential example of transnational harm which affects 'things' whether these are thought to have intrinsic worth or are valued because they enrich human lives. There is no doubt, however, that the concern with harm to things has been a crucial factor in the revival of cosmopolitan sentiments in recent times. This is a key element of current discussions about how contemporary international society can be reworked in support of cosmopolitan moral imperatives.

A second and related question is whether all harms have equal moral importance, and indeed whether all forms of transnational harm are undesirable and whether international society should endeavour to reduce all of them. These are matters that are best left to specialist moral philosophers. However, two points are worth making. The first is that it is far from obvious that all forms of transnational harm are equally undesirable and reprehensible. Some may think that it is appropriate that international society uses economic sanctions to punish aggressive states or despotic regimes, while others may protest that sanctions – such as those currently in place against Iraq – cause unnecessary and indefensible suffering to innocent populations. The second and more central point from the vantage-point of a sociology of transnational harm is how such disputes impinge on the normative structure of international society, and what they mean for the dominant harm conventions. At present, the emphasis of international society has been on tackling what the dominant states regard as the primary forms of indefensible harm. Steps have been taken to reduce concrete harm anchored in false assumptions about the superiority of some groups over others. Doctrines of racial or ethnic superiority have been delegitimated in recent times, and several barriers to the enjoyment of equal respect and recognition have been dismantled. We shall return to this in the next section. Many protest, however, that international society has not made equivalent investments in protecting human beings from abstract harm; and, as noted earlier, others have argued that the agenda needs to be broadened to include harm to non-human species and nature. No other international system has confronted such complex questions about how to reduce these diverse forms of harm.

Progress, modernity and transnational harm

The shifting relationship between concrete and abstract harm invites the question of how modern international relations should be viewed in a comparative context, and specifically whether it is meaningful to regard modernity as an advance beyond earlier types of international system. One purpose of the sociology of transnational harm is to consider judgements of this kind. An earlier work identified systems of states, empires and inter-civilisational relations as the three types of international system which are especially relevant to this project (Linklater, 1998).[15] They are relevant to a comparative sociology of states systems modelled on the work of comparative sociologists such as Mann, students of comparative government such as Finer and earlier studies of states systems undertaken by Watson and Wight.[16] An initial task is to analyse the main harm conventions in different international systems. The focus is on what the dominant actors – or the majority of actors – regard as harm, what they deem to be acceptable, permissible and proscribed. A related task is to discover whether key political actors believed there was a duty to create cosmopolitan harm conventions: conventions designed to protect vulnerable peoples everywhere from the effects of transnational harm. An inevitable question is whether historical comparisons of this kind will suggest that the modern international system represents progress beyond what has gone before.

One proposition stands out given that war and conquest have been the main determinants of world history for five millennia. Harm conventions

---

[15] Relations between early societies form a separate category which warrants attention. That said, important conceptual issues arise about how the three different inter-societal systems differ and overlap. The main point concerns the inter-civilisational domain. Clearly, inter-civilisational relations exist within states systems and within empires, but some do not have these containers. Examples are relations between Christendom and Islam, and Rome and Carthage.

[16] The comparative-historical method is also associated with the Weberian tradition, specifically with Weber's sociology of religion and with Nelson's approach to civilisational complexes and inter-civilisational relations. For an analysis of different approaches to historical sociology, see Burke (1980), Abrams (1982), Skocpol (1984: 374ff.) and Smith (1991). Interestingly, Nelson is a neglected figure in this literature. Kalberg (1994) is an exception. Smith (1991: 1) makes the important point that one function of historical sociology is to enlarge human understanding about what is 'possible' or 'impossible' in history. This is to link historical sociology with a 'critical perspective' (Smith, 1991: 1) which has affinities with the Frankfurt School and other forms of radical scholarship.

in most – if not all – societies have contained morally relevant distinctions between *us* and *them* which entitle insiders to harm outsiders in ways that are forbidden in relations between members of the same group. Examples include allegedly morally relevant distinctions between the civilised and the savage, between fellow believers and infidels, which have legitimated harm in the form of war, conquest, the expulsion of peoples, ethnocide and so forth.[17] Distinctions of this kind have been the norm in world history. An enormous variety of distinctions between the civilised and the barbaric, and between co-nationals and enemy peoples, were central to European harm conventions in the age of conquest and in the era of total war.

Challenges to such harm conventions are one of the chief characteristics of modernity. Natural hierarchies of the kind supported by notions of the Great Chain of Being have been discredited, as have quasi-scientific accounts of racial supremacy. Doctrines of historical progress which once granted European and North American societies the right to dominate supposedly 'primitive' or 'backward' ones have been challenged. The abolition of slavery and the slave trade, the process of decolonisation, the revolt against white supremacism and the struggle undertaken by indigenous peoples are illustrations of the struggle to overthrow the harm conventions which prevailed during the age of European conquest. As for the moral relevance of the distinction between the citizen and the alien, rising levels of transnational harm have led many to challenge this constitutive principle of modern political life. Many transnational social movements argue for and express new solidarities which deny that the distinction between the citizen and the alien is as morally significant as it has been in the past. These are principal themes in the struggle to create harm conventions which protect the interests of all.

More radical possibilities are suggested by influential movements in contemporary social and political thought, and particularly by those that deny that there is some Archimedean standpoint, or 'view from nowhere', in the sphere of international ethics. From this vantage-point, notions of human rights and human equality must be freed from erroneous and dangerous assumptions that universal truths have been discovered by

---

[17] Theories of progress in the nineteenth century justified the extermination of indigenous peoples, and theories of natural hierarchies were used to justify colonial domination and acts of ethnocide. At first glance, arguments that citizens stand together in special relationships which exclude outsiders do not carry the same connotations of domination and extermination. However, an earlier reference to the indiscriminate harm caused by strategic bombing is a reminder that citizens have been prepared to tolerate acts of violence to outsiders, especially in war, which bear comparison with the atrocities committed to conquered peoples.

any one society or civilisation. There is, in consequence, an obligation to submit all claims on others to a universal tribunal in which each has a duty to 'think from the standpoint of everyone else' (Kant, quoted in Bohman, 1997: 185). Perhaps these moral themes reveal that modernity has a unique capacity to embed robust cosmopolitan harm conventions in international society; perhaps they suggest that it may yet surpass earlier international systems in this respect.

Some support for the view that modernity contains unusual possibilities for eradicating inter-state violence can be found in studies of the rise of the trading state (Rosecrance, 1986), the obsolescence of force (Mueller, 1989; Ray, 1989) and the liberal zone of peace (Doyle, 1983; Fukuyama, 1991; Maoz and Russett, 1993). The explicit question raised by these studies is whether core industrial states or liberal-democratic societies have largely abolished war between themselves. Underlying this question is the issue of whether national differences have lost much of their former moral relevance for the societies concerned.

It is impossible to exaggerate the importance of these pacifying trends which have released modern generations from the anguish of war, but it is essential not to take the triumphalist position that modernity is more advanced than other periods rather than more recent in the scheme of things. In many other periods of human history, societies did not attach as much moral and political importance to differences of race as the European world has done (Snowden, 1983). Any progress that the modern world has made in the direction of the 'age of equalisation' has to be considered in the light of its long history of subjugating others because of racial characteristics – just as any progress made in developing strong commitments to dialogue has to be seen in the light of the fact that modernity has been the site for terrible acts of violence.

Of course, modernity may yet come to represent a major advance beyond all earlier epochs even if this progress has its origins in forms of domination which have few parallels in the past. Complex issues arise at this point which cannot be discussed here. Suffice it to add that Lyotard's question of whether it is still possible to write a universal history with progress as a central theme remains a fascinating one (Rorty, 1991: 211ff.). The progress that exists is not uniform but patchy; hostility to other nations and race is far from abolished in the pacified core, and advances in reducing the level of concrete transnational harm may not survive indefinitely in any case. Crucially, the pacification of core areas and the reduction of concrete harm may only mean that the dominant modes of harm are being reconfigured rather than eliminated in the modern world. The level of abstract transnational harm has increased in the modern world despite progress in this other domain, and it is not impossible that the reconfiguration of the dominant forms of harm marks the beginning of a new phase of world history.

These two developments – declining concrete harm in some parts of the world, increasing abstract harm almost everywhere – can be regarded as different sides of the same coin. Geras (1999) argues that the 'monetarisation' and 'marketisation' of human relations are perfectly compatible with advances in reducing the moral relevance of human differences. In this statement one can hear echoes of Marx's claim that industrial capitalism dissolves national and other differences as it incorporates the whole of humanity in global relations of production which exploit all human beings irrespective of their nationality or race. Racial, national and gender hierarchies can lose much of their importance as organising principles of society but harm may revolve around another axis because of the global economic and social forces which engulf the human race.[18] One of the paradoxes of modernity is that its reproduction and legitimation require the dismantlement of systems of exclusion based on those hierarchies as well as a commitment, however shallow or disingenuous, to dialogue and consent. But this may be small progress when the fate of increasing numbers of the human race is decided by global forces and when cosmopolitan national and international law remains weak.

The paradoxical character of modernity may not be unique. Many have pointed to similarities between the modern states system and the Hellenistic civilisation which existed between the collapse of Alexander the Great's empire and the rise of Rome (Toynbee, 1978) but it may be that certain parallels with the Roman Empire may turn out to be more important. It has been argued that the Roman Empire granted citizenship rights to the conquered groups in order to secure its legitimation and promote its reproduction.[19] But especially during the Severan dynasty between 77 BC and 235 AD this condition of legal equality was undermined by new distinctions between the affluent and powerful elites and the disadvantaged and marginal – between the *honestiores* and the *humiliores* (Garnsey, 1974). Of course, any parallels between the preindustrial Roman Empire and post-industrial modernity should not be pressed too far. The commitment to the language of equality is much stronger in the modern world, and nation-states as well as international society have been reconfigured as a result. Various means of dealing with

---

[18] See also Beck (1992: 101, 23).

[19] The extension of citizenship rights throughout the empire meant the end of active citizenship in the sense of participation in civic life. Citizenship conferred legal rights on persons rather than the right of active involvement in the public sphere.

abstract transnational harm have been proposed, particularly concerning harm to industrialising societies and to the environment,[20] and it is not impossible that modern international society will devise effective means of reducing abstract as well as concrete harm. The fact that modernity can succeed in this respect is associated with the Enlightenment tradition. Against it we must recall Foucault's claim that history is no more than a series of forms of domination and Toynbee's argument that there is no progress in history other than in the technological sphere (Toynbee, 1978).

Conclusions

The dominant strands of historical sociology have shed considerable light on the interplay between society, state, geopolitics and war but moral and cultural forces in international relations have not received the attention they deserve. This chapter has argued for broadening the sociological object of analysis to include harm conventions in different forms of world political organisation. Analysing harm conventions in different forms of world political organisation is an important way of linking historical sociology with the critical theory of international relations.

It has been argued that concrete harm has been the main form of transnational harm in the history of international relations. Harm was exported from one society to another rather than transmitted across frontiers by global forces or transnational actors as is so often the case in the modern world. Throughout international history, particular societies have set out to injure the populations of other societies who were regarded as moral inferiors or unequals. Harm conventions have frequently stressed the moral relevance of racial, cultural, ethnic and related differences. In recent times, these have come under challenge, and an intriguing question is whether the 'age of equalisation' means that the era of concrete transnational harm is drawing to a close in the core regions of the world-system.

The possibility of inter-state violence has been reduced in those areas because of the interpenetration of post-national elites wedded to the project of globalisation. This extraordinary development may free further generations from the scourge of war but it does not of itself mean that one of the paradoxes of modernity (powerful resistance to unjust exclusion and increased vulnerability to remote and invisible sources of power) has been eradicated. A central task of historical sociology is to reflect on the world-historical significance of the changing relationship between

---

[20] The precautionary principle is the best-known example.

concrete and abstract transnational harm. Whether counter-hegemonic movements will be overpowered by sectional interests and global forces promoting 'monetarisation' and 'marketisation', or whether the former will succeed in creating cosmopolitan harm conventions which are unprecedented in human history, is the most important question of all for the historical sociology of transnational harm.

9 Critical historical materialism and international law: imagining international law as praxis

A. Claire Cutler

Introduction

This chapter argues that there is an urgent need to reconceptualise some of the basic assumptions of international relations and international law. This is particularly so with regard to dominant understandings of the nature of the relationship, or nexus, between international law and international relations. In both law and politics, conventional approaches tend to peripheralise the role of law in the global political order, thus obscuring a critical understanding of the contribution that law makes to the constitution of political practices. Moreover, both disciplines are dominated by ahistorical and state-centric theories that are incapable of dealing analytically, theoretically and normatively with contemporary transformations in global power and authority. This inability is responsible, in no small part, for an increasingly acute legitimacy crisis for international law.

The two dominant approaches in international relations, neorealism and neoliberal institutionalism, tend to regard international law unhistorically as an interest-based order used or neglected by states in the furtherance of their goals (Waltz, 1979; Keohane, 1984). In international law, liberal theories form the dominant approach and tend to regard law in a similarly ahistoric, instrumental way (Franck, 1990). Neither engages law as a constitutive element of a global order with roots in diverse historical conditions or historic blocs (Gramsci, 1971; Cox, 1987; Gill, 1993; Cutler 1999c). Both produce formalistic, mythical and artificial understandings of international law that obscure its profound impact on lived experience. Neither thus captures the significance of international law in the creation and perpetuation of asymmetrical power relations and oppressive political practices. Conversely, neither is able to envision law as a potential liberating and emancipatory force, capable of promoting progressive ends and purposes.

This chapter asserts the need for the development of a critical theory of international law that captures the integral role of the law and legal theory in the construction of the political practices and, indeed, the history

181

of the states system. This involves recognising that law, like theory, is always *'for* someone and *for* some purpose' and cannot be 'divorced from a standpoint in time and space' (Cox, 1996: 87). Critical theory engages one in imagining international law as praxis, as a unity of theory and practice, through a radical critique of the dominant approaches to international law and international relations. This involves an interrogation of the historical processes through which dominant approaches to international law (and international relations) both create and perpetuate social injustices and repressive interests and then make them appear as neutral and objective ontological conditions. The objective of critical theory is to reveal the internal contradictions in, and incoherence of, international law, with a view to fostering 'reflexivity, a capacity for fantasy, and a new basis for praxis in an increasingly alienated world' (Bronner, 1994: 3).

Critical theory as here conceived consists of a 'cluster of themes inspired by an emancipatory intent' (Bronner, 1994: 3), although it has much in common with Marxist sociology. The latter is historical, as opposed to 'ahistorical, formalistic sociology'; materialist, 'as opposed to idealistic social theorizing'; empirical, as opposed to 'speculative theorizing'; has as its subject matter the research of social relations that result from the relations of production, 'which determine the objective structure of historically concrete societies'; makes use of the concept of 'totality', 'including the analysis of socioeconomic base and that of the political, cultural and ideological superstructure, in its reciprocal interrelationship'; and is 'value committed' in that it is 'optimistic that society can become perfect and just' (Tar, 1977: 42). However, as will become apparent, critical theory as here conceived, unlike Marxist sociology, rejects a purely materialist conception of history and resists the rigid distinction between the base and superstructure of capitalism. Rather, history is regarded as the movement of forces involving a unity of material and ideational influences operating economically, politically and ideologically (Cox, 1986: 218). Critical theory aims at 'the grasping of the societal process in its totality and presume[s] the possibility of comprehending forces active underneath the chaotic surfaces of historical events. History may appear arbitrary, but its dynamics are dominated by laws . . . Thus history is concerned with all the factors of economic, psychic, and societal nature that determine social life' (Tar, 1977: 27).

For the dominant modes of theorising about international law and international relations, history, if considered at all, provides a 'quarry providing materials with which to illustrate variations on always recurrent themes' (Cox, 1986: 212). These themes revolve around a state-centric universe in which international anarchy establishes the foundational historic condition, from which all else flows in recurring patterns. History provides a material context for action, providing certain incentives or disincentives for states who function more or less autonomously, in response to cues from their environment (see Krasner, 1993). History thus provides a framework or field for action for states who are theorised to function in response to external influences. As Cox notes, 'the mode of thought ceases to be historical', even though the materials used are taken from history, and 'dictates that the future will always be like the past' (Cox, 1986: 212). The analysis misses the crucial role of states and other entities in the construction of their own history. In addition, historical differentiation in political authority structures is flattened out in theorising the timelessness of international anarchy and the continuing relevance of state-centric theorisation (Krasner, 1993, 1997).

In contrast, critical historical sociology, as here conceived, adopts an historical materialist understanding of international law and international relations that puts the state back into history, as an integral element in the constitution of lived experience, and puts history back into our understanding of international relations and law. Critical historical sociology reasons historically and dialectically and is concerned with past and continuing processes of historical change (Cox, 1986: 208). It is a 'Marxism which reasons historically and seeks to explain as well as to promote, changes in social relation' (Cox, 1986: 214). The dialectic is the 'potential for alternative forms of development arising from the confrontation of opposed social forces in any concrete situation' (Cox, 1986: 215). An examination of the dialectical operation of international law is crucial in capturing the analytical significance of transformations that are occurring in world order and in providing an adequate understanding of their theoretical importance and normative implications. Such examination reveals that while there are influential legal doctrines that continue to establish the state as the centre of the political/legal universe, there are also sources of tension and opposition to state-centric orthodoxy that seek to establish a host of entities and identities that are rivalling the state as effective historical forces.

However, the need for a critical understanding of international law is even more urgent than a need for analytical, theoretical and normative clarity. Here we come to the nature of the dialectic and the purposes of critical theory. The dialectic is not just a methodology of analysis. As Theodor Adorno said of the dialectic and art: 'Dialectics is not some rule on how to handle art, but something that inheres in it' (quoted in Bronner, 1994: 192). Dialectics thus inhere in international law, which is evident in the legitimacy crisis facing international law. This crisis stems from ahistoric and state-centric modes of theorising that create a dialectical tension between the theoretical foundations and practical applications of the law. International legal theory remains committed to a state-centric orientation that precludes the recognition of challenges to state authority coming from individuals, corporations and a number of social movements. However, state practice is increasingly recognising the authority of these claims, thus producing a disjuncture between theory and practice. This disjuncture between theory and practice is in turn a reflection of a more profound disjuncture between law and politics. As law becomes ever more formalistic, artificial and mythical in its theorisation of power and authority, the political practices of those challenging legal formalism are making inroads on the monopoly by the state of political authority and control. This is creating a legitimacy crisis for international law because the law has ceased to have relevance and meaning for actual political practices. However, this state of affairs is obscured by conventional theoretical approaches that lack historical depth, over-theorise the state and under-theorise the nature and role of international law in the global order. Critical theory provides a crucial insight into this disjuncture for it assists in separating mythologies of the law from the law as it actually exists and operates. It also facilitates the development of a constitutive theory of law that recognises law not only as internal to the constitution of international society, but also as a powerful dialectical means for regulating and, hence, transforming social relations. Indeed, central to the purposes served by critical theory is belief in the unity of thought and action or theory and practice as a precondition for human self-expression and emancipation.[1] In contrast to 'traditional' or 'problem-solving' theory, which 'is bent on the preservation and gradual reformation of society', the purpose of critical theory is directly opposed to and aims at the radical transformation of societal arrangements through the unity of thought and action or theory and practice in emancipatory human praxis (Tar, 1977: 31–2; Cox: 1986: 210).[2] Understanding the historical, dialectical nature of international law is the first step towards imagining international law as praxis.

[1] Tar (1977: 151) traces the earliest 'call for the unity of theory and practice' to Platonic philosophy and faith that the unification of the rational thought of the Philosopher-King with the practice of politics would produce the ideal state, and to a rejection of Comtean social philosophy that separated values, theory and practice and 'abandoned the idea of radical intervention into societal mechanisms'.

[2] Critical theorists, like Max Horkheimer and Theodor Adorno, lost faith in the revolutionary potential of praxis, in part because of the horrors associated with Nazism and declining faith in the revolutionary potential of the proletariat or, indeed, any historical agent (Tar, 1977: 34–5, 43, 202–3). This separated them from more orthodox Marxism. However, as Martin Jay notes (1973: 78), in their earlier days they had faith, along with Herbert Marcuse, that the 'integration of rational theory, aesthetic imagination, and human action seemed at least a hope, however uncertain and fragile'. Tar (1977: 28) notes that Horkheimer's view of critical theory drew on a number of sources including German idealist philosophy, Judaic ethics, Gestalt psychology and elements of Marxism.

It is also significant for developing a critical historical sociology of the nexus between international law and international relations. The chapter begins with an examination of the crisis of international law. A review of conventional approaches to international law and politics illustrates their analytical and theoretical inadequacy in capturing and explaining transformations in the nature of the units or subjects and the sources of normative regulation in the global political order. Conventional approaches to international law and politics reify both chronofetishist and tempocentric ontologies[3] of international relations and are thus of limited value in understanding the dynamics of global change and historic transformation in both the subjects and the sources of normative regulation. In addition, the chapter posits that conventional approaches obscure the dialectical nature of international law, neglect the acute disjunction between its theory and its practices, and are consequently unable to contemplate the potential for law to work towards progressive or emancipatory ends and purposes. The chapter then considers what a critical historical materialist theory of international law might look like.

International law in crisis

International law is facing a crisis relating to its inability to account for fundamental transformations in global power and authority. It is a crisis of legitimacy of empirical, theoretical and normative dimensions. There is an increasingly acute asymmetry between legal theory and state practice regarding the dominant identifications of the legitimate units or subjects of the political/legal order and its authoritative sources or voices (Cutler, 2001a). Moreover, this asymmetry has significant normative implications. The dominant approaches in international relations, neorealism and neoliberal institutionalism, are associated with scepticism regarding the capacity of international law to alter significantly the posited condition of international anarchy associated with a system in which the preservation of state sovereignty is the pre-eminent interest of states (see Waltz, 1979; Keohane, 1984). In international law, the dominant approach, legal positivism, posits international law to be a law created for states by acts of positive will or state consent, in effect delimiting the law to areas of convergent state interests and agreement (see Brownlie, 1990; Beck, Arend and Vander Lugt, 1996). Conventional theories in both domains are remarkably similar in their theorisation of a state-centric order in which only states and their agents are regarded as the legitimate subjects and units of the order, while state consent (through the entry into treaties

---

[3] These terms are defined below, taken from Hobson (this volume, pp. 5–13).

and creation of custom) provides the authoritative source and voice of the law (Cutler, 2001b). International lawyers refer to these as subject and sources doctrine, while international relations scholars tend to conflate the two analytically in the analysis of the legitimate units or agents of the global polity (Krasner, 1993).

Conventional wisdom in both disciplines identifies the advent of the state-centric order with the Peace of Westphalia and the articulation of the doctrine of sovereignty as the fundamental constitutional principle of the international political/legal order (Bull, 1977; Falk, 1985). Conventional legal theory established the premise that states are the proper 'subjects' of international law, while state consent became the litmus test of 'sources' of law. Concerning legal subjects, only a state has full and originating international legal personality in terms of the capacity 'of possessing international rights and duties and having the capacity to maintain its rights by bringing international claims' (Brownlie, 1990: 58). In theory, states have full and exclusive jurisdiction over their territory and personal jurisdiction over their nationals (Malanczuk, 1997: 91). Thus, only states can declare war, enter into treaties, appoint ambassadors, be full members of the United Nations, be parties to contentious proceedings before the International Court of Justice and claim immunities and privileges under international law.

Somewhat predictably, given the state-centric nature of the law governing legal subjects, sources doctrine also constitutes a state-centric order. Article 38 of the Statute of the International Court of Justice is generally regarded as a definitive statement of the formal sources of international law. It identifies the two primary sources of law, international conventions (treaties) entered into by states and international custom, as evidence of a general practice of states accepted by them as law. The two subsidiary sources include general principles of law recognised by civilised nations and judicial decisions and teachings of the most highly qualified publicists. Conventional international legal theorists tend to prefer treaties over custom as authoritative sources because the former are based on positive acts of state consent. Custom, in contrast, is harder to fit into a consent-based legal order (Kennedy, 1987: 24–5). In order to do so, theorists have reinterpreted custom in a manner consistent with consent-based sources: custom binds only those states that have consented to it. Clearly, proving consent to be bound by historic customs proves problematic when new states are concerned and when there is no historical record. As a result, state consent is implied from the repeated practice of the custom by states and the belief that the conduct is legally obligatory (Kennedy, 1987: 25–6). Thus the criteria determining when state practice has evolved into customary law are collapsed into the test for positive consent-based law. Both subject and sources doctrine thus establish a state-centric legal universe.

Conventional international relations theory reproduces these state-centric tendencies, although international relations scholars refer to agents or actors and conflate the analytical concepts of source and subject. States as the essential actors in international relations are also the legitimate voices of the global polity. Structural realists are steadfastly committed to the view that states remain the essential actors in international relations (see Krasner, 1993, 1995; Mearsheimer, 1995a, 1995b). Neoliberal institutionalists also continue to regard the state as the main agent of international regimes, despite the fact that the generally accepted definition of international regimes did not limit them to participation by states but to 'actors around which expectations converge' (Krasner, 1983: 2). The initial promise of regime analysis to net in a broader set of actors was not met as regime analysis became progressively more state-centric. This led Miles Kahler to observe that regimes analysis was 'captured' by a neorealist synthesis of realism and neoliberalism. Neoliberals had initially challenged the excessive state-centrism of realism in studies of interdependence and transnational relations that were the precursors to regime analysis. However, over time a synthesis emerged and 'Neo-liberalism was redefined away from complex interdependence toward a state-centric version more compatible with realism' (Kahler, 1997: 35).

Neorealists clearly regard states as the legitimate voices, recognising the authority of the pronouncements of international organisations only in so far as states have empowered them to speak. Recognising the voice of individuals is regarded as potentially subversive of the authority of states and is thus discouraged (see Cutler, 1999b: 290–1), while the activities of transnational corporations are ultimately regarded as conditioned by states (Krasner, 1995: 279). However, as noted elsewhere, there are problems with these theories and this story of origins (Cutler, 2001a; and see Krasner, 1993, 1997). One problem with the state-centric order theorised by conventional approaches is that it no longer bears any reasonable relation to empirical practices, if ever it did. Historically, the existence of significant departures from the state's monopoly over political authority as the subject of the law is evident in the legal significance accorded the Holy See, chartered companies and belligerents under international law. Today, challenges to the state authority emanate from supranational regional associations, like the European Union, while the developing international human rights regime challenges the domestic authority of states, and a globalising modernity or postmodernity, of ubiquitous influence economically and culturally, is marginalising the authority of national governments (Koskenniemi, 1991; Twining, 1996; Fried, 1997). Claims for recognition under international law are increasingly emanating from individuals, international organisations, business enterprises, human rights and environmental movements, ethnic minorities and indigenous peoples. Individuals are acquiring significant attributes of international legal personality through the operation of international human rights agreements that provide individual claimants direct access to human rights tribunals and courts in order to challenge the conduct of states (Janis, 1984; Higgins, 1985; Keohane, Moravcsik and Slaughter, 2000). In practice, states are endowing a number of non-state entities like international organisations and regional associations with elements of legal personality (Brownlie, 1990: 63; Malanczuk, 1997: 92–6).

In addition, private, non-governmental organisations, like Amnesty International, Greenpeace and Médecins Sans Frontières, international business corporations and their private associations, like the International Chamber of Commerce and the International Air Transport Association, and international federations of trade unions and employers are increasingly participating in the international legal system (Malanczuk, 1997: 96–7; Cutler, Haufler and Porter, 1999; Higgott, Underhill and Bieler, 1999). Finally, states are endowing multi- and transnational corporations with many of the elements of international legal personality required in order to assert their rights against states. Bilateral investment treaties entered into by states under the auspices of the World Bank's International Center for the Settlement of Investment Disputes, the Canada–US Free Trade Agreement, the North America Free Trade Agreement and the failed Multilateral Agreement on Investment all provide corporations with the legal personality required to sue states directly under international law (Eden, 1996; Cutler, 2000, 2001a).

Notwithstanding these significant challenges to the state's status as the only full and originating 'subject' of the law, legal theory remains steadfastly state-centric. The legal personality of international organisations remains derivative of state personality, while individuals and transnational corporations remain 'objects' and not 'subjects' of the law (Higgins, 1985). Indeed, the transnational corporation is 'invisible' according to international legal theory (Johns, 1994).

Sources doctrine exhibits similar inadequacies. Conventional legal theorists rank the sources in a hierarchy of declining consent and, hence, declining strength. The strongest source is treaties; next comes custom; next come general principles of law; and weakest are judicial decisions and the writings of publicists. Moreover, unlike in many domestic legal systems where the principle of *stare decisis* (the binding force of judicial decisions upon subsequent proceedings) applies, under international law such decisions are only subsidiary and not primary sources. This leaves states very much at the centre as the sources of law, for not even the judicial decisions of the International Court of Justice can trump state consent as a legal source. Notably, however, the resolutions of international organisations do not figure in this hierarchy of sources, notwithstanding their significant contribution to law-making. Neither do the normative claims of individuals, human rights or environmental movements, or indigenous people constitute sources of law. More often than not, these rest upon extra-consensual sources like appeals to 'justice', 'equity' and 'fairness' that do not figure in traditional sources doctrine. Nor do the legal regulatory mechanisms developed by transnational corporations and private business associations figure as legitimate sources, notwithstanding the enhanced significance of informal standards, 'soft law' and non-binding codes of conduct often negotiated by private business associations (see generally, Seidl-Hohenveldern, 1980; Malanczuk, 1997: 54). Soft law is becoming the norm in the regulation of international economic relations, reflecting the concern of commercial actors that rules be flexible, adaptable, porous and not too constraining on state sovereignty and freedom of action (see Cutler, 1999a; Abbott and Snidal, 2000). It is also very common in the regulation of international environmental matters (Burhenne, 1993).

Indeed, there has been a shift in commercial preference, at least in the developed world, away from the negotiation of binding multilateral conventions to optional, non-binding rules that must be understood as part of a more profound transformation in the nature and operation of capitalism. This shift is not embraced by many states on the periphery of the global economy who prefer the negotiation of hard laws in the form of multilateral conventions that provide transparency in rule-making and tend to level the playing field somewhat (see Sempas, 1992). The transformation involves the 'privatisation' of economic legal regulation through increasing reliance on private, non-transparent and discretionary sources that are developed and applied through the agency of private actors in international trade, banking, taxation and dispute resolution (Dezalay and Garth, 1996; Cutler, Haufler and Porter, 1999; Scheuerman, 1999). It reflects 'international capital's preference for porous, open-ended law' that is flexible and adaptable to the exigencies of international competition (Scheuerman, 1999: 4).

Changes associated with late capitalist production are thus transforming the nature and role of law and rendering traditional positivist forms of legal regulation quite anachronistic and even irrelevant (Sousa Santos, 1993: 115). Soft law and flexible, porous, discretionary and nontransparent standards are some of the mechanisms of flexible accumulation facilitating transformations in capitalism. David Harvey (1990: 147) associates post-Fordism with enhanced capital mobility and flexibility, which he refers to as 'flexible accumulation' (flexibility with respect to labour processes, labour markets, products, and patterns of consumption; the emergence of new sectors of production, new financial services and markets; and intensified rates of technological, commercial and organisational innovation). This 'flexible accumulation' results in a process of time-space compression as the time-horizon for decision-makers shrinks. In some cases, this process of time-space compression is obviating the need for hard law, while the growing ideological unity of transnational business interests reduces the need for formal legal unification and harmonisation and opens up space for informal and privatised legal regimes (Dezalay and Garth, 1996; Cutler, 1999a, 1999c; Scheuerman, 1999).

However, the formalistic emphasis on state-based subjects and sources obscures the nature of these transformations that are occurring in contemporary capitalism. In addition, formalistic and state-centric theories are incapable of capturing the role that law plays in affecting these transformations. To the extent that these transformations are inconsistent with democratic notions of the rule of law (generality, clarity, publicness, prospective application and stability), they signal the crucial role that increasingly privatised law is playing in the constitution and reconstitution of global capitalism, suggesting a fundamental contradiction between contemporary capitalism and democracy (Abel, 1991; Wood, 1995; Scheuerman, 1999).

These developments suggest that there is increasing pluralism as regards both subjects and sources of legal regulation. They thus raise significant normative issues concerning the private interests and values that are being represented and advanced by these transformations in the effective subjects and sources of the law. But conventional theories are incapable of inquiry into the political and normative implications of these practices. For both international relations and law, the formalism of the dominant approaches concerning subjects and sources precludes theorising about the authority of non-state actors or subjects and sources of law. Formalism defines the political/legal order as a state-based order, thus rendering non-state subjects and sources to be of theoretically impossible analytical significance. Their inconsistency with the logic of state sovereignty rules them out of consideration as legitimate subjects and sources. However, we have argued that non-state subjects and sources are, in fact, functioning as legal subjects and sources, causing a disjuncture of theory and practice and of law and politics.

As a consequence of these transformations, international law no longer speaks authoritatively to its subjects, who increasingly form a privatised world of transnational legal practice, and suffers from internal incoherence in sources and subject doctrine. Non-state actors in fact operate authoritatively, notwithstanding their theoretical insignificance. Both state consent and the practices of states are identified as sources, but the test of customary law has been eclipsed by the test of consent-based law. This incoherence stems from the dialectical tension between positive-consent-based law and customary law that is built into the structure of sources doctrine. The recognition of non-consensual and 'soft' sources is simply irreconcilable with the consent-based and positivist foundation of international law, as too is the practical significance of private actors in the law-making process. As a result of this incoherence, international law is unable to analyse, theorise or regulate its subjects and sources in any but the most formalistic and artificial way.

All legitimate constitutional orders require some measure of correspondence between their constitutive theories and their political practices and incongruence suggests a crisis of legitimacy. The crisis of legitimacy for international law is precisely its inability to conceptualise, theorise or discipline its subjects and sources. This brings us to the dialectical nature of, and internal contradictions within, international law.

International law as dialectic

Conventional approaches to international law and international relations reify a chronofetishised world order by freezing the Westphalian moment in time. International law and international relations are all about states: the state is naturalised as the primordial entity. The present is thus 'sealed off', appearing as a 'static and reified entity' (see Hobson's discussion of 'chronofetishism' in this volume, pp. 6–9). In an equally important 'tempocentric' move, conventional theories are then 'extrapolated backwards through time' positing the past to be much like the present (Hobson, this volume, pp. 9–13). The way in which the state has created its own subjectivity under international law and given authority to its own voice as a source of the law is lost in presumptions of the timelessness and enduring character of the Westphalian order. As the critical legal scholar, David Kennedy observes, Westphalia marked a crucial break with the past:

International legal scholars are particularly insistent that their discipline began in 1648 with the Treaty of Westphalia closing the Thirty Years' War. The originality of 1648 is important to the discipline, for it situates public international law as rational philosophy, handmaiden of statehood, the cultural heir to religious principle. As part of the effort to sustain this image, public international legal historians have consistently treated earlier work as immature and incomplete – significant only as precursor for what followed. Before 1648 were facts, politics, religion, in some tellings a 'chaotic void' slowly filled by sovereign states. Thereafter, after the establishment of peace, after the 'rise of states', after the collapse of 'religious universalism', after the chaos of war, came law – as philosophy, as idea, as word (Kennedy, 1988–9: 14).

According to this narrative, the law brought order to chaos and rationality to the irrational. The state appeared at the centre of the rationalised universe. Thus the Westphalian moment stands frozen and transfixed for all time, while sources and subject doctrine disciplines anti-statist tendencies in what appears to be an objectively rational state of affairs and the best-of-all-possible-worlds. However, conventional approaches are unable to recognise the increasing heterogeneity and differentiation in legal subjects and sources over time because their analytical and theoretical assumptions preclude an understanding of the nature of international law as an historically specific dialectical process. Through movements of legal doctrine, the law operates dialectically in a number of dimensions. In one dimension, it operates as both a constitutive and a regulative influence. It creates and constitutes the state as 'subject', mirroring the sovereign subject through sources and subject doctrine. Then it steps outside and 'law is set up *against* the state' to objectively police, measure and regulate state action (Kennedy, 1988–9: 23). Through a process of objectification common to all legal orders, the law is objectified and becomes the embodiment of sovereign will, letting the subjective nature of the state-based order slip from sight. The objectification and sublimation of the subject are formalistic moves to give the law the appearance of neutrality and objectivity and, hence, to render law stable and legitimate (Schlag, 1991: 1627). This enables theorists to believe in their 'objectified thought-structures as off the shelf, stand-alone, self-sufficient, self-sustaining systems, completely independent of the activity of the subjects' (Schlag, 1991: 1640). The state is no longer responsible for legal doctrines governing who matters as a subject and what counts as a source, because sources and subject doctrine steps in and does the job as the embodiment of rationality and objectivity. The fairness or equity or inclusivity or even accuracy of sources and subject doctrine simply cannot be raised in this analytical and theoretical framework. Sources and subject doctrine is quite simply placed beyond consideration and contention.

This move to objectify the law is of crucial significance to our understanding of contemporary transformations in world order. By attributing objective status to statist subject and sources doctrine, both the law and the state are removed from the subjective determination of who counts and who does not count in the global polity. It results in the fetishism of international law whereby the law becomes 'an "independent", "autonomous" reality to be explained according to its own "internal dynamics", i.e., conceives it as an independent subject, on whose creativity the survival of the society depends . . . [I]ndividuals [or states] affirm that they owe their existence to the law, rather than the reverse, inverting the real causal relationship between themselves and their product' (Balbus, 1977: 583). As a result, the possibility for human intervention to challenge and displace conventional theories becomes ontologically infeasible.

Of equal significance is the way in which another dimension of the dialectical operation of the law also slips from view. This is the dialectical tension between positive law theory and state practice built into sources and subject doctrines. We have argued that international law reifies a state-centric ontology through legal doctrines governing subjects and sources. However, it simultaneously empowers anti-statist tendencies by recognising attributes of legal personality possessed by non-state actors, like individuals, corporate entities and a potentially growing list of aspiring subjects, such as indigenous people and women. Paradoxically, it is international law that gave voice to revolutionary aspirations for subjectivity and voice coming from women, indigenous people, colonised people, individuals and a host of social movements. Interestingly, many of these aspirations eventually materialised through state practice and customary sources of law, as articulated in resolutions of the United Nations General Assembly and other international organisations. The right to national self-determination, permanent sovereignty over natural resources, the condemnation of apartheid, and the recognition of war crimes, crimes against humanity, the crime of genocide and the imposition of individual responsibility for such crimes under international law, all emerged in part through the mechanism of customary sources of law (see Malanczuk, 1997: 326–7, 354). However, their recognition is potentially disruptive of, if not revolutionary for, statist orthodoxy. Thus conventional theories have written customary law (and its agents or subjects) out of sources (and subject) doctrine, thereby obscuring the internal tension between consent-based positive law and extra-consensual customary law. In this sense, law operates dialectically, moving between formal consent-based law and law emerging through the evolution of state practice. But by collapsing practice into formal law, the revolutionary potential of emerging practices is lost and the orthodoxy of consent-based state law prevails. Conventional theories thus arrest the dialectical movement of law between consensual theory and state practice, excluding the agency of non-state subjects in the face of statist orthodoxy. The fetishism of international law then renders this state of affairs and the law to be unproblematic by definition, for 'when Society is said to be a result of the Law, rather than the law to be a result of one particular type of society, then the Law by definition is unproblematical' (Balbus, 1977: 583).

What is needed is a new type of theory that captures the integral role of international law in the constitution of political practices and restores the role of human agency in effecting change. In a word, what is required is the re-engagement of law and politics. Conventional theories have lost sight of the symbiotic nature of the relationship between law and politics in the effort to create law in the form of a rational and objective order. The resulting fetishism of law produces analytical and theoretical paralysis, while undue formalism blinds the dominant modes of thought to major transformations in the subjects and sources of law. Both prevent inquiry into the practical and normative implications of these developments for democracy and the future viability of an inclusive and democratic rule of law. We will now turn to consider how we might remedy this situation by imagining international law as praxis.

International law as praxis

If the analytical and theoretical foundations of conventional theories pose problems for capturing contemporary global transformations, Marxist theories are no less troubled. The problem stems in part from ambiguity in Marx's treatment of law and subsequent interpretations that relegated law to the superstructure of capitalism and instrumentalist theories that accorded little historical effectivity to the law. Moreover, as part of the superstructure of capitalism, along with others forms of 'social conscious-ness', like ideology, law is hard to reconcile with a materialist conception of history. Neither Marx nor Engels developed a systematic theory of law, although Marx's writings did engage in negative critique of bourgeois law (Vincent, 1993). Marx never succeeded in developing an understanding of the law in relation to the mode of production and commodity form of capitalism (Balbus, 1997). As a result of certain ambiguity in Marx's view of law and notwithstanding the consideration that he never aban-doned law nor called for its destruction, as Vincent notes (1993: 378), subsequent Marxists tended to regard law as part of the superstructure and not of the base of capitalism (Fraser, 1978; Vincent, 1993; Balbus, 1997). As such, the law was not an effective historical force.

Instrumentalist theories developed an understanding of law as merely the tool or instrument of the dominant classes or a reflection of the con-sciousness and ideology of the dominant class. Accordingly, all that is analytically or theoretically necessary in order to capture the significance of law is to analyse the law in terms of its role in disciplining and ma-nipulating the subordinate elements of society. However, critics of such thinking argue that instrumentalism 'fails to pose the problem of the specific *form* of the law and the way in which this form articulates with the overall requirements of the capitalist system in which these social actors function' (Balbus, 1997: 571). Moreover, like legal positivism, instrumentalist theories fall victim to the tendency to separate law from the 'social totality', 'disintegrating the unity of law and economic process' and thus obscuring the fact that 'law is literally the effected voice of the relations of production' (Gable, 1977: 622). In the following passage, Fraser captures the problems generated by both instrumentalist and positivist theories of law:

> Such an instrumentalist conception of law precludes the possibility of developing a sensitive awareness of the legal process as a form of creative social praxis in its own right. To conceive of law as an inert tool deprives it of any social character and treats it instead as something like a physical fact external to the concrete individuals who create, apply, and are affected by it. Marxist instrumentalism, like bourgeois positivism, conceives the law as only a formal structure of rules, categorically distinct from social context within which that set of rules is placed (Fraser, 1978: 152).

For Fraser, Marxist instrumentalist theories present law divorced from 'human subjects in the process of making their own history' (Fraser, 1978: 160).

Considerable dissatisfaction with this rather rudimentary and crude understanding of the law has led a number of Marxists to develop the idea of the 'relative autonomy of the law'.[4] According to this notion, law is autonomous of the will of social actors, but 'entails at the same time an essential *identity* or homology between the legal form and the very "cell" of capitalist society, the commodity form' (Balbus, 1997: 573). Others, like E. P. Thompson, articulate the view that the law is 'deeply imbricated within the very basis of productive relations', rejecting its attribution to the superstructure of capitalism (Thompson, 1975: 261). Thompson (1975: 262) submits that law functions in three ways: as an instrument 'mediating and reinforcing existent class relations'; as ideology, legitimating class relations; and as a material expression of class relations through legal forms. He counters superstructural theories of law thus:

> The rules and categories of law penetrate every level of society, effect vertical as well as horizontal definitions of men's rights and status and contribute to men's self-definition or sense of identity. As such law has not only been *imposed* upon men from above: it has also been a medium within which other social

---

[4] See Jessop (1980) for an insightful review of three leading Marxist approaches to theorising the nature of domestic law: the capital logic approach of Eugen Pashukanis and others, Althusserian structuralism and Gramscian analysis.

conflicts have been fought out. Productive relations themselves are, in part, only meaningful in terms of their definitions at law: the serf; the free labourer; the cottager with common rights, the inhabitant without; the unfree proletarian, the picket conscious of his rights; the landless labourer who may still sue his employer for assault (Thompson, 1975: 267).

Ellen Meiksins Wood too notes that 'relations of production themselves take the form of particular juridical and political relations – modes of domination and coercion, forms of property and social organization – which are not mere secondary reflexes, nor even just external supports, but *constituents* of the productive relations' (Wood, 1995: 27).

These approaches challenge the continuing relevance of the base–superstructure distinction, purely materialist conceptions of history and the resulting tendency to peripheralise the significance of law. They suggest that there is a need to review the analytical foundations of historical materialism, particularly in light of transformations in late capitalism that are rendering the distinction of increasingly dubious analytical and theoretical utility. Karl Klare (1979) argues against the viability of the base–superstructure distinction in the face of changes in capitalist production involving the politicisation of the base with government involvement in the economy, the transformation of the superstructure with the increasing infusion of private matters into public affairs (labour, education, welfare) and changes in the nature of the capitalist state in terms of its corporativism, bureaucratisation and the legitimation functions of the state (see, too, Unger, 1976). In a similar vein, Fraser (1978) identifies the need to understand the role of new forms of law that are enabling the fusion of public and private authority making possible new forms of rationalised and objectified domination. He asserts 'law must be a central category in any theory of sociality within advanced capitalist societies' (1978: 148). However, Marxist instrumentalism has resulted in the disappearance of the human subject, who 'has been swallowed up by the capitalist mode of production' (Fraser, 1978: 167). In an effort to restore human beings as effective agents of historical change, Fraser thus urges that we take seriously Gramsci's observation that all people, as political beings, are also legislators in the sense that 'every man, inasmuch as he is active, i.e. living, contributes to modifying the social environment in which he develops . . . ; in other words, he tends to establish "norms", rules of living and of behavior . . . Liberation requires that radical lawyers . . . acknowledge the extent to which we are active participants in our own oppression and alienation' (Fraser, 1978: 184–5).

Marxist instrumentalism thus obscures the extent to which law participates in the constitution of capitalist productive and social relations through moves that, while very distinct from those characterising conventional theory, nevertheless remove human agency from the picture. One way of dealing with this problem is to accept the criticisms raised above of the base–superstructure distinction and to begin to theorise law as part of the base of capitalism. This requires investigating the role that law plays in the constitution of the mode of production. This is the route taken by Balbus (1977), Gable (1979) and others (see Jessop, 1980), and the position this author has taken elsewhere in analysing transformations in world order from medieval, through capitalist to late capitalist modes of production (Cutler, forthcoming). These transformations are analysed in the context of changing property rights and competing theories of property law that are argued to be constitutive of the mode of production for different historical blocs. The contemporary historical conjuncture is said to reflect a dialectical tension between two conceptions of property. One conception of property as 'bundles of rights' works in favour of patterns of transnational capital accumulation. In opposition, the conception of property as 'ownership of things' works in favour of patterns of national capital accumulation.

Relatedly, it is possible to draw on a 'looser materialism' that conceptualises Marxism as a form of praxis uniting theory and practice in a symbiotic and reciprocal relationship, and thus denying unidirectional claims of base over superstructure or the material over the ideational (Klare, 1979; Vincent, 1993; Cutler, forthcoming).

The alternative looser materialism can be observed in the elusive Marxist doctrine of 'praxis' (where 'theory' and 'practice' have symbiotic and reciprocal relations). The basic logic of praxis argument denies the basic premise of the unidirectionality claim [that material conditions causally determine thought and political/legal structures]; that is it asserts that reflective thought and consciousness (as embodied in philosophical, economic, or legal thought) can actually affect our material conditions. We can accommodate our theory to our practices and vice versa. Put simply, human reflective thought has definitive efficacy; it is not just an epiphenomenon of the material conditions of life (Vincent, 1993: 379).

Accordingly, one might conceive of law as praxis through analysis of the role of law in constituting the mode of production and the dialectical tension between class interests for different historical blocs. Drawing on Antonio Gramsci's understanding of hegemony and the mechanisms by which laws become internalised in the consciousness of people, we might begin to theorise law as an effective agent in history.[5] Operating

---

[5] See Cutler (1999c) for analysis of the nature of Gramsci's conception of hegemony and see Vincent (1993: 383–4) for analysis of Gramsci's notion of the hegemony of legal ideas. It is also instructive to consider the work of Franz Neumann and Otto Kirchheimer, two critical theorists associated with the Frankfurt School, who engaged in considerable analysis of the political and ideological significance of law. While neither theorised the

predominantly by consent and persuasion, but at the margin by coercion, legal hegemony assists in creating 'a social conformism which is useful to the ruling group's line of development' (Gramsci, 1971: 247; and see Benney, 1983 and Cutler, 1999c). Law thus, in addition to creating the material conditions of existence, serves important legitimating functions. But equally importantly, law-making may be regarded as a 'form of praxis' and a 'constitutive component of the social totality' whose dialectical operations give rise to potentially emancipatory and liberating practices (Klare, 1979: 128).

Drawing upon these insights, we might conceive of international law as a form of praxis involving a dialectical relationship between theory and practice, thought and action, and law and politics. This involves developing a constitutive theory of international law in which the law is understood as operating in a dialectical movement between legal theory and the practices of the actors. Following Gramsci, the philosophy of praxis and the unity of theory and practice is not a 'mechanical fact', but a 'part of a historical process' (Gramsci, in Forgacs, 2000: 334). Theory and practice are not factors that 'stand apart from and influence each other in a this-then-that fashion', but 'are to be grasped as constituents of living form which are elaborated within the movement of a social totality' (Gable, 1977: 635–6). The objective is to 'free Marxist theory of law from its deterministic integument – i.e., the notion that law is a mere instrument of class power – and to conceive the legal process, at least in part, in a manner in which class relationships are created and articulated, that is, to view law-making as a form of praxis' (Klare, 1979: 128). This involves demystifying international law and making its theory relevant to the practices of politics and the lived experiences of people.

International law-making is thus to be understood in dynamic terms as a process giving rise to material, institutional and ideological conditions embodying both oppressive and potentially emancipatory social relations. At present, sources and subject doctrine controls the law-making process by determining who counts as a legal subject and who has voice as a source of law. It functions as a mechanism of exclusion, repressing and excluding actual social difference in the face of statist orthodoxy (Kennedy, 1988–9: 25). However, it does not have to be this way, for the law-making process also provides opportunities for reconceiving sources and subject doctrine to create a more inclusive and equitable order. This requires recognising the inadequacy of chronofetishist and tempocentric appeals to Westphalia as definitive of contemporary political practices and

law as constitutive of the mode of production of capitalism, their work reflects an acute awareness of the significance of law in establishing the basic material, institutional and ideological framework for society (see Scheuerman, 1996).

recognising the historical differentiation in legal subjects and sources as an empirical reality. It also requires analysing and incorporating into legal doctrines and law-making institutions the claims to subjectivity and voice coming from a multiplicity of identities. The materiality of the law must be critically analysed in the context of the representativeness and inclusiveness of the interests and rights promoted by contemporary law. For example, the claims made by women that international legal doctrines in the area of development operate to disadvantage women must be taken seriously and examined with a view to equalising their distributional impact (Charlesworth *et al.*, 1991). Similarly, claims for the recognition of indigenous peoples' property rights as protected rights under the World Intellectual Property Law regime must also be examined in the context of the continuing relevance of traditional property law regimes (Doucas, 1995; Cutler, forthcoming). Progressive law and practices must extend into the institutional framework of international law. For example, the inclusion of women and the representatives of human rights and environmental groups and other people claiming recognition as subjects and voice in the operations of international organisations and other bodies involved in law-making, like the meetings of the World Trade Organisation and the Organisation of Economic Cooperation and Development, must be addressed. Finally, critical analysis of the ways in which legal doctrines, like sources and subject doctrine, have historically operated to exclude marginalised and repressed peoples and developing countries by favouring existing positive law over potentially destabilising, if not revolutionary, customary law, is a necessary step in beginning to understand the ideological operation of the law. These are modest but necessary beginnings for the development of a theory of international law as praxis. While unquestionably a challenging undertaking, 'to engage in praxis is not to tread on alien ground, external to the theory [of historical materialism]', because revolutionary theory is already contained in historical materialist theory: 'The theory itself is already a practical one; praxis does not only come at the end but is already present in the beginning of the theory' (Marcuse, 1972: 5).

Imagining international law as praxis is not just an intellectual engagement, but a very material one upon which turns the future viability, relevance and, indeed, the desirability of the rule of law in international relations.

10 International systems in world history: remaking the study of international relations

Barry Buzan and Richard Little

Introduction

This chapter offers a new way of looking at international systems that enables us to examine them from a world historical perspective. Existing approaches to the study of international relations are almost all premised on a remarkably 'thin', often unidimensionally political, conception of the international system, as most clearly exemplified in neorealism. Although parsimony in theorising is a virtue, without a 'thicker' conception of the international system we believe that there is much about international relations that simply cannot be adequately understood. The recent influence of historical sociology in international relations has also introduced a world historical dimension into the discipline, but has had relatively little impact because it continues to work on the basis of the prevailing thin conception of the international system (Hobden, 1998). From our perspective, this thin conception of the international system is the product of a number of weaknesses in the discipline. Our approach aims to overcome these weaknesses and, in the process, to reassess how international relations should be studied.

Instead of tracing the history of the contemporary international system back 350 years to the Treaty of Westphalia in 1648 AD – the date conventionally used to mark the origins of the contemporary international system – our approach makes it possible to provide a much longer and more complex story of the multiple international systems that have formed over a period of more than five millennia. Our starting point is 3500 BC, when the interaction among the Sumerian city-states constituted the first known fully-fledged international system (cf. Gills, this volume). But we find it both fruitful and necessary to investigate the pre-international systems that evolved during several tens of thousands of years before the rise of city-states. These systems not only provided the precursors for international systems, but they also existed alongside them

The chapter attempts to provide a summary of *International Systems in World History* (Buzan and Little, 2000).

right down to the twentieth century. Over five millennia between 3500 BC and 1500 AD a range of very different international systems came into existence around the world. These systems have been largely ignored within mainstream international relations, in part because of the assumption fostered by neorealism that they can be accounted for by established theory. In this view, there is little purpose served by investigating them, because although they provide additional historical depth, they give no extra theoretical purchase on the understanding of international systems. We fundamentally disagree with this position.

From our perspective, existing frameworks in international relations are seriously crippled by their failure to build on a long view of history. Because mainstream international relations theories are derived almost exclusively from the model of the Westphalian international system established in the seventeenth century, they inadvertently, but effectively, isolate the whole discourse of international relations from the wider debates about world history. International relations theorists have largely failed to follow the English School injunction that history requires 'the elucidation of the unlikeness between past and present' (Butterfield, 1949: 10). On the contrary, to the extent that international relations theorists have turned their attention to world history, they have been mainly impressed by how similar previous international systems have been to our own.

This position reflects a long-standing tradition of thought in Europe. Nearly 200 years ago, Heeren (1809) produced a manual charting the history of the European 'states system'. In outlining his theoretical framework, Heeren observed how similar to the European states system were the Greek and Italian city-states, as well as the Diadochi Empires, formed after the collapse of Alexander the Great's empire. In the context of this volume, it is disappointing to note that a prominent historical sociologist asserts, albeit controversially, that the emergence of international relations is 'coeval with the origins of nation-states', thus implying that Europe provides the first, and only, example of an international system (Giddens, 1985: 4). Like Giddens, we think that there is something very distinctive about the international system that formed in Europe after 1500. But we disagree strongly that the modern European system is the only relevant case, and we want to paint our picture of international systems on a much broader historical canvas. In doing so, we eschew the route followed by Heeren, as well as many contemporary international relations theorists, who focus exclusively on the limited number of international systems in world history that appear, superficially, to resemble the contemporary international system.

To develop a really effective world history of international systems it is necessary to rethink entirely how to approach the conceptualisation of the international system. There are two problems with existing mainstream conceptualisations. First, because they are so closely modelled on the Westphalian system, they are unable to capture the huge swathes of world history where international systems have taken a radically different form. Second, even where they appear to fit the Westphalian model, earlier international systems are only embraced by it because its conceptualisation of what constitutes an international system is so narrowly defined. Existing conceptualisations fail to expose important differences between the modern international system and its predecessors. A theoretical framework that can reveal how international systems have evolved across the entire spatial and temporal sweep of human history needs to be more elaborate than anything that currently exists, yet still retain a powerfully simplifying theoretical scheme. When one confronts the existing concepts of international systems with the task of providing a world historical narrative, it becomes apparent just how seriously underdeveloped they are.

Setting up an enriched theoretical framework of the international system pays significant dividends. Although there are other theoretical frameworks available to examine world history, we argue that the framework presented here generates a version, and a vision, of world history that is more coherent and comprehensive than any of the rival world historical narratives that have emerged in recent years. We suggest that Westphalia-based international relations theory is not only incapable of understanding pre-modern international systems, but also that its lack of historical perspective makes it unable to answer, or in many cases even address, the most important questions about the modern international system. And we argue that the historical narrowness of most international relations thinking goes a long way towards explaining why international relations debates have had so little impact on debates in the other social sciences and history. Our view is that international relations has failed to occupy a proper role in the macro-debates of the social sciences and history, and our hope is to show how this disastrous underachievement might begin to be rectified. Our historical account thus propels us to challenge the most fundamental theoretical assumptions about international systems that are found in the contemporary study of international relations.

The impoverished view of the international system in most international relations thinking prevents the discipline from taking full advantage of the many valuable insights available in established world historical accounts of the past. But it is also the case that these accounts have not been informed in any way by the theoretical developments made in international relations. By contrast, historical sociologists, according to Mann

(1996), went on a 'raiding party' and returned with a certain amount of 'loot' taken from the realists. But this analysis is made with a degree of hindsight, the link with realism being made after the historical sociologists had independently reached the long-standing international relations realist position that 'war makes the state and the state makes war' (Tilly, 1975b: 42). Moreover, by focusing on the militaristic side of international relations, the work of these historical sociologists reflects the familiar, thin view of the international system (Hobden, 1998). Mann goes on to argue that analysts in international relations, for their part, engaged in a similar raid on the work of historical sociologists, returning with some of the essential elements of the world systems literature. Wallerstein's ideas have been revamped and used to considerable effect in disciplines like archaeology and anthropology (Chase-Dunn and Hall, 1997), which were looking for ways to extend their spatial framework. But these ideas have not had the same impact in international relations, which continues to work on the basis of the traditional, underdeveloped conception of the international system.

Our approach is built on three basic premises. The first is that none of the existing conceptualisations of the international system in international relations can describe and analyse how international systems have emerged and evolved through the course of world history. The second is that the level of theoretical understanding in international relations has been held back by a failure to examine international systems from a world historical perspective. The third premise is that the international system constitutes the most effective unit for developing world history, as well as for helping social scientists to advance a macro-analysis of social reality.

If these premises hold water, then it is surprising that so few links have been forged between world historians and international relations theorists. Nevertheless, it has to be acknowledged that, up to now, mainstream international relations theorists have shown virtually no interest in examining international relations from a world historical perspective, and nor have world historians shown much inclination to use an international systems framework to analyse world history. So our theoretical framework and our world historical account of international systems are intended to address, and encourage, a closer collaboration between international relations theorists and world historians.

In the next section of the chapter we explore how weaknesses in contemporary international relations have helped to maintain a very thin conception of the international system. In the third section we outline the essential features of our thicker conception of the international system, and in the fourth section we explore some of the theoretical implications of using a thicker understanding of the international system. In the final section of the chapter we sketch out an overview of what world history looks like through our analytical scheme.

The underdeveloped conception
of the international system

Despite more than a century of intensive discussion about the nature of the international system, it is difficult to deny how underdeveloped the concept continues to be. Even the more sophisticated accounts of the international system fail to address some of the most elementary questions. Waltz (1979: 91), for example, talks about the international political system in terms of independent units co-acting, but he does not specify how much interaction, or what type, is necessary for a system to exist. Will any interaction suffice, or must we identify a boundary (or perhaps boundaries) defined by levels, types and frequencies of interaction? On one side of this boundary will be international systems, and on the other will be sets of lightly interacting parts not yet defined as international systems. Neorealism suggests (without specifically addressing the question) that an international system does not come into being until quite high levels of (military-political) interaction exist. On this basis, an international system does not necessarily form from the first point at which units begin to co-act.

This line of thinking points towards some interesting questions. Exactly what are the criteria for specifying that an international system exists? Is it useful or necessary to conceive of different types of international system – strategic, economic, cultural – in order to register the significance of different types of interaction? How far back in time can we apply the idea of international system? What does the history of international systems look like, and are there patterns in its development? When can we say that a fully global international system came into being? Existing research does not suggest obvious or uncontroversial answers to any of these questions, and before proceeding to suggest some possibilities, it is worth considering why this is so. Why is it that such extremely basic questions about what is arguably the core concept in the discipline remain not only unaddressed, but almost unasked in international relations? At least five complementary lines of explanation suggest themselves: presentism, ahistoricism, Eurocentrism, anarchophilia and state-centrism.

Presentism

The discipline of international relations has been mainly focused on contemporary history and current policy issues. The fast-moving nature of the subject, and the pressing demand for expertise on current events, encourage a forward- rather than a backward-looking perspective. Consequently, rather few specialists within the discipline have had either a broad historical knowledge or an interest in acquiring it.

Occasionally, authors will raid further back and further afield, but these forays are usually guided more by the search for particular parallels with the modern European experience than by any interest in capturing the character of the international system in history overall (Holsti, 1967: 2; Wight, 1977). Following Burke (1993: xi), we refer here to this perspective as presentism, which suggests that the dictum about using the past to understand the present is reversed. As a consequence, the few historical times and places that resemble the international anarchy of modern Europe get a disproportionate amount of attention, most notably classical Greece, Renaissance Italy, the 'warring states' period in China during several hundred years of the first millennium BC, and, to a lesser extent, 'warring state' periods in South Asia. Because these attempts to break away from presentism impose the present on the past, they reinforce the problem of ahistoricism in the analysis of the international system.

Ahistoricism

Ahistoricism does not imply that the past is of no concern to social scientists, but rather that they should be searching for general laws that apply to the past as well as the present. Such a goal is dictated by the desire to emulate the invariant laws of natural science that hold across time and space. Social scientists of a positivist predisposition, anxious to emulate the natural sciences, also seek to identify laws that are immune to historical variation. In most areas of social science there has been a persistent debate about the relative merits of ahistoricism and historicism.

Debates of this kind have rarely taken place in international relations. Until recently it was widely accepted that the 'texture' of international politics did not change over time, because 'patterns recur, and events repeat themselves endlessly' (Waltz, 1979: 66). Twentieth-century realists have assumed that the balance of power provides the basis for a transhistorical theory that accounts just as well for behaviour in the Greek city-states as it did for relations between the Soviet Union and the United States. In the last quarter of the twentieth century the ahistoricism of realism has come under increasing criticism. The easy assumption that we can compare the conflict between Athens and Sparta with the conflict between the United States and the Soviet Union rests, it is argued, on a 'gigantic optical illusion' (Rosenberg, 1994: 90). The comparison requires the analyst to distort beyond recognition the underlying social structures that form the Greek city-states. Similar criticisms have been levelled at attempts to apply realist thinking to the feudal era (see Hall and Kratochwil, 1993 on Fischer, 1992).

Eurocentrism

Eurocentrism has bedevilled every aspect of the social sciences, and it has had a particularly big impact on international relations. At first sight, it might appear that there is nothing untoward about the familiar Eurocentric account of how the contemporary international system emerged. It seems to be almost self-evidently true that Europeans created the first global international system by bringing all parts of humankind into regular economic and strategic contact with each other. They occupied whole continents and stamped upon them a system of territorial boundaries, trading economies and colonial administrations. The few places that they did not reduce to colonial status (Japan, Siam, Persia, Turkey, China) were forced to adapt to European models in order to preserve themselves. But as with ahistoricism, this story can only be told in this way by ignoring or distorting large tracts from the past. In particular, as writers such as Hodgson (1993) have demonstrated, Eurocentric accounts invariably ignore the Afro-Eurasian system that existed long before the Europeans began to extend across the globe.

Rather than tracing the origins of Europe, we argue that it is this much wider history that constitutes the real antecedent of the contemporary global international system. Indeed, one can only explore the origins and significance of the idea of international system, and fully understand what is happening to it now, by comprehending its non-European dimension. Such comprehension requires more than selecting the handful of times and locations from the ancient and classical era during which anarchic structures similar to modern Europe's briefly held sway. It means addressing the whole sweep of ancient and classical history in terms of the international system, and asking just what kind of system(s), if any, existed before the Europeans subordinated everything to their own anarchic model. Only by following this course can one bring the historical record to bear on the question of what are the necessary and sufficient conditions for an international system to come into being.

Anarchophilia

The fourth reason why basic questions about the core concept in the discipline remain not only unaddressed but almost unasked is anarchophilia, which is very much a consequence of ahistoric and Eurocentric perceptions. By anarchophilia we mean the disposition to assume that the structure of the international system has always been anarchic, that this is natural and (more selectively) that this is a desirable thing. This normative assumption is strongest in neorealism. Classical realists have often expressed more mixed feelings about the virtues of anarchy, and liberals have tended to see it as the main cause of war and disorder.

Adam Watson (1992, 1997) has opened an attack on anarchophilia, arguing that much of the international history of the last 5,000 years has not been anarchic, but has ranged across a spectrum with anarchy at one end, empire at the other, and hegemony, suzerainty and dominion in between. Moreover, he argues that both anarchy and empire are extreme conditions, the natural instabilities of which tend to push the norm into the middle ranges of the spectrum. It is not easy for international relations to break free from the grip of anarchophilia because its mainstream theories conceptualise international systems exclusively in anarchic terms. Other disciplines are not so constrained. Historians like Gallagher and Robinson (1953), for example, find it appropriate to depict the links between Britain and Latin America in the first part of the nineteenth century in terms of an informal empire. As a consequence, it might be easier to tell the story of the British empire, or the Soviet empire, for that matter, if they are identified as subglobal or regional international systems rather than as states in the international system. Watson's framework raises the possibility that even the most abstract and successful theoretical development in the discipline has been profoundly, and probably unwittingly, shaped by an undue reliance on the peculiarities of the European and contemporary world experience.

State-centrism

Although almost inseparable from anarchophilia, state-centrism (or politicophilia) is a distinct reason for the underdeveloped conceptualisation of international systems. There has, of course, been extensive attention paid to the economic, social and environmental dimensions of international relations within the discipline. But attempts to conceptualise international systems have focused overwhelmingly on the military-political sector. Perhaps even more important, politics has been linked almost indissolubly with the state. This is perhaps not that surprising after the Second World War, an era when the idea of the political system became little more than a synonym for the state (Easton, 1953, 1981). A previous generation of pluralists in both Britain and the United States had endeavoured to dispense with the idea of the state when analysing politics (Little, 1991, 1996). At the beginning of the twentieth century, pluralists began to argue that links between financial centres around the world were now closer than cities within the state had been in the past (Angell, 1912: viii). The state was characterised as a 'metaphysical spook' by the pluralists and during the inter-war era there were tentative attempts to analyse international relations from a non-state pluralist perspective (Fox, 1975; Wilde, 1991). It seemed possible in the 1960s and 1970s that the pluralist perspective would be resurrected and that a multi-centric and multi-layered image of the international system might be developed (Burton, 1968; Keohane and Nye, 1971). But the putative pluralists very rapidly drew back and refocused their attention on the state (Keohane and Nye, 1977; Keohane, 1984). Although Rosenau (1990) advocated the need to combine the pluralist and realist images of the international system, others have failed to follow this route, and the most sophisticated attempts to conceptualise the international system have been restricted to the state-centric perspective. Curiously, historical sociology has also been largely seduced by state-centrism.

The alternative

Within mainstream international relations the concept of international system has almost invariably been depicted in one-dimensional, usually military-political, terms. The resulting assessment is necessarily partial, and there is generally no acknowledgement that a more comprehensive approach to the task of conceptualising such a complex phenomenon is required. The underdeveloped concept of the international system has acted as a Procrustean straitjacket on the discipline. We hope to transcend the weaknesses discussed in this section by developing a very open-ended approach to the international system which does not prejudge the nature of the dominant units in the system, privilege one sector of activity over another (for example, politics over economics), or give precedence to one mode of explanation over another (for example, structure over process, or material over social). To achieve these objectives we need to draw extensively on both history and theory.

Conceptualising a 'thick' international system

In *The Logic of Anarchy* (Buzan, Jones and Little, 1993) we argued that despite the persistent criticism that has been levelled at neorealism, we nevertheless saw this approach as a useful 'foundation on which to construct a more solid and wider ranging Structural Realism' (Buzan, Jones and Little, 1993). We employ a similar strategy here. We have deliberately favoured methodological pluralism over methodological monism. Many elements of both structure and realism are still prominent, but there is much else besides. The range and diversity of our borrowing also forbids calling the result a theory, for it contains no single line of cause and effect. Our position is that phenomena as massive and complex as international systems cannot be understood by any single method. The first task for international systems theorists must therefore be to show how existing theories stand in relation to each other. To say that they are simply different, or opposed, or mutually exclusive is not adequate. The job is to differentiate them in such a way as to expose their complementarities, to make clear how static and dynamic elements of systems can co-exist, and to show how a division of labour can be constructed amongst them. We hope we have made a substantial start in this direction by deploying a matrix of levels and sectors of analysis as a way of organising existing theories. We do not pretend to have produced a grand theory. But what follows might count as a grand theoretical framework within which a meta-theory might one day be constructed. And it does generate some of the meta-theoretical questions that such a theory will need to answer, and some of the meta-theoretical concepts it may find useful.

Our theoretical framework draws upon three types of tool. First, we argue that international systems need to be sectorally differentiated. International relations theory has tended to assume that international systems are, first and foremost, political systems. We argue that it is essential to separate out the military-political, economic, societal and environmental sectors of international systems. Focusing exclusively on the international military-political system makes it impossible to provide a comprehensive account of how international systems have evolved. For example, it is important to recognise that for most of world history, international economic systems have been more extensive than international political systems. This approach makes it possible to think of classical Afro-Eurasia as a weak international economic system linking together a number of separate international military-political systems. This divergence between economic and military-political systems has profound theoretical and practical implications which simply cannot be opened up for inspection if the international system is treated in undifferentiated terms.

The second set of tools highlights the fact that there are different analytical levels on which international systems can be investigated. This idea is already firmly embedded in the literature and does not require elaboration here. We distinguish five levels of analysis: system, subsystem, unit, subunit and individual, though given the high level of generalisation necessary to look at things on a world historical scale, we concentrate mostly on the first three of these.

The third set of tools comprises three sources of explanation that can help us to understand how systems are maintained and transformed:

interaction capacity, process and *structure*. Interaction capacity focuses on the system-wide capability of units to maintain contact with each other by moving goods, people and information around the system. It is about the speed, range and carrying capacity of physical systems (e.g., caravans, ships, railways, aircraft) and social systems (norms, rules and institutions) for transportation and communication. Process is about the types of interaction that actually take place (e.g., fighting, political recognition, trade, identity formation, transplantation of flora and fauna) and the recurrent patterns of behaviour that form as a consequence (e.g., war, diplomacy, money, religion, plague). Structure concerns the principles by which the units in a system are arranged, and the effects of those arrangements on the behaviour of the units (e.g., anarchy, market, international society).

Interaction capacity and process are quite straightforward, but the very idea of structure remains controversial. Our methodological pluralism will probably add to the controversy about the place of structure in international relations theory. We extend the challenge to Waltz's conception of structure that we first opened up in *The Logic of Anarchy*, using world history to show just how hugely mistaken is Waltz's closure of the second tier (structural and functional differentiation of units). And because sectoral differentiation is such a crucial feature of our framework, we extend the idea of structure beyond the military-political sector to embrace the economic and socio-cultural sectors. International economic systems are structured by either the market or by some form of authoritative allocation mechanism – thereby closely mirroring the structures that regulate international military-political systems. Socio-cultural structures are more difficult to specify in any international system. But drawing on the work of the English School and the constructivists, who have focused on the idea of an international society, it seems clear that international units within an empire or an anarchic arena can be constrained by a common ideology or set of beliefs about appropriate norms and rules of behaviour. In what might be seen as a radical move, we take the English School concepts of international and world society as constituting structure in the societal sector.

Some implications of using a thicker understanding of international systems

Our approach differentiates three general types of system:

(1) *full international systems*: these normally contain the full range of nested sectors, though in principle one might envisage (as in some

science fiction space-war scenarios) military-political interaction without economic or socio-cultural exchange;

(2) *economic international systems*: these lack military-political interaction, but would normally embody both economic and socio-cultural exchange;

(3) *pre-international systems*: these comprise mainly socio-cultural interactions, though they may also contain elements of non-commercial trade. They are the main type of large-scale system found amongst non-urban, pre-civilisational peoples.

These three types can be seen both as a hierarchy from more comprehensive (1) to less (2 and 3), and as a development sequence (from 3, through 2 to 1).

This classification still leaves the problem of how much interaction is necessary to constitute an international system. This is an empirical question to which at this stage it is probably impossible (given limitations on data), and perhaps unwise (given the range of historical conditions), to try to give a definitive universal answer. But our general guidelines for thinking of interaction of any type as sufficient to form a system are as follows:

• It must be sustained, in the sense of recurring on a regular basis over a substantial period of time. One does not want to preclude the possibility of short-lived systems, but longevity is important in order for structural pressure to take effect.
• It must be substantial, in the sense that it penetrates the units involved more than superficially. This might mean either or both of penetrating widely into society and/or penetrating the ruling elite. It is important to avoid defining the degree of interaction in terms of its effects. Doing so conflates cause with effect and negates the possibility of theory.

In order to understand the full character of international systems we have to ask three further questions: what types of units can constitute international systems? Are international systems a mechanical phenomenon or a socially constructed one? And what is the relationship between an international system's units and its structure?

What units?

There is controversy within international relations over the question of what units should be allowed to define international systems. This controversy arises primarily because of realism's strong commitment to the political sector, and its consequent privileging of the state. Given the long dominance of realism (and neorealism) in international relations, and given the obvious importance of the state in almost any perspective on the modern international system, state-centrism has tended to squeeze out or marginalise other units. Our more open, multi-sectoral framework allows, and our longer historical view requires, a more pragmatic approach to units. That said, however, we do retain the idea from neorealism that in understanding international systems it is very useful to focus on the dominant unit – i.e., the unit whose arrangements and activities do most to define the system. We define units in international systems as entities composed of various subgroups, organisations, communities and many individuals, sufficiently cohesive to have actor quality (i.e., to be capable of conscious decision-making), and sufficiently independent to be differentiated from others and to have standing at the higher levels (e.g., states, nations, transnational firms). This definition quite easily admits units other than the state, but the specification that units must be capable of self-directed behaviour, and that they must possess fairly high levels of cohesion, rules out diffuse entities such as civilisations. Using this understanding, the Roman Catholic Church, NATO, Microsoft and Hizbullah can be seen as units, but Christian, Western or Islamic civilisation cannot.

Using this definition of units, we take an empirical view of what units define any particular system. In pre-international systems, the main units are pre-civilisational ones such as bands, tribes, clans and perhaps chiefdoms. Such units display no or low levels of specialisation and division of labour, and cannot easily be analysed or differentiated by sector. They display behaviour in all the sectors – fighting, governing, trading and identity-formation and maintenance – but these activities are closely blended together. It is far from clear, for example, that the exchange of goods among such units can be understood in terms of modern economic logic, with its emphasis on monetary value, profit and individual motivation (Polanyi, 1971).

Economic international systems typically involve a range of units including tribes, empires, city-states, clans and early forms of firm. Compared to pre-civilisational ones, many of these units had sophisticated forms of internal specialisation (priests, kings, soldiers, scribes, slaves, artisans, etc.) and, therefore, a much more elaborate division of labour. But as a rule they lacked much differentiation into sectorally specialised types of international unit. One finds tribes, city-states and empires playing the key roles in both the military-political and economic sectors. Cities normally grew and flourished as nodal points on trade routes. Empires were typically attempts to control a trading system and its revenues. Barbarian tribes played mixed roles, sometimes as raiders and wreckers, and sometimes as intermediaries in the long-distance trading systems that connected different centres of civilisation. That said, individual merchants were also important players in economic systems, as were communities of merchants organised as 'trade diasporas' (Curtin, 1984).

Full international systems can also involve different types of unit. Such systems may be homogeneous, as Waltz's structural logic of military-political relations says they should be. They might be composed entirely of city-states, as in ancient Sumeria and classical Greece, or entirely of national states, as in the modern world system. Such homogeneous systems will tend to bind together closely the military-political and economic sectors, with the main political unit also being the main economic one. Mercantilist approaches to political economy in eighteenth-century Europe illustrate such a fusion of the political and the economic. But *contra* Waltz, full international systems can also be composed of unlike units. Much of the history of ancient and classical international systems can be told in these terms, with strong military and economic interplay among empires, city-states and barbarian tribes sustained for thousands of years.

In our view more is lost than gained by ignoring the *de facto* diversity of units in order to hang on to the conceptual neatness of a system defined in terms of a single type of unit. In some times and places such neatness may actually reflect the empirical world. But when it does not, the difficulties of diversity have to be faced rather than avoided. Embracing diversity of units also means abandoning the conventional (though little considered) assumption in much of international relations that the dominant units must be territorial. States, of course, are the archetypal territorial unit, which is why this assumption is so strong in international relations. Empires, city-states and some tribes can also be conceptualised in territorial terms. But many bands and tribes are nomadic, as, in a different way, are many types of economic actor. In international systems both ancient and modern, non-territorial actors often play alongside territorial ones, sometimes amongst the dominant units.

In sum, we take a pragmatic, empirical approach to determining what units compose and structure international systems in any given time and place. In practice, much of the story can be told in terms of five basic units – hunter-gatherer bands, tribes (including clans and chiefdoms), city-states, empires and national states – operating in our three types of international system. The five types of unit, can, like the three types of system they inhabit, in part be seen as stages in a process of development. The pre-civilisational units of pre-international systems, for example, were largely defined by the social ties of kinship. But kinship ties were inadequate for the larger and more complex units that followed on from the founding of cities, and were in many respects overlaid (though certainly not eliminated, even now) by cultural ties that constructed identity in terms of shared ideas such as religion and nation. Carneiro defines this process as 'the most important single step ever taken in the process of political development' (1978: 207). But while they are in one sense stages of development, these units also have to be seen as co-existing within full international systems, as most of them do even today, albeit with some no longer as dominant units. These basic five types can, and often do, stretch across all the main sectors of activity. But in economic and full international systems there is also space for sectorally specialised units, most obviously varieties of economic actor ranging from merchants, guilds and trade diasporas, through banks and some chartered companies to transnational corporations.

Mechanically versus socially constructed systems

We differentiate structure by sector into military-political, economic and societal (or socio-political). In doing so we note that by using the English School concepts of international and world society to stand for societal structure, we can introduce a constructivist element into thinking about the structure of international systems. That remark hinges on the view that most realist and economic views of system and structure are essentially mechanical, and it is worth explaining this distinction in more depth (see also Reus-Smit and Barnett, this volume).

A mechanistic or materialist view derives easily both from general systems theory and from analogies between the social and physical worlds, and is particularly strong in the American tradition of international relations thinking about international systems. In this view, international systems are similar to physical ones. Mechanical systems are about units interacting in ways that are structurally determined by some set of physical governing laws. In this view it makes no difference whether the units are lifeless (like planets) or sentient (like humans and their collective organisations). The behaviour of both types of unit will still be subject to objective mechanical laws deriving from material conditions, and the analyst's main job is to discover what these laws are.

An alternative view thinks that sentience makes a difference, and on this basis separates social from physical systems. When units are sentient, how they perceive each other is a major determinant of how they interact. If the units share a common identity (a religion or a language), or even just a common set of rules or norms (about how to determine relative status, and how to conduct diplomacy), then these inter-subjective understandings not only condition their behaviour, but also define the boundaries of a social system. This way of thinking has traditionally been stronger in European than in American approaches to international relations, though the current upsurge of social constructivism in international relations may rectify this imbalance. It goes back at least as far as Grotius (Cutler, 1991), and its classical roots are found in the notion that international law constitutes a community of those participating in the international legal order (Mosler, 1980: xv). Within international relations, this approach has so far been mainly embodied in the concept of *international society* put forward and developed by writers of the English School, including Manning (1962), Wight (1966b, 1977), Vincent (1974, 1986) Bull (1977, 1984), Gong (1984), Watson (1987, 1990, 1992), Mayall (1990) and Wæver (1998).

Bull and Watson's (1984: 1) classic definition of international society is:

a group of states (or, more generally, a group of independent political communities) which not merely form a system, in the sense that the behaviour of each is a necessary factor in the calculations of the others, but also have established by dialogue and consent common rules and institutions for the conduct of their relations, and recognise their common interest in maintaining these arrangements.

This definition captures both the mechanical side of systems (units interacting), and the socially constructed one (the establishment and maintenance of rules and institutions). We broadly accept the English School framework as a way of understanding international systems. We think that a purely mechanical conception is insufficient, and that the socially constructed elements provide valuable criteria both for benchmarking the development of international systems and for comparing them.

In tracing the story of international systems, both mechanical and social constructivist views of the phenomenon are required. One problem is that these two approaches have tended to develop separately within international relations, and not much thought has been devoted to how they relate to each other. At first glance, for example, Waltzian neorealism might seem to be purely mechanical and materialist in conception. But its strong dependence on sovereignty and high levels of interaction suggest that the theory in fact depends on constructivist elements. Sovereignty only works if it is recognised by other units, and this is one of the benchmark conditions for modern international society. Ruggie (1998b: introduction) has noted the anomaly of Waltz's dependence on the constructivist process of 'socialization' in order to produce the 'like' (i.e., sovereign) units on which his theory depends. It is beyond the scope of this chapter to resolve the question of whether mechanical international systems can exist apart

from socially constructed ones. What is clear is that both understandings
are relevant to the development of international systems.

Structuration

What disturbs many historians and some social scientists about the mechanical perspective on social systems in general and international systems in particular is the way that human beings get treated as cogs in a
machine over which they have no control. The historian E. P. Thompson
(1978: 267), for example, wrote a fierce denunciation of what he saw as a
dehumanised view of the world where 'systems and subsystems, elements
and structures are drilled up and down the pages pretending to be people'.
But as Archer (1988) has stressed, the problem with endowing human
beings with unfettered powers of agency and free-will is that human beings are invariably aware that they are, in fact, constrained by structural
forces. At the heart of the constructivist programme is the desire to make
provision for both structures and human agents. Wendt (1987) moves in
this direction by arguing that structures and agents are mutually constituted. What this implies is that practices habitually carried out by agents
to maintain and define their own interests and identity, simultaneously
reproduce the social structures that make up the larger system of which
they form a part. So, as argued in the previous section, when states engage in mutual recognition, they determine not only their own identity,
but also the societal structure of the system of which they form a part.
Subsequent actions that are premised on mutual recognition, such as
diplomatic codes of practice, simultaneously reproduce the component
states and the international system of which they form a part.

The mutual constitution of agent and structure was originally identified
by Giddens (1979: 93) as *structuration* and this concept indicates that, far
from being a cog in a machine, social agents are knowledgeable and skilful
players who constantly monitor their own behaviour and the behaviour of
others in order to ensure their own survival. In doing so, whether intentionally or not, they reproduce the structure of the system within which
they operate. The idea of structuration provides a way of conceptualising
the relationship between mechanical and socially constructed systems.
Because there is always a possibility that states will pursue competitive
rather than co-operative strategies in an anarchic system, the assumption
is often made that knowledge of this possibility will push all the actors
to pursue competitive strategies. Theories about arms races and markets
draw on this logic. But we know that states can build up co-operative rule-
governed relations and that these relations will persist so long as none of
the parties defects. In game-theoretic terms, this suggests that there is a

dominant strategy that mechanistically pushes all parties to compete. But if states move into a position where they are all co-operating, they can form an unstable equilibrium that will persist so long as no state breaks rank. The very knowledge that defection from co-operation will lead to the reassertion of competitive strategy can help to maintain the unstable equilibrium. Structuration is operating in both instances but the logic is different. We are seeing the competitive logic as mechanical and the co-operative logic as social.

A sketch of our perspective on world history

We do not have the space here to set out fully the perspective on world history that comes from adopting an international systems approach. But the main outlines of the story can be summarised as follows.

Precursors of international systems can be found in the extensive patterns of socio-cultural, and to a lesser extent economic, interaction that were typical of hunter-gatherer and tribal peoples who interacted for many millennia before the rise of cities and civilisations. Archaeological evidence reveals that around 40,000 years ago goods began to move considerable distances from where they originated, sometimes hundreds or even thousands of miles. Although this movement is often explained in terms of trade, we do not think that it is appropriate to relate the movement of these goods to the emergence of a proto-international economic system. Instead, we accept the argument that goods were exchanged between these units in order to consolidate relations with their immediate neighbours. Although there may often have been an economic dimension to the exchange, we assume that the goods changed hands primarily in order to maintain links with neighbouring bands and tribes because these units were too small on their own to form viable breeding groups. Long-term survival, therefore, depended upon the maintenance of these social links. We also accept the argument that these links played a vital role in helping humans to move into territory that had previously resisted colonisation. In particular, they were able to move into the Americas from Afro-Eurasia. All of these interactions, however, were local, although the goods that were exchanged locally could be moved over very considerable distances, being passed 'down the line' from one unit to another. The archaeological evidence, therefore, supports the idea that these early units formed direct links with neighbouring units and indirect links, through the movement of goods, over very much more extensive distances. Before the emergence of the sedentary and hierarchical units that we associate with cities and civilisations, there existed 'thin', but very extensive, pre-international systems.

What we will treat as fully fledged international systems – those having substantial economic and military-political interaction – began with the rise of city-states, and grew up within these precursor systems. The Sumerian city-states, for example, emerged around 3500 BC in the context of much more expansive pre-international systems of tribes and hunter-gatherer bands. The 'thin' pre-international systems created the potential for indirect links to be established with other international systems emerging further afield. Within a relatively short space of time these indirect links generated more direct links, with the Sumerian city-states, for example, engaging in trade with the cities in the Harappan civilisation that formed in Northern India. Once these links were consolidated, a sectorally layered arrangement emerged in which fully fledged international systems were typically embedded in geographically much more extensive systems of socio-cultural and economic interaction. This layered arrangement became the distinctive form of international system in the ancient and classical world of Afro-Eurasia. It was in some ways a scaled-up version of pre-international systems, with, for example, goods moving 'down the line' between Rome and Han China, without those two great empires ever coming into direct political or military contact.

Much of human history since the rise of civilisation in Afro-Eurasia can be told in terms of multiple international systems structured in this layered arrangement. A marked distinction has to be drawn, however, between Afro-Eurasia and the Americas, where there is much less evidence of contact between full international systems. As far as we know, no contact developed between the Meso-American and Andean international systems. The divergence can partially be explained by the fact that the Americas lacked animals, like horses, camels, sheep and cattle, that were domesticated in Afro-Eurasia and played an essential role in the formation of the tribes of pastoral nomads that roamed across the steppes and deserts of Afro-Eurasia. These tribes provided a vital transmission belt linking the full international systems that formed in Afro-Eurasia. The absence of these domesticated animals in the Americas had important consequences for the nature and level of interaction capacity that developed respectively in the Americas and Afro-Eurasia. On the other hand, in both the Americas and Afro-Eurasia, the geographical size of socio-cultural, economic and military-political systems tended to expand. Although socio-cultural and economic interaction tended nearly always to be wider in extent than military-political systems, the general expansion meant that over time, more and more of the human population were absorbed into military-political international systems as well. For the last five millennia there has been a steady tendency for international systems to expand at the expense of the pre-international ones out of which they originally formed.

In Afro-Eurasia, much more than in the Americas, conditions prevailed which encouraged the progressive merging of what had been distinct international systems. The wars between the Greeks and the Persians some 2,500 years ago, for example, marked the merging of Middle Eastern and Mediterranean international systems. By the fifteenth century, the maritime skills developed in Afro-Eurasia opened up the possibility of traversing the Atlantic and Pacific Oceans, changing what had been barriers into highways. These links were fostered in the sixteenth century, with the result that by the end of that century a rudimentary global economic system was in place. In subsequent centuries, European power expanded to all corners of the planet. By the nineteenth century, the Western powers were able to defeat the last and remotest remnants of the classical world, China and Japan, so extending the military-political sector to the global scale achieved in the economic sector three centuries earlier. This produced for the first time a geographically co-terminous set of systems in all three sectors. The contemporary global international system that we so take for granted is in fact only a century and a half old, and its story covers only 3 per cent of the world history of international systems.

Although geographic disjuncture between the sectors no longer exists, it might be argued that interaction in the economic sector still races ahead of developments in the military-political one. This creates a disjuncture of relative development, with the economy much more advanced in its global organisation than either the apparatuses of governance or the patterns of human identity.

Conclusions

Our approach rests on two fundamental and interrelated assumptions: first, that international relations theory has the potential to provide a framework that will foster a coherent and intelligible approach to the task of writing world history, and second, that world history provides the most appropriate setting for developing and testing international relations theory. Our intention, therefore, is to make a contribution to both world history and international relations, and our aim has been to show that harnessing international relations theory and world history has mutually beneficial and synergistic consequences.

World historians have regularly acknowledged the need for a stronger and more inclusive framework. Although Wallerstein's conception of world systems is still seen by McNeill (1998: 26–7), and others, as the 'leading candidate', it is far from being generally acknowledged as providing a satisfactory framework for the analysis of world history; indeed, McNeill has noted that world historians are 'still fumbling around in search of a more adequate conceptualization of human history'. And according to Green (1998: 62), 'debate on this matter is just beginning'. We are anxious to ensure that international relations theorists make a contribution to this debate.

At the heart of our project is the belief that the theory surrounding the idea of an international system provides the basis for an effective, although obviously not the only possible, framework for examining world history. In making this claim we also wish simultaneously to undermine the widespread assumption inside and outside of the discipline that international relations represents a retarded social science. Our approach forms a direct challenge to the view of the philosopher Alan Ryan (1998: 27), who has noted 'the feebleness of theorising in international relations and the superiority of good narrative history to what is passed off as "theory"'. As the search for an effective conceptual framework by world historians amply demonstrates, the distinction between history and theory drawn by Ryan rests on a false dichotomy.

From our perspective, international relations theory has been sold, and has sold itself, short on two main counts. On the one hand, there has been a widespread failure to look for ways of integrating the rich and divergent areas of theory that have been developed across the discipline over many years. On the other hand, the attention of international relations theorists has too often been restricted either to the contemporary international system or to an earlier system made up of European states. We take these two deficiencies as being largely responsible for the failure of international relations thinking to make any significant impact on either history or the other social sciences, and we have made a concerted effort to rectify them. In terms of the concerns of this chapter, our view is that English School theory provides by far the most congenial linkage point at which the discourses of international relations and historical sociology should be connected.

Part III
Conclusion: The future of historical
sociology in international relations

11 Historical sociology and international relations theory

Steve Smith

Introduction

Historical sociology faces an identity crisis because it is no longer clear just what is entailed by the approach. Once it was very clear: historical sociology was an approach that, by disputing both the mono-causal logic of realism, and the functional undifferentiation of its core unit (the state), challenged the fundamental assumptions of realism, and thus was one of a group of approaches said to be alternatives to realism. From the late 1980s onwards, historical sociology was grouped together (by myself amongst others) as one of the 'reflectivist' approaches that were challenging the neorealist/neoliberal orthodoxy. I am now clear that this is a mistaken view of where historical sociology fits into the discipline of international relations, since historical sociology is at base a rationalist enterprise that can fit relatively easily with the mainstream. I want to spend the first part of this chapter substantiating this claim, and then I want to look at what a more reflectivist historical sociology might look like. I want to use the previous chapters as pegs on which to hang my argument, and also to give the editors (whom I do not think for a moment will agree with my claims) clear reference points to respond to. Let me say at the outset that my claim does not mean that I think that historical sociology is any the less important as an approach to the understanding of world politics just because it seems to me to be essentially rationalist. All I want to claim is that the form of historical sociology represented so strongly and persuasively in this volume is a narrow form of what the sociological imagination might have constructed.

Let me start by briefly saying something about the preceding chapters. Broadly speaking they fall into three main groups: the first, which comprises the vast majority of the contributions, sees the shadows of Marx and Weber in the background. These chapters, by Hobson, Hobden, Cutler, Shaw, Gills, Linklater and Halliday, adopt an essentially causal (albeit multi-causal) approach. The second 'group' comprises just one chapter, that by Buzan and Little, which offers a powerful realist-inspired account of the historical development of various 'thick' international systems. The third group contains two chapters, those by Barnett and Reus-Smit: they develop social constructivist approaches to historical sociology. The first two of these groups, whilst differing on questions of what the world is like (ontology), share very similar views on the ways in which that world operates: Buzan and Little are no less causal than the authors of the chapters in the first group. This leaves the third group, and here I think that there is a noticeable and critically important difference between Barnett and Reus-Smit in that Reus-Smit offers a significantly deeper notion of the influence of ideas on the social world. Indeed, I would go so far as to claim that of all the chapters only Reus-Smit's offers any real diversion from what is an overwhelmingly materialist account of historical sociology. I am most in agreement with Reus-Smit, and not surprisingly, therefore, my argument will be closest to the position taken in his chapter, although this does not mean that he would necessarily agree with the main themes of this chapter, which centre on pointing out just how materialist and mainstream is the vast bulk of historical sociology, and offering an alternative view of what a more reflectivist or ideational historical sociology might look like.

The identity crisis of mainstream historical sociology: reflectivism or rationalism?

The rationalist roots of mainstream international relations theory

My first task is to say something about where historical sociology fits into contemporary international theory. I am not going to write at length about the current state of the discipline of international relations since I have recently done so at length elsewhere (Smith, 1995, 1996, 1997, 2000a, 2000b, 2000c). However, I do need to summarise the developments of the last decade in order to be able to trace the way in which historical sociology has been seen as relating to the mainstream.

Since the early 1990s the mainstream position in international relations theory has been that of a research programme comprising neorealism and neoliberalism. The most common term for this mainstream is *rationalism*. In essence, rationalism represents the merging of the long-term rivalry between liberal and realist accounts of international relations. Since the development of a separate discipline of international relations, there has been an ongoing debate between those approaches. It was these differing world-views that lay at the core of the 'debate' in the 1930s between what later became known as idealism and realism. The main differences between these positions focused on the nature of international anarchy and of the state. Broadly speaking, realism has assumed that unitary, egotistical states were the key actors in world politics, and that international anarchy was the main determinant of state behaviour, resulting in a world whereby state leaders were preoccupied with power, security and above all survival. In contrast, liberal approaches saw a different world: states were not always central to key areas of international relations, were not unitary actors, and reacted to the pressures of both the international and the domestic environments; state leaders were not only concerned with survival and security, but also with economics, and therefore co-operation was more achievable than was assumed by realists. These differences between the two approaches were the historical focus of the main theoretical debates in the discipline for over fifty years. Generations of international relations students were trained to see this as the core debate within the discipline. But by the early 1980s, the research programmes of the two approaches started to merge. This was due to three main factors. First, there was the publication of Waltz's *Theory of International Politics* (1979), which outlined a parsimonious research programme based on a much tighter model of social science than had hitherto been the case with realist work. Second, there was the growing interest of liberals in the ability of international institutions to mitigate the effects of international anarchy, especially in the area of international political economy, which offered the prospect of significant overlaps with the emerging research programme of Waltzian neorealism. Thirdly, there was the increasing influence of one specific methodology within the social sciences, rational choice theory.

The impact of rational choice theory is to my mind the most important of these influences, because it provided a methodology suitable for both neorealism and neoliberalism, whereas previously they had been seemingly divided because of different ontologies. By the 1990s they had effectively merged into one research programme, what Ole Wæver has termed the 'neo-neo synthesis' (Wæver, 1996), and it is of crucial importance to note that in the early 2000s they are being taught in the main graduate schools in the United States as the twin, and complementary, elements of the core research programme of the discipline. This is reflected in Charles Kegley's (1995) review of the two approaches. He concludes that, despite their different assumptions about human nature, the possibility for improvement, the nature of war and the character of international society, the two approaches are basically similar. He calls for the development of 'that hybrid combination of both realist and liberal concepts around which a new paradigm might be organized . . . [one] that integrates the most relevant features of both theoretical traditions' (Kegley, 1995: 17). Similarly, David Baldwin (1993), in his discussion of the debate between neorealism and neoliberalism, concludes that, despite important differences, there are four issues over which they are in agreement: first, 'the current debate does not revolve around techniques of statecraft', notably the role of military force; second, 'both sides argue from assumptions that states behave like egoistic value maximisers. Moral considerations are hardly mentioned'; third, 'both sides treat states as the primary actors'; fourth, 'this is not a debate between conflict theorists and cooperation theorists... both sides have moved beyond the simple dichotomy between cooperation and conflict that characterized earlier discussions' (Baldwin, 1993: 9). Taking the differences and the similarities into account, Baldwin suggests that the two approaches can together contribute to a 'better understanding of the conditions that promote or inhibit international cooperation' (Baldwin, 1993: 22), and he notes three focal points for the debate between them which provide a 'a rich research agenda for both neoliberal and neorealist scholars' (Baldwin, 1993: 22–3). These are the nature of international co-operation, the role of domestic politics in international relations, and the relative utility of various tools of statecraft, notably military force and economic measures. Baldwin sees these as facilitating a synthesis between neorealism and neoliberalism. However, despite all the talk of the two approaches merging to form the dominant research programme, it is important to note John Mearsheimer's comment that 'liberal institutionalism in its latest form is no longer a clear alternative to realism, but has, in fact, been swallowed up by it. The most recent variant of liberal institutionalism is realism by another name' (Mearsheimer, 1995b: 85).

This rationalist mainstream dominates the discipline because it dominates its main academic community, namely that of the United States, a dominance that has been powerfully illustrated by Kal Holsti (1985) and Ole Wæver (1998b) (see also Smith, 2000b). As argued above, at first sight rationalist approaches may seem to share much in terms of ontology, but the more important point is that they share a similar conception of social science, the impact of which will be discussed below. By this I simply mean that they share assumptions about the appropriate (and inappropriate) methodologies and epistemology for studying the social world. The main ones are those of positivism, by which I mean a belief in naturalism in the social world (that is to say that the social world is amenable to the same kinds of analysis as the natural world); a separation between facts and values, by which is meant both that 'facts' are theory-neutral, and that normative commitments should not influence what counts as facts or as knowledge; a commitment to uncovering patterns and regularities in the social world, patterns and regularities that exist apart from the methods used to uncover them; and finally a commitment to empiricism as the arbiter of what counts as knowledge. Clearly, several of these assumptions would not be shared by historical sociology, but the commitment to naturalism, as revealed in an appeal to causal analysis, is indeed shared, and I want to say more about that below.

As for alternatives to the rationalist mainstream, there are two main contenders: the first comprises what are usually termed 'reflectivist' approaches; the second is social constructivism. The main shared feature of reflectivist approaches is what they are opposed to, namely the ontological, and especially the epistemological, assumptions of the rationalist mainstream. Reflectivism is typically said to include feminist, postmodern, Critical Theory, post-colonial and normative approaches, as well as historical sociology. Clearly there are major differences between these approaches, most notably in the area of epistemology, but each is critical of rationalism, and together they have been portrayed as a challenge (or even *the* challenge) to rationalism. I have certainly argued this myself (Smith, 1995, 1996, 1997), but in recent years I have become more interested in the differences among reflectivist approaches. Historical sociology is the approach that fits least well, because it shares much with rationalism in terms of its underlying epistemological assumptions.

Constructivism as an alternative to mainstream rationalism?

The other alternative, originally seen as one approach, but now clearly dividing into a set of importantly different approaches, is social constructivism. Social constructivism is commonly located as an approach lying between rationalism and reflectivism (see Adler 1997; Checkel, 1998; Wendt, 1999). Its main theme is that the social world is what we make it; we construct the key features. Within constructivism there is a division, with more radical authors, such as Chris Reus-Smit, Friedrich Kratochwil and Nick Onuf, tending to a version of constructivism that stresses the role of rules and inter-subjective understandings, and the dominant tendency, that of Wendt, Adler and Checkel, being more concerned with developing a constructivism that shares with the mainstream the assumptions about both the furniture of the social world and agreement on how to study that world. I would go so far as to say that social constructivism in its dominant (mainly North American) form is very close to the neoliberal wing of the rationalist paradigm. As will be noted below, this is precisely why it is seen as acceptable by many mainstream writers: it is acceptable because it adopts not only the ontology but also, much more importantly, the epistemology of the mainstream. This distinction between fundamentally different forms of constructivism fits with my long-stated claim that there are always at least two stories to tell about the social world (see Hollis and Smith, 1990), one to do with explaining that world, the other with understanding it.

Many constructivists are at pains to differentiate constructivism from reflectivism, with the litmus test being a commitment to 'the social science enterprise'. The strongest justification of this position is Wendt's (1987; 1992: 393–4, 422–5; 1994; 1999). As he put it in an article he co-wrote with Ronald Jepperson and Peter Katzenstein, 'The term *identity* here is intended as a useful label, not as a signal of commitment to some exotic (presumably Parisian) social theory' (Jepperson, Wendt and Katzenstein, 1996: 34). In his 1999 book *Social Theory of International Politics*, Wendt spends a lot of time discussing issues of epistemology. One quote gives a flavour of his argument: 'Epistemologically, I have sided with positivists . . . our best hope is social science . . . [but] on ontology – which is to my mind the more important issue – I will side with post-positivists. Like them I believe that social life is "ideas all the way down" (or almost anyway . . .)' (Wendt, 1999: 90). He is, he states, 'a strong believer in science . . . I am a positivist' (Wendt, 1999: 39). Thus, much constructivist work is much closer to rationalism than it is to reflectivism, because it shares methodological and epistemological assumptions with rationalism (most obviously, with neoliberal institutionalism). By contrast, the gap between this version of social constructivism and reflectivist work is fundamental. These constructivists can agree with rationalists that states are the main actors and that social science is the method of study. With reflectivists, these scholars can agree that ideas matter more than is represented by the neo-institutionalists. But as long as the method of study is to be social science, the linkage with rationalism is much stronger.

Wendt's constructivism is coming under increasing challenge from a variety of writers, Reus-Smit being prominent among them (see Price and Reus-Smit, 1998; Reus-Smit, 1999), who want to develop a distinctly different form of constructivism. The clearest contrast is between the work of Wendt and that of two of the other, earlier founders of the approach, Nick Onuf and Friedrich Kratochwil (see Kratochwil and Ruggie, 1986; Kratochwil 1989; Onuf, 1989, 1998). The basic difference concerns the type of theory appropriate for analysing the social world. Wendt is fundamentally a positivist and a naturalist on questions of knowledge and this means that analysis is limited to certain kinds of things in the social world, and these things can be analysed using the same methods as in the natural sciences. The problem with all this is that there is an important intellectual tradition that sees these worlds as distinct, requiring distinct and different analytical approaches, and this tradition is the one that is the basis of the form of constructivism preferred by Onuf and Kratochwil. Thus, the crucial distinction is that, whereas Wendt ends up painting a world that seems very similar to that painted by rationalists, the social worlds seen by Onuf and Kratochwil are very different to those of the rationalists: for Onuf and Kratochwil it is a world in which actors are governed by language, rules and choices. This view of the social world, which has its intellectual roots in the work of writers such as Wittgenstein and Winch, is one that does not share Wendt's naturalism.

This epistemological difference between the two forms of constructivism has enormous consequences for their relationship with the mainstream. Increasingly, constructivism, of the Wendtian variety, is being accepted as a (the?) debating partner of rationalism. This has recently been illustrated in an article by three former editors of the US journal *International Organization*, Katzenstein, Keohane and Krasner, in which they argue that 'rationalism . . . and constructivism now provide the major points of contestation for international relations scholarship' (Katzenstein, Keohane and Krasner, 1998: 646; see also Walt, 1998). But not all of constructivism is included in their definition, only that which acknowledges 'the possibility of a social science and a willingness to engage openly in scholarly debate with rationalism' (Katzenstein, Keohane and Krasner, 1998: 677). They claim that postmodern constructivism (by which I assume they mean the work of many of those labelled reflectivists) by contrast denies 'the use of evidence to adjudicate between truth claims. In contrast to conventional and critical constructivism, postmodernism falls clearly outside of the social science enterprise, and in IR research it risks becoming self-referential and disengaged from the world, protests to the contrary notwithstanding' (Katzenstein, Keohane and Krasner, 1998: 678).

This threat of the marginalisation of work that stands outside the social science canon was originally famously used by Robert Keohane in his address as the new president of the International Studies Association in 1988. He simply claimed that reflectivism suffered from the weakness of

the lack of a clear reflective research program . . . Until the reflective scholars or others sympathetic to their arguments have delineated such a research program and shown in particular studies that it can illuminate important issues in world politics, they will remain on the margins of the field, largely invisible to the preponderance of empirical researchers, most of whom explicitly or implicitly accept one or another version of rationalistic premises (Keohane, 1989: 173).

Mainstream historical sociology in international relations: a rationalist neorealism

Where does historical sociology fit into this picture of contemporary international relations theory? As I imagine is now clear, because I consider the bulk of work within historical sociology as dependent on a materialist and naturalist social theory, I see considerable overlaps between it and rationalism, and few similarities with reflectivism. Indeed, I would go so far as to claim that, contrary to the self-image of historical sociology as a radical account of human history, there are in fact few barriers to a fruitful debate between materialist historical sociology and rationalism. Given the importance of the two main intellectual influences on historical sociology, Marx and Weber, this is not surprising. Of course, there are considerable differences between historical sociology and the neoliberal/neorealist mainstream. The central ones are historical sociology's challenge to the notion of the state as an undifferentiated actor by focusing on how states emerged and changed according to the influence of domestic and international forces, its claim to be a critical theory, and its forcing of a rethinking of the origins of the state. These result in a picture of the state that is significantly different to that found within neorealism: the state becomes a construct of a variety of social forces, some domestic, some international, rather than a unit that is essentially the same throughout history. This is directly opposed to Waltz's claim that states are functionally undifferentiated, a claim that lies at the core of neorealism's theory of international relations. In this sense, historical sociology undermines what is probably the central theoretical assumption of neorealism; this is why historical sociology is seen as a reflectivist approach.

However, there are two main problems with this assessment. The first is that historical sociology's differences from the mainstream have lessened in the last decade as a result of related developments in the historical sociology and neorealism literatures. Within historical sociology, the Weberian influence has overshadowed the Marxist influence in historical sociology. The first major works on historical sociology were indebted to both Marx and Weber (see Wallerstein, 1974, 1980; Tilly, 1975; Skocpol, 1979; Giddens, 1985; Hall, 1986; Mann, 1986, 1993), but since then, Weber has, I believe, become the more influential (see Evans, Rueschemeyer and Skocpol, 1985; Hall, 1986, 1996; Jarvis, 1989; Smith, 1991; Shaw, 1994; Spruyt, 1994; Thomson, 1994; Rueschemeyer and Skocpol, 1996; Hobson, 1997). And, as Steve Hobden has shown, in the work of the 'founding figures' it is Weber's notion of the state that underpins the historical sociology of Tilly, Skocpol and Mann (Hobden, 1998: 190); similarly, John Hobson, in outlining his own neo-Weberian sociology of international relations, cites a list of other neo-Weberian historical sociologists including Skocpol, Mann, Giddens and Hall (Hobson, 1997: 3). This does not mean that Marxist-influenced historical sociology has disappeared – far from it (see, notably, Halliday,

1987, 1999; Rosenberg 1994); but it has become the minor partner to Weberian historical sociology. One result of this is that the vast majority of the historical sociology literature has not followed up the emancipatory and normative imperatives of Marxism. Within neorealism, a similar move has been underway, questioning the idea of an undifferentiated state to enquire into the influence of the variety of state forms on historical international systems (Buzan, Jones and Little, 1993; Buzan and Little, 2000). In this sense, historical sociologists and some neorealists have been moving towards overlapping, if not common, research agendas. In both developments looms the spectre of Weber, as each examines the relationship between the international and the domestic in terms of historical configurations of social power. In a crucially important sense, this should not be surprising, given Weber's enormous influence on the development of the disciplines of sociology and international relations.

The second problem is that despite these differences the two approaches share much, both in terms of ontology and, to me more importantly, epistemology. In terms of the kinds of worlds that they see, both realism and historical sociology agree on the key actor in world politics, that is, the state; more than this, they are statist, in that both see world politics through the lens of the state. Their commitment to the centrality of the state in politics is more than a methodological convenience, since, because of the influence of Weber, both see the state as the central political actor. As Weber argued in 'Politics as a Vocation' (1948), 'We wish to understand by politics only the leadership, or the influencing of the leadership, of a *political* association, hence today, of a *state*' (Weber, 1948: 77). From this follows his definition of the state, namely that

a state is a human community that (successfully) claims the *monopoly of the legitimate use of physical force* within a given territory ... Hence, 'politics' for us means striving to share power or striving to influence the distribution, either among states or among groups within a state ... When a question is said to be a 'political' question ... what is always meant is that interests in the distribution, maintenance, or transfer of power are decisive ... He who is active in politics strives for power (Weber, 1948: 78).

As Michael Smith puts it: 'More than any other modern figure Weber established the discourse of the realist approach to international relations' (Smith, 1986: 53). Similarly, both historical sociology and neorealism agree on the influence of both the domestic and international environments on the nature and behaviour of the state; and both see the key issue to be explained as the nature of war. Just one quotation will illustrate this influence: in the memorable words of Charles Tilly, 'War made the state, and the state made war' (Tilly, 1975: 42). This is a quintessentially

Weberian statement, which could be equally at home in either the neo-realist or the historical sociological literature. These similarities between historical sociology and the neorealist component of the rationalist main-stream has led Barry Buzan to claim that 'several historical sociologists . . . have come to analytical conclusions remarkably similar to a rather crude view of classical Realism . . . The result of their enquiries has been to support a harsh, social Darwinistic, interpretation that shares much with the main assumptions of realism' (Buzan, 1996: 60).

However, although there are these similarities in the onotological commitments of historical sociology and neorealism, I think that of more relevance to contemporary debates within international relations theory is the extent to which they share epistemological assumptions. Both historical sociology and rationalist international relations accept one model of how to analyse the social world. Both, therefore, are part of the social science enterprise, in the narrow sense used in the United States. Accordingly, both deem causal analysis as appropriate to the social world. The leading historical sociology scholars, for example Hall, Mann, Skocpol, Tilly and Wallerstein, all accept a broadly explanatory form of social theory, one in which causal, albeit multi-causal, analysis is the way to study the development of state–society relations. Steve Hobden has extensively analysed the epistemological commitments of four of these writers (Hall is the exception), and he shows how all of them rely on a notion of explanation (Hobden, 1998: 174–5). I will simply provide examples from each author.

Skocpol states that to understand revolutions it is necessary that 'the analyst take a nonvoluntarist, structural perspective on their causes and processes . . . all existing approaches theorize on the basis of a voluntarist image of how revolutions happen' (Skocpol, 1979: 14). She goes on to criticise those 'purposive' theorists for fundamentally misunderstanding the 'causes' of revolutions: 'The purposive image is just as misleading about the processes and outcomes of historical revolutions as it is about their causes. For the image strongly suggests that revolutionary processes and outcomes can be understood in terms of the activity and intentions or interests of the key groups . . . Any valid explanation of revolution depends upon the analyst's "rising above" the viewpoints to find important regularities across given historical instances' (Skocpol, 1979: 17–18).

Tilly's work is less explicit on its epistemological and methodological assumptions, and he does show far more interest in questions of agency than does Skocpol. But his methodological position is well summed up in the title of his 1984 book *Big Structures, Large Processes, Huge Comparisons.* He is interested in how large structural forces influence the processes by which human beings interact so as to form societies and states, and to find out what these are, he wants to use those methods which best capture 'the actual structure of the social world' (Tilly, 1984: 146). More generally, his work focuses on the two 'master processes' of world history, namely, the rise of capitalism and the growth of states and the states system. In his major work (Tilly, 1990) he explains the rise of these two 'master processes' in terms of two key variables, the ways in which capital and coercion were organised and concentrated. The first chapter of the book is a sophisticated analysis of the relationship among three internal factors (cities, coercion and capital), and of the influence of the international environment, specifically the need for a war-making capability. Crucially, he sees the international environment, specifically war, as having causal power: 'war drove not only the state system and the formation of individual states, but also the distribution of power over the state' (Tilly, 1990: 187). Steve Hobden has noted that Tilly is ambiguous in his writings, in that there are several places in which he speaks in more constructivist language (Hobden, 1998: 106–16), but it is clear that Tilly's model of the linkage between cities, coercion, capital and war-making requires an almost hydraulic, or rigidly structuralist, causal mechanism to work. There is little room for active agents, as distinct from agents reacting to these internal and external causal processes.

Michael Mann's work aims at developing an account of social power 'from the beginning', and his core claim is that 'A general account of societies, their structure, and their history can best be given in terms of the interrelations of what I will call the four sources of social power: ideological, economic, military and political (IEMP) relationships' (Mann, 1986: 2). Mann is ambiguous as to how these sources are to be evaluated; at times he writes as if causal analysis is appropriate, while at other times he writes in terms of shared norms and rules, which implies a much more hermeneutic social theory. Steve Hobden has powerfully documented this ambiguity in Mann's work (Hobden, 1998: 134–41); indeed, Hobden argues that they are inconsistent and thus constitute a 'serious weakness' in Mann's analysis (Hobden, 1998: 139). In my view, Mann's sources of social power ultimately have to be causal. Though there are pointers to a more 'insider' account in the two volumes of his history of social power, I think these are intended to be read as accounts of how the four external causal forces operate on and through agents. Even though he states that ideology is one of the four sources of social power, it is important to note that he limits his definition of ideology to it being a potential power resource – those who can successfully claim authority over meaning thereby have power: 'To monopolize norms is thus a route to power' (Mann, 1986: 22). Ideology is not something that constitutes the identities or interests of actors; instead, it intensifies 'the cohesion, the confidence, and, therefore, the power of an already-established social group...it largely strengthens whatever is there' (Mann, 1986: 24). In other words, understanding is ultimately reducible to explanation. Maybe Mann will say more on this when he publishes the fourth volume of the series, on the theory of social power, but from reading the first two volumes it is clear to me that he conceives of social power in a decidedly causal manner.

Wallerstein's work, as might be predicted from his preference for Marx over Weber, is explicitly structuralist and causal (Wallerstein, 1974, 1980, 1989). His model of the world system treats economic structures as external to actors (and it is worth noting that the key actors for Wallerstein are classes) and sees these structures being ultimately determining. The world economic system is primary, with other aspects of the social world being produced by it. As Hobden has noted, Wallerstein is closer to Waltz than to any of the other historical sociologists discussed in this chapter (Hobden, 1998: 1655). Wallerstein's account focuses primarily on economic structures and he treats these in a deterministic manner. In the three volumes of his history of the world system, there is little in the way of discussion of what economic structures and processes meant for the actors, and the story is told in terms of a series of factors external to individuals causing their behaviour.

John Hall's first major work, *Powers and Liberties* (1986), contains a strong plea for a particular kind of social theory. Hall wants to trace the development of human society by looking at the interaction between three forms of power – economic, political and ideological – and in so doing he wants to 'counteract the tendency in modern thought to lend too great weight to the power of "ideas", especially when no attempt is made to examine why a particular belief system has a specific content, why it spreads and why its hold is maintained over time' (Hall, 1986: 20). For him, there are two main arguments against the view that social meanings are important in understanding human history: the first is that beliefs do not 'exist in a vacuum...they can be explained in other more structural terms' (Hall, 1986: 19). Second, 'most belief systems are adaptable, and change considerably over time...[they] are loose and baggy monsters, full of saving clauses and alternatives that can be brought out by an interested group when occasion demands. This process needs to be explained in traditional social structural terms. In other words, we are returned to the position that there is an affinity between people's beliefs and their circumstances' (Hall, 1986: 19–20). This position is again clear in Hall's 1996 book *International Orders*, where he bemoans the 'idealism which so plagues the social sciences, that is, the view that ideas make the world go round – and thereby that we can study ourselves rather than fulfil our proper duty of conducting research into actual structures of society' (Hall, 1996: 27).

In summary, the 'founding figures' of historical sociology, or to be more precise, those who have been cited by those working at the historical sociology/international relations borderline (thus omitting such key sociologists as Bloch, Braudel, Barrington Moore, Perry Anderson and Giddens), have tended to base their work on explanatory and causal social theory. The main influences have been Marx and Weber. Marx's holist explanatory approach, but especially his materialism, leads fairly straightforwardly into causal analysis and a social theory that fits within 'the social science enterprise'. The influence of Weber is more nuanced. In my view, historical sociology has privileged one aspect of Weber's social theory, resulting in a rather starkly causal and materialist neo-Weberian historical sociology. This is also the argument of Chris Reus-Smit in his chapter in this volume. As he puts it: 'Important though the neo-Weberian contribution has been, it exhibits a subterranean rationalism and materialism that handicaps the development of an heuristically powerful historical sociology of international relations' (Reus-Smit, this volume, p. 121). Similarly, Michael Barnett in this volume notes that 'Historical sociologists . . . were more significantly influenced by the Marx–Weber debate on various macro-historical outcomes; accordingly, their arguments tended to be rooted in the disputed relationship between the political economy, class structure and class conflict, and the state' (Barnett, this volume, p. 104).

Yet, another reading of Weber is possible, and this reading stresses a rather different model of the social world. This reading comes from Weber's comments at the start of *Economy and Society* where he states that 'We shall speak of "action" insofar as the acting individual attaches a subjective meaning to his behaviour' (Weber, 1978: 4). This meaning cannot be objectively determined: meaning cannot 'refer to an objectively "correct" meaning or one which is "true" in some metaphysical sense. It is this which distinguishes the empirical sciences of action, such as sociology and history, from the . . . disciplines . . . which seek to ascertain the "true" and "valid" meanings associated with the objects of their investigation' (Weber, 1978: 4). He goes on to differentiate between two main forms of understanding, direct observational and explanatory, with his key concern being to build a sociology based in the meaning that actions had for actors. As he puts it: 'Interpretative sociology considers the individual . . . and his action as the basic unit . . . the individual is also the upper limit and the sole carrier of meaningful conduct . . . the task of sociology is to reduce . . . concepts to "understandable" action, that is, without exception, to the actions of participating individual men' (Weber, 1948: 55).

Many commentators read Weber's aim as being that of bringing together explaining and understanding. To quote the first sentence of *Economy and Society*, in which Weber defines sociology: 'Sociology . . . is a science concerning itself with the interpretive understanding of social action and *thereby with a causal explanation of its course and consequences*' (Weber, 1978: 4, emphasis added). He wants to develop an account of meaning that is both 'adequate at the level of meaning' and causally adequate (Weber, 1978: 11). The relationship between the two is that 'A correct causal interpretation of typical action means that the process which is claimed to be typical is shown to be both adequately grasped on the level of meaning and at the same time the interpretation is to some degree causally adequate' (Weber, 1978: 12). Weber's social theory is importantly different to those of Marx and Durkheim, and it is his interest in the subjective meaning that action has for agents that lies at the heart of this. However, my reading of Weber is that, despite his interest in subjective meaning, his sociology ultimately depends more on causality than interpretation. Weber, after all, wants to develop a sociological science. This is illustrated by his insistence, in *Economy and Society*, on the need for subjective understanding to be causally adequate, by which he means that 'according to established generalizations from experience, there is a probability that it will always actually occur in the same way . . . causal explanation depends on being able to determine that there is a probability . . . that a given observable event . . . will be followed or accompanied by another event' (Weber, 1978: 11–12). In short, there is ambiguity in Weber's work over the exact relationship between subjective understanding and causal analysis. In his empirical work, Weber seems to drop most of the material on subjective meaning, and instead concentrates on the issue of causal adequacy.

The 'switchmen' analogy, used in his study of the social psychology of world religions, epitomises this ambiguity. Reus-Smit has mentioned this in his chapter in this volume. On the one hand, Weber seems to be saying that ideas determine action, yet on the other, he undermines this by the second part of the relevant sentence: 'Yet, very frequently, the "world images" that have been created by "ideas" have, like switchmen, determined the tracks along which action has been pushed by the dynamic of interest' (Weber, 1948: 280). Indeed, the preceding sentence reads: 'Not ideas, but material and ideal interests, directly govern men's conduct' (Weber, 1948: 280). The switchmen do nothing other than direct actors to routes for achieving their goals, which are themselves determined by material interests. As John Hall puts it: 'The essential problem is that the metaphor takes for granted that the railway lines or tracks have already been laid' (Hall, 1993: 48). In this light, the role of the ideational is secondary to the role of the material in the social world.

In other words, the materialism of Marx and this materialist reading of Weber has resulted in an historical sociology focused on large-scale social 'forces' such as war, capitalism and industrialisation. This is clear both in the work of the founders of historical sociology and in the contributions to this volume, virtually all of which talk in decidedly materialist ways: multi-causal they might be, but causal nonetheless.

A Foucauldian historical sociology as an alternative to the rationalist mainstream

What might be alternatives to this form of historical sociology? There are two points that I want to make. The first is that historical sociology as it has developed is curiously vocal about some, and silent about other, 'material' factors. Class, nation and state get considerable attention, but gender and, to some extent, non-Western voices are much less pronounced. I do not mean that women are absent, only that the framework within which questions to do with gender and women are discussed is overwhelmingly that of class, state and nation. Mann's work is full of references to issues such as female employment, but gender is not one of his focal points. There are of course many different ways to undertake gender analysis, some of which would want to replace the economic materialism of Marx, and the multi-causal materialism of Weber, with a patriarchal materialism; others would want to ask the seemingly innocent, and limited, liberal question of where women have been in historical sociological processes. Others still would want to link the normative and emancipatory elements of an historical sociology informed by Critical Theory to a focus on women. Finally, others would want to pose similar questions about the role of ideas and material factors in constructing the identities and subjectivities of historical agents, including the gendered aspects of these identities and subjectivities. My purpose is not to offer some exhaustive list, but only to make the point that there are many ways in which feminist, or gender-based, historical sociology might be developed. It is curious that gender is so absent in historical sociology, given its importance in the discipline of sociology, but it is remarkably absent. Similarly, although much historical sociology deals at length with various regions of the world, it remains the case that the lens through which it is viewed is very much the Western state. The story is one about modernising and industrialising states operating within a states system: the great processes are indeed those mentioned by Tilly, the rise of capitalism and the development of the states system, and this means that the framework is clearly one aimed at telling the story of the emergence of the Western state in terms of the relationships between classes, nations and states. Therefore, one alternative to the bulk of historical sociology would be to develop non-materialist accounts that focus on issues connected to women/gender, ethnicity or colonialism.

But, of course, there are other alternatives, and I want to conclude this chapter by putting forward a very different form of historical sociology. What follows is obviously open to the major objection that it is simply a theoretical possibility, since there will be no empirical study to back it up. Let me be clear: I think that the empirical work undertaken by historical sociology is enormously strong and impressive, and I am offering nothing to compare to that record of scholarship. However, I do firmly believe that historical sociology, apart from being silent about some material factors, is also open to the charge that it tends to operate within one model of the social world, one in which great processes cause or determine history. Put simply, I want to point to a different notion of what the social world is like. Let me immediately accept that some historical sociologists do share this aim, notably Anthony Giddens (1984), but these are not the writers who have been at the forefront of the debate between historical sociology and international relations (presumably, precisely because they do not share rationalist international relations' notion of structure). But with that proviso, what is most noticeable is that all the key figures in the historical sociology/international relations area work within a very different social theory, one that is both materialist and explanatory.

The intellectual influences for an alternative, or, more accurately, a complementary, historical sociology would be Wittgenstein, Winch and Foucault, writers who see the social world as something in which the causal mechanism does not hold in the way assumed by Marx and ultimately by Weber. I will concentrate on the work of Foucault, whose work stands in most marked contrast to the historical sociologists discussed above; but the work of Winch and Wittgenstein also offers a clear alternative to the kind of social theory underlying the historical sociology, in that they focus on social behaviour as rule-governed, not causal, behaviour. There is a massive debate about this approach, especially over the issue of whether reasons can be causes, and many would argue that, ultimately, rule-governed social theory is compatible with seeing reasons as causes; nonetheless, I think that it does offer a very different, and non-materialist, route for historical sociology.

Turning to Foucault, my aim is not so much to propose a ready-formed alternative to historical sociology as it is to argue that there is a significant contrast between the kinds of historical inquiries that Foucault undertook and those of historical sociology. In a broad sense, Foucault did historical sociology when he analysed the historical development of the prison, of mental illness and of sexuality; but he did it in a very different way. The clearest contrast comes when we look at power. In direct contrast to the statements of the historical sociologists discussed above, Foucault does not see power as something external to actors. As he describes his position, in a lecture given in 1976:

Power must be analysed as something which circulates, or rather as something which only functions in the form of a chain. It is never localised here or there, never in anybody's hands, never appropriated as a commodity or a piece of wealth. Power is employed and exercised through a net-like organisation ... individuals ... are always in the position of simultaneously undergoing and exercising this power ... individuals are the vehicles of power, not its points of application (Foucault, 1980: 98).

As he put it in an interview, 'I don't think power is built on "wills" (individual or collective) or that it derives from interests' (Foucault, 1989: 210). In a series of propositions outlined in the first volume of his history of sexuality, and in direct contrast to the position of Michael Mann, Foucault claimed that

Power is not something that is acquired, seized, or shared, something that one holds on to or allows to slip away ... Relations of power are not in a position of exteriority with respect to other types of relationships ... relations of power are not in superstructural positions ... Power comes from below; that is, there is no binary and all-encompassing opposition between rulers and ruled at the root of power relations ... no such duality extending from the top down and reacting on more and more limited groups ... Power relations are both intentional and nonsubjective. If in fact they are intelligible, this is not because they are the effect of another instance that 'explains' them ... Where there is power, there is resistance, and yet, or rather consequently, this resistance is never in a position of exteriority in relation to power (Foucault, 1990: 94–5).

This conception of power is very different to that used within historical sociology, which Foucault calls *sovereign power*. In its place he wants to propose a notion of power as *disciplinary power*, which produces normalised bodies and identities: this power

is exercised rather than possessed; it is not the 'privilege', acquired or preserved, of the dominant class, but the overall effect of its strategic positions ... this power is not exercised simply as an obligation or a prohibition on those who 'do not have it'; it invests them, is transmitted by them and through them; it exerts pressure on them, just as they themselves, in their struggle against it, resist the grip it has on them (Foucault, 1979: 26–7).

One of Foucault's most infamous claims, one that results from this view of power, concerns the individual. He writes in *The Order of Things*: 'As the archaeology of our thought easily shows, man is an invention of recent date. And one perhaps nearing its end' (Foucault, 1973: 387). For Foucault, the individual is an effect of power: 'it is one of the prime effects of power that certain bodies, certain gestures, certain discourses, certain desires, come to be identified and constituted as individuals . . . The individual is an effect of power . . . The individual which power has constituted is at the same time its vehicle' (Foucault, 1980: 98). The subject, as distinct from the individual, is both an effect of power discourses and is the venue for power. As Judith Butler puts it: 'This does not mean that the subject can be *reduced* to the power by which it is occasioned, nor does it mean that the power by which it is occasioned is *reducible to* the subject. Power is never merely a condition external or prior to the subject . . . If conditions of power are to persist, they must be reiterated; the subject is precisely the site of such reiteration, a reiteration that is never merely mechanical' (Butler, 1997: 16).

This picture has considerable consequences for how we study the past. The first of these is that Foucault is critical of traditional historical inquiry, preferring instead a genealogical approach. Following Nietzsche, he is opposed to any search for the 'real' origins or for an uncovering of what happened in the past: the genealogist 'finds that there is "something altogether different" behind things: not a timeless and essential secret, but the secret that they have no essence' (Foucault, 1986b: 78). Thus, for example, he claims that the concept of liberty was an invention of the ruling classes and not something fundamental to human nature. He is sceptical about the notion of historical truth because 'From the vantage point of an absolute distance . . . the origin makes possible a field of knowledge whose function is to recover it . . . Truth, and its original reign, has had a history within history from which we are barely emerging' (Foucault, 1986b: 79–80). In place of a history which seeks to uncover the origins of the present, genealogy 'does not pretend to go back in time to restore an unbroken continuity . . . its duty is not to demonstrate that the past actively exists in the present . . . Genealogy does not resemble the evolution of a species and does not map the destiny of a people' (Foucault, 1986b: 81). Instead of 'the erecting of foundations . . . it disturbs what was previously considered immobile; it fragments what was thought unified; it shows the heterogeneity of what was imagined consistent within itself' (Foucault, 1986b: 82). The focus of genealogy is the body, 'the inscribed surface of events . . . Its task is to expose a body totally imprinted by history' (Foucault, 1986b: 83).

According to this view of how to study the past, the key focus is on the process of domination, and this is not a story of a gradual triumph of a particular type of society or ideology:

In a sense, only a single drama is ever staged in this 'non-place', the endlessly repeated play of domination . . . this relationship of domination . . . is fixed throughout its history, in rituals, in meticulous procedures that impose rights and obligations. It establishes marks of its power and engraves memories on things and even within bodies. It makes itself accountable for debts and gives rise to the universe of rules ... the law ... permits the perpetual instigation of new dominations ... Humanity does not gradually progress from combat to combat until it arrives at universal reciprocity, where the rule of law finally replaces warfare; humanity installs each of its violences in a system of rules and thus proceeds from domination to domination (Foucault, 1986b: 85).

This process implies that 'The successes of history belong to those who are capable of seizing these rules, to replace those who had used them' (Foucault, 1986b: 86). Foucault wants to replace traditional historical inquiry with 'effective' history, by which he means historical inquiry that introduces discontinuities and 'deprives the self of the reassuring stability of life and nature' (Foucault, 1986b: 88). Effective history also alters what is studied. Rather than focusing on the development of large forces and processes, effective history 'shortens its vision to those things nearest to it – the body, the nervous system, nutrition' (Foucault, 1986b: 89). Finally, effective history alters the relationship between the historian and knowledge. Whereas historians 'take unusual pains to erase the elements in their work which reveal their grounding in a particular time and place' (Foucault, 1986b: 90), effective history sees knowledge as, by necessity, reflecting the perspective of the writer.

A second consequence concerns the nature of historical truth and knowledge. Again in direct contrast to the assumptions of historical sociology, Foucault argues that truth and knowledge are functions of power:

truth isn't outside power ... truth isn't the reward of free spirits, the child of protracted solitude, nor the privilege of those who have succeeded in liberating themselves. Truth is a thing of this world ... Each society has its regime of truth, its 'general politics' of truth: that is, the types of discourse which it accepts and makes function as true; the mechanisms and instances which enable one to distinguish true and false statements ... 'Truth' is to be understood as a system of ordered procedures for the production, regulation, distribution, circulation, and operation of statements. 'Truth' is linked in a circular relation with systems of power which produce and sustain it ... A 'regime' of truth (Foucault, 1986a: 72–4).

Similarly, for knowledge:

we should abandon a whole tradition that allows us to imagine that knowledge can exist only where the power relations are suspended and that knowledge can develop only outside its injunctions, its demands and its interests ... We should admit rather that power produces knowledge ... that power and knowledge directly imply one another; that there is no power relation without the correlative constitution of a field of knowledge, nor any knowledge that does not presuppose and constitute at the same time power relations (Foucault, 1979: 27).

Importantly, the person who studies truth and power is not someone free from the effects of power, but 'must be regarded as so many effects of these fundamental implications of power–knowledge' (Foucault, 1979: 28).

Taken together, these aspects of Foucault's methods for undertaking studies of the past constitute an alternative to the methods and assumptions of historical sociology. In place of an approach that seeks to develop the causal analysis of the effects of 'external' material forces on pre-existing subjects, it is possible to develop a more genealogical sociology of history, one that looks at factors such as regimes of truth, disciplinary power, the creation of agents' identities and subjectivities, and the interaction and relationship between truth, knowledge and power. This would be different to the forms of historical sociology adopted in this volume. My claim is not that such a form of historical sociology should replace the forms represented in this volume, only that the approach has tended to adopt one version of what might constitute historical sociology. More importantly, historical sociology does tend to work within one model of social theory, and my concern is that this both limits the kinds of studies that can be undertaken, and builds on a model of the social world that I consider inappropriate. Ultimately, I do not think that reasons can be causes, and I find Foucault's analysis of power and its implications for identity and subjectivity to be persuasive.

Conclusion

My purpose in this chapter has been to argue one simple point: historical sociology has been overwhelmingly materialist and explanatory. This is not surprising given that the two main influences on its development have been Marx and Weber, especially when Weber has been read in a very specific way. This claim is true of both the founding figures in historical sociology and the contributors to this volume. Only Reus-Smit and Barnett write about historical sociology in a way that challenges this explanatory materialism. This feature of the majority of the writing on historical sociology means that although it challenges the rationalist mainstream of international relations in important ways, it shares with it an epistemological and methodological stance that facilitates debate between the two. Indeed, historical sociology might possibly provide the theory of the state required by neorealism and neoliberalism. For these reasons, historical sociology is not part of the reflectivist challenge to rationalism; it could become complementary to rationalism. Michael Barnett's chapter takes this one step further in that he proposes a merging of historical sociology and constructivism; this fits exactly with my claim noted above that the dominant form of constructivism can easily develop a dialogue with the rationalist mainstream. Therefore, even Barnett's extension of historical sociology will retain its links with rationalist international relations. Of the other contributions to this volume, the overlap between realist international relations and historical sociology is clearest in Buzan and Little's chapter; but all bar Reus-Smit would fit within a broadly Marxist or Weberian approach, and in every case the epistemology is close to that of rationalist international relations. To reiterate, historical sociology differs from rationalist international relations in terms of its ontology; but for me this is less important than what is shared, namely assumptions about epistemology and methodology.

I have also argued that the form of historical sociology found in the contributions to this volume is but one possible form. I noted the absence of gender and ethnicity as material factors to be studied; but more fundamentally I pointed to the kinds of problems with the assumptions of historical sociology that a Foucauldian perspective might identify. My main aim has been the simple one of pointing to the form of social theory that underlies historical sociology, and to argue that there are other social theories that would permit a different historical sociology, one that did not treat the relationship between the great material processes and the unfolding of states, nations and classes as one of cause and effect. Rather, such a perspective would problematise the notion that power, materiality and subjectivity are things that sit on pre-formed actors; such processes construct the very subjectivity and identity of the individual. As such, there are many alternative narratives to be told by historical sociologies, narratives that inquire into the truth regimes within which individual subjects are produced and disciplined. This is not a call for a less structural account of history, but is a call for a very different notion of structure. In the language of my work with Martin Hollis (Hollis and Smith, 1990), I am calling for a more 'top-right' (i.e., a holistic 'insider' account) notion of structure in historical sociology, an approach that to date (despite its claims to the contrary as illustrated in its reading of Weber) seems to me to work overwhelmingly within a 'top-left' (i.e., a holistic 'outsider' account) notion of structure. Not all structures are material; not all structures are external to agents; and not all structures exercise power on agents. There are other models of the social world to that assumed by historical sociologists, and the central aim of this chapter has been to call for a more reflexive historical sociology, one that would thereby fit less easily with either the rationalist mainstream or the constructivist middle ground. All of this brings me back to epistemology, and its role in determining not just how we can speak about the social world but also what kind of social world we see.

12   For an international sociology

Fred Halliday

From historical sociology to international sociology

The interaction of historical sociology and international relations has been one of the most creative dimensions of the latter subject over the past ten years. Building on insights pioneered by Aron in the 1950s, on work in Marxist political sociology in the 1960s and on work within Anglo-American historical sociology itself over the 1970s and 1980s, the writings that have followed have allowed at once for development of a new inter-disciplinary field, and for a reconceptualisation within international relations of core categories – state, conflict, society, modernity.[1] Such an endeavour has, moreover, long been present in much existing sociological and international relations literature. Of historical sociology we can include the work on the state (Nettl, Mann, Anderson and Migdal), on forms of international domination and empires (Wallerstein and Eisenstadt), on capitalism (Polanyi and Schumpeter), on cultures (Braudel and McNeill) and on movements of revolt (Skocpol and Tilly). It has been present, above all, in the work of the classic theorists of sociology (particularly Saint-Simon, Marx and Weber), where there is a combination of historical perspective, social totality and analysis of modernity with analysis of the international.[2]

The *existing* international agenda of historical sociology has, therefore, a rich potential for international relations. At the same time, there is already a long-standing strong, if unacknowledged, concern within international relations for sociological issues. Raymond Aron himself combined, as perhaps no one else since has done, the double commitment (Aron, 1966). The work of E. H. Carr, for example, rests on a set of premises about long-run macro-social change – a secular trend towards collectivism and at the same time towards greater emancipation and

---

[1] There is a rich literature registering and criticising this interaction: see especially Jarvis (1989), Little (1994), Hobden (1998) and Hobson (1998a).

[2] Of course, there are some notable exceptions: Moore (1967) is an example of an historical sociological work of genius that ignores the international factors in the shaping of states.

internationalisation – that contrasts with his more short-term pessimism.[3] The 'realism' of the English School, as articulated in Hedley Bull, rests on a set of premises about the nature of 'society', on the one hand, and the transnational diffusion of norms, on the other. More recently the work of Christopher Coker, drawing on some of the less eirenic trends in nineteenth-century thinking on war and power, has invoked a set of cultural and social explanations for inter-state relations (Coker, 1998). Alexander Wendt's constructivism combines respect, arguably overstated, for a neorealist structure of inter-state relations with an examination, derived from Durkheim and other sociologists, of the role of structures of collective perception (Wendt, 1999). On the other hand, international political economy has come to an increasing extent to examine the ways in which domestic political *and* social trends are formed by international factors (Keohane and Milner, 1996). John Hobson's 'fiscal sociological' approach is an exemplar in this field (Hobson, 1997). We thus see a transition from the focus of the 1970s literature on transnational linkages between societies to one on the transnational, and international, as constitutive of the domestic.

This rethinking of international relations has at the same time allowed for the development of a new conception of history. In his formulation of the tasks of historical sociology, Raymond Aron rightly saw it as countering the claims, most common in international relations, and now fatuously reinforced by biologism, about underlying and determinant continuities in social and political life (Aron, 1957). Thus historical sociology provides for a very different account of the development of the international system as a whole, since its inception around 1500, and for different national, 'nation-state', histories that take sociological and international factors into account. The term 'historical sociology' itself is in one respect too condensed, for it contains two distinct claims: the historicisation of the state on the one hand, and the location of that history within an international context on the other. It is this double challenge – to produce a sociology at once historical *and* international – which the broader agenda encompassed within 'historical sociology' can meet.

The range of such contributions is itself striking, ranging from Weberian studies of the state through to Marxist work. The classic writings of Karl Polanyi, and more recent work by Immanuel Wallerstein, Charles Tilly, Michael Mann, John Hobson and Justin Rosenberg (the last pioneering the application of the concept of 'modernity' to international relations and relating this to other conceptions of the rupture associated

---

[3] I have explored this in Halliday (2000).

with industrialisation and political revolution), have been among the most important in this field. At the same time, the writing of history itself has been informed and enriched by the incorporation of historical sociological perspectives; the work of Bayley Stone (1994) on the French revolution and of Robin Blackburn (1997) on New World slavery are recent examples. Nor are we only looking at a debate that has taken place in the universities of Britain and the USA. Some works of historical sociology have broken out of the confines of the academic: Le Roy Ladurie's *Montaillou*, Simon Schama's *Citizens*, Paul Kennedy's *The Rise and Fall of the Great Powers*, Fukuyama's *The End of History*, to name but four bestsellers. At the same time, in continental Europe, debate on parallel themes, and drawing sometimes more explicitly on the classical literature from which historical sociology originates, has continued (Badie and Smouts, 1992; Senghaas, 1994). Against this background, it is possible to recognise the impact of this literature in terms of what it has achieved, and of the broader fulfilment of the agenda formulated in the 1980s.

The promise of historical sociology is, therefore, a double one – international *and* historical. In this perspective, it is pertinent to register what the potential range of this subject would be. In the first place, we should not confine discussion to the state. The historicisation of social relations in historical sociology has involved not only those of the state, but also those of other aspects of social life: the family, economy, culture, power and social movements. Marx, Weber and Durkheim were above all concerned with the impact of something novel, industrial modernity, on these areas of social life. It has also, classically, involved the study of international and transnational developments: empires, wars, geographical spaces and regions, and the relation of human society to the environment.[4] The eighteen historical sociologists studied by Dennis Smith cover everything from the most particular to the universal (Smith, 1991). Historical sociology has been closely related to another historical approach, economic history; indeed, the study of social forms has been matched, perhaps surpassed, in the study of the economic, where, equally, the historical and the international dimensions combine to shed light on the formation of modern economies. Work on the formation of the world economy, and on contemporary forms of global hierarchy, is of direct relevance to international relations. Recent examples of economic historical studies that have multiple implications for international relations, not least the study of international institutions, are the work of David Landes on

[4] For general surveys, see Abrams (1964), Skocpol (1984) and Sillitoe (1998). For critique, see Goldthorpe (1991).

global economic hierarchy and of Alan Milward on the formation of the European Union.

The power of such historicisation is not only analytic – the revealing of how institutions and practices were formed – but also emancipatory – denaturalising that which is presented, in any specific context, as inevitable. Hence the link, evident in classical theorists from Adam Smith to Karl Marx, with normative argument. Forms of gender, social, political, even academic power that are legitimated as natural, or inevitable, or the culmination of human progress, are laid open to critique by such an historicisation. Polanyi's long research detour through pre-modern forms of market was intended to cast such a critical light on the supposedly given, unmanageable market of his, and our, time. For its part, the historicisation of nations, something that nationalists cannot tolerate, challenges perennialism. That insight alone would be of great relevance, analytic and normative, to international relations. For the historicisation of the supposedly eternal entities – state, nation, war, power, the international and the 'real' itself – has this double function, denaturalising and emancipatory, within international relations. This is so in general, but is specifically cogent when linked to a particular historical and sociological view of modernity: the force of Polanyi's and Rosenberg's work, different in theoretical orientation but convergent in its denaturalising intent, is precisely that it links the apparently given international system to the conditions of emergence of the modern world. In so doing, it suggests a realistic framework for challenges to the given.

Establishing both the historical and international context for social analysis would denaturalise in one further respect, namely by removing the myth of the bounded society, or what Herminio Martins has aptly termed 'methodological nationalism'. This is, at its simplest, the narration of history, or the explanation of social behaviour, in purely national terms. Thus the development of the electoral system, or of education, or of language is described in purely national or endogenous terms. This serves not only a methodological function, in the narrowest sense, of limiting and simplifying the range of explanation, but also an ideological one, of keeping foreign influence at bay. A recurrent example is the British Chancellor of the Exchequer who in his annual budget speech focuses all attention on what *he* is going to do, and its immediate impact on purchasers of cigarettes, petrol and alcohol; he says nothing about the international context that will, for better or worse, determine much of what he does and what consumers actually experience. This may seem a simple matter but it is not: for the assumption of the bounded society pervades much social and political theory and has, as will be noted later, significant normative implications as well. Once the international is seen

not as intruding on the national, but as participating in its very constitution, then different analytic, and ethical, conclusions may follow.[5]

Barriers in theory

While we are, therefore, somewhere on the road towards such an integrated, international, sociology, there are at the same time considerable
difficulties in the way. On the one hand, there is a substantive problem: the integration of the social, the historical and the international
too often runs up against the incorporation into this new perspective of
untransformed theoretical elements. The use in contemporary discussions of international relations of ahistorical and hypostatised concepts
of culture is one example. Its caricature is in Huntington's *The Clash of
Civilisations*; but there is, in both contemporary political theory and international relations, a pervasive, ahistorical and asociological, tendency
to take as given the 'Asian', the 'Islamic', the West, even the 'other', and
treat these as explanatory variables. Most of those who pronounce on the
Islamic or Middle Eastern 'other' have no detailed familiarity with this
material. Equally, the relation of state to international relations too easily
assumes a determinist, 'realist', view of the latter. While much of this has
been laid at the door of more recent historical sociologists – Mann and
Skocpol, to name but two (Hobden, 1998: chs. 4, 6) – the real origina-
tor, the *radix malorum* of this determinist view of the international, is Max
Weber himself. His baneful, and ethically endorsed, view of inter-state
relations as inevitably one of conflict and war has influenced not only
conservative thinking, but also such supposedly emancipatory thinkers
as C. Wright Mills (1958). Wright Mills's work, democratic in value and
astute in analysis at the domestic level, is, at the international, reduced
to grand conspiracy theory and bureaucratic-technological determinism
(Halliday, 1994a). He exemplified that uneasy conjoining of radical, and
potentially emancipatory, critique of foreign policy with a disabling pessimism that has reached its apogee in the work of Noam Chomsky and
was reflected in E. P. Thompson's (1982) 'exterminism'. One person
who escaped from, even as he made creative use of, his Weberian legacy
was Raymond Aron. Fluent in both idioms, Aron produced work that
integrated sociological and international relations analysis without the
conventions of either.

This substantive difficulty is replicated in the field of methodology
and theory itself. If historical sociology, as it was revived in the 1970s

[5] To take one example of the international constitution of society, all four of the forms of
power identified by Mann – ideological, economic, military and political – have significant
international preconditions and consequences.

and 1980s, reflected a favourable intellectual conjuncture, the situation today is in some respects less so. Within sociology, the requirement to study classical texts, the better to be aware of the history of ideas themselves, has been eroded by a fashionable presentism. At the same time, the endeavour of macro-social theory has been challenged by the advance of rivals: a fetishised micro-theory, derived from economics, that denies the relevance of history or structural context, and a postmodernist anti-foundationalism that rejects the very project of macro-social theory and rational analysis. Both of these have, of course, had their impact on international relations itself. One further challenge to macro-social theory in its original form is also pertinent: constructivism. This involves the application to the international of a theoretical framework represented within sociology as ethno-methodology or symbolic interactionism. Roles, perceptions and self-definitions replace the realist concepts of state, power and economy (Wendt, 1999). The very questions that historical sociology might ask – how has such a set of ideas or values emerged, who controls and defines them, and with what mechanisms are they reproduced and enforced – are displaced. At the same time, there is a debatable slippage from analysing the subjective dimensions of individual behaviour – in terms of roles, perceptions and identity – and transposing these to collective entities – states, nations and people. The result is an international relations that runs a risk of returning to unitary, ahistorical entities, which would be a regression beyond the very questioning of such unitary analysis that behaviouralism and transnationalism pioneered three decades ago. Needless to say, this is the opposite of what a sociological inquiry, properly understood, should entail.

State and society revisited: three questions

Any general assessment of this interaction has, however, to be combined with an engagement with more general questions within social theory and with analysis of substantive questions. This is, quite rightly, the agenda that Justin Rosenberg (1994), following Mills, laid out for international relations. In what follows, I want to touch on three theoretical issues which fall within the realm of a putative international sociology. In the subsequent section I shall address some substantive contemporary questions. By way of conclusion I shall address normative issues.

Agency

The problem of agency has been central to much of sociological thought, and to much of historiography. The pendulum has swung from theories that stress agency to those that circumscribe or deny it. Agency is not, however, going to go away, either as an analytic question – how far can conscious human subjects determine their own history? – or as a normative one – since any critique of society or international relations must be linked to a view of how, and by whom, change can be brought about. Classically, international relations has denied the question of agency: the whole bent of the subject has been that of reducing the claims and expectations of actors. Structure is a disciplinary idea. This is as true of conventional international relations realism, which both denies the capacity for agency and stresses the *dangers* of any attempt to improve the system, as it is for more recent structural writing, be this Marxist (dependency theory), Weberian, culturalist or political-economic (Strange). Yet the briefest of surveys of contemporary international relations – from work on NGOs and civil society, through invocations of emancipation by critical theory, to the study of global governance – indicates that premises, and values, about agency abound.

There are two straightforward ways to address the question of agency in international relations. The first is historical. Who made the international system? And who goes on making, i.e., reproduces, it? We can ask this question either of the international system as a whole from, say, 1500, or of particular processes within international history: the abolition of slavery or the end of the European empires, the arms race or the formation of the European Union, globalisation or the collapse of communism, shifts in the world economy or currency fluctuations. The fluctuations of oil prices are a fascinating case of the interaction of agency and structure.

An alternative approach is to list the candidates for agency. This list would include states, international organisations, the 'international community', NGOs, firms, social movements, anti-systemic movements and individual leaders. Some have needed to invoke God, or gods; some still do. Within each of these actors it would be possible to identify the role of ideas. Clarification of this issue of agency, in theory and in regard to specific historical events, would not only serve the explanatory and normative functions mentioned earlier, but would also make a contribution to the broader debate within social science on structure and agency. It might, in so doing, deprive determinists of their favourite source of authority. The international would cease to be the realm of necessity, but, like the domestic, a domain where necessity and agency interacted.

The standard counterpoint to agency is, of course, structure, that set of determinations which limits or denies the choices of individuals and states alike. International relations is, like sociology, centred on the recognition of structure against the untutored common sense of agency.

Yet this emphasis on structure, in both cases, conceals a deeper problem, not just that of the role of agency, but also that of the contrast between what one may term static and dynamic concepts of structure. By static concepts of structure I mean those conceptions which stress the enduring, unchangeable limits which structure imposes: the plurality of states, the limits of human nature. A similar function is played by the incorporation into international relations of game theory and its set-piece routines: here the conventions of, in origin, micro-economic theory have their macro-historical payoff, all of history being reduced to a set of 'stag-hunts', 'prisoners' dilemmas' and other routines, a grand continuity without content or change. Such static concepts of structure therefore tend towards *limiting* the movement of individual actors. They incline against change.

Yet structure may operate in quite a different manner, producing change even where the actor does not want it; we are all familiar with such dynamic structural change from the changes of climate, time and ageing. Here the terms of the argument are reversed: common sense inclines towards the static, structure towards change. In society, both domestic and international, similar processes can be noted, be they those of the development of modernity, or technology, or social attitude, of language or fashion. Some of these are long-term, tectonic, or *longue durée*. Social science seems unable, for long, to resist the temptations of cyclical theory: Ibn Khaldun, Arnold Toynbee, Paul Kennedy, Francis Fukuyama. But some are most certainly not so long-term: what the *Annales* school terms the *événementiel* can be the most dramatic – earthquakes, volcanoes, tornadoes. Here structure seizes the individual agents and tosses them hither and thither. Such processes in social affairs include economic booms and crashes, wars and revolutions; human agency can do little to arrest them or, despite the feckless and iterated pleases of behaviourists, to predict them – accidents, heart attacks, *coups de passion*. The twentieth century has seen many such international upheavals; here agency consists, at best, of short-term, anticipated, well-timed intervention and a sense of survival. The challenge of analysing agency in international relations is therefore a double one – at once identifying, historically and theoretically, those areas where agency operates, while recognising where structure, far from constraining, may be the precipitant of change and conflict.[6]

---

[6] A fine test of such alternative explanations is provided by the events in Yugoslavia over the past ten years: how much can be ascribed to structural change – the collapse of communism, international realignments, the resurgence of an already latent, atavistic nationalism, demography – how much to the decisions of individual leaders and parties, and how much to the decisions, indecisions and non-decisions of the international community?

Revolutions

The role of agency and structure is nowhere more present than in the analysis of revolutions, and of their international impact.[7] Here sociological analysis has been conventionally polarised between explanations stressing one or other, while international relations literature has debated the degree to which revolutions, understood as upheavals in one country, can and do affect the international system as a whole. As a broad generalisation it can be argued that over the past two decades the balance of opinion has, in both cases, tended towards the structural.

Yet this structuralist consensus, apparently reinforced by sociological theory, is open to challenge from within international sociology itself. In the first place, the downplaying of the international impact of revolutions is detached from an account of the broad – structural and transnational – causes of revolutions themselves. In the aftermath of 1989 it has become commonplace to stress the fruitless, utopian character of communism (Furet, 1995). As far as its goal, of creating a fundamentally distinct and competitive political order, is concerned, this is valid. But this retrospective dismissal, this sigh of relief at the disappearance of the greatest challenge capitalist modernity has faced, misses the point that it was this very capitalist modernity, in its contradictory and international form, which generated communism in the first place. The revolutions that punctuated twentieth-century history, the wars preceding and following such revolutions, the mass mobilisations of millions of people in revolutionary upheaval and post-revolutionary construction, and the spread of radical democratic ideas reflected a rejection of a system that had, for many, failed. This failure was international in its diffusion, causes and manifestations: the inequalities of North–South relations, the pervasive failure of European democracies in the inter-war years, the supine response to fascism in the 1930s and 1940s, the rejection of imperial domination – all located within a world system marked by inequalities of wealth and power – produced a world-wide revolt that shaped the twentieth century.

Equally, the history and analysis of this movement illustrate the question of agency. This is evident in three interrelated respects: leadership, organisation and ideas. It is no return to voluntarism – be it that of heroic leaders or sinister subversives – to argue that in the midst of these structural upheavals, individuals and groups of politically motivated leaders played a decisive role, in revolution as they do in war. Lenin, Mao, Castro, Khomeini marked the twentieth century in part because through intuition and intelligence, and luck, they gauged the tide of events. Equally, those

---

[7] I have gone into this in greater detail in Halliday (1999).

who presided over the collapse, often rapid and unanticipated, of established states systems also played a role, through their encouragement of,
or permission for, the disarticulation of the states they governed: Louis
XVI, Nicholas II, the Shah, even Gorbachev fall into this category. Lenin's
two famous preconditions for the success of revolutions – the failure of
existing states and the revolt of those who are ruled – *both* involve, and
often require, the intervention of consciously purposive individuals.

This applies equally to the role of movements. There has been much
misinterpretation of the role of movements in historical change: those opposed to them see them as manipulated, deluded by leaders and elites –
the Kedourie view of nationalism, and that of many elite theorists of
revolution; those in favour of them often exaggerate their autonomy
from structural factors (e.g., Thompson, 1963), or, as in regard to many
contemporary emancipatory movements, overstate their influence and
cohesion. Yet movements express more than the wishes and goals of their
leaders, even as they operate within realities – of state and economic
power – that they often ignore.

Again the twin examples of nationalist and communist movements
within modern history are a striking instance of this. We need an account
of the structural factors that generate and sustain them, and we need
to locate them in their transnational context, social and ideological. We
need at the same time to develop the concepts for analysing collective
social action and the forms of intention and achievement they embody.
For international relations the challenge is acute: between a realist or
structuralist history, that denies the efficacy of social movements, and
one that in a naive contrary mode vaunts their efficacy, we need a proper
compass of evaluation. As we shall see when we come to 'critical' theory, such a compass is essential for any plausible normative reflection on
contemporary international relations.

Ideas too play a significant role in such processes of structural upheaval. It is not a question of saying that ideas accurately describe reality, or indicate the goal towards which, in retrospect, actors are moving.
But they guide leaders and led alike, they provide a basis for the dele-
gitimation of existing orders, and they suggest a model towards which
those in revolt are striving. The history of social movements over the past
two centuries – nationalism, communism, feminism, religious fundamen-
talism, to name but four – cannot be separated from the formulation *and
impact* of ideas.

Here, in recent literature, there has been a curious exchanging of positions. Those most sceptical of voluntarist explanations, for example
Skocpol, have been most resistant to analysing the role of ideas even as

they have stressed the deep historical roots of revolutions. The ideological component of that 'world-historical' context that Skocpol in other respects identifies as important as causing revolutions is downplayed in her work, as it is in Tilly's. On the other hand, those who downplay structural and class factors, such as Furet and Schama, do lay considerable emphasis on the role of ideas, be it in regard to 1789 or 1917. They do not ask how these ideas were generated. Yet both structural and ideological factors form part of the international context that generates and transmits revolutions; they are not alternatives, but complementary forces in the onset and development of revolutionary crises.

The study of ideas has one further contribution to make to such an international sociology. Conventionally, the transnational impact of ideas is presented in terms of the disruptive consequences of external ideological influence: revolutionary, religious, political or even gender ideas come from outside, from abroad. In sociological models based on equilibrium, or in other models of a structural-functional kind, the external, ideological and other, is disruptive. Here orthodox sociology merges with the conventions of methodological nationalism. States and nations, like individuals, and academic disciplines, like international relations, present themselves as unique, denying the formative and contextual factors that affect them. Yet here, as elsewhere, this presumption of national insulation, and of endogenous determination as the norm, is misleading. Ideas, like economics, are never confined within a national or bounded system. Ideological stability within any one society presupposes external factors, what I have elsewhere, following Aron, termed 'homogeneity'. States and societies are not discrete entities, but more like terraced houses: they presuppose the physical and social similarity of others. Here was the great insight of Burke into the international impact of the French revolution: it was not because France attacked other countries that it was an enemy, it was because it based its legitimacy on different principles. The same is true today in an era where, in political forms, in law, in gender relations and in economics and culture, the pressures for homogeneity are so strong. States may not draw attention to this, but the stability of any one society requires that others be like it.

One may here suggest an internationalisation of Gramsci's insights into the role of hegemony, of a dominant ideology, as common sense: as long as others are like you – have kings or parliamentary systems – your own system, presented as natural and specifically national, is more secure. Therefore, the lesson that is drawn from the study of revolutions, that externally generated ideas can be disruptive, can be revised to take account of ideological homogeneity as a stabilising factor in society in general. The dominant ideas of any society require and draw on similar ideas beyond the frontier.[8]

Homogeneity and fragmentation

The broader issue of homogeneity and the pressures for it in international relations are central to modern social theory. The balance of much sociological and international relations literature stresses this tendency, be it in analysis of the pressures of modernity itself, and now of globalisation, or in those strands within international relations that stress the impact of 'international society'. In my own work I have argued – in a comparison of Burke, Marx and Fukuyama – not only that homogenisation is a dominant process, domestically and internationally, but also that it underlies the analysis of the Cold War (Halliday, 1994b). Beyond its political and military dimensions, the Cold War, and its conclusion, reflected a competition between two rival blocs, heterogeneously constituted and inherently competitive, which could only end, however, with the homogenisation and subordination of 'the other'. This is more or less, I would argue, what has happened. The former communist countries have been reincorporated, and their political and economic distinctness has been eliminated. They are back in the global capitalist hierarchy from which they temporarily escaped. Like runaway slaves, they are being taught a lesson: for the CIS countries, an average 50 per cent fall in GDP since 1989, with no end in sight.

That said, there are aspects of this process that may require further elaboration, within the perspective of an international and historical sociology. The first is the most obvious form of heterogeneity of all, the inequality of wealth and power in the contemporary world. This has always been present, and colonialism was one, transient, form of this permanent system of allocation. The facts show that in economic and social terms the inequality is growing not reducing, that the hierarchy initiated in 1500 is now more pronounced than ever. Linked to this is the extraordinary historical continuity of the allocation: as Giovanni Arrighi has pointed out, the top group of states has remained the same for a century and a half, with the single addition of Japan. Yet the recognition of this is matched by a continued failure of social scientists or anyone else

[8] A world-wide example: elected legislatures the world over affect a national, ancestral character, even as they conform, in substance and political context, to a universal modernity. Duma and Sejm, Hural and Shura, Diet and Majlis, Knesset and Bundestag, Dáil and House of Commons are superficially heterogeneous, but substantively homogeneous. The same goes for football teams, international relations departments, flags, etc.

to provide a convincing explanation of why it is so; the set of explanatory factors adduced – culture, climate, natural endowment, governance and global trading patterns – have remained much the same for decades. Here historical sociology subsists as *bricolage*. This is the greatest analytic *and normative* challenge facing social science today.

Heterogeneity also takes the form of cultural diversity. It is a striking feature of globalisation that it appears to co-exist with, and in some cases generate, both greater cultural diversity and nationalism. Contemporary diversity of multi-culturalism, and of artistic creation, allows of new cultural forms in music, art, cuisine and language. At the same time, in tandem with economic integration, forms of nationalist and religious assertion drawing on established traditions proliferate. To say that globalisation has contradictory impacts – in politics and culture – is a justified initial step. But there are other questions lying beneath this. One is that of assessing how far, beneath the appearance of national and cultural diversity, there are fundamentally different models of political life. Many who analyse distinct forms of capitalism, or political discourse, identify a commonality of cause and content where its proponents proclaim originality. The claims of a distinct Asian or Islamic economics are dubious. The discourse of Ayatollah Khomeini, or of Confucian leaders, rests upon such familiar friends as the state, sovereignty, economic development and equality of rights. Equally, we can examine how far, within this contradictory process of globalisation, the heterogeneous prevails over the homogeneous; any one example – Islamic radicalism, Serbian nationalism, Chinese outrage – can be read in different ways. The homogenists will argue, as does Fukuyama, that the globalisation of unity, a combination of modernity itself and international pressure, is in the significant responses prevailing. There are protests and revolts; but we are not looking at viable alternatives in political or economic terms. Quebec is something you do at 'the end of history'. Others do identify a greater challenge from heterogeneity: Huntington, John Gray and the proponents of alternative routes themselves.

This issue, beyond its theoretical and analytic importance, touches on two vital questions for international relations at the start of a new millennium. One is that of the future cohesion of states. The map of 200-odd sovereign states in the world is deemed by the international community to be relatively stable. The creation of over twenty new entities after the collapse of communism was accepted, reluctantly. With the exception of one or two candidates already in the race, Palestine, Kosovo, New Caledonia and, if it wants it, Quebec, the parking lot is rather full. Yet this presumption in favour of the finality of the map is countered by those who argue for the possibility and desirability of multiple fissure, a product

of technological and normative change. Graham Fuller has talked of a
possible 'amoebisation' of state over the next two decades, linked to the
refusal of the populations of modern states to fight to prevent secession: if
California seceded no one would kill to stop it. Some libertarians envisage
a world of hundreds of states. Any such fragmentation would, of course,
have an economic basis, but in an era of decentralisation and 'small is
beautiful' this may not be hard to envisage. Fragmentation would, however, also require a cultural base – existing or invented – within which
language and religion would play a role.

Heterogeneity is relevant to the other, more ominous issue in international relations, namely that of the emergence of new militarised blocs,
and the possibility of strategic wars. Here, of course, the trend is not
towards fragmentation but towards cohesion. There can be little doubt
that the more significant trend of the post-1989 period has not been the
breakup of states but their fusion – Germany, China, Korea. The simplest,
not necessarily mistaken, expectation is that large states and their allies –
China, and perhaps also Russia, India, Iran and Germany – will become
the centres of new cultural, but also military and strategic, blocs that
will reintroduce a world of power politics. This is the practical import of
Huntington's *Clash of Civilisations* as of much related, alarmist but not
necessarily unfounded, 'realist' prognostication about the next century.
The question is not whether globalisation has this contradictory character but how far the homogeneous will prevail over the heterogeneous,
and in what respects the latter will endure. A world of diverse and constantly renegotiated cuisines and languages is very different from nuclear
proliferation and strategic rivalry.

Contemporary analysis

If the matter of engagement with theory is one challenge, that of engagement with issues of substantive analytic significance within contemporary
social science itself is another. Here the challenge, relevance and opportunity of historical sociology is enormous, a point that can be illustrated
by reference to four issues of contemporary debate. We can start with
the most momentous historical event of the second half of the twentieth
century, the collapse of Soviet communism. Explanation of this process
requires an historical sociological perspective, with an analysis of the varying contributions of state and society, agency and structure, economics
and ideology, and external and internal change. It is at once a laboratory
for social scientists and a challenge for historical explanation, one that
has occasioned much, theoretically limited, empirical explanation as well
as precipitate theoretical resolution.

Second, globalisation, in its various renderings, posits a set of changing relations among state, society, economy and culture, and a claim to historical rupture associated with the past two decades. Discussion of this ranges from denial to 'hyperglobalisation'. Adjudication of this issue, indeed the establishment of the very criteria by which the claims to continuity or change within globalisation may be judged, is something that requires historical and sociological analysis. A degree of conceptual precision and historical perspective would not be amiss.

Third, there is the issue which interrelates the history of the developed, formerly imperial world with its present and future, that of postcoloniality. Interest in the post-colonial, initially a theorisation of the continued impact on formerly colonial states of the imperial experience, has now come to focus on the formative role of the colonial 'other' in the metropolitan countries themselves, be this in literature, migration or economics. The colonial 'other' is held to constitute the metropolitan self. Beyond a recognition of historical and continuing connections, however, this runs the risk of replacing one partial analysis – denial of the imperial as constitutive – by another – the post-colonial as determinant. A measured analysis, historical and contemporary, of the role of the colonial in the economics, politics and ideology of formerly imperial states would be pertinent here; the formative role of the colonial 'other' would be weighed against other formative experiences – in the case of European states, interimperial wars in Europe, endogenous social and political change and the influence of the non-colonial 'other', North America.

Finally, historical sociology has a direct relevance to the most overarching issue in contemporary social theory and analysis, one with many implications for international relations, that of a transition from modernity to postmodernity. The claim of 'postmodernity' has at least three constituent elements: aesthetics, social theory and modern social life (Anderson, 1999). If the first is unquestionable, but not necessarily determinant of the other two, the second oscillates between a claim about a new late-twentieth-century epistemological era and an assertion of the permanent, historical falseness of rationalistic and Enlightenment claims. What concerns us most here is the third, the claim that, over the past quartercentury or so, society domestically and internationally has moved from a modern to a postmodern phase. Here again, the perspectives of history and sociology are most relevant. Whether this be in regard to the disappearance of classic forms of state, territoriality, identity or sovereignty, or in more general claims about the destabilising and nomadic consequences of global movements of finance and ideas, there is an opportunity, and necessity, for a coherent analytic and historical framework. Beyond establishing what the criteria and claims may be, such a perspective may, as with globalisation, allow us to identify those ways in which we do, and do not, inhabit a significantly changed world.

Normative agenda

As noted above, the classical texts of historical sociology were intertwined with a set of normative issues, reflections on general ethical questions on the one hand, and interventions in debates on contemporary policy on the other. For many, reflections on historical sociology have arisen out of the tumultuous events, and dangers, of their own lifetime; this was as true for those writers formed in the crucible of early-twentieth-century history – Weber, Polanyi, Schumpeter – as for the critical theorists of the Frankfurt School and those of the 1970s and 1980s – Skocpol, Anderson, Giddens. In his overview of historical sociology in the 1990s, Dennis Smith points to the central critical role of historical sociology in examining the question of democracy and concludes: 'The best contribution historical sociology could make in the 1990s would be the discovery and dissemination of knowledge relevant to the development of capitalist democracy...' (Smith, 1991: 182–3).

A parallel argument can be made with regard to issues in international relations. Without engaging in denial of the distinction between fact and value, which David Hume, one of the founders of historical sociology, insisted on, it is evident how far speculation about the normative direction of human affairs involves a set of assumptions about humanity, in its biological, historical and social dimensions. A fine recent example of such work, linking historical sociology and international relations, is John Hall's *International Orders*, an Aronite reflection on the link between democracy and the inter-state system. Four examples of the pertinence of the normative may suffice.

Identity and difference

The contrast has already been made between theories of culture that rest on the acceptance of difference and those which question this assertion of difference and point to the construction of identity as a function of power. The latter school also lays greater stress on the shared context of modernity which all societies experience. This argument has direct implications for what is, in conventional terms, presented as an issue in moral and political philosophy. Those who, in the name of communitarian or multicultural theory, question universalism assume that the difference they are defending is something with objective validity. For example, they accept that cultures and related moral systems are formed as distinct, discrete entities, and that the formalised presentation of these, as national tradition or as codes of legal practice such as *shari'ah* or Confucianism, are givens. The moral question of what to do about such difference is, therefore, constructed upon a set of historical and sociological presuppositions. If it is shown that the tradition is a contemporary, elite-created construct, or that what is presented as one variant of law or custom is challenged by others within that system, then the scope for transcultural, perhaps even universal, dialogue may be all the greater. The homogeneity and historical continuity of cultures are proper subjects for inquiry with direct relevance to this, perhaps the dominant issue in contemporary political philosophy. It is equally of direct relevance to the debate on human rights, as between international and national standards; what is often presented as a conflict between different, culture-specific values may turn out to reflect notions, formed in terms of interest. Here the challenge to international relations is precisely to identify how far the diffusion of 'international society' has reached a common normative discourse. The thin/thick distinction, espoused by Walzer, simplifies this spread of shared values on democracy, rights and independence.

Intervention

The issue of intervention, by which is meant forcible or military involvement in another country's internal affairs, has been central to debate in the 1990s. Yet it has rested upon, quite properly, a set of arguments that go back a long way in international political theory, most famously to the writings of John Stuart Mill (Walzer, 1978: ch. 6). One of Mill's central arguments is the need for self-help, that peoples, even when seriously oppressed, should liberate themselves. Only in this way may 'the virtues needful for maintaining freedom' be developed. The paradoxical, but not inconsistent, conclusion is that intervention is legitimate where it may be less needed – i.e., where a people have begun, in a substantial way, to liberate themselves and so have already demonstrated the virtues of self-help.

Mill's judgement was made in the 1840s. Without explicitly saying so, it presumes a set of (historically contingent) arguments about the capacities of states and their ability to repress their own peoples. On this basis, he feels it is possible to make some judgement about whether a people are serious, and virtuous, enough in pursuit of their own freedom. But the capacity of states to repress is not a transhistorical constant; it can, on the contrary, be argued that just as state power has increased massively in other respects – to tax or to control frontiers – over the ensuing century and a half, so has its capacity to monitor and repress. If state intervention in the economy has risen by, say, ten times, then the capacity to repress has also done so – surveillance, mobility and firepower have all risen spectacularly. So too has the willingness of states to employ mass terror, very much a feature of modern times. The implications of this shift, both historical and sociological, for the argument on intervention may be considerable; the margin of self-help in, say, contemporary Iraq or North Korea is rather less than it was in the Austro-Hungarian, Russian or British empires of the mid-nineteenth century.

Critical theory and global civil society

The advance of emancipatory philosophies within international relations, be these world society theory, critical theory or postmodernism, rests upon a set of claims about the possibility of change in the real world. Early examples would be peace through law and dependency theory. Here Runciman's distinction between the 'improbably plausible' and the 'probably impossible' needs to be borne in mind (Runciman, 1998: ch. 9). Equally Carr's critique in *The Twenty Years' Crisis* rested upon insistence on the real world, or historical sociological, presuppositions of any project for improving inter-state relations.

The origins of these alternative projects elucidate these real world pre-suppositions. 'Critical theory' originated in the Frankfurt School. Beginning as a form of Marxist reflection upon the emancipatory subject in twentieth-century Europe, it has, at various stages, encompassed radical students, Third World revolutionaries, the social movements of the 1970s and 1980s and an international civil society: in other words, agency. Robert Cox's (1996) work seeks to identify such emancipatory forces. Of all these subjects of change, the question of plausibility has to be asked. Rather too often, as we have seen, in classical and contemporary critical theory, the argument on agency is vague: a mystical invocation of the working class, or colonial liberation movements, is replaced by a hypo-statisation of social movements, or by gestural invocations of selected, distant examples – indigenous peoples in India, recycling collectives in Cologne, Comandante Marcos in Chiapas. The challenge of realism remains in large measure unanswered.

Any project for changing or reforming the world has to address this issue, and pay, at each stage, close attention to the distinction between 'ought' and 'is'. Transnational social movements did not, in the twentieth century, stop wars: while they may, as in Europe during World War I

or as in Northern Ireland in the 1970s or in former Yugoslavia in the
1990s, have gone on articulating an independent voice, they did not prevent states, and combative social movements, from prevailing. Equally,
the interventions of gender-based or ecological NGOs over the past two
decades may have altered agendas, but this is not the same thing as saying they have altered state policy. In some cases they have, but in others
rhetoric, and formal acceptance, contrast with inaction. At the end of the
1990s there was much talk of global civil society and of a new global citizenship, but it was not much in evidence in the more developed OECD
countries, where international awareness was in decline. A careful, sober
study of institutions and of political attitudes is a precondition for the
advocacy of any such 'critical' or 'emancipatory' project. The oldest
error in politics, as Machiavelli and Carr remind us, is to mistake wish
for reality.

Appeals to respect 'other' voices are also, in this regard, insufficient.
On the one hand, the question of *which* other voices has to be answered:
what of Khomeini, or *Sendero Luminoso*, or the PKK, or the IRA, or the
UVF, or, for that matter, the KLA? On closer examination neither Fanon
nor Mao may be all they appear to be. Their respect for human rights or
the dialogic interaction with their own local alterities leaves much to be
desired. On the other hand, few of those who invoke the 'other' engage
in a serious analysis of how 'other' it really is. Abstracted denunciations
of 'the West' are rarely matched by concrete studies of the alternatives:
the work of Edward Said, and of such later relativists as Maria Mies or
Gayatry Spivak, avoid this issue, even as they play into forms of nativism
and obscurantism that would, in all likelihood, clash with the values of
those who in the first instance propound dialogue.[9]

The state

If the starting point for the analytic contribution of international relations has been the state, it should, quite fittingly, be the conclusion of the
normative discussion. Historical sociology has already made a distinctive contribution (e.g., in the work of Charles Tilly and John Hall) to
the normative discussion of the state, by analysing its origins in coercion and spoliation. In this, work on the state has been reinforced by
the modernist work on the nation, questioning the perennialist derivation of modern national entities. Neither of these should, in themselves,
deny the legitimacy of modern nation-states; rather, they should move

[9] A striking instance of such simplified analysis is the work of Arrighi, Hopkins and
Wallerstein (1989) on 'anti-systemic movements'.

legitimation away from any supposedly dynastic or contractual bases, let alone divine legitimation, towards contemporary, and repeatedly reaffirmed, democratic principles.

Discussion of the contemporary state involves, however, a further set of issues to which, as Dennis Mack rightly argues, historical sociology has a contribution to make. Mack was most concerned with the domestic dimensions of this, with changing functions of the state and with changing definitions of citizenship. Yet an international concomitant of this domestic debate is not hard to find: in the creation of democratic supranational bodies, in the broader democratisation of global governance and the democratic control of corporate and other unelected bodies, and in the regulation of global problems. Here historical sociology, by criticising existing norms, and by advancing 'improbably possible' forms of future organisation, can contribute as much to the international debate as to the nation.

We are not without historical precedents here: the campaigns against slavery and colonialism, the construction of the post-1945 United Nations system and the construction of the European Union are all examples of the 'improbably possible' being realised. Part of this visionary work has, however, to involve a recognition of dangers, established and new. An analysis of the contemporary world cannot ignore trends which run against any such democratic regulation of state and global governance: the rise of uncontrolled corporate power, oligarchic control of the media, declining levels of education and interest in international issues, a crisis of an ethic of global responsibility matching that within societies, the increasing rapidity and complexity of the technologies and processes of global interaction, the increasing complexification and uncertainty of science. Above all, we see a dramatic shift, in public discourse at once uninformed and supposedly informed, away from the assertion of the possibilities of rational, and purposive, human control, be this in the new determinism of evolutionary biology or in the apparent capitulation of the world as a whole to the supposedly objective, technologically determined requirements of the IT industry (monopoly capitalism if ever there was one!).

The central import of critical theory, in its Frankfurt School variant, as of the early Marx, as indeed of the founder of empirical science, Francis Bacon, is critical – the insistence on the human, social, origins of modern society and its supposedly given, i.e., alienated, manifestations. This international, civic responsibility has other, self-evident implications for contemporary society. In a world where myths about cultural and religious conflict abound, where conspiracy theory has become a prevalent form of popular imagination in all continents, the corrections of history, sociology, even facts play their role. Historical sociology is, above all, a part of the attempt by human beings to take mastery of their own surroundings, their past and their present, the better to emancipate themselves from it and determine, within the constraints of structure of course, their future.

13 On the road towards an historicised world sociology

John M. Hobson and Stephen Hobden

In this concluding chapter we draw on the findings and arguments made in this book in order to present our own case for an historical sociology of international relations. In particular we focus on a set of questions and issues which revolve around our calling for the development of what we term 'world sociology'. Fred Halliday's notion of '*international* sociology' is important and complementary to ours – as is Scholte's (1993) conception of *world historical sociological studies*. We prefer the label '*world* sociology' only because we are unhappy with the traditional meaning that the term 'international' conveys – i.e., the tendency to focus on inter-state relations to the exclusion of domestic, transnational and global *social* relations (even though Halliday's approach is decidedly not state-centric). This chapter is framed around four fundamental questions that are pertinent to our calling for a world sociology of international relations.

(1) Why do we need an historicised world sociology?
(2) What place in the discipline should world sociology occupy?
(3) What does world sociology look like?
(4) What research agenda does world sociology bring to light?

Why do we need an historicised world sociology?

In order to make our case, we could start by examining several basic questions that underpin traditional or conventional understandings of international relations:

• Is the international system anarchic or hierarchic?
• When did the modern states system emerge?
• At what point did the modern conception of sovereignty become institutionalised?
• When did states become functional 'like units' based on a centralised state with a triple monopoly of the means of rule, violence and taxation?

265

Few would dispute that these questions are basic, and most international relations scholars would almost certainly consider this an easy test of their knowledge: 'anarchic' is the answer to the first question, and as for the remaining questions – an emphatic '1648 of course!' It might, therefore, come as a surprise to learn that many of the contributors to this volume would provide an alternative set of answers. To the first question, most would reply: 'Both: the international system has always shown a co-existence of hierarchic and anarchic forms – even today.' For example, the British and French empires in the nineteenth and twentieth centuries, as well as US hegemony and the Warsaw Pact after 1945, are four examples of mini-hierarchies existing under 'anarchy'. And in answering the remaining questions, a range of quite different dates are supplied by our historical sociologists. Reus-Smit, for example, shows us that in 1648, pre-modern 'dynastic' conceptions of international relations were in full swing, with the modern conception of sovereignty only emerging at the international level in the nineteenth century (cf. R. Hall, 1999). Moreover, in 1648 no state had internal sovereignty; and as late as the early twentieth century all the units remained 'functionally differentiated' (i.e., there was more than one source of domestic political authority). Even then, many First World states have been embedded within various 'mini-hierarchies', as noted above. Furthermore, it was only *after* 1945, with the process of decolonisation, that many Third World states became internally sovereign (i.e., functionally undifferentiated units) on the Western model – even though many of these remained within the mini-hierarchy of the Warsaw Pact. And even today, many Third World states remain functionally differentiated, whether they be 'quasi-states' (Jackson, 1990) or 'failed states'.

The lesson of this exercise is fundamental to why we need an historicised world sociology: if we do not even know the answers to some of the most basic questions in international relations, then clearly, there is a problem with the current way in which the discipline is constructed. But if it was *only* a problem of dates, then the purpose or rationale of historical sociology would be simply to supply us with better factual historical knowledge (i.e., 'add historical sociology and stir'). The main rationale for world sociology is that it enables us to rethink and problematise some of the most basic assumptions that international relations scholars hold about the modern system, assumptions that reflect traditional ahistorical modes of theorising.

At a more profound level, we would argue that there are a number of issues or questions which are seldom considered or problematised, the first of which concerns the appropriate 'starting point' for international relations inquiry, both for research and teaching. How many courses in international relations take '1945' as their starting date ('Intro to World Politics Since 1945'), and regurgitate the 'usual suspects' – US hegemony, the Cold War, the security dilemma, nuclear deterrence, international regimes, interdependence and, last but not least, globalisation? And increasingly, international relations courses are being historically situated post-1989, and at times resemble 'current affairs' spliced with unproblematised traditional assumptions. It is *as if* the world was born in 1945 (though with a tacit nod to '1648 and all that'), and that all that went before 1945 is 'surplus to requirements', i.e., 'all very interesting but what has any of this got to do with the "real international relations issues" since 1945?' But the revealing thing here is the implicit assumption that a 'history' of international relations would begin *before* 1945 and might go 'as far back' as 1648 (the alleged but mythical starting date of the modern states system); the assumption is revealing because such a course would only encapsulate the modern period (at least according to conventional thinking), rather than the historical periods, thus showing the subconscious level at which ahistoricism pervades the discipline. And no less problematic is that our insistence on the need for history and sociology is usually answered by the *seemingly* appropriate question, 'Why don't you go to a history department, or better still a sociology department, if you want to pursue *your* interests?'

But such a question turns out to be an unwitting part of the 'traditional international relations' *gatekeeping strategy*. It is as if the historical sociology traveller, when trying to gain entry into the traditionally defined 'legitimate' terrain of international relations, is taken discreetly aside by 'international relations immigration officers' at the border, and told that she needs a visa, the conditions of which stipulate clearly that her baggage must be quarantined, but that it will be returned on departure conditional upon satisfactory behaviour during her stay (i.e., behaviour that conforms to the 'real international relations'). 'You *can* be seen,' say the international relations immigration officers, 'but you must *not* be heard.' And she will be told that any violation of these rules will be met with the usual refrain, 'you're not an *international relations* scholar', and will, therefore, lead to her immediate deportation (understood as permanent excommunication from the international relations discipline). In short, the seeming appropriateness of the above-mentioned question ('Why don't you go elsewhere to pursue *your* interests?') turns out to be symptomatic of an academic prejudice – what we will call *disciplinism* – which seeks to maintain an essentialist or 'intellectually pure' conception of the discipline, free of 'contamination' from so-called 'unpure' extra-disciplinary insight.

A further set of questions can be added to that concerning the 'starting point' for international relations inquiry, most notably:

• Who acts in global and world-historical politics?
• How can we explain change?
• What are states, and how have they emerged and changed through time?
• How can we understand the ever changing connections among, and configurations of, the global, the international, the national and the local, as they shift through long-run historical time?
• Is there only one international system, or many?

Most important here is the point that only an *historicised* world sociology allows the possibility of exploring, contextualising and rethinking not just the conventional stuff of international relations (the so-called 'real issues' since 1945), but also the answers to the deeper questions posed above, which, we argue, *should* be fundamental to the study of international relations.

Such questions are ignored because the mainstream international relations research agenda is inherently ahistorical, or suffers from what Hobson in chapter 1 calls *chronofetishism* and *tempocentrism*. He claims that mainstream international relations is *chronofetishist*, which is defined as 'a mode of ahistoricism which conveys *a set of illusions that represent the present as an autonomous, natural, spontaneous and immutable system that is self-constituting and eternal, and which necessarily obscures the processes of power, identity/social exclusion and norms that gave rise to, and continuously reconstitute, the present as an immanent order of change*' (Hobson, this volume, p. 12). All of the approaches in this volume seek implicitly or explicitly to overcome chronofetishism. For example, critical historical materialism, Critical Theory and postmodernism denaturalise the present by revealing the processes of social exclusion that gave rise to the present as well as pointing to the dialectical processes which are challenging and seeking to transcend the present order (and for a full discussion, see Hobson, this volume, pp. 31–9).

In this context, as Halliday argues, one of the most important benefits that an international sociology (or world sociology) provides is its ability to 'denaturalise' the present. One of the various ways in which this is achieved is through the rejection of 'methodological nationalism', which connotes the tendency of sociological theorists to explain domestic institutions and social practices in isolation from international forces. He argues that methodological nationalism obscures the constitutive impact of 'foreign' forces. And 'once the international is seen not as intruding on the national, but as participating in its very constitution then different analytic and ethical conclusions may follow'. The same holds for the tendency of international relations to invoke what might be termed 'methodological internationalism'. Paraphrasing Halliday, once the domestic is seen as participating in the very construction of the international, different analytical and ethical considerations follow. In particular, the traditional view of the 'great divide' that separates the 'good life' of domestic politics from the international as the 'realm of conflict' (e.g., Wight, 1966a; Waltz, 1979) largely disappears when we recognise the mutual impact of the national on the international and vice versa. Reus-Smit's constructivism, for example, shows how changes in the moral purpose of the state lead on to new forms of inter-state relations and international institutions (such that both the international and domestic realms share the same ethical principles). Moreover, Hobson's neo-Weberianism argues that the more states co-operate with their domestic societies (i.e., the more state–society complexes are 'socially embedded'), the greater becomes their ability to create a more co-operative international society. In other words, the domestic co-operative properties of state–society relations are internationalised to create an international society. From a different angle, Smith's postmodernism and Linklater's and Cutler's critical approaches reveal how domestic processes of social exclusion in turn create an international realm which embodies the repression and exclusion of various nations and identity groups.

A world sociology would also seek to break fundamentally with the ahistorical mode of *tempocentrism*, where the theorist takes a reified (i.e., chronofetishised) conception of the present and extrapolates this back in time to tarnish all historical international systems as isomorphic. This leads on to the *tempocentric paradox* in so far as tempocentrism 'conveys *the illusion that all international systems are equivalent (isomorphic) and have been marked by the constant and regular tempo of a chronofetishised present, which paradoxically obscures some of the most fundamental constitutive features of the present international system*' (Hobson, this volume, p. 12). An historicised world sociology is important because it can shed light on those constitutive features of the present system that are currently obscured by tempocentric international relations theory. For example, our contributors reveal that international history has witnessed a range of different international systems/societies, which have been governed by social principles that beat to a rhythm that is different to that of the present. Reus-Smit's constructivist approach sees that the 1648–1789 period is very different to the subsequent post-1815 period, the latter being governed by multilateralism as individual reciprocal norms of domestic society become internationalised. Linklater's approach reveals the different forms of identity and exclusion that differentiate ancient from modern states, and ancient from modern international relations. Buzan and

Little show that there have been three ideal types of international system through history. And Hobson shows that the free trade regimes of the mid-nineteenth century and post-1945 era are radically different, so an historical sociological explanation of the present trade regime is required.

The main implication of all this is that neither of these two disciplines can any longer stand in not-so-splendid isolation, precisely because domestic society or the international system do not exist as independent and self-constituting entities. Of course, to purists in each of these disciplines who are resistant to this message (for whatever reason), none of this will appear welcome. Perhaps the strongest objection concerns what might be called the 'incommensurability problem' (or what Halliday calls the 'substantive problem'): that not only do sociology and international relations scholars seek to explain different things, but they operationalise seemingly similar concepts (power, hegemony, state, etc.) in differing ways and with different results. Thus they might conclude that even with the best will in the world, it is simply not possible for practitioners of these different disciplines to enter into a mutual dialogue, precisely because they are talking fundamentally different languages.

But we argue that mainstream historical sociologists have little choice but to rethink the purpose of their discipline and engage with international relations for three principal reasons. First, when world systems theorists and neo-Weberians discovered the importance of the international to their theories of social change, whether they liked it or not, they necessarily entered the terrain of international relations. Second, largely unbeknown to them, Weberian historical sociologists operationalised an unproblematised traditional (neorealist) conception of the international, which led them, at best, to produce inconsistent analyses (Hobden, 1998), and, at worst, to contradict the objectives that their theory was designed to achieve – unwittingly leading them to 'kick the state back out', produce a reductionist 'base–superstructure' model, and deny any causal linkages that might flow from the national to the international (Hobson, this volume, pp. 70–3; Hobson, 2000: ch. 6; cf. Smith, this volume, pp. 230–5). Third, and most ironically, by operationalising chronofetishist and tempocentric analysis (derived from their employment of a neorealist definition of the international), they ended up by denying the rationale for historical sociology in the first place (Hobson, this volume, ch. 3). For these three reasons, therefore, historical sociologists can no longer afford to stand alone and defect from co-operation with international relations. Equally, mainstream international relations theorists have no choice, as we have argued all along, but to engage with historical sociology precisely because their chronofetishist and tempocentric approaches obscure crucial aspects and processes that constitute the present international system.

All of this underlines the need for a *reconstructed* historical sociology, which can overcome inconsistencies in the employment of shared concepts. Thus, for example, world sociology, as already noted, can only be developed by transcending methodological nationalism and methodological internationalism. But however we seek to resolve these problems, the key point is that we *must* do so if we are to advance both international relations theory as well as sociological theory. And drawing on the multiple insights that international relations and historical sociology bring can help us add dimensions to concepts that are employed in a monolithic way by each of the disciplines in isolation. It is precisely this that 'adds value' and constitutes one of the most important reasons for synthesising them into world sociology in the first place. This, of course, begs the question as to the place that world sociology might occupy within the discipline of international relations.

Specifying a place for world sociology within international relations

Before we can specify a place for world sociology within international relations, it is necessary to begin by reiterating what we mean by world sociology. This was defined in chapter 1 of this volume as *a critical approach which refuses to treat the present as an autonomous entity outside of history, but insists on embedding it within a specific socio-temporal place, thereby offering sociological remedies to the ahistorical illusions that chronofetishism and tempocentrism produce.* And, as already noted, such a definition is no less critical of mainstream historical sociology as it is of mainstream international relations. This provides one of the most compelling reasons why we believe that historical sociologists working outside of international relations (no less than mainstream international relations scholars) *should* engage in the project outlined in this volume if they are to enhance their own discipline. Thus it should be clear that we are not simply transplanting an unproblematised historical sociological approach into the study of international relations. Instead, we have sought to reformulate the definition of historical sociology in order to historicise international relations. So what place for world sociology within international relations?

While clearly we do *not* seek to replace international relations with historical sociology, nevertheless to establish historical sociology only as a *complement* to, or as a subdiscipline of, international relations would be insufficient. For we are not simply asking to 'add historical sociology and stir'. Re-importing a reproblematised historical sociology into international relations enables us to rethink many of the fundamental categories and assumptions about international relations theory and its research agenda. Moreover, as we noted in chapter 1, it has been the obsessive quest for scientific certainty, and a celebration of positivism which sees 'legitimate international relations inquiry' as defined only by the acquisition of objective knowledge, that prompted Waltz and others to find in international politics 'law-like patterns' of recurrence and continuity, patterns which could *not* be revealed through an historical sociological lens. Accordingly, our project entails a *rejection* of this definition of 'legitimate international relations inquiry', which has merely imposed an historically sanitised and totalising logic on past and present international relations.

It is at this point, however, that we are faced with a particular irony: for it is the central claim of Steve Smith's chapter that the historical sociological project outlined in this volume shares little with reflectivism and is, therefore, 'at base a rationalist enterprise that can fit relatively easily with the mainstream [of international relations theory]'. He makes this claim on the basis that historical sociology is allegedly materialist rather than idealist, 'causal' rather than interpretivist, and is ultimately statist and realist. This of course is ironic, if not perplexing, given that we have defined our historical sociological project negatively against the mainstream of international relations theory, most notably neorealism. What are we to make of this interesting and provocative claim? From the outset, it is worth emphasising that we welcome Smith's critical comments, no less than the Foucauldian approach that he offers us. Not surprisingly though (as he himself explicitly and correctly anticipates), we do not agree with his critique that historical sociology is part (potentially or actually) of mainstream international relations theory.

We have three main responses to Smith's argument. First, we see that his reading tends to stress the importance of epistemology, and his critique of the historical sociological enterprise tends, in our view, towards a binary view of international relations theory – a view that we see as both problematic and misunderstanding of the nature and purpose of the contribution that we believe historical sociology can provide for international relations. In his preferred lexicon, if you are not idealist (in the sense that ideas construct or shape the world), and if you support an 'outsider' as opposed to an 'insider' account, then *ipso facto* you are deemed to be part of positivist mainstream international relations theory. It is, we believe, not overly dramatic to state that his claim that historical sociology is part of the mainstream comes as something of a shock to us as editors – not least because the central purpose of this volume is not just to make the argument for historical sociology, but also to push the project from its present peripheral position towards the core of international relations. Moreover, we see that historical sociology's prime mandate is to redefine rather than complement or reflect the present mainstream international relations research agenda. But if epistemology is the main criterion used to evaluate theory, then everything that is neither radical constructivist nor postmodern is necessarily included in the same 'mainstream' category. This bifurcation glosses over the numerous positions that lie in between the extremes (i.e., reflectivism and mainstream international relations theory). Thus some of the historical sociology variants fit within a reflectivist tradition while others do not. But the crucial point is that of the latter (materialist) variants, *none* of their representatives in this volume would in any way support a neorealist approach. In short, evaluating the position of historical sociology within international relations through an epistemological lens leads to conclusions with which we would disagree regarding the nature and purpose of the historical sociology enterprise and its potential contribution to international relations.

Our second response to Smith revolves around what we see as a tension in his argument. On the one hand he very politely dismisses the majority of historical sociology as a part of mainstream international relations theory, but on the other hand he sees in constructivism, especially its more radical versions (outlined in Reus-Smit's chapter), an acceptable form of historical sociology. Thus he concedes that a certain type of historical sociology is, in his terms, 'non-mainstream'. But this is no small concession on his part because we see that the critical version of constructivism (especially Reus-Smit's approach in this volume), in certain key respects, is entirely commensurate with all the other approaches outlined in this volume. All of these contributors, in particular Reus-Smit, speak the *same* language – *all* are interested in *causal* explanation, *all* are interested in *explaining* international change, *all* are interested in developing *empirically based* and historically informed analyses of international relations, and *all* are interested in theorising the state (albeit in different ways). Smith criticises all streams of historical sociology bar radical constructivism as problematic because they are materialist (rationalist), and are necessarily 'causal' in that they seek to explain the world through an 'outsider' account (naturalism or positivism). But as we see it, the only real difference between Reus-Smit's version and all the others in this volume (bar Barnett and Smith) revolves around ontological concerns – the constructivists focusing on the causal centrality of norms while the remainder focus more (though not exclusively) on material structures. Moreover, it is as well to emphasise that the role of norms (as *constitutive* and not just regulatory as Smith suggests) enters, at least to some extent, the analyses of Mann, Hobson, Cutler, Linklater, Shaw, and Buzan and Little. We sincerely believe, therefore, that Smith has made a straw-person out of the bulk of historical sociology.

The third problem we have with Smith's argument concerns our rejection of his claim that historical sociology (in its non-constructivist form) is essentially statist and (politically) realist. He makes this claim on the basis that the majority of writers of historical sociology are neo-Weberian, and that Weberianism is essentially realist. But the writers whom he singles out – especially Skocpol and Tilly – are part of what Hobson calls the neorealist 'first wave' of Weberian historical sociology, and he sees a viable Weberian approach *only* in the *non*-realist second-wave theory that he has outlined in his chapter. Moreover, such writers do *not* represent the majority of historical sociologists working within international relations, even though many international relations scholars continue to assume otherwise (and arguably such writers are part of a defunct Weberian approach to international relations, if Hobson's claims are correct). And ironically neither Skocpol nor Tilly is, or ever has been, formally part of the international relations discipline, and neither has sought to engage with the discipline. A further point – and this one is undeniably controversial so we shall not make too much of it here – is the view of Hobson and Seabrooke (2001) that Max Weber was *not* a realist, a claim which, if correct, undermines the basis of Smith's claim here (even though we recognise his, as well as Reus-Smit's, qualifier – that Weber's work also contains cues for a non-materialist approach). But most importantly, we view historical sociology as a broad church of approaches, of which Weberianism, though perhaps the most prominent, is but one variant. And it is the problematic tendency among many international relations scholars to equate historical sociology with neo-Weberianism that provided us with one of the most compelling motivations for editing this volume in the first place – i.e., to display the seven major approaches to the international relations community. Finally, even if all the writers here adopt a causal and naturalist approach (which, we would argue, they do not), this does not make them neorealist as Smith seems to think. As noted already, all our contributors are in fundamental disagreement with neorealism. And central to our call for the development of historical sociological approaches to the study of international relations is our view that historical sociology *undermines* neorealism (see Hobden, 1998: ch 8; cf. Hobson, 1998a). Thus if historical sociology poses a challenge to mainstream international relations theory, as we contend, then it remains to be ascertained what the nature of this challenge is.

Though we argue that historical sociology poses a challenge for orthodox international relations, it is vital to note that our call for an historical sociologically informed international relations turns out to be somewhat less radical, or subversive of the discipline as a whole, than might at first appear (though not for the reasons pointed out by Steve Smith).

First, we are *not* asking international relations scholars to abandon their traditionally preferred topics (hegemony, the balance of power, the security dilemma, nuclear deterrence, international regimes, etc.), nor are we trying to say that the knowledge that they have painstakingly acquired over many years is in any way irrelevant. We are merely trying to suggest that they might enhance their studies further by engaging with world sociology. And second, it seems as though international relations scholars are presently suffering from a kind of collective 'disciplinary amnesia' in that for many, the division between historical sociology and international relations appears to be perfectly 'natural'. Clearly, it has been forgotten that international relations began as a *multi-disciplinary body of thought*, and was firmly grounded within history and sociology, as well as political theory, law and economics (Hobden, this volume). In short, as Hobden points out, it was only with the rise of the now defunct 'behavioural revolution' that international relations was socially reconstructed and defined negatively against historical sociology – a move that reached its apogee with Waltz (even though the original behaviouralist move did not go unchallenged, not least by Hedley Bull and the English School). This is perhaps *the* crucial point, given that some, though clearly not all, international relations scholars seem resistant to a broadening of 'their' *pure* discipline, in that the reimportation of historical sociology is viewed suspiciously as a mere contamination. But such an assumption appears unwarranted precisely because the present boundary line that has been imagined or constructed between mainstream international relations and historical sociology is *unnatural*, given that international relations did not begin as an exclusive discipline but was a thoroughly broad and inclusive school of thought in which historical sociology played an important and 'legitimate' part.

Accordingly, for both these reasons, we are *not* advocating a battle over academic property rights, but are merely suggesting that international relations should revitalise or *recapture* the historical and sociological sensitivity that it had originally accepted as a core part of its identity until the latter part of the twentieth century. To borrow Andrew Linklater's phrase, we are calling for the creation of an open *dialogic community* of scholars not only from historical sociology and international relations, but also from economics, economic history, world history, comparative politics/economics, anthropology and political/historical geography. Our central message, then, is offered in a spirit of *inclusiveness*, for we seek neither to subvert the discipline nor to substitute historical sociology for international relations. Rather, the point is to *reintroduce* historical sociology to the wider international relations community. And in the same way that, as this book argues, a more broadly based multi-disciplinary conception of international relations would considerably improve the discipline, these 'other', complementary disciplines would significantly benefit from a dialogue with international relations. It is for this reason, as we argue in our introductory chapters, that we seek to 'bring historical sociology *back* into international relations', no less than we propose that historical sociology should bring international relations theory and research into the core of its approach.

As to the *specific* place that we are seeking for world sociology, it helps to conceive of a Venn diagram with four elements, in which international relations, international political economy and historical sociology all appear as separate elements. World sociology might be thought of as a fourth element that overlaps with the other three. It not only sheds light on and reconfigures the other three, but it can also be seen as the *via media* between all three. This is very much reflected in the research agenda that our world sociology entails (to be discussed in the fourth section of this chapter). However, before addressing the agenda of an historicised world sociology, we turn to examine the third question posed above: what might such an approach look like?

Theoretical foundations of world sociology

Constructing a volume that separately considers each of the seven major historical sociology approaches tends in the first instance to exaggerate the appearance of differences, and obscures the fundamental commonalities of these approaches. Considering these similarities helps point to particular ingredients that an historicised world sociology should embody. It could be argued that the two central and most general commonalities are, first (to borrow Buzan and Little's term), a 'thick' conception of the international system and, second, a 'thick' conception of the state–society complex.

Mainstream international relations tends to utilise a 'thin' conception of the international system (as noted by Buzan and Little). Thin conceptions are problematic because they lead to tempocentric analysis, which obscures differences between international systems through history. Elaborating on Buzan and Little's arguments, we define a thin conception of the international as one in which *the international is extracted out of its specific historical context and is treated as 'temporally isomorphic' (i.e., that its features never change) as well as being conceived of as autonomous, self-constituting and monolithic – both sectorally and spatially – such that it obscures the specific spatio-temporal, domestic and global social processes that both constitute and continuously redefine the international.* More specifically, this definition can be unpacked into its five components (though six if we include Buzan and Little's emphasis on 'interaction capacity'):

(1) the international system is deemed to be an *autonomous* or self-constituting structure which is entirely separate from influences emanating from the domestic realm;
(2) the international is viewed as *monolithic* in that it is *sectorally* undifferentiated (i.e., it is purely constituted as either economic, military or political);
(3) the international is viewed as *monolithic* in that it is *spatially* undifferentiated (focusing only on territorial inter-state relations);
(4) the social dimensions of the international are obscured;
(5) structure is exaggerated over agency (ignoring state–society complexes or global non-state actors as constitutive of the international).

How then does historical sociology remedy the blindspots of mainstream (thin) conceptions of the international? Put differently, what does a thick conception of the international system look like?

Taking each of the five aspects of the international in turn, we begin by noting that virtually all our contributors envisage the international as *in part* constituted by domestic forces, whether these be based on class (Cutler's critical historical materialism), domestic norms and social identity (Reus-Smit's constructivism, Linklater's Critical Theory and Smith's postmodernism), *socially embedded* state–society relations (Hobson's second-wave Weberianism), or state–society relations (Buzan and Little's structural realism). Second, most envisage the international as 'sectorally differentiated', whether this is based on norms and international institutions (constructivism), economic, military, political and normative features (second-wave Weberian historical sociology and structural realism), class forces and international institutions (Cutler's critical historical materialism), or social, moral and global economic forces (Linklater's Critical Theory). Third, all approaches perceive the 'international' as embedded not just in the domestic but also in the global environment (with Shaw, Barnett, Linklater and Gills paying special attention to the global). Fourth, all approaches emphasise the social dimensions of the international, and, fifth, most insist that the international is in part shaped by agential power forces, either at the international/global or domestic levels. Accordingly, all insist that the international system has taken on different faces through time.

A thick conception of the state at the domestic level is explicitly argued for by Hobson, who suggests that prevailing conceptions of the state in international relations are premised on thin conceptions. A thin conception of the state is one in which *the state is extracted out of its specific historical context and treated as absolutely autonomous of society, 'temporally isomorphic' (such that its features and behaviour never change) and territorially marked off from other states (i.e., exhibits sovereignty), such that it obscures the specific spatio-temporal, domestic and global social processes that constitute and continuously redefine both the state and state behaviour in the international and global realms.* Hobson argues specifically for a second-wave Weberian historical sociology which can open up the 'black box' and consider the state–society complex as a constitutive feature of the international, while at the same time emphasising the international or even global social forces that shape the 'national'. Halliday's work provides an important cue for developing such a thick conception of state–society relations by showing that particular forms of state–society relations generate war in the international system, and that the international in turn shapes the state–society complex (Halliday, 1994b, 1999). Shaw does likewise but emphasises a set of 'global–domestic–global' linkages. Reus-Smit's constructivist approach embeds the state within prevailing moral conceptions of the domestic social realm, which in turn guide the moral direction of inter-state relations. International norms and institutions then react back and shape states. Smith's postmodernism, as well as Linklater's Critical Theory, also focus on the identity of the state and the construction of the 'moral community' which, as in Reus-Smit's analysis, has important ramifications for the conduct of international relations and vice versa. Cutler's critical historical materialism fundamentally embeds the state within hegemonic social and class forces, which in turn guide state behaviour internationally, while simultaneously showing that international institutions (especially international law) also shape the domestic realm. Moreover, Buzan and Little's structural realism pays attention to the way in which the units affect the international and vice versa (see, especially, Buzan, Jones and Little, 1993).

In sum, by adopting thick conceptions of the state and the international system, world sociology is able to remedy tempocentrism and choronfetishism, thereby revealing change through time. Moreover, we can draw out from the previous discussion four main areas of theoretical overlap, which underpin our world sociological approach. Interestingly, these four areas are fundamental to Jan Aart Scholte's six-point programme that underpins what he calls 'world-historical-sociological' studies (Scholte, 1993: 143–4). These comprise, first, a commitment to ontologically complex models of causality and a simultaneous rejection of parsimony; second, a commitment to 'neo-integrationism' which involves a rejection of 'methodological nationalism' and 'methodological internationalism'; third, a commitment to structurationism and a rejection of agent-centrism and structuralism; and fourth, a commitment to some form of 'Critical Theory' and a rejection of 'problem-solving theory'.

But perhaps the more important aspect, and indeed the *most* unifying element that draws each of the different approaches into a single 'world sociology school', is the research agenda that such a school offers, around which all our contributors gather in one way or another.

A world sociological research agenda: ten analytical areas for empirical and normative research

Embracing world sociology not only enhances the current international relations research agenda, but more importantly, can bring into focus new areas for research that have remained obscured by the present mainstream research agenda. Moreover, we also suggest that historical sociologists working outside of international relations might also engage with such a research agenda, not least to enhance their own discipline's focus on 'structural historical change'. In this final section, we highlight ten analytical areas for future empirical and normative research.

(1)   *Inter-systemic/trans-systemic and inter-societal/trans-societal analysis*

Given that international anarchy is not pure but differentiated, it is clear that there has always been a variety of anarchic and hierarchic international systems. This requires an analysis that can trace the various configurations and relations between different hierarchies and anarchies in international systems, and thereby develop a taxonomy of different international systems through time (Spruyt, 1998: 348). And in considering whether we are moving into a new global era that is qualitatively different to the Westphalian era, we need to rethink previous examples of systems change, most notably the shift from medieval heteronomy to sovereignty, as well as consider the differing constitutions of the medieval and contemporary international political architectures. Moreover, we also need to differentiate 'inter/trans-systemic' from 'inter/trans-societal' analyses; the former are constructed around territorial boundaries whereas the latter considers societies which are differentiated along moral boundaries.

(2)   *Intra-systemic and intra-societal change*

Not only do we need to understand changes between different international systems/societies, but we also need to focus on changes *within* particular international systems/societies. Halliday, in his chapter, specifies the general issue of revolutions, as well as the particular instance of the collapse of Soviet communism and the end of the Cold War, as urgent areas for analysis, though he insists that this can only be done through a long-run historical sociological approach. And while historical sociology might appear to take the lead in this area, only by developing *thick* conceptions of the state and international system (by carefully synthesising insights from historical sociology and international relations) can such a task be adequately undertaken.

(3)   *Inter-spatial analysis*

The fact that the units have been spatially configured in different ways through time means that we cannot presuppose sovereign relations, but must explain these. Moreover, the fact that the units have been embedded within anarchies *and* hierarchies means that we need to develop not just a spatial 'architecture and arrangement of the parts' (Spruyt, 1998: 349), but also an analysis that can examine the different *behavioural* patterns of the units under different forms of spatial relations. Clearly states and non-state actors behave differently under different historical-spatial architectures. And if hierarchy and anarchy co-exist today, what effect does this have on inter-state as well as global relations?

(4)   *Spatio-temporal analysis*

As noted already, tempocentric international relations theory presupposes that international systems in world history have all marched to the same beat. In mainstream international relations theory, space is static and equated with the specific territoriality of the sovereign state, a problem that has been referred to as the 'territorial trap' (Agnew, 1994). But rather than assume that space was static prior to 1945 and has since become more fluid (an assumption that is common to most theories of globalisation), an historical sociology of space-time reveals that space has always been fluid, though such fluidity has *varied* through time. Thus a world sociology does not call merely for a 'spatial turn', but rather, for a 'spatio-temporal turn'. Such a 'world sociology of space-time' asserts, first, that space-time is variable, and second, that space-time is not a dependent, but a partially independent, variable, in that its changing configurations impact upon, and constitute the conduct and development of, international and domestic systems – a notion that lies at base of Buzan and Little's concept of 'interaction capacity', and Giddens's (1984) concept of 'time-space distanciation' (see also Massey, 1992; Agnew, 1994, 1999; Ruggie, 1998b; Brenner, 1999). To use a scientific analogy, historical sociology seeks to replace traditional international relations' 'Newtonian' conception of (international) space with Einstein's conception of relativity.

Given that world history cannot be understood in terms of a constant tempo, the following research questions are worthy of consideration:

- How immanent is the propensity for change within the present system?
- If pre-modern international systems were governed by a 'dialectic' between anarchies and hierarchies (Mann, 1986; Watson, 1992), has the modern system resolved this contradiction, or is the continuation of this dialectic leading to a new, more hierarchic international or global system?
- If world history is not unilinear and temporally constant, how can we understand its changing space-time configurations?
- Is world historical change governed by moments of 'punctuated equilibrium' (e.g., Spruyt, 1994), moments of 'episodic' change (e.g., Gellner, 1964), 'discontinuous' ruptures (e.g., Giddens, 1984), 'revolutionary' moments (Marxism), or some other mode of change? This is clearly a difficult issue precisely because, as Scholte put it,

> In every social development the past, the present and the future are linked together by continuity as well as distinguished by change . . . In the end continuity and change are only separable analytically; in concrete social history persistence and transformation are interwoven and mutually defining (Scholte, 1993: 7).

But it would be too limited to link space only to time, because space is also connected to power (the 'space-power nexus'). That is, different forms of power (economic, normative, military and political) have had different spatial configurations through time. Owen Lattimore has argued that for long periods of history, military power has had the most extensive reach, and political power has eclipsed economic power (Lattimore, 1962: 480–91, 542–51). Conversely, in the modern world, economic power has the most extensive reach, eclipsing political and military power. On the other hand, Barry Gills suggests that economic power has always had the most extensive reach (Gills, this volume; Frank and Gills, 1996). Drawing on Mann (1986), who argues that 'extensive' power predominated in pre-modern systems, while 'intensive' forms have predominated in the modern world, we can ask:

- How has the space-power nexus differed between systems over time, and with what ramifications for past and present international relations?
- Given that the 'time-space edges' (Giddens, 1984) that 'separate' societies within international systems have changed through time, how can we theorise these changes (an area that returns us to 'inter-spatial analysis')?

In this way, world sociology provides an important means to escape the 'territorial trap'.

(5)   *From the inter-state to a global analytic framework*

Although inter-state relations are important, they necessarily obscure the impact of global and international social forces and normative environments. World sociology supports a move away from a monolithic inter-state analysis to a 'multi-spatial' approach – i.e., 'neo-integrationism' (see also Scholte, 1993). Of course, such an approach can take a variety of forms (compare Linklater, Shaw, Gills and Barnett, all of whom emphasise different aspects of what Shaw calls 'globality'). And of course, this raises a series of further questions – not the least of which is whether modern globalisation represents a new and distinct period of world relations (again, compare Shaw and Gills for two opposed answers).

(6)   *Unit-based analysis*

The fact that unlike-units have taken precedence over like-units for about 99 per cent of world history means that we cannot presuppose the existence of like-units but must explain their origins, as well as recognise that, even today, the existence of unlike-units persists within the Third World. We also need to consider the different ways in which the units shape the international system, as well as to develop a taxonomy of different units in different international systems over time. And we need to inquire as to how the construction of 'sovereignty' has changed within particular international systems, and what ramifications this has for the conduct of international as well as domestic relations. Moreover, we need to think about whether the present global era has ushered in a period of 'state de-formation' in the First World, and whether the Third World is undergoing a process that leads to 'state deformity', something which, we believe, can only be adequately analysed through historical sociological analysis.

(7)   *Social power-based analysis*

Given the premise of ontological complexity, it is apparent that different social power sources will configure in a variety of combinations through time. Accordingly, we need to ask:

• 'Why at given points in time [do] certain configurations come to dominate?' (Spruyt, 1998: 349).
• Do different international systems demonstrate identifiable patterns of social power interaction?
• To what extent are the various sources of social power materially prescribed or socially constructed?

(8)   *Structurationist analysis*

While structures are important, a systemic analysis that ignores the impact of agents necessarily leads to ahistoricism. A world sociology approach is only possible because of the assumption that agents and structures are mutually co-constituted. Such an approach should, therefore, inquire into the relationship between structures and agents, and how these relationships differ over time and with what consequences for international and domestic relations. Clearly, it needs to be asked who are the actors and which structures are important, and how can we conceptualise the co-constitution of agents and structures? Finally, with the rise of constructivism in international relations, the term 'structurationism' has become almost a buzz-word. But, as noted above, it seems to have been forgotten by some, though by no means all, constructivists, that when Giddens (1984) originally laid out his theory of structuration, it was inextricably embedded within an historical sociological framework. In other words, to abstract from his approach only the co-constitutive relationship between agents and structures, divorced from their historical environment, undermines the rationale for structurationism in the first place.

(9)   *Identity-formation analysis*

World sociology places considerable emphasis on how the identities of the agents are, in part, shaped by the intentional and unintentional impact of structures, which are, in turn, partially shaped by the intentional and unintentional actions of the agents. Such analysis would inquire into the processes through which agent identities, such as sovereignty, are formed, and would examine the impact of international institutions no less than the domestic normative environments within which states are embedded.

(10)   *Critical and normative analysis*

As our definition of world sociology implies (pp. 271, 13), such an approach is necessarily 'critical' and normative, in that it forces us to rethink the origins of international systems, states and international institutions, as well as to *denaturalise* such historical forms, and to consider the potential and actual processes which are reconstituting, if not transforming, the present into possible and desirable futures. More specifically, drawing on Linklater's contribution, we can ask:

• How have 'moral communities' been defined through time, and what processes are responsible for shifts in moral communities through time?

- Is the modern conception of the moral community radically different to previous moral formations?
- Are we moving into a post-sovereign world, and is there a process through which 'moral deficits' (Linklater) are being reduced?
- How and what processes have led to the contraction and expansion of the moral boundaries of international societies through time?
- How have different international societies and civilisations communicated through moral dialogue with each other?

Last, but not least, Fred Halliday and Steve Smith signal the importance of thinking about post-colonial issues, and the degree to which the 'West' has defined itself negatively against the 'East', as well as the importance of gender issues. This, of course, takes us back to our ninth proposed area of analysis (identity-formation).

Conclusion: international relations in the light of historical sociology

Finally, a more general consequence of ahistoricism (i.e., chronofetishism and tempocentrism) is that the international relations research agenda has come to suffer from what might be called a 'weather-vane syndrome', in which international relations scholars are constantly blown around in different directions with the rapid toing and froing of almost daily events and crises. Thus, one day the obsolescence of war and the victory of liberalism over realism, the next day the second Gulf War and the victory of realism; one day the end of strategic studies, the next day the Indo-Pakistani nuclear rivalry and the revival of security studies; one day the end of US capitalism, the retreat of liberalism and the rise of (East Asian) statism, the next day Asian meltdown, the resurgence of the US economy, the end of statism and the triumph of liberalism, and so on and so forth. Such a research agenda is propelled by an 'instrumental' understanding of 'present history', in that current history serves as little more than a battleground in which theorists compete for ideological hegemony or supremacy. In this way, history is forced into the background, while theorists compete for ideological hegemony in the foreground.

By contrast, world sociology rejects such an 'instrumental' reading of either past or present history, and by bringing 'constitutive' history into the foreground, enables us to move away from the eternally shifting sands of the 'weather-vane' research model, to reconsider and problematise some of the most fundamental theoretical assumptions upon which the discipline is founded, assumptions which the weather-vane model fails to problematise. Historical sociology can, therefore, provide a much stronger foundation for the international relations research agenda, one that would no longer be constantly buffeted by the latest event or fad to emerge within 'current affairs'. This in particular, we argue, is one of the most compelling rationales for an historicised world sociology.

But more generally, we suggest that the volume's 'intellectual success' should be evaluated in terms of three further criteria: first, whether the reader is persuaded by the rationale and usefulness of this ten-point world sociology research agenda, rather than whether he/she is convinced by any one of the individual approaches that are proposed in this volume. Second, we suggest that perhaps the ultimate litmus test for the success of this volume lies in whether the reader is convinced of the inappropriateness of the oft-made claim that 'historical sociology is simply *not* international relations', and that 'real international relations' can only be defined by the study of unproblematised contemporary topics. Put differently, this book will have served its purpose if it succeeds in persuading international relations scholars of the inherent problems with 'disciplinism'. Finally, one ironic sign of the success of our world sociology manifesto might be in the form of a silence, in which traditional international relations campaigners come to recognise the intellectual sterility or even absurdity of the 'disciplinist' question, 'why don't you historical sociologists join a sociology or history department if you want to pursue your interests?' (and, no less, the disciplinist claim that 'you're not an international relations scholar'), to the extent that they refrain from asking the question at all, not for reasons of inter-subjective politeness, but on the grounds of inter-subjective reflection.

References

Abbott, Kenneth and Snidal, Duncan (2000), 'Hard and Soft Law in International Governance', *International Organization* 54 (3): 421–56.

Abel, Richard (1991), 'Capitalism and the Rule of Law: Precondition or Contradiction?', *Law and Social Inquiry* 15 (4): 685–97.

Abrams, Philip (1982), *Historical Sociology*, Ithaca: Cornell University Press.

Abu-Lughod, Janet (1989), *Before European Hegemony*, Oxford: Oxford University Press.

Adams, Henry Brooks (1895), *The Law of Civilization and Decay*, London: Sonnenschein.

Adas, Michael (1989), *Machines as the Measure of Men*, Ithaca: Cornell University Press.

Adler, Emanuel (1997), 'Seizing the Middle Ground: Constructivism in World Politics', *European Journal of International Relations* 3 (3): 319–63.

——— (1998), 'Seeds of Peaceful Change: The OSCE's Security Community-Building Model', in Emanuel Adler and Michael Barnett (eds.), *Security Communities*, New York: Cambridge University Press, pp. 119–60.

Adler, Emanuel and Haas, Peter M. (1992), 'Conclusion: Epistemic Communities, World Order, and the Creation of a Reflective Research Program', *International Organization* 46 (1): 367–90.

Agnew, John A. (1994), 'The Territorial Trap: The Geographical Assumptions of International Relations Theory', *Review of International Political Economy* 1 (1): 53–80.

——— (1999), 'Mapping Political Power Beyond State Boundaries: Territory, Identity, and Movement in World Politics', *Millennium* 28 (3): 499–521.

Albrow, Martin (1996), *The Global Age*, Cambridge: Polity.

Amin, Samir (1988), *Eurocentrism*, London: Zed Press.

——— (1996), 'The Ancient World-Systems versus the Modern Capitalist World-System', in Frank and Gills (eds.), pp. 247–77.

Amoore, Louise, Dodgson, Richard, Germain, Randall, Gills, Barry K., Langley, Paul and Watson, Iain (2000), 'Paths to a Historicized International Political Economy', *Review of International Political Economy* 7 (1): 53–71.

Anderson, Perry (1974), *Passages from Antiquity to Feudalism*, London: New Left Books.

——— (1980), *Arguments Within English Marxism*, London: New Left Books.

——— (1999), *The Origins of Post-Modernity*, London: Verso.

Angell, Norman (1912), *The Great Illusion*, London: Heinemann.

Archer, Margaret S. (1982), 'Morphogenesis versus Structuration: On Combining Structure and Action', *British Journal of Sociology* 33 (4): 455–83.

(1988), *Culture and Agency*, Cambridge: Cambridge University Press.

(1995), *Realist Social Theory*, Cambridge: Cambridge University Press.

Archibugi, Daniele, Held, David and Kohler, Michael (eds.) (1998), *Reimagining Political Community*, Cambridge: Polity.

Armstrong, David (1998), 'Globalization and the Social State', *Review of International Studies* 24 (4): 461–78.

Aron, Raymond (1957), 'Historical Sociology as an Approach to International Relations', in *The Nature of Conflict* (Paris: UNESCO), reprinted in abbreviated form in Evan Luard, *Basic Texts in International Relations*, London: Macmillan (1992), pp. 578–83.

(1966), *Peace and War*, London: Weidenfeld & Nicolson.

Arrighi, Giovanni (1994), *The Long Twentieth Century*, London: Verso.

Arrighi, Giovanni, Hopkins, Terence and Wallerstein, Immanuel (1989), *Antisystemic Movements*, London: Verso.

Ascher, William (1983), 'New Development Approaches and the Adaptability of International Agencies: The Case of the World Bank', *International Organization* 37 (3): 415–39.

Ashley, Richard K. (1986), 'The Poverty of Neorealism', in Keohane (ed.), pp. 255–300.

(1989), 'Living on Borderlines: Man, Poststructuralism and War', in J. Der Derian and M. J. Shapiro (eds.), *International/Intertextual Relations*, Lexington: Lexington Books, pp. 259–321.

Badie, Bertrand and Smouts, Marie-Claude (1992), *Le Retournement du Monde*, Paris: Presses de la Fondation National des Sciences Politiques et Dalloz.

Balbus, Isaac (1977), 'Commodity Form and Legal Form: An Essay on the "Relative Autonomy" of the Law', *Law and Society* 11 (Winter): 571–88.

Baldwin, David (1993), 'Neoliberalism, Neorealism, and World Politics', in David Baldwin (ed.), *Neorealism and Neoliberalism: The Contemporary Debate*, New York: Columbia University Press, pp. 3–25.

Barnet, Richard J. (1981), *The Lean Years*, London: Abacus.

Barnett, Michael and Finnemore, Martha (1998), 'Power and Pathologies of International Organizations', unpublished work.

(1999), 'The Politics, Power, and Pathologies of International Organizations', *International Organization* 53 (4): 699–732.

Bartelson, Jens (1995), *A Genealogy of Sovereignty*, Cambridge: Cambridge University Press.

Bauslaugh, Robert A. (1991), *The Concept of Neutrality in Ancient Greece*, Berkeley: University of California Press.

Baylis, John and Smith, Steve (eds.) (1997), *The Globalization of World Politics*, Oxford: Oxford University Press.

Beck, Robert, Arend, Anthony and Vander Lugt, Robert (eds.) (1996), *International Rules: Approaches from International Law and International Relations*, Oxford: Oxford University Press.

Beck, Ulrich (1992), *Risk Society*, London: Sage.

Beetham, David (1985), *Max Weber and the Theory of Modern Politics*, Cambridge: Polity.

(1996), *Bureaucracy*, Minneapolis: University of Minnesota Press.

Bendix, Reinhard (1978), *Kings or People*, London: University of California Press.

Benney, Mark (1983), 'Gramsci on Law, Morality, and Power', *International Journal of Sociology of Law* 11 (2): 191–208.

Bentley, Jerry H. (1993), *Old World Encounters*, New York: Oxford University Press.

Biersteker, Thomas J. and Weber, Cynthia (eds.) (1996), *State Sovereignty as Social Construct*, Cambridge: Cambridge University Press.

Blackburn, Robin (1997), *The Making of New World Slavery*, London: Verso.

Blaut, James M. (1992), '1492', *Political Geography* 11 (4): 355–85.

(1993), *The Colonizer's Model of the World*, New York: Guilford Press.

Bloch, Marc (1967), 'Natural Economy or Money Economy: A Pseudo-Dilemma', in Marc Bloch (ed.), *Land and Work in Medieval Europe*, London: Routledge & Kegan Paul, pp. 230–43.

Blundell, Mary W. (1989), *Helping Friends and Harming Enemies*, Cambridge: Cambridge University Press.

Bodin, Jean (1967), *Six Books of the Commonwealth*, Oxford: Blackwell.

Bohman, James (1997), 'The Public Spheres of the World Citizen', in James Bohman and Mattias Lutz-Machmann (eds.), *Perpetual Peace*, London: MIT Press, pp. 179–200.

Boli, John (1999), 'Conclusion: World Authority Structures and Legitimations', in Boli and Thomas (eds.), pp. 267–300.

Boli, John and Thomas, George (eds.) (1999), *Constructing World Culture*, Stanford: Stanford University Press.

Booth, Ken (1996), '75 Years On: Rewriting the Subject's Past – Reinventing its Future', in Smith, Booth and Zalewski (eds.), pp. 328–39.

Booth, Ken and Smith, Steve (eds.) (1995), *International Relations Theory Today*, Cambridge: Polity.

Bottomore, Tom (ed.) (1991), *A Dictionary of Marxist Thought*, Oxford: Blackwell.

Brenner, Neil (1999), 'Beyond State-Centrism? Space, Territoriality, and Geographical Scale in Globalization Studies', *Theory and Society* 28: 39–78.

Brenner, Robert (1977), 'The Origins of Capitalist Development: A Critique of Neo-Smithian Marxism', *New Left Review* 104: 25–92.

Bronner, Stephen (1994), *Of Critical Theory and its Theorists*, Oxford: Blackwell.

Brown, Chris (1992), *International Relations Theory*, London: Harvester Wheatsheaf.

Brownlie, Ian (1990), *Principles of Public International Law*, 4th edn, Oxford: Clarendon Press.

Bukovansky, Mlada (1997), 'American Identity and Neutral Rights from Independence to the War of 1812', *International Organization* 51 (2): 209–44.

Bull, Hedley (1966a), 'International Theory: The Case for a Classical Approach', *World Politics* 18 (3): 361–77.

(1966b), 'The Grotian Concept of International Society', in Butterfield and Wight (eds.), pp. 51–74.

(1977), *The Anarchical Society*, London: Macmillan.

(1984), *Justice in International Relations*, Waterloo, Ont.: University of Waterloo Press.

Bull, Hedley and Watson, Adam (eds.) (1984), *The Expansion of International Society*, Oxford: Oxford University Press.

Burch, Kurt and Denemark, Robert A. (eds.) (1997), *Constituting International Political Economy*, London: Lynne Rienner.

Burhenne, W. E. (ed.) (1993), *International Environmental Soft Law: Collection of Relevant Instruments*, Dordrecht: M. Nijhoff.

Burke, Edmond, III (1993), 'Introduction: Marshall G. S. Hodgson and World History', in Hodgson, pp. ix–xxi.

Burke, Peter (1980), *Sociology and History*, London: Allen & Unwin.

Burton, John W. (1968), *Systems, States, Diplomacy and Rules*, Cambridge: Cambridge University Press.

Butler, Judith (1997), *The Psychic Life of Power: Theories in Subjection*, Stanford: Stanford University Press.

Butterfield, Herbert (1949), *The Whig Interpretation of History*, London: Bell.

Butterfield, Herbert and Wight, Martin (eds.) (1966), *Diplomatic Investigations*, London: Allen & Unwin.

Buzan, Barry (1996), 'The Timeless Wisdom of Realism?', in Smith, Booth and Zalewski (eds.), pp. 47–65.

Buzan, Barry, Jones, Charles and Little, Richard (1993), *The Logic of Anarchy*, New York: Columbia University Press.

Buzan, Barry and Little, Richard (1994), 'The Idea of "International System": Theory Meets History', *International Political Science Review* 15 (3): 231–55.

(2000), *International Systems in World History*, Oxford: Oxford University Press.

Campbell, David (1998), *Writing Security*, Minneapolis: University of Minnesota Press.

Carley, M. and Spapens, P. (1998), *Sharing the World*, London: Earthscan.

Carneiro, Robert L. (1978), 'Political Expansion of the Principle of Political Exclusion', in Ronald Cohen and Elman R. Service (eds.), *Origins of the State*, Philadelphia: Institute for the Study of Human Issues, pp. 205–23.

Carr, Edward H. (1951), *The New Society*, London: Macmillan.

(1961), *What is History?*, Harmondsworth: Penguin.

Cerny, Philip (1990), *The Changing Architecture of the State*, London: Sage.

Charlesworth, Hilary, Chinkin, Christine and Wright, Shelley (1991), 'Feminist Approaches to International Law', *American Journal of International Law* 85 (4): 613–45.

Chase-Dunn, Christopher K. (1989), *Global Formation*, Oxford: Blackwell.

Chase-Dunn, Christopher K. and Hall, Thomas D. (1997), *Rise and Demise: Comparing World Systems*, Boulder: Westview Press.

Chaudhuri, Kirti N. (1985), *Trade and Civilisation in the Indian Ocean*, Cambridge: Cambridge University Press.

(1990), *Asia Before Europe*, Cambridge: Cambridge University Press.

Checkel, Jeff (1998), 'The Constructivist Turn in International Relations Theory', *World Politics* 50 (2): 324–48.

Childe, Gordon (1942), *What Happened in History*, Harmondsworth: Pelican.

Church, William F. (ed.) (1969), *Impact of Absolutism in France*, New York: Wiley.

Clark, Ian (1998), 'Beyond the Great Divide: Globalization and the Theory of International Relations', *Review of International Studies* 24 (4): 479–98.

Coker, Christopher (1998), *Twilight of the West*, Oxford: Westview Press.

Collins, Randall (1986), *Weberian Sociological Theory*, New York: Cambridge University Press.

Corrigan, P. and Sayer, D. (1985), *The Great Arch*, Oxford: Blackwell.

Cox, Robert W. (1980), 'The Crisis of World Order and the Problem of International Organization in the 1980s', *International Journal* 35 (2): 370–95.

—— (1986), 'Social Forces, States and World Orders: Beyond International Relations Theory', in Keohane (ed.), pp. 204–54.

—— (1987), *Production, Power, and World Order*, New York: Columbia University Press.

—— (1996), *Approaches to World Order*, Cambridge: Cambridge University Press.

Cupitt, Richard, Whitlock, Rodney and Whitlock, Lynn (1997), 'The (Im)mortality of International Governmental Organizations', in Paul F. Diehl (ed.), *The Politics of Global Governance: International Organizations in an Interdependent World*, Boulder: Lynne Rienner, pp. 7–23.

Curtin, Philip D. (1984), *Cross-Cultural Trade in World History*, Cambridge: Cambridge University Press.

Cusack, Mary Frances (1995), *An Illustrated History of Ireland*, London: Bracken Books.

Cutler, A. Claire (1991), 'The "Grotian Tradition" in International Relations', *Review of International Studies* 17 (1): 41–65.

—— (1999a), 'Public Meets Private: The International Unification and Harmonization of Private International Trade Law', *Global Society* 13 (1): 25–48.

—— (1999b), 'Private Authority in International Trade Relations: The Case of Maritime Transport', in Cutler, Haufler and Porter (eds.), pp. 283–329.

—— (1999c), 'Locating "Authority" in the Global Political Economy', *International Studies Quarterly* 43 (1): 59–81.

—— (2000), 'Globalization, Law, and Transnational Corporations: The Deepening of Market Discipline', in Theodore Cohn, Stephen McBride and David Wiseman (eds.), *Power in the Global Era*, London: Macmillan, pp. 53–66.

—— (2001a), 'Critical Reflections on Westphalian Assumptions of International Law and Organization: A Crisis of Legitimacy', *Review of International Studies* 27 (2): 133–150.

—— (2001b), 'Law in the Global Polity', in Richard Higgott and Morten Ougaard (eds.), *Understanding the Global Polity*, London: Routledge.

—— (forthcoming), 'Historical Materialism, Globalization, and Law: Competing Conceptions of Property', in Mark Rupert and Hazel Smith (eds.), *The Point is to Change the World: Socialism through Globalization?*, London: Routledge.

Cutler, A. Claire, Haufler, Virginia and Porter, Tony (eds.) (1999), *Private Authority and International Affairs*, New York: State University of New York Press.

Dandeker, Christopher (1990), *Surveillance, Power and Modernity*, New York: St Martin's Press.

De Ste. Croix, Geoffrey E. M. (1981), *The Class Struggle in the Ancient Greek World*, London: Duckworth.

Denemark, Robert, Friedman, Jonathan, Gills, Barry K. and Modelski, George (eds.) (2000) *World System History*, London: Routledge.

De-Shalit, Avner (1998), 'Transnational and International Exploitation', *Political Studies* 46 (4): 693–708.

Dezalay, Yves and Garth, Bryant (1996), *Dealing in Virtue: International Commercial Arbitration and the Construction of a Transnational Legal Order*, Chicago: University of Chicago Press.

Donelan, Michael D. (1990), *Elements of International Political Theory*, Oxford: Clarendon.

Doty, Roxanne-Lynn (1996), 'Sovereignty and the Nation: Constructing the Boundaries of National Identity', in Biersteker and Weber (eds.), pp. 121–47.

Doucas, Margaret (1995), 'Intellectual Property Law – Indigenous Peoples' Concerns', *Canadian Intellectual Property Review* 12 (1): 1–5.

Doyle, Michael (1983), 'Kant, Liberal Legacies and Foreign Affairs', *Philosophy and Public Affairs* 12 (3 & 4): 205–34 and 323–52.

Dunne, Timothy J. (1998), *Inventing International Society*, Basingstoke: Macmillan.

Easton, David (1953), *The Political System*, New York: Knopf.

(1981), 'The Political System Besieged by the State', *Political Theory* 9 (3): 303–25.

Eden, Lorraine (1996), 'The Emerging North American Investment Regime', *Transnational Corporations* 5 (3): 61–98.

Eisenstadt, Shmuel N. (1963), *The Political Systems of Empires*, New York: Free Press of Glencoe.

Ekholm, Kasja and Friedman, Jonathan (1982), '"Capital" Imperialism and Exploitation in Ancient World Systems', *Review* 4 (1): 87–109.

Elias, Norbert (1978), *What is Sociology?*, London: Hutchinson.

(1994) [1939], *The Civilising Process*, vol. II, Oxford: Blackwell.

Escobar, Arturo (1995), *Encountering Development*, Princeton: Princeton University Press.

Evans, Peter, Rueschemeyer, Dietrich and Skocpol, Theda (eds.) (1985), *Bringing the State Back In*, Cambridge: Cambridge University Press.

Falk, Richard (1985), 'The Interplay of Westphalia and Charter Conceptions of the International Legal Order', in Richard Falk, Friedrich Kratochwil and Saul Mendlovitz (eds.), *International Law: A Contemporary Perspective*, Boulder: Westview Press, pp. 116–42.

(1997), 'State of Siege: Will Globalization Win Out?', *International Affairs* 73 (1): 123–36.

Feldstein, Martin (1998), 'Refocusing the IMF', *Foreign Affairs* 77 (2): 20–33.

Ferguson, James (1990), *The Anti-Politics Machine*, New York: Cambridge University Press.

Ferguson, Yale and Mansbach, Richard (1996), *Polities*, Columbia: University of South Carolina Press.

Finer, Samuel E. (1997), *The History of Government from the Earliest Times*, vol. III: *Empires, Monarchies, and the Modern State*, Oxford: Oxford University Press.

Finnemore, Martha (1996a), 'Norms, Culture, and World Politics: Insights from Sociology's Institutionalism', *International Organization* 50 (2): 325–47.

(1996b), *National Interests in International Society*, Ithaca: Cornell University Press.

Finnemore, Martha and Sikkink, Kathryn (1998), 'International Norm Dynamics and Political Change', *International Organization* 52 (4): 887–918.

Fischer, Markus (1992), 'Feudal Europe, 800–1300: Communal Discourses and Conflictual Practices', *International Organization* 46 (2): 427–66.

Fisher, William (1997), 'Doing Good? The Politics and Antipolitics of NGO Practices', *Annual Review of Anthropology* 26: 439–64.

Forgacs, David (ed.) (2000), *The Antonio Gramsci Reader: Selected Writings 1916–1935*, New York: New York University Press.

Foucault, Michel (1973), *The Order of Things: An Archaeology of the Human Science*, New York: Vintage Books.

(1979), *Discipline and Punish: The Birth of the Prison*, London: Peregrine Books.

(1980), 'Two Lectures', in *Power/Knowledge: Selected Interviews and Other Writings, 1972–1977*, edited by Colin Gordon, New York: Pantheon Books, pp. 78–108.

(1986a), 'Truth and Power', in Rabinow (ed.) pp. 51–75.

(1986b), 'Nietzsche, Genealogy, History', in Rabinow (ed.), pp. 76–100.

(1989), *Foucault Live: Collected Interviews, 1961–1984*, edited by Sylvere Lotringer, New York: Semiotext(e).

(1990), *The History of Sexuality*, vol. I: *An Introduction*, New York: Vintage Books.

Fox, William T. R. (1975), 'Pluralism, the Science of Politics and the World System', *World Politics* 27 (4): 597–611.

Franck, Thomas (1990), *The Power of Legitimacy Among Nations*, Oxford: Oxford University Press.

Frank, André Gunder (1967), *Capitalism and Underdevelopment in Latin America*, London: Monthly Review Press.

(1996), 'Transitional Ideological Modes: Feudalism, Capitalism, Socialism', in Frank and Gills (eds.), pp. 200–17.

(1998) *ReOrient*, Berkeley: University of California Press.

Frank, André Gunder and Gills, Barry K. (eds.) (1996), *The World System*, London: Routledge.

Fraser, Andrew (1978), 'The Legal Theory We Need Now', *Socialist Review* 40–41: 147–87.

Fried, J. (1997), 'Globalization and International Law – Some Thoughts for States and Citizens', *Queen's Law Journal* 23 (1): 259–76.

Fuat Keyman, E. (1997), *Globalization, State, Identity/Difference*, Atlantic Highlands, N.J.: Humanities Press.

Fukuyama, Francis (1991), 'Liberal Democracy as a Global Phenomenon', *PS: Political Science and Politics* 24 (4): 659–64.

(1992), *The End of History and the Last Man*, London: Hamish Hamilton.

Furet, François (1995), *Le Passé d'une Illusion*, Paris: Laffont.

Gable, Peter (1977), 'Intentions and Structure in Contractual Conditions: Outline of a Method for Critical Legal Theory', *Minnesota Law Review* 61: 601–43.

Gallagher, John and Robinson, Ronald (1953), 'The Imperialism of Free Trade', *Economic History Review* 6 (1): 1–15.

Garnsey, Peter (1974), 'Legal Privilege in the Roman Empire', in M. Finley (ed.), *Studies in Ancient Society*, London: Routledge & Kegan Paul, pp. 141–65.

Gellner, Ernest (1964), *Thought and Change*, London: Weidenfeld & Nicolson.

Geras, Norman (1999), 'A View from Everywhere', *Review of International Studies* 25 (1): 157–63.

Giddens, Anthony (1979), *Central Problems in Social Theory*, London: Macmillan.

(1984), *The Constitution of Society*, Cambridge: Polity.

(1985), *The Nation-State and Violence*, Cambridge: Polity.

(1990), *The Consequences of Modernity*, Cambridge: Polity.

(1991), *Modernity and Self-Identity*, Cambridge: Polity.

Gill, Stephen (1990), *American Hegemony and the Trilateral Commission*, Cambridge: Cambridge University Press.

(ed.) (1993), *Gramsci, Historical Materialism, and International Relations*, Cambridge: Cambridge University Press.

Gills, Barry K. (1989), 'International Relations Theory and the Processes of World History: Three Approaches', in Hugh C. Dyer and Leon Mangasarian (eds.), *The Study of International Relations*, London: Macmillan, pp. 103–54.

(1993), 'Hegemonic Transitions in the World System', in Frank and Gills (eds.), pp. 115–40.

(1995), 'Capital and Power in the Processes of World History', in Sanderson (ed.), pp. 136–62.

(1996) 'The Continuity Thesis in World Development', in Sing C. Chew and Robert A. Denemark (eds.), *The Underdevelopment of Development*, London: Sage, pp. 226–45.

(2001) 'Re-directing the New (International) Political Economy', *New Political Economy*, 6 (2): 233–45.

Gills, Barry K. and Frank, André Gunder (1990), 'The Cumulation of Accumulation: Theses and Research Agenda for 5000 Years of World System History', *Dialectical Anthropology* 15 (1): 19–42.

(1992), 'World System Cycles, Crises, and Hegemonic Shifts, 1700 BC to 1700 AD', *Review* 15 (4): 621–87.

Gilpin, Robert (1975), *U.S. Power and the Multinational Corporation*, New York: Basic Books.

(1981), *War and Change in World Politics*, Cambridge: Cambridge University Press.

(1986), 'The Richness of the Tradition of Political Realism', in Keohane (ed.), pp. 301–21.

Goldstein, Joshua S. (1988), *Long Cycles*, London: Yale University Press.

Goldstone, Jack A. (1991), *Revolution and Rebellion in the Modern World*, Berkeley: University of California Press.

Goldthorpe, John H. (1991), 'The Uses of History in Sociology: Reflections on Some Recent Tendencies', *British Journal of Sociology* 42 (2): 211–30.

Gong, Gerrit W. (1984), *The Standard of 'Civilisation' in International Society*, Oxford: Clarendon Press.

Goody, Jack (1996), *The East in the West*, Cambridge: Cambridge University Press.

Gramsci, Antonio (1971), *Selections from Prison Notebooks*, edited and translated by Quintin Hoare and Geoffrey Nowell Smith, London: Lawrence & Wishart.

Green, William A. (1998), 'Periodising World History', in Philip Pomper, Richard Elphick and Richard T. Vann (eds.), *World History*, Oxford: Blackwell, pp. 53–65.

Groom, A. J. R. and Taylor, Paul (eds.) (1998), *International Institutions at Work*, New York: St Martin's Press.

Haas, Ernst (1987), *When Knowledge is Power*, Berkeley: University of California Press.

Habermas, Jürgen (1980), *Moral Consciousness and Communicative Action*, Cambridge: Polity.

Hall, John A. (1986), *Powers and Liberties: The Causes and Consequences of the Rise of the West*, Harmondsworth: Penguin.

(1993), 'Ideas and the Social Sciences', in Judith Goldstein and Robert Keohane (eds.), *Ideas and Foreign Policy: Beliefs, Institutions, and Political Change*, Ithaca: Cornell University Press, pp. 31–54.

(1996), *International Orders*, Cambridge: Polity.

Hall, Martin (1998), 'International Political Economy Meets Historical Sociology: Problems and Promises', *Cooperation and Conflict* 33 (3): 257–76.

(1999), 'Constructing Historical Realism', Ph.D. dissertation, Lund University, Sweden (Studenlitteratur).

Hall, Rodney Bruce (1997), 'Moral Authority as a Power Resource', *International Organization* 51 (4): 591–622.

(1999), *National Collective Identity*, New York: Columbia University Press.

Hall, Rodney Bruce and Kratochwil, Friedrich V. (1993), 'Medieval Tales: Neorealist "Science" and the Abuse of History', *International Organization* 47 (3): 479–91.

Halliday, Fred (1987), 'State and Society in International Relations: A Second Agenda', *Millennium* 16 (2): 215–29.

(1994a), 'Theory and Ethics in International Relations: The Contradictions of C. Wright Mills', *Millennium* 23 (2): 377–86.

(1994b), *Rethinking International Relations*, London: Macmillan.

(1999), *Revolution in World Politics*, London: Macmillan.

(2000), 'Reason and Romance: Revolution in the Work of E. H. Carr', in Michael Cox (ed.), *E. H. Carr*, London: Macmillan, pp. 258–79.

Halperin, Sandra (1998), 'Shadowboxing: Weberian Historical Sociology vs State-Centric International Relations Theory', *Review of International Political Economy* 5 (2): 327–39.

Hanson, Victor D. (1998), *Warfare and Agriculture in Ancient Greece*, Berkeley: University of California Press.

Harvey, David (1990), *The Condition of Postmodernity: An Inquiry into the Origins of Cultural Change*, Oxford: Blackwell.

Hawdon, James (1996), *Emerging Organizational Forms: The Proliferation of Intergovernmental Regional Organizations in the Modern World-System*, Westport, Conn.: Greenwood Press.

Heeren, Arnold H. L. (1809), *A Manual of the History of the Political System of Europe and Its Colonies* (translated in 1857 from 5th edn), London: Henry G. Bohn.

(1829), *History of the Political System of Europe and Its Colonies*, vol. I, Boston: Butler and Sons.

(1833), *Historical Researches into the Politics, Intercourse, and Trade of the Principal Nations of Antiquity*, vol. I, Oxford: D. A. Talboys.

Hegel, Georg W. F. (1952), *The Philosophy of Right*, Oxford: Clarendon Press.

Held, David (1995), *Democracy and the Global Order*, Cambridge: Polity.

(1996), *Models of Democracy*, Cambridge: Polity.

Heller, Agnes (1987), *Beyond Justice*, Oxford: Blackwell.

Herzfeld, Michael (1993), *The Social Production of Indifference*, Chicago: University of Chicago Press.

Higgins, Rosalyn (1985), 'Conceptual Thinking about the Individual under International Law', in Richard Falk, Friedrich Kratochwil and Saul Mendlovitz (eds.), *International Law: A Contemporary Perspective*, Boulder: Westview Press, pp. 476–94.

Higgott, Richard, Underhill, Geoffrey and Bieler, Andreas (eds.) (1999), *Non-State Actors and Authority in the Global System*, London: Routledge.

Hill, Christopher (1985), 'History and International Relations', in Steve Smith (ed.), *International Relations*, Oxford: Blackwell, pp. 126–45.

(1991), 'Diplomacy in the Modern State', in Cornelia Navari (ed.), *The Condition of States*, Milton Keynes: Open University Press, pp. 85–101.

Hintze, Otto (1975), *The Historical Essays of Otto Hintze*, Oxford: Oxford University Press.

Hirst, Paul and Thompson, Grahame (1996), *Globalization in Question*, Cambridge: Polity.

Hobden, Stephen (1998), *International Relations and Historical Sociology*, New York: Routledge.

(1999a), 'Theorising the International System: Perspectives from Historical Sociology', *Review of International Studies* 25 (2): 257–71.

(1999b), 'Can Historical Sociology be Critical?', *Alternatives* 24 (3): 391–413.

Hobsbawm, Eric (1994), *The Age of Extremes*, London: Michael Joseph.

Hobson, John M. (1994), 'The Poverty of Marxism and Neorealism: Bringing Historical Sociology Back In to International Relations', School of Politics, La Trobe University, Melbourne, Working Paper no. 2.

(1997), *The Wealth of States*, Cambridge: Cambridge University Press.

(1998a), 'The Historical Sociology of the State and the State of Historical Sociology in International Relations', *Review of International Political Economy* 5 (2): 284–320.

(1998b), 'For a "Second-Wave" Weberian Historical Sociology in International Relations', *Review of International Political Economy* 5 (2): 354–61.

(2000), *The State and International Relations*, Cambridge: Cambridge University Press.

Hobson, John M. and Seabrooke, Leonard (2001), 'Reimagining Weber: Constructing International Society and the Social Balance of Power', *European Journal of International Relations* 7 (2).

Hodgson, Marshall G. S. (1974), *The Venture of Islam*, vol. III, Chicago: Chicago University Press.

(1993), *Rethinking World History*, Cambridge: Cambridge University Press.

Hoffmann, Stanley (1959), 'International Relations: The Long Road to Theory', *World Politics* 11 (3): 346–77.

Hollis, Martin and Smith, Steve (1990), *Explaining and Understanding International Relations*, New York: Oxford University Press.

Holsti, Kalevi J. (1967), *International Politics*, Englewood Cliffs, N.J.: Prentice-Hall.

(1985), *The Dividing Discipline: Hegemony and Diversity in International Theory*, London: Allen & Unwin.

Hopf, Ted (1998), 'The Promise of Constructivism in International Relations Theory', *International Security* 23 (1): 171–200.

Human Rights Watch (1999), *Leave None to Tell the Story*, New York: HRW Press.

Inoguchi, Takashi (1988), 'Four Japanese Scenarios for the Future', *International Affairs* 65 (1): 15–28.

International Security (1997), 'Symposium on "History and Theory"', *International Security* 22 (1).

Jackson, Robert H. (1990), *Quasi-States*, Cambridge: Cambridge University Press.

Jacobs, Norman (1958), *The Origins of Modern Capitalism and Eastern Asia*, Hong Kong: Hong Kong University Press.

Janis, M. W. (1984), 'Individuals as Subjects of International Law', *Cornell International Law Journal* 17 (1): 61–78.

Jarvis, Anthony (1989), 'Societies, States and Geopolitics: Challenges from Historical Sociology', *Review of International Studies* 15 (3): 281–93.

Jay, Martin (1973), *The Dialectical Imagination: A History of the Frankfurt School and the Institute of Social Research 1923–1950*, Boston: Little, Brown.

Jepperson, Ronald, Wendt, Alexander and Katzenstein, Peter (1996), 'Norms, Identity, and Culture in National Security', in Peter Katzenstein (ed.), *The Culture of National Security: Norms and Identity in World Politics*, New York: Columbia University Press, pp. 33–75.

Jessop, Bob (1980), 'On Recent Marxist Theories of Law, the State, and Juridico-Political Ideology', *International Journal of the Sociology of Law* 8 (4): 339–68.

Jessup, Philip (1956), *Transnational Law*, New Haven: Yale University Press.

Johns, Fleur (1994), 'The Invisibility of the Transnational Corporation: An Analysis of International Law and Legal Theory', *Melbourne University Law Review* 19: 893–923.

Jones, Eric L. (1988), *Growth Recurring*, Oxford: Clarendon Press.

Josephy, Alvin M. (1995), *500 Nations*, London: Random House.

Kahler, Miles (1997), 'Inventing International Relations: International Relations Theory After 1945', in Michael W. Doyle and G. John Ikenberry (eds.), *New Thinking in International Relations Theory*, Boulder: Westview Press, pp. 20–53.

Kalberg, Stephen (1994), *Max Weber's Comparative Historical Sociology*, Cambridge: Polity.

Kaldor, Mary (1979), *The Disintegration of the West*, Harmondsworth: Penguin.

(1999), *New and Old Wars*, Cambridge: Polity.

Kaplan, Morton (1957), *System and Process in International Politics*, New York: Wiley.

(1961), 'Problems of Theory Building and Theory Confirmation in International Politics', *World Politics* 14 (1): 6–24.

Katzenstein, Peter J. (1996a), *Cultural Norms and National Security*, Ithaca: Cornell University Press.

(ed.) (1996b), *The Culture of National Security*, New York: Columbia University Press.

Katzenstein, Peter, Keohane, Robert and Krasner, Stephen (1998), 'International Organization and the Study of World Politics', *International Organization* 52 (4): 645–86.

Keck, Margaret and Sikkink, Kathryn (1998), *Activists Without Borders*, Ithaca: Cornell University Press.

Kegley, Charles (1995), 'The Neoliberal Challenge to Realist Theories of World Politics: An Introduction', in Charles Kegley (ed.), *Controversies in International Relations Theory: Realism and the Neoliberal Challenge*. New York: St Martin's Press, pp. 1–24.

Kelstrup, Morten and Williams, Michael (eds.) (2000), *International Relations Theory and the Politics of European Integration*, London: Routledge.

Kennedy, David (1986), 'International Refugee Protection', *Human Rights Quarterly* 8 (1): 1–69.

(1987), 'The Sources of International Law', *American University Journal of International Law and Policy* 2 (1): 1–96.

(1988–9), 'A New Stream in International Law Scholarship', *Wisconsin International Law Journal* 7 (1): 1–49.

Kennedy, Paul M. (1988), *The Rise and Fall of the Great Powers*, London: Unwin Hyman.

Keohane, Robert O. (1984), *After Hegemony*, Princeton: Princeton University Press.

(ed.) (1986), *Neorealism and its Critics*, New York: Columbia University Press.

(1988), 'International Institutions: Two Approaches', *International Studies Quarterly* 32 (4): 379–96.

(1989), *International Institutions and State Power: Essays in International Relations Theory*, Boulder: Westview Press.

Keohane, Robert O. and Milner, Helen V. (eds.) (1996), *Internationalization and Domestic Politics*, Cambridge: Cambridge University Press.

Keohane, Robert, Moravcsik, Andrew and Slaughter, Anne-Marie (2000), 'Legalized Dispute Resolution: Interstate and Transnational', *International Organization* 54 (3): 457–88.

Keohane, Robert O. and Nye, Joseph S. (1971), *Transnational Relations and World Politics*, Princeton: Princeton University Press.

(1977), *Power and Interdependence*, Boston: Little, Brown.

Klare, Karl (1979), 'Law-Making as Praxis', *Telos* 40: 123–35.

Korsch, Karl (1963), *Karl Marx*, New York: Russell and Russell.

Koskenniemi, Marti (1991), 'The Future of Statehood', *Harvard International Law Journal* 32 (2): 397–410.

Kramer, Samuel Noah (1959), *History Begins at Sumer*, Garden City, N.Y.: Anchor Books.

Krasner, Stephen D. (1978), *Defending the National Interest*, Princeton: Princeton University Press.

(ed.) (1983), *International Regimes*, Ithaca: Cornell University Press.

(1993), 'Westphalia and All That', in Judith Goldstein and Robert O. Keohane (eds.), *Ideas and Foreign Policy*, Ithaca: Cornell University Press, pp. 235–64.

(1995), 'Power Politics, Institutions, and Transnational Relations', in Risse-Kappen (ed.), pp. 257–79.

(1997), 'Pervasive Not Perverse: Semi-Sovereigns as the Global Norm', *Cornell International Law Journal* 30 (3): 651–80.

Kratochwil, Friedrich (1989), *Norms, Rules, and Decisions*, Cambridge: Cambridge University Press.

Kratochwil, Friedrich and Ruggie, John (1986), 'International Organization: A State of the Art or an Art of the State', *International Organization* 40 (4): 753–75.

Landes, David S. (1998), *The Wealth and Poverty of Nations*, New York: Norton.

Larsen, Mogens (1967), 'Old Assyrian Caravan Procedures', Nederlands Historisch-Arekaeologish Institut te Istanbul, 22.

(1976), *The Old Assyrian City-State and its Colonies*, Copenhagen: Akademisk Forlag.

Latham, Robert, Kassimer, Ron and Callaghy, Thomas (forthcoming), *Transboundary Formations*.

Lattimore, Owen (1962), *Studies in Frontier History*, London: Oxford University Press.

Lincoln, Bruce (1994), *Authority*, Chicago: University of Chicago Press.

Linklater, Andrew (1990), *Beyond Realism and Marxism*, London: Macmillan.

(1998), *The Transformation of Political Community*, Cambridge: Polity.

(1999), 'The Evolving Spheres of International Justice', *International Affairs* 75 (3): 473–82.

Little, Richard (1991), 'Liberal Hegemony and the Realist Assault: Competing Ideological Theories of the State', in Michael Banks and Martin Shaw (eds.), *State and Society in International Relations*, Hemel Hempstead: Harvester Wheatsheaf, pp. 19–38.

(1994), 'International Relations and Large-Scale Historical Change', in A. J. R. Groom and Margot Light (eds.), *Contemporary International Relations*, London: Pinter, pp. 9–26.

(1996), 'The Growing Relevance of Pluralism', in Smith, Booth and Zalewski (eds.), pp. 66–86.

Lombard, Maurice (1975), *The Golden Age of Islam*, Amsterdam: North-Holland.

Love, John R. (1991), *Antiquity and Capitalism*, London: Routledge.

Malanczuk, Peter (ed.) (1997), *Akehurst's Modern Introduction to International Law*, 7th revised edn, London: Routledge.

Mandel, Ernest (1970), *Europe versus America?*, London: Verso.

Mann, Michael (1984), 'Capitalism and Militarism', in Martin Shaw (ed.), *War, State and Society*, London: Macmillan, pp. 25–46.

——— (1986), *The Sources of Social Power*, vol. I, Cambridge: Cambridge University Press.

——— (1988), *States, War and Capitalism*, Oxford: Blackwell.

——— (1993), *The Sources of Social Power*, vol. II, Cambridge: Cambridge University Press.

——— (1996), 'Authoritarian and Liberal Militarism: A Contribution from Comparative and Historical Sociology', in Smith, Booth and Zalewski (eds.), pp. 221–39.

——— (1997), 'Has Globalization Ended the Rise and Rise of the Nation-State?', *Review of International Political Economy* 4 (3): 472–96.

Manning, Charles A. W. (1962), *The Nature of International Society*, London: LSE.

Maoz, Zeev and Russett, Bruce (1993), 'Normative and Structural Causes of Democratic Peace, 1946–1986', *American Political Science Review* 87 (3): 624–38.

Marcuse, Herbert (1972), 'Foundations of Historical Materialism', in Herbert Marcuse, *Studies in Critical Philosophy*, translated by Joris de Bres, London: New Left Books.

Martin, Lisa (1993), 'The Rational State Choice of Multilateralism', in Ruggie (ed.), pp. 91–121.

Marx, Karl (1950), *The Eighteenth Brumaire of Louis Bonaparte*, in Marx and Engels, *Selected Works*, vol. I, London: Lawrence & Wishart.

——— (1954), *Capital*, vol. I, London: Lawrence & Wishart.

——— (1976), *Preface and Introduction to 'A Contribution to the Critique of Political Economy'*, Beijing: Foreign Languages Publishing House.

Massey, Doreen (1992), 'Politics and Space/Time', *New Left Review* 196: 65–84.

Mayall, James (1990), *Nationalism and International Society*, Cambridge: Cambridge University Press.

McDonald, Terrance (ed.) (1996), *Historic Turn in the Human Sciences*, Ann Arbor: University of Michigan Press.

McKeown, Timothy J. (1983), 'Hegemonic Stability Theory and Nineteenth Century Tariff Levels', *International Organization* 37 (1): 73–91.

McNeill, William H. (1963), *The Rise of the West*, Chicago: University of Chicago Press.

——— (1998), 'The Changing Shape of World History', in Philip Pomper, Richard Elphick and Richard T. Vann (eds.), *World History*, Oxford: Blackwell, pp. 21–40.

Mearsheimer, John (1990), 'Back to the Future: Instability in Europe after the Cold War', *International Security* 15 (1): 5–56.

——— (1995a), 'The False Promise of International Institutions', *International Security*, 19 (3): 5–49.

——— (1995b), 'A Realist Reply', *International Security*, 20 (1): 82–93.

Mennell, Stephen (1989), *Norbert Elias*, Oxford: Blackwell.

Meyer, John W. and Rowan, Brian (1977), 'Institutionalized Organizations: Formal Structure as Myth and Ceremony', *American Journal of Sociology* 83 (2): 340–63.

Meyer, John W. and Scott, W. Richard (1992), *Organizational Environments*, Newbury Park, Calif.: Sage.

Moore, Barrington (1967), *Social Origins of Dictatorship and Democracy*, London: Penguin.

Moravcsik, Andrew (1999), 'A New Statecraft? Supranational Entrepreneurs and International Cooperation', *International Organization* 53 (2): 267–306.

Morgenthau, Hans J. (1985), *Politics Among Nations*, New York: McGraw-Hill.

Mosler, Hermann (1980), *The International Society as a Legal Community*, Alphen aan den Rijn: Sijthoff & Noordhoff.

Mostecky, Vaclav (1965), *Index of Multilateral Treaties*, Cambridge, Mass.: Harvard Law School Library.

Mouzelis, Nicos (1967), *Organization and Bureaucracy*, Chicago: Aldine.

Mueller, John (1989), *Retreat from Doomsday*, New York: Basic Books.

Muppidi, Himadeep (1999), 'Economic Liberalization in Comparative Context', unpublished manuscript.

Murphy, Craig N. (1994), *International Organization and Industrial Change*, New York: Oxford University Press.

Needham, Joseph (1954), *Science and Civilization in China*, Cambridge: Cambridge University Press.

Nelson, Benjamin (1973), 'Civilisational Complexes and Inter-Civilisational Relations', *Sociological Analysis* 74: 79–105.

Nelson, Paul (1995), *The World Bank and Non-Governmental Organizations*, New York: St Martin's Press.

Neuman, Iver (1996), 'Self and Other in International Relations', *European Journal of International Relations* 2 (2): 139–74.

New Left Review (1999), 'The Imperialism of Human Rights', *New Left Review* 235.

Ohmae, Kenichi (1995), *The End of the Nation-State*, New York: Free Press.

O'Neill, Onora (1991), 'Transnational Justice', in David Held (ed.), *Political Theory Today*, Cambridge: Polity, pp. 276–304.

Onuf, Nicholas (1989), *World of Our Making*, Columbia: University of South Carolina Press.

—— (1995), 'Levels', *European Journal of International Relations* 1 (1): 25–58.

—— (1998), 'Constructivism: A User's Manual', in Vendulka Kubalkova, Nicholas Onuf and Paul Klowert (eds.), *International Relations in a Constructed World*, Armonk, N.Y.: M. E. Sharpe, pp. 58–78.

Orentlicher, Diane F. (1999) 'Genocide', in Roy Guttman and David Rieff (eds.), *Crimes of War*, New York: Norton, pp. 153–7.

Paris, Roland (1997), 'Peacebuilding and the Limits of Liberal Internationalism', *International Security* 22 (2): 54–89.

Paul, Darel E. (1999), 'Sovereignty, Survival and the Westphalian Blind Alley in International Relations', *Review of International Studies* 25 (2): 217–31.

Pirenne, Henri (1925), *Medieval Cities*, Princeton: Princeton University Press.

—— (1939), *Mohammed and Charlemagne*, London: Allen & Unwin.

Poggi, Gianfranco (1978), *The Development of the Modern State*, London: Hutchinson.

Polanyi, Karl (1971), *Primitive, Archaic, and Modern Economics*, Boston: Beacon Press.

Pollack, Mark (1997), 'Delegation, Agency, and Agenda-Setting in the European Community', *International Organization* 51 (1): 99–134.

Powelson, John P. (1994), *Centuries of Economic Endeavour*, Ann Arbor: University of Michigan Press.

Price, Richard (1997), *The Chemical Weapons Taboo*, Ithaca: Cornell University Press.

(1998), 'Reversing the Gun Sights: Transnational Civil Society Targets Land Mines', *International Organization* 52 (3): 575–612.

Price, Richard and Reus-Smit, Christian (1998), 'Dangerous Liaisons? Critical International Theory and Constructivism', *European Journal of International Relations* 4 (3): 259–94.

Pufendorf, Samuel (1927), *The Two Books on the Duty of Man and Citizen According to the Natural Law*, New York: Classics of International Law.

Rabinow, Paul (ed.) (1986), *The Foucault Reader*, London: Penguin.

Randsborg, Klavs (1991), *The First Millennium A.D. in Europe and the Mediterranean*, Cambridge: Cambridge University Press.

Ray, James L. (1989), 'The Abolition of Slavery and the End of War', *International Organization* 43 (3): 405–39.

Raz, Joseph (1990), 'Introduction', in Joseph Raz (ed.), *Authority*, New York: New York University Press, pp. 1–9.

Reus-Smit, Christian (1999), *The Moral Purpose of the State*, Princeton: Princeton University Press.

Rich, Paul (1995), 'Alfred Zimmern's Cautious Idealism: The League of Nations, International Education and the Commonwealth', in David Long and Peter Wilson (eds.), *Thinkers of the Twenty Years' Crisis*, Oxford: Clarendon Press, pp. 79–99.

Risse-Kappen, Thomas (ed.) (1995), *Bringing Transnational Relations Back In*, Cambridge: Cambridge University Press.

Roberts, Adam and Guelff, Richard (eds.) (1982), *Documents on the Law of War*, Oxford: Clarendon Press.

Robertson, Roland (1992), *Globalization*, London: Sage.

Rodinson, Maxime (1974), *Islam and Capitalism*, London: Allen Lane.

Rorty, Richard (1991), 'Cosmopolitanism Without Emancipation: A Response to Jean-François Lyotard', in Richard Rorty (ed.), *Objectivity, Relativism and Truth*, Philosophical Papers, vol. I, Cambridge: Cambridge University Press, pp. 211–22.

Rosecrance, Richard (1973), *International Relations*, New York: McGraw-Hill.

(1986), *The Rise of the Trading State*, New York: Basic Books.

Rosenau, James N. (1990), *Turbulence in World Politics*, London: Harvester Wheatsheaf.

Rosenau, James N. and Czempiel, Ernst O. (eds.) (1992), *Governance Without Government*, Cambridge: Cambridge University Press.

Rosenberg, Justin (1994), *The Empire of Civil Society*, London: Verso.

Ross, George (1995), *Jacques Delors and European Integration*, New York: Oxford University Press.

Rostovtzeff, Michael (1957), *Social and Economic History of the Roman Empire*, Oxford: Oxford University Press.

Rousseau, Jean-Jacques (1970), 'Fragments on War', in Murray Forsyth *et al.* (eds.), *The Theory of International Relations*, London: Allen & Unwin, pp. 178–80.

Rueschemeyer, Dietrich and Skocpol, Theda (eds.) (1996), *States, Social Knowledge, and the Origins of Modern Social Politics*, Cambridge: Cambridge University Press.

Ruggie, John G. (1983), 'Continuity and Transformation in the World Polity: Towards a Neo-Realist Synthesis', *World Politics* 35 (2): 261–85.

(ed.) (1993a), *Multilateralism Matters*, New York: Columbia University Press.

(1993b), 'Multilateralism: The Anatomy of an Institution', in Ruggie (ed.), pp. 3–47.

(1993c), 'Territoriality and Beyond: Problematizing Modernity in International Relations', *International Organization* 47 (1): 139–74.

(1998a), 'What Makes the World Hang Together', *International Organization*, 52 (4): 855–86.

(1998b), *Constructing the World Polity*, London: Routledge.

Runciman, W. Gary (1989), *A Treatise on Social Theory*, vol. II, Cambridge: Cambridge University Press.

(1998), *The Social Animal*, London: HarperCollins.

Ryan, Alan (1998), 'A Theory of Growing Concerns' (Review of F. Zakaria, *From Wealth to Power*), *Times Higher Educational Supplement*, 27 November 1998, p. 27.

Sahlins, Marshall (1976), *Culture and Practical Reason*, Chicago: University of Chicago Press.

Sanderson, Stephen K. (ed.) (1995), *Civilizations and World System*, London: Sage.

Scheuerman, William (ed.) (1996), *The Rule of Law under Siege: Selected Essays of Franz L. Neumann and Otto Kirchheimer*, Berkeley: University of California Press.

(1999), 'Economic Globalization and the Rule of Law', *Constellations: An International Journal of Critical and Democratic Theory* 6 (1): 3–25.

Schlag, Pierre (1991), 'The Problem of the Subject', *Texas Law Review* 69 (7): 1627–742.

Schmandt-Besserat, Denise (1992), *Before Writing*, vol. I, Austin: University of Texas Press.

Schmidt, Brian (1998), *The Political Discourse of Anarchy*, Albany: State University of New York Press.

Scholte, Jan Aart (1993), *International Relations of Social Change*, Milton Keynes: Open University Press.

Schroeder, Paul (1994), 'Historical Reality versus Neorealist Theory', *International Security* 19 (1): 108–48.

Seabrooke, Leonard (2001), *US Power in International Finance*, London: Palgrave.

Seidl-Hohenveldern, Ignaz (1980), 'International Economic Law as Soft Law', in *Recueil des Cours 1979*, vol. II, Collected Courses of the Hague Academy of International Law, The Netherlands: Sijthoff & Noordhoff, pp. 173–246.

Sempas, Samson (1992), 'Obstacles to International Commercial Arbitration in African Countries', *International and Comparative Law Quarterly* 41: 387–413.

Senghaas, Dieter (1994), *Wohin Driftet die Welt?*, Frankfurt: Suhrkamp.

Sewell, William (1996), 'Three Temporalities: Toward an Eventful Sociology', in McDonald (ed.), pp. 245–80.

Shanks, Cheryl, Jacobson, Harold K. and Kaplan, Jeffrey H. (1996), 'Inertia and Change in the Constellation of Intergovernmental Organizations, 1981–1992', *International Organization* 50 (4): 593–627.

Shaw, Martin (ed.) (1984a), *War, State and Society*, London: Macmillan.

   (1984b), 'War, Imperialism and the State System: A Critique of Orthodox Marxism for the 1980s', in Shaw (ed.), pp. 47–70.

   (1988), *Dialectics of War*, London: Pluto.

   (1989), 'War and the Nation-State', in David Held and John B. Thompson (eds.), *The Social Theory of Modern Societies*, Cambridge: Cambridge University Press, pp. 129–46.

   (1991), *Post-Military Society*, Cambridge: Polity.

   (1994), *Global Society and International Relations*, Cambridge: Polity.

   (1996), *Civil Society and Media in Global Crises*, London: Pinter.

   (1998), 'The Historical Sociology of the Future', *Review of International Political Economy* 5 (2): 321–6.

   (1999a), 'Globality as a Revolutionary Transformation', in Martin Shaw (ed.), *Politics and Globalisation*, London: Routledge, pp. 159–73.

   (1999b), 'The State of International Relations', in Sarah Owen Vandersluis (ed.), *The State and Identity Construction in International Relations*, London: Macmillan, pp. 7–30.

   (1999c) 'War and Globality', in Ho-won Jeong (ed.), *The New Agenda for Peace Research*, Aldershot: Ashgate, pp. 61–80.

Shaw, Martin and Creighton, Colin (eds.) (1987), *The Sociology of War and Peace*, London: Macmillan.

Shore, Cris and Wright, Susan (1997), 'Policy: A New Field of Anthropology', in Cris Shore and Susan Wright (eds.), *Anthropology of Policy*, New York: Routledge, pp. 3–39.

Shue, Henry (1981), 'Exporting Hazards', in Peter G. Brown and Henry Shue (eds.), *Boundaries*, Towota, N.J.: Rowman & Littlefield, pp. 107–45.

Sillitoe, Alan (1998), *Key Issues in Historical and Comparative Sociology*, London: Routledge.

Singer, J. David (1961), 'The Level of Analysis Problem in International Relations', *World Politics* 14 (1): 77–92.

Sked, Alan (1987), 'The Study of International Relations: A Historian's View', *Millennium* 16 (2): 251–62.

Skinner, Quentin (1978), *The Foundations of Modern Political Thought*, vol. I, Cambridge: Cambridge University Press.

Skocpol, Theda (1979), *States and Social Revolutions*, Cambridge: Cambridge University Press.

   (1984), *Vision and Method in Historical Sociology*, Cambridge: Cambridge University Press.

(1985), 'Bringing the State Back In: Strategies of Analysis in Current Research', in Evans, Rueschemeyer and Skocpol (eds.), pp. 3–42.

(1988), 'An "Uppity Generation" and the Revitalisation of Macroscopic Sociology', *Theory and Society* 17 (5): 627–43.

Smith, Adam (1937), *The Wealth of Nations*, New York: Random House.

Smith, Dennis (1991), *The Rise of Historical Sociology*, Philadelphia: Temple University Press.

Smith, Jackie, Chatfield, Charles and Pagnucco, Ron (eds.) (1997), *Transnational Social Movements and World Politics*, Albany: State University of New York Press.

Smith, Michael (1986), *Realist Thought from Weber to Kissinger*, Baton Rouge: Louisiana State University Press.

Smith, Steve (1995), 'The Self-Images of a Discipline: A Genealogy of International Relations Theory', in Booth and Smith (eds.), pp. 1–37.

(1996), 'Positivism and Beyond', in Smith, Booth and Zalewski (eds.), pp. 11–44.

(1997), 'New Approaches to International Theory', in Baylis and Smith (eds.), pp. 165–90.

(2000a), 'Wendt's World', *Review of International Studies*, 26 (1): 151–63.

(2000b), 'The Discipline of International Relations: Still an American Social Science?', *British Journal of Politics and International Relations*, 2 (3): 374–402.

(2000c), 'International Theory and European Integration', in Kelstrup and Williams (eds.), pp. 33–56.

Smith, Steve, Booth, Ken and Zalewski, Marysia (eds.) (1996), *International Theory*, Cambridge: Cambridge University Press.

Snidal, Duncan (1996), 'Political Economy and International Institutions', *International Review of Law and Economics* 16 (1): 121–37.

Snowden, Frank M. (1983), *Before Color Prejudice*, Cambridge, Mass.: Harvard University Press.

Sousa Santos, Bonaventura de (1993), 'The Postmodern Transition: Law and Politics', in Austin Sarat and Thomas Kearns (eds.), *The Fate of Law*, Ann Arbor: University of Michigan Press, pp. 79–118.

Speigel, Henry W. (1991), *The Growth of Economic Thought*, 3rd edn, Durham: Duke University Press.

Spruyt, Hendrik (1994), *The Sovereign State and Its Competitors*, Princeton: Princeton University Press.

(1998), 'Historical Sociology and Systems Theory in International Relations', *Review of International Political Economy* 5 (2): 340–53.

Stein, Arthur A. (1984), 'The Hegemon's Dilemma: Great Britain, the United States and the International Economic Order', *International Organization* 38 (2): 354–86.

Stone, Bayley (1994), *The Origins of the French Revolution*, Cambridge: Cambridge University Press.

Taira, Koji (1993), 'Japan as Number Two: New Thoughts on the Hegemonic Theory of World Governance', in Tsuneo Akaha and Frank C. Langdon (eds.), *Japan in the Post Hegemonic World*, Boulder: Lynne Rienner, pp. 250–63.

Tar, Zoltán (1977), *The Frankfurt School: The Critical Theories of Max Horkheimer and Theodor Adorno*, New York: Wiley.

Tawney, Richard H. (1938), *Religion and the Rise of Capitalism*, Harmondsworth: Penguin.

Thakur, Ramesh, and Malley, William (1999), 'The Ottawa Convention on Landmines: A Landmark Humanitarian Treaty in Arms Control?', *Global Governance* 5 (3): 273–302.

Thomas, Hugh (1998), *The Slave Trade*, London: Papermac.

Thompson, Edward P. (1963), *The Making of the English Working Class*, London: Gollancz.

(1975), *Whigs and Hunters: The Origins of the Black Act*, London: Penguin.

(1978), *The Poverty of Theory and Other Essays*, London: Merlin.

(1982), 'Notes on Exterminism, the Highest Stage of Civilization', in Edward Thompson (ed.), *Exterminism and Cold War*, London: Verso, pp. 1–33.

Thomson, Janice (1994), *Mercenaries, Pirates, and Sovereigns*, Princeton: Princeton University Press.

Tilly, Charles (ed.) (1975a), *The Formation of National States in Western Europe*, Princeton: Princeton University Press.

(1975b), 'Reflections on the History of European State-Making', in Tilly (ed.), pp. 3–83.

(1978), *From Mobilization to Revolution*, Reading, Mass.: Addison-Wesley.

(1981), *As Sociology Meets History*, New York: Academic Press.

(1984), *Big Structures, Large Processes, Huge Comparisons*. New York: Russell Sage Foundation.

(1990), *Coercion, Capital, and European States, AD 990–1990*, Oxford: Blackwell.

(1992), 'War in History', *Sociological Forum* 7 (1): 187–95.

(1994), 'Entanglements of European Cities and States', in Charles Tilly (ed.), *Cities and the Rise of States in Europe, AD 1000 to 1800*, Boulder: Westview Press, pp. 1–27.

(1995), *Popular Contention in Great Britain, 1758–1834*, Cambridge, Mass.: Harvard University Press.

Toynbee, Arnold (1978), *Mankind and Mother Earth*, London: Paladin.

Tronto, Joan C. (1993), *Moral Boundaries*, London: Routledge & Kegan Paul.

Turner, Bryan S. (1974), *Weber and Islam*, New York: Humanities Press.

Twining, William (1996), 'Globalization and Legal Theory: Some Local Implications', *Current Legal Problems* 49 (2): 1–42.

Unger, Roberto (1976), *Law in Modern Society: Toward a Criticism of Social Theory*, New York: Free Press.

Union of International Associations (1996), *Yearbook of International Organizations, 1996/97*, 33rd edn, Munich: K. G. Saur.

van der Pijl, Kees (1984), *The Making of an Atlantic Ruling Class*, London: Verso.

(1994), 'The Cadre Class and Public Multilateralism', in Yoshikazu Sakamoto (ed.), *Global Transformation*, Tokyo: United Nations University Press, pp. 200–27.

Veblen, Thorstein (1994), *The Theory of the Leisure Class*, London: Penguin.

Vincent, Andrew (1993), 'Marx and Law', *Journal of Law and Society* 20 (4): 371–97.

Vincent, R. John (1974), *Nonintervention and International Order*, Princeton: Princeton University Press.

(1986), *Human Rights and International Relations*, Cambridge: Cambridge University Press.

Wade, Robert (1996), 'Japan, the World Bank, and the Art of Paradigm Maintenance: The East Asian Miracle in Political Perspective', *New Left Review* 217: 3–38.

Wæver, Ole (1996), 'The Rise and Fall of the Inter-Paradigm Debate', in Smith, Booth and Zalewski (eds.), pp. 149–85.

(1998a), 'Four Meanings of International Society: A Trans-Atlantic Dialogue', in Barbara A. Roberson (ed.), *International Society and the Development of International Relations Theory*, London: Pinter, pp. 80–144.

(1998b), 'The Sociology of a Not so International Discipline: American and European Developments in International Relations', *International Organization* 52 (4): 687–727.

Walker, Rob (1993), *Inside/Outside*, New York: Cambridge University Press.

Wallerstein, Immanuel (1974), *The Modern World-System*, vol. I, New York: Academic Press.

(1980), *The Modern World-System*, vol. II, New York: Academic Press.

(1989), *The Modern World-System*, vol. III, New York: Academic Press.

(1992), 'The West, Capitalism, and the Modern World-System', *Review* 15 (4): 561–619.

(1995), 'Hold the Tiller Firm: On Method and the Unit of Analysis', in Sanderson (ed.), pp. 239–47.

(1996), 'World System versus World-Systems: A Critique', in Frank and Gills (eds.), pp. 292–6.

Walt, Stephen (1998), 'International Relations: One World, Many Theories', *Foreign Policy* 110: 29–46.

Waltz, Kenneth N. (1979), *Theory of International Politics*, New York: McGraw-Hill.

(1986), 'Reflections on *Theory of International Politics*: A Response to My Critics', in Keohane (ed.), pp. 322–45.

Walzer, Michael (1965), *The Revolution of the Saints*, Boston: Beacon Press.

(1970), *Obligations*, New York: Simon & Schuster.

(1978), *Just and Unjust Wars*, Harmondsworth: Pelican.

Watson, Adam (1984), *Diplomacy*, London: Methuen.

(1987), 'Hedley Bull, State Systems and International Studies', *Review of International Studies* 13 (2): 147–53.

(1990), 'Systems of States', *Review of International Studies* 16 (2): 99–109.

(1992), *The Evolution of International Society*, London: Routledge.

(1997), *The Limits of Independence*, London: Routledge.

Weber, Cynthia (1995), *Simulating Sovereignty*, Cambridge: Cambridge University Press.

Weber, Marianne (1926), *Max Weber*, Tübingen: J. C. B. Mohr.

Weber, Max (1948), *From Max Weber*, edited by H. H. Gerth and C. Wright Mills, London: Routledge & Kegan Paul.

(1976), *The Agrarian Sociology of Ancient Civilizations*, London: New Left Books.

(1978), *Economy and Society*, Berkeley: University of California Press.

Weiss, Linda (1998), *The Myth of the Powerless State*, Cambridge: Polity.

Weiss, Linda and Hobson, John M. (1995), *States and Economic Development*, Cambridge: Polity.

Wendt, Alexander (1987), 'The Agent–Structure Problem in International Relations Theory', *International Organization* 41 (3): 335–70.

(1992), 'Anarchy is What States Make of It: The Social Construction of Power Politics', *International Organization* 46 (2): 391–426.

(1994), 'Collective Identity Formation and the International State', *American Political Science Review* 88 (2): 384–96.

(1995), 'Constructing International Politics', *International Security* 20 (1): 71–81.

(1996), 'Identity and Structural Change in International Politics', in Yosef Lapid and Friedrich Kratochwil (eds.), *The Return of Culture and Identity in IR Theory*, Boulder: Lynne Rienner, pp. 47–64.

(1998), 'On Constitution and Causation in International Relations', *Review of International Studies*, 24 (Special Issue): 101–17.

(1999), *Social Theory of International Politics*, New York: Cambridge University Press.

Wendt, Alexander and Duvall, Raymond (1989), 'Institutions and International Order', in Ernst-Otto Czempiel and James N. Rosenau (eds.), *Global Changes and Theoretical Challenges: Approaches to World Politics for the 1990s*, Lexington: Lexington Books, pp. 51–73.

Wendt, Alexander and Friedheim, Daniel (1996), 'Hierarchy under Anarchy: Informal Empire and the East German State', in Biersteker and Weber (eds.), pp. 240–77.

Wheeler, Nicholas J. (1992), 'Pluralist or Solidarist Conceptions of Humanitarian Intervention: Bull and Vincent on Humanitarian Intervention', *Millennium*, 21 (3): 463–87.

(2000), *Saving Strangers*, Oxford: Oxford University Press.

Wight, Martin (1966a), 'Why is There no International Theory?', in Butterfield and Wight (eds.), pp. 17–34.

(1966b), 'Western Values in International Relations', in Butterfield and Wight (eds.), pp. 89–131.

(1977), *Systems of States*, Leicester: Leicester University Press.

Wilde, Jaap H. de (1991), *Saved from Oblivion*, Aldershot: Dartmouth.

Williams, Eric (1964), *Capitalism and Slavery*, London: Deutsch.

Wilson, James (1998), *The Earth Shall Weep*, London: Picador.

Wolf, Eric (1982), *Europe and the People Without History*, Berkeley: University of California Press.

Wood, Ellen M. (1995), *Democracy Against Capitalism: Renewing Historical Materialism*, Cambridge: Cambridge University Press.

Wright, Susan (1994), '"Culture" in Anthropology and Organizational Studies', in Susan Wright (ed.), *Anthropology of Organizations*, New York: Routledge, pp. 1–31.

Wright Mills, C. (1958), *The Causes of World War III*, New York: Simon & Schuster.

—— (1970), *The Sociological Imagination*, Harmondsworth: Pelican.

Yalvaç, Faruk (1991), 'The Sociology of the State and the Sociology of International Relations', in Michael Banks and Martin Shaw (eds.), *State and Society in International Relations*, Hemel Hempstead: Harvester, pp. 93–114.

Index

Abu-Lughod, Janet, 30
Adams, Henry Brooks, 156
Adorno, Theodor, 183, 184n2
agent–structure, 66, 132, 216, 249–53
Agnew, John, 116
ahistoricism, modes of
  chronofetishism, 5–13, 19, 72, 78–80,
    191, 268
  historical sociology as remedy, 7, 10–13,
    15–41, 73–81, 93–8, 134-9, 164–80,
    181–5, 191–9, 200–17, 244–59,
    265–71, 276–85
  presentism, 204–5, 284
  tempocentrism, 5, 6, 7, 9–15, 17, 19,
    78–80, 191, 269–70
Amin, Samir, 152
anarchy, 15, 18–19, 54, 67, 135, 206–7,
  278
  as differentiated, 18
Angell, Norman, 168n7
Archer, Margaret, 216
Aron, Raymond, 169n8, 244, 245, 248
Arrighi, Giovanni, 255
Ashley, Richard, 8

Baldwin, David, 225–6
Barnett, Michael, 5, 24–7, 224, 235, 242–3
behaviouralism, 49–50, 56
Blaut, Jim, 151–2
blocs, 257
Bodin, Jean, 138
Braudel, Fernand, 147
Brown, Chris, 49
Bucher, Karl, 153
Bull, Hedley, 34, 50–1, 245
  Anarchical Society, The, 52
Bull, Hedley and Watson, Adam, 215
  Expansion of International Society, 53, 167
bureaucratisation, 106–10
  and international organisations, 26–7,
    112–19
  and war, 109–10

Burke, Edmund, 254
Butler, Judith, 240
Butterfield, Herbert and Wight, Martin
  Diplomatic Investigations, 51
Buzan, Barry, 232
Buzan, Jones and Little
  Logic of Anarchy, The, 39–40, 208, 210
Buzan, Barry and Little, Richard, 41, 223,
  224, 269–70, 276–7, 278, 280

capital, 144–5, 146–7, 152–6, 159, 161
capital accumulation, 141, 144, 145, 146,
  158
  in Asia, 148
  continuity thesis, 141, 148
capitalism, 149–52, 159, 170–1
  and international law, 189–90
  transition to, 159–60, 161
Carneiro, Robert, 214
Carr, Edward H., 46, 130, 244–5
  Twenty Years' Crisis, The, 48, 261
Cerny, Philip, 88
Chaudhuri, Kirti, 145, 151, 159
Chernobyl, 171n13
Childe, Gordon, 153
chronofetishism, 5–9, 13, 19, 72, 78–80,
  191, 268
  defined, 12
  historical sociology as remedy for, 278
civilisation, 145–6, 153, 167–8
class, 86, 195, 197–8
  capitalist, 147, 149, 153
  conflict, 32, 109, 153, 158, 160–1,
    172
  merchant, 149
  propertied, 153
Coker, Christopher, 245
Cold War, 82, 88–9, 255
community
  dialogic, 34–5
  moral, 278, 283–4
  political, 33–4, 37–8, 165–6